Natural Health for DOGS & CATS

Natural Health for DOGS & CATS

Richard H. Pitcairn, D.V.M., Ph.D.
and Susan Hubble Pitcairn

PRION

First published in the United States by
Rodale Books, Rodale Press, Inc.
33 East Minor Street, Emmaus, PA 18049

This edition published in 1989 by
PRION
an imprint of Multimedia Books Limited,
32–34 Gordon House Road, London NW5 1LP

Editor (English edition): Susan Rea
Veterinary advisor (English edition): Roger Harrison MRCVS
Design: Jerry O'Brien
Line illustrations: Frank Fretz

British Library Cataloguing in Publication Data
Pitcairn, Richard
    Natural health for dogs and cats
    1. Livestock: Dogs. Care   2. Pets. Cats. Care
    I. Title   II. Pitcairn, Susan Hubble
    636.7'083

ISBN 1-85375-091-3

Typeset by Vision Typesetting, Manchester, UK
Printed in the United Kingdom by The Bath Press

*This book is intended to supplement the advice and guidance of a
qualified veterinary practitioner. Neither the authors nor the
publisher can be held responsible for unsupervised treatments
administered at home.*

Contents

Foreword

It is a refreshing change to write a foreword for a book such as this, written by a kindred spirit who, in grasping the holistic principles of health and disease with courage and conviction, dares to go against the narrow mainstream and consensus of veterinary medicine, to open up new frontiers.

As a recent graduate in veterinary medicine two decades ago, I wrote a clinical treatise on 'sympathy-lameness' in dogs, describing how emotionally disturbed dogs and those soliciting the attentions of their owners will actually feign injury to one of their legs. Some vets publicly ridiculed this study, since it was inconceivable that animals could be afflicted with emotional and psychosomatic disorders.

Today there is more widespread recognition of such phenomena: humans are not the only intelligent, sensitive beings on earth. Our animal kin can also suffer from a wide variety of emotional problems, as Dr Pitcairn describes in this book. Yet the suggestion that animals have emotions which can affect their health will still be met with strong resistance, because many 'experts' believe that such interpretations are anthropomorphic.

Similarly, most people never even consider that animals should be accorded 'rights' and become part of the community of moral concern. The usual view is that animals are inferior to us, so we can exploit them as we choose without a twinge of conscience.

Above and beyond the ethical consideration of our dealings with animals is the pervading view that mind and body are separate. Nature is demystified or desanctified into a mere resource to be conquered and exploited for our own exclusive use. And humanity is likewise dehumanized, the body being considered just a survival machine for our genes or a bio-chemical container holding the mind. Furthermore, with this fragmented world view, humanity becomes increasingly separated and alienated from nature, animals and from the totality of its own being and becoming.

Such erroneous beliefs and values are being challenged today, since they lie at the roots of our contemporary social and environmental ills. Modern physics, various Eastern philosophies and ecology all have shown that we live in a unified field. It is imperative for our own health and future survival that we think and act *eco*centrically rather than *ego*centrically. Our values, beliefs and wants must become attuned to the totality of life, so that enlightened self-interest is in concord with the greater good. This new, world-embracing ethic includes a universal reverence for all life, including animal life. It is urgently needed.

Such is the philosophy behind the holistic medicine that Dr Pitcairn and a handful of other vets are now applying to animals. As is often the case, Dr Pitcairn's introduction to holistic medicine began with personal experience, first with experiencing the effects of changing his dietary habits and then of treating his own child with herbal medicine.

This led him to the realization 'that many chronic and degenerative diseases we see today are caused or complicated by inadequate diets'. Since the immune system is especially vulnerable to dietary imbalances, Dr Pitcairn did graduate research, obtaining a Ph.D. in advanced studies in immunology. Yet such specialization had limited practical application, and seemed to confuse rather than clarify the nature of health and disease. So, after his graduate studies were completed, he reassessed the modern approach to animal health problems, and realized the narrowness and ineffectuality of such an approach, especially in chronic, degenerative and psychosomatic disorders.

He knew intuitively that it is bad medicine not to see health problems 'in relation to the whole and to become lost in the divisions of our artificial labels and definitions'. Furthermore, he learned through personal experience that healing (and health maintenance) entails not only specific therapies, but also major lifestyle changes.

As an animal doctor, with such insight and knowledge he has made the obvious and most intelligent decision: to develop a holistic health care and maintenance programme for pets, together with a valuable encyclopaedia of treatments for vets and pet owners (ideally under the supervision of their pets' doctors) to use. Certainly much more research is needed especially in veterinary chiropractic, herbalism and homeopathy. Veterinary acupuncture is being practised by an increasing number of vets and my own book on pet massage opens up new vistas for pet owners and vets to help pets through sickness and also maintain their overall physical and psychological well-being.

Holistic medicine respects and is attuned to the 'wisdom of the body'. This body wisdom – the connection between body-sensitivity and mind-awareness – has almost been lost to modern civilization, which separates mind from body, man from animal, and humanity from nature. We have to relearn the fact that our bodies are not machines, nor are animals'.

Albert Schweitzer, the great humanitarian and healer, said that the good doctor simply awakes 'the physician within' the patient. Similarly, as Dr Pitcairn so ably shows in this book, both the good veterinary surgeon and the pet owner can help awaken and support the natural processes within the animal to help prevent illness and combat stress and disease.

The presence of the healer is part of the healing process. Talking to a person or animal in a quiet, gentle voice has a very similar effect to comforting (stroking) or gentle, rhythmic massage. Researchers have shown that the effect is quite profound, the cardinal signs being a dramatic decrease in heart rate and a general relaxation in muscle tension. The change in heart rate is an indication that the parasympathetic nervous system is being stimulated. This is, I believe, part of the healing or tonic effect of gentle vocal or physical contact. When the parasympathetic nervous system is stimulated, the digestive system is stimulated; this is why the tender loving care of a mother rocking her baby and singing it a lullaby, or a cat or dog licking its offspring or companion, facilitates the digestive process.

Being emotionally deprived of the essential energy of another's affection is as bad as being deprived of some essential dietary nutrient. In fact, there are many physical, social and emotional 'nutrients', such as exercise and play and recreation, proteins, vitamins, affection, touch and companionship, that are vital components of total health care for man and beast alike.

The healer, by influencing the mind of the patient, together with directly affecting the body (via drugs, massage, and so on), activates the 'physician within', restoring balance. Therefore, an animal is more likely to benefit if it is emotionally attached to the healer than if it were not attached or were being treated by a stranger. This is why the therapies suggested by Dr Pitcairn for home use hold such great potential for pets and pet owners. Their effectiveness is enhanced by the close emotional bond between pet and owner.

Holistic living is living in harmony with ourselves, each other, and with nature as a whole; it is knowing that the quality of relationships influences our state of health as much as our temperament, perceptions, genetic constitution and such. The same holds true for the health of our pets. And the more removed we and they are from nature, the more disharmony and privation, the more sickness and suffering there are in the world.

This book will help pet owners make a better life for their pets and for themselves as well. Dr Pitcairn provides the essential enlightenment for a fully responsible, fulfilling and healthful relationship between humans and animals.

With this book, pets have never had it so good!

MICHAEL W. FOX, D.SC., PH.D.,
B. VET. MED., M.R.C.V.S.

Director, Institute for the Study of Animal Problems, a Division of the Humane Society of the United States

PART ONE

Natural Health
for Pets

CHAPTER ONE

The Need for a New Approach

'**W**hy don't you take care of this one?' my colleague asked me, with the look of someone about to unload an unwelcome problem. He pointed through the door to a little middle-aged dog standing forlornly on the examining table. If his coat had ever been sleek, soft and healthy, it was no more. His hair had been falling out for some time now, revealing large greasy patches with a rancid,

unpleasant odour. Even his spirits were low. Unfortunately, I'd seen cases like his all too often.

Waiting nearby were the dog's equally dejected guardians, an ageing couple who had 'tried it all' but still seemed to care enough about their little companion to try once more. The dog's record showed a long history of treatments – cortisone injections, medicated soaps, ointments, more injections, more creams – all without any noticeable improvement.

'Oh, he is so *miserable*,' Mrs Wilson told me sadly. 'We would do anything if we thought it could help him.' It didn't take me long to decide to try nutritional therapy. We were at a medical dead end and there was nothing to lose. But more important, I knew there was a good chance it might work. I'd been doing a lot of learning about the importance of good nutrition, and as I examined Tiny I explained to the Wilsons why I thought an improved diet was their animal's best chance for recovery.

'Skin problems like his are probably the most common and frustrating of the conditions we try to deal with. Because the skin is such a visible area of the body, it can show the first signs of underlying problems, particularly those caused by inadequate diet. The skin grows very rapidly – it usually makes a whole new crop of cells about every three weeks. It needs a lot of nourishment, so if the diet lacks what it really needs, it will be one of the first tissues to break down and show abnormalities like the kind we see here in Tiny.'

As we went on talking about the effects of diet, the Wilsons saw that a change could make a big difference. So next we worked out a suitable feeding programme for Tiny, emphasizing fresh foods rather than preprocessed commercial pet food. Now Tiny would eat meat, whole grains and fresh vegetables. In addition, the Wilsons would give him several supplements rich in nutrients important to the health of the skin, as well as the whole body – brewer's yeast, vegetable oil, cod-liver oil, kelp, bone meal, vitamin E and zinc. I also recommended that they bath him occasionally with a mild shampoo to help remove irritating toxic secretions from his skin.

For the next few weeks I wondered how Tiny was doing on this treatment. A month after their first visit, the Wilsons returned with the results. Tiny was a new dog.

'You wouldn't believe the difference,' Mrs Wilson exclaimed. 'He runs around and plays like a puppy again.'

He was indeed full of life, jumping around excitedly on the table. His coat was much healthier and the hair was rapidly filling in the previously bare spots. It was very rewarding to all of us, but most of all to Tiny himself. For the Wilsons there was the added benefit of realizing that their dog's health was now in their control and they no longer needed to depend on monthly injections of cortisone or on other medications.

Tiny's case was one of my first clinical attempts to apply the results of a long process of learning about the vital role of nutrition in health. Though it now seems obvious to me that a proper diet is an essential aspect of treatment, I had not always approached cases in such a manner. My veterinary school training in nutrition had included little more than the admonition: 'Tell your clients to feed their animals balanced commercial pet foods and to avoid table scraps.' In most of my professional studies the subject of nutrition was generally considered unimportant, or else was altogether ignored. I accepted this attitude at face value and after graduation set out to conquer disease armed with a vast array of conventional methods gleaned from my years of schooling.

Faced with the day-to-day challenges of my job in small and large animal practice, however, I soon learned that many diseases simply did not respond to treatments as I had been told they would. In fact, it often seemed that what I did mattered very little. I was like a bystander in the battle for recovery – doing a lot of cheering and occasionally making a contribution of sorts – but often feeling ineffectual.

I tried to make sense of what I saw and gradually several basic questions arose. I wondered, for example, why some animals recover easily, while others never seem to do well regardless of which drugs I use. And why some animals in a group seem to have all the fleas and catch all the diseases going around while others remain unaffected. I knew there must be something basic that I just didn't grasp about the body's ability to defend and heal itself.

When you ask a question long enough and deeply enough, life seems to provide you with the opportunity to find an answer. Indeed, I was soon given a chance to become a full-time graduate student studying veterinary immunology, virology and biochemistry. Surely here, I thought, I could learn the secrets of the body's defence systems, and I eagerly set about studying and researching various problems, particularly the body's immune response to cancer.

Some five years and a Ph.D. later, I found that the answers to my questions still eluded me. Though I had acquired an even greater wealth of facts and information about the mechanisms of immunology and metabolism, I still did not feel a sense of real insight about the issues that concerned me.

The holistic approach

Yet I had begun to realize in a vague way that part of the difficulty was the way that knowledge is broken up and fragmented into narrow academic disciplines. One group of immunologists had one particular viewpoint and a second group another. And then there were the microbiologists, the virologists, the biochemists, the pathologists and a host of others, all of whom tended to see things through different sets of filters! Our research problems had become so narrowly defined and carried out that we were missing the whole picture. Though I didn't completely realize it at the time, what was really needed was a holistic approach to the problem of disease.

As a result, I started doing two things that were decisive and that have continued to be my 'style of operation' ever since. One was to read broadly in many fields and from many sources to get a larger scope of concepts and ideas. The other was to experiment with new ideas that made sense by trying them out on myself first.

My first priority was to learn more about nutrition. After some studying, I was amazed to find that despite what I'd been told, the right diet is *tremendously* important for maintaining health and preventing disease. I learned that a number of specific vitamins are essential to the normal functioning of the immune system – though they'd never been mentioned once in my years of graduate study. At last I began to find some answers to my questions. As a result, I started using whole grains, cutting out sugars and other junk foods, reducing my intake of meat and taking supplements like brewer's yeast, wheat germ and various vitamins. Before long I was feeling better than I had in years.

Along with dietary changes and vitamins, exercise, herbs and self-inquiry all eventually played a part in removing from my life some things I didn't need – like a developing potbelly, as well as colitis, ear infections, excess tension, susceptibility to colds and flu, and a number of psychological conditionings.

Though these personal explorations didn't constitute 'statistically significant' studies, they were tremendously valuable. There is nothing more convincing than feeling better. You don't need the interpretation or opinion of any authority to perceive positive changes in your own body!

After helping myself, I began to apply my new knowledge to animals — first my own pets and then, as I returned to clinical practice, some 'hopeless' cases like Tiny. At one point I adopted a stray kitten, half-starved and ragged from life in the woods. At first I fed her conventional things like dry cat food, and she did all right. But when she became pregnant a year or two later, I decided to boost her strength. I faithfully added fresh raw ox liver, raw eggs, bone meal, fresh chicken, brewer's yeast and other nutritious foods to her daily fare. Unlike many cats I've seen, she never lost any weight or hair during pregnancy and her delivery was exceptionally fast, easy and calm. She always had plenty of milk to nurse her three large, thriving kittens, and all of them grew up to be much larger than she. I kept one of them and continued adding supplements to both cats' diets. I was always amazed at how remarkably healthy they were. I never needed to resort to any flea control. And if one of them got scratched or bitten in a fight, the injury healed quickly and never developed into an infection or abscess.

One thing led to another and soon I took an interest in herbs as well. Nothing convinced me more that these natural remedies could bring about almost miraculous cures than one particular occasion. It was late one Sunday night and one of my children (then about six) was suffering from a high fever, flushed face, swollen throat glands and incipient bronchitis (to which he was prone). He was very restless and cried with extreme discomfort and pain. I had nothing in the house to give him except some aspirin, which neither reduced his fever nor enabled him to get to sleep.

I felt stuck. Not knowing what to do, I grasped about desperately in my mind. Then all at once I remembered I had some herbal capsules – goldenseal, about the only herb I happened to have on hand at the time. I gave him one with a little water and about five to ten minutes later he suddenly got up and, for the first time in hours, went to the bathroom and voided a large quantity of urine.

Afterward he lay down, relaxed and fell asleep. His fever began to diminish rapidly and the next morning he was normal. As you can imagine, this experience was very intriguing.

Looking back, I can now see that goldenseal was an appropriate herb to use for the symptoms my child showed. I was fortunate to have hit it so perfectly. These remarkable results inspired me to pursue many fruitful directions later on, such as herbalism, naturopathy and homeopathy. Though I eventually branched out into these other directions (as this book will also), I have found over the years that proper nutrition is of the utmost importance and is indeed the basic foundation of a holistic approach. Without it there is little to work with in restoring an animal's health. And I feel certain that many of the chronic and degenerative diseases we see today are caused by or complicated by inadequate diet.

After all, the physical body requires certain substances that cannot be made internally. Like any complicated and delicate machinery, one missing part can bring the whole to a standstill. It appears that the immune system with its production of specialized white blood cells and antibodies is particularly susceptible to nutritional imbalance. Perhaps it is because these specialized cells in the body grow fast and have a complex job that deficiencies show up here sooner than they might with bone, for example.

Therefore, let's look at what your animal friend is eating every day. What is and *isn't* in the diet can make a big difference in your animal's well-being.

CHAPTER TWO

What's Really in Pet Food

Preparation of pet foods is such that moulds . . . and toxins from condemned meats, hormones, mixed allergens, plus any exogenous [added] material needed to meet basic requirements for manufacturing, are present in the available diets on the market.

In commercial foods, dry foods are the easiest to mask impure protein additives, canned foods next, then fresh frozen foods the most difficult. . .

—Alfred J. Plechner, D.V.M.

Imagine that somebody has just developed and marketed a 'complete' packaged diet for human beings – called 'Insta-Meal.' It contains everything thought necessary to sustain life – all the officially recommended daily amounts of protein, fats, carbohydrates, vitamins and minerals. To compensate for the loss of natural nutrients in processing, the manufacturer has added an array of chemically isolated vitamins and minerals bearing such impressive titles as pyridoxine hydrochloride, calcium pantothenate, iron carbonate, potassium chloride and manganous oxide.

To make Insta-Meal more colourful and long lasting, the manufacturer has added a sprinkling of Allura Red, E129, butylated hydroxyanisole (the common preservative known as BHA or E320) and, for extra flavour appeal, a dash of disodium guanylate (a flavouring common in instant soups and processed Chinese foods).

The least expensive version of this new product has been moulded and baked into crunchy bite-size chunks about the size and texture of croutons. According to the package directions you can now have a complete diet for less than half the price you usually pay for food, and with much greater ease of preparation. All you need do is pour it into a bowl and serve a little tap water on the side.

For extra flavour appeal, you can try the following variations:

- To every three cups of dry mix add one cup of hot water. Mix, and let it stand a couple of minutes. New Insta-Meal makes its own tasty sauce.
- Mix two cups of Insta-Meal with two cups of water in your blender. Pour into a greased bread tin and bake at 350°F for 20 minutes. Presto! Insta-Casserole!
- For that occasional sweet tooth, try new soft-moist Insta-Meal Chunks. Or if your prefer a hearty, meaty style, try one of five tinned varieties of complete Insta-Meal.

Think about eating Insta-Meal for the rest of your life. Certainly you'd refuse such a diet – even if there were a 'health food' variety, free of artificial preservatives and other additives. I have yet to meet anyone willing to adopt such a diet. Not only would we long for the taste of a varied and natural diet, but we would somehow know we were missing something. Before long most of us would be climbing the walls looking for a salad or some fresh fruit – *anything* relatively whole and fresh! Or just different!

Surely, if you follow my line of reasoning, I need say no more. But for those who feel that the cost and convenience of processed pet foods make up for any minor shortcomings they may have, or for those who would just like to be informed, read on. As you do, please bear in mind that I have nothing personal against the makers of animal foods nor do I seek to put them out of business. Many of them do their best to provide what they consider to be decent products which meet animals' needs at reasonable prices. It's just that I don't think *any* kind of completely cooked, dried, tinned or frozen prepared food constitutes the most favourable diet for the good health of either human or beast.

Although we have come to accept commercial foods as being normal and natural ways to feed animals (and indeed ourselves), in fact, they are not. They are simply what we've grown used to in the last few decades. But nothing we can produce commercially ever can rival those mysteriously complex foods manufactured for aeons by nature itself. And even compared to many foods processed for people, most pet foods leave much to be desired.

The many objections we can make about the nutritional quality of animal convenience foods boil down to two basic types: these foods *don't* contain things we wish they did, and *do* contain things we wish they didn't. The missing ingredients are mostly adequate quantities and/or qualities of various nutrients, particularly proteins, fats, vitamins and minerals, as well as the more intangible qualities unique to live, fresh foods. Those ingredients that are present, but unwelcome, comprise a larger group and include various slaughterhouse wastes, non-nutritive fillers, heavy metal contaminants, sugar, and artificial colours, flavours and preservatives.

The two basic problems are linked together as an unhappy pair because the presence of various toxins and pollutants actually *increases* the body's needs for high-quality nutrients necessary for combating or eliminating these contaminants. When the overall nutrition is *already* lower than it should be, we are inviting trouble.

What's missing in pet foods?

Pet food makers go through a lot of effort to manufacture products drawn from a fluctuating market of available ingredients. Using these, they must create a product that meets or exceeds officially accepted levels of various nutrients, while also matching the analyses guaranteed on the label. Along with a list of ingredients (which can be vague terms like 'meat meal' or 'poultry by-products'), the labels tell you what percentage of the food is protein, fats, fibre, and sometimes ash and carbohydrates.

The purpose of these analyses is to give you, the purchaser, a basis of comparison among different products, as well as the assurance that a given food contains what the label says. Let's say you want to buy a high-protein food for your dog. All you need do is compare several foods by their stated percentages of proteins and their costs to find the best food at the best value, right? Unfortunately, no.

Two factors make such easy evaluations more difficult. First, the biological useful-

ness of one type of protein can be quite different from that of another. Second, a more mathematical problem is that you can't realistically compare the listed percentages of two or more products unless you also take into account any differences in their moisture content – a considerable element in judging dry and tinned foods. Let's consider each factor in turn.

Labels can be misleading

In considering protein, which is one of the most important nutrients your animal requires, we must first understand the meaning of a few terms.

A protein's *biological value* (which has also been called the nitrogen balance index) depends on the food's composition of essential amino acids, the building blocks which the body must have in order to construct its own particular protein tissues. On a relative scale, eggs are given an ideal value of 100, whereas fish meal is 92, beef and milk 78, rice 75, soya beans 68, yeast 63 and wheat gluten 40.

The *digestibility* of a protein (or any food) is simply the extent to which the gastro-intestinal tract can actually absorb it. For example, one source might be 70 per cent digestible while another is 90 per cent. Some protein – like the protein in hair – is less digestible because it is harder to break down. Other proteins are compromised by the way they are processed. The prolonged high temperatures used to prepare some pet foods can destroy much of the usefulness of even proteins with high biological value, because the heat can cause some proteins to combine with certain sugars to form compounds that can't be broken down by the body's digestive enzymes.

Now, because manufacturers list only the

crude amount of protein rather than the amount your pet can actually use, they can include relatively inexpensive sources that may supply your pet with much less protein than you would imagine. Most people don't realize that the terms referring to meat industry by-products can actually mean poultry feather meal, connective tissues, leather meal, faecal waste from poultry and other animals, and horse and cattle hair. All these are reputedly used in pet food. Such ingredients would boost the *crude* protein content, but provide relatively little nourishment.

To understand how deceptive this crude protein figure can be, imagine two cans of dog food, each claiming a content of 10 per cent protein. One comes from good-quality beef with a biological value of 78, carefully processed so it will be about 95 per cent digestible. The first can of dog food, then, actually contains about 7.4 per cent net usable protein (78 × .95 × 10 per cent). The protein in the second can, on the other hand, comes mostly from chicken feather meal with a biological value of 40 and a digestibility of 75 per cent, which means it has less than half the usable protein of the first can, or 3 per cent. Obviously, a pet will fare much better on the first type of food. But remember, both labels *correctly* state an identical protein content.

As a result of the use of such poor ingredients, dogs are able to utilize only about 75 per cent of the protein in meat meal (dry weight basis) because of the tough, fibrous tissues present. All meat meal is made even less digestible by the high cooking temperatures. Protein from another cheap ingredient, dried blood meal, is even less usable.

Like protein, other basic ingredients such as carbohydrates, fats and fibres can vary widely in their quality and digestibility. For example, the carbohydrates in a soft-moist dog food product could come largely from such dubious sources as sugar (sucrose), dextrose and propylene glycol. But the carbohydrates in other products may come mostly from whole grains. You have to read the label carefully.

Fats might come from wholesome ingredients or from rancid animal fats that have been condemned as unfit for human consumption. The fibre content may simply reflect the amount naturally found in various ingredients, or it can mean extra fibre has been added from sources like peanut shells, hair or even newspapers.

So by itself the chemical analysis on the label does not mean a whole lot. To underscore this point, a vet is said to have concocted a product containing the same number of nutrients as one brand of dog food by deriving his protein, fats and carbohydrates from old leather shoes, crankcase oil and wood shavings, respectively. Things are not quite *that* bad, but the point is that labels don't always tell us enough. Be especially wary of pet food that lists its ingredients in vague terms like 'meal', 'by-products' or 'digest of [meat] by-products'.

The Pet Food Institute, which represents the industry in the United States, has repeatedly tried to get permission from the Food and Drug Administration (FDA) to use more of these collective ingredient terms. They say it will let them continuously choose a 'least cost mix' from each class of ingredients. Some of the proposed collective ingredient terms include 'processed animal and marine protein products', 'vegetable products' and 'plant fibre products'. Suppose some of these terms are used by less reputable manufacturers to include such questionable ingredients as feathers, hair and sawdust in your pet's dinner. The supposition isn't as far-fetched as you might imagine – a commercial bakery was found to be using wood pulp as a fibre source in its widely distributed product.

The mathematics of moisture variations

The second factor that makes it hard to interpret what's in pet food requires you to do sums to figure out how the moisture content affects the nutritional analysis.

For instance, the label on a tin of pet food may say that the protein content is 6 per cent. The label on a box of dry food may say the contents are 20 per cent protein. At first glance, it seems that the dry food contains significantly more protein than the tinned food. However, that conclusion may be untrue. To compare the amounts of protein better, it is helpful to work out the percentage of protein as a portion of total dry *solids* – excluding any liquid. To understand what this figure represents, imagine squeezing every single drop of water out of the food, and then measuring the amount of protein in the solids that remain. That figure is the percentage of protein in the total dry solids. With the water removed, the tinned food may have more protein than the dry food.

Therefore, to compare the nutritional content of different brands accurately, you need – in theory – to omit the moisture content. Here's how: subtract the moisture content of the food (say, 75 per cent for the tinned example and 10 per cent for the dry food) from 100 per cent to find out what percentage of the total is actually solid. This is where the nutrients are. Then divide the percentage of protein (or other nutrients) listed on the label by the percentage of solids in the food. Our examples come out like this:

tinned product:
$$\frac{6\% \text{ protein (label)}}{25\% \text{ dry solids}} = \begin{array}{l}24.0\% \text{ protein} \\ \text{(dry weight basis)}\end{array}$$

dry product:
$$\frac{20\% \text{ protein (label)}}{90\% \text{ dry solids}} = \begin{array}{l}22.2\% \text{ protein} \\ \text{(dry weight basis)}\end{array}$$

It's not as hard as it may look at first! When calculated on this basis, most dog foods contain at least 22 per cent crude protein, while cat foods contain at least 32 per cent. Generally, tinned foods contain more. (Realize the significance of the term 'crude', as just discussed! You may have a harder time trying to compare the approximate usable protein.)

What about vitamins and minerals?

Vitamins and minerals usually are not listed in terms of amounts. Therefore, you have no real way of knowing exactly how much a product contains. Certain vitamins present in the original ingredients or added by the manufacturer may be lost before your animal ever eats the food. They can be destroyed by heat processing, especially in the presence of oxygen, and by interactions with other ingredients during shelf storage.

Vitamins A, E and B_1, all important in fighting disease, are particularly susceptible to such loss. In fact, researchers have found that a number of American cat foods are so low in vitamin B_1 that they produce deficiencies after only a few weeks of feeding. Another study found that the processing method used in a certain cat food changed its vitamin B_6 so that cats' bodies could not use it, also creating signs of a deficiency. Furthermore, cats fed low-fat diets have been found to absorb vitamin A rather poorly. This problem should be particularly worrying to people who feed their cats dry food – which is fairly low in fat.

As far as minerals go, a food may be chemically complete according to accepted nutritional standards, but may lack the complex organic structures found in natural foods. Many nutritionists contend that the body digests and assimilates the minerals and vitamins in natural foods much better than those nutrients in a synthetic or isolated form. Why natural nutrients should be more valuable to the body than their synthetic copies is unknown. It seems many important factors involved in the way nutrients act inside the body still remain undiscovered. This means that even though many manufacturers add a long list of synthetic or isolated vitamins and minerals, these may not fully replace those natural forms that have been lost in processing or insufficiently supplied in the first place.

Another missing ingredient: life

All processed pet foods – whether sold in tins, bags or frozen packages, in either giant supermarket chains or local health food stores – are missing something that seems to me to be one of the most important 'nutrients' of all. This key ingredient is something nutritional scientists have practically ignored. But when it's there, you and I can know it and feel it. It is a quality found only in freshly grown, uncooked whole foods. It's *life energy*.

To a mind accustomed to mechanistic explanations of the universe, this statement might sound a bit far-fetched. Yet in recent years some researchers have been confirming through laboratory tests something described by many people around the world for centuries. It is a subtle force field that permeates and surrounds all living things. What exactly this field is, and how it operates, is still mostly a mystery, although there are a number of successful therapies (such as acupuncture, homeopathy and various Oriental disciplines) which seem to work at this level.

Through a special medium of photography developed in Russia by the Kirlians, a husband and wife team, a number of investigators are now discovering a whole new world of colourful and complex emissions and 'auras' of energies given off by living organisms. They seem to vary according to the individual's emotional state, health and use of drugs, as well as other factors.

The Kirlians were the first to discover that the field around 'a withered leaf (shows) almost no flares. . . . As the leaf gradually dies, its self-emissions also decrease correspondingly until there is no emission from the dead leaf.' What are the implications of this finding for animals (or people) who never or rarely eat anything still fresh or raw enough to retain this mysterious energy?

Almost everyone knows that raw food contains more vitamins and minerals than cooked food. Yet live foods seem to have other benefits as well, some of them apparently related to their greater vitality. As summarized by Paavo Airola, a respected authority on natural nutrition, research and experimentation with raw foods have revealed that they:

- help the body resist ageing by increasing a subtle micro-electric tension found in cell tissues, thus improving and stimulating the cell's oxygenation, metabolism and renewal;
- contain substances that help the body fight disease-producing agents;
- are actually easier to digest than cooked foods in most cases, and contain many enzymes (all of which are destroyed by cooking) that are essential for optimal digestion and assimilation.

The living testimony of many people and animals who thrive on diets that include plenty of fresh raw vegetables, fruits, dairy products and other foods is enough to convince me that a diet of cooked foods alone will not keep your pets in top-notch condition.

One example that comes to mind to illustrate this point is that of a remarkable experiment run by a doctor stationed in India some years ago – Sir Robert McCarrison. Impressed by the degree of health enjoyed by the Hunza, Pathan and Sikh peoples in that part of the world, he wondered whether or not a diet similar to theirs could produce comparable physique and health in experimental rats.

So for a period of 27 months, Dr McCarrison fed more than a thousand rats a number of live foods, including sprouted beans, fresh raw carrots and cabbage and raw whole milk, along with whole-wheat pita bread and (once a week) a bit of meat and bones. He also provided the rats with good air, sunlight and clean living quarters.

At the close of the experiment, when the rats had reached an age equivalent to about 55 years in human terms, he killed them and examined them thoroughly for signs of disease. To his amazement he could find none. The only deaths that *had* occurred were due to accidental causes. Later Dr McCarrison fed two other diets to groups of rats, diets typical of poor people from England and parts of India. Rats who lived on the poor Indian diet had disease in every organ they possessed! Those who lived on the boiled, sweetened and tinned foods commonly eaten by the English poor grew so highly-strung that they ate each other – the weaker rats succumbing first.

In my own practice I have seen case after case in which an animal given a diet of natural, including some raw, foods achieved levels of vitality and spark not seen for years! So if you want your pet to enjoy the greatest health potential, then it's pretty clear that you can't get by on commercially processed foods alone.

Potentially harmful ingredients in pet foods

Not long ago *Prevention* magazine published a letter from a reader. She gave an inside glimpse of the pet food industry in America.

> *In 1978 I worked in a chicken butchering factory in Maine. Our average daily output was 100,000 chickens. . . . Directly ahead of me on the conveyor line were the USDA inspectors and their trimmers. The trimmers cut the damaged and diseased parts off the chickens and dropped them in garbage cans, which were emptied periodically. These parts were sent to a pet food factory.*
>
> *So the next time you hear a pet food company talk about the fine ingredients they use in their product, don't you believe it.*

Probably most of us have heard stories of this type. They make you wonder just what kind of quality control, if any, governs the manufacturing of pet foods.

According to the U.S. Department of Agriculture (USDA), there is no mandatory federal inspection of ingredients used in pet food manufacturing, though some states may oversee the canning processes used. (This bacteriological safety, however, is not assured for dry pet foods.) In all but two or three states the laws allow pet food makers to use what are called '4-D' sources – that is, tissues from animals that are dead, dying, disabled or diseased when they arrive at the slaughterhouse.

Other pet food ingredients include food rejected by the USDA for human consumption, such as mouldy grains or rancid animal fats.

It is doubtful whether most pet food makers use hooves, hair, feathers and some of the unsavoury fillers about which we hear rumours. But it is common knowledge that the pet food industry cleans up the leftovers of the food industry that are not desirable for human use.

American manufacturers can, however, voluntarily submit to continuous government inspection of the ingredients of their products, and of their plant facilities. Such products bear a legend saying that they have been packed under continuous inspection by the USDA.

Although such compliance to human-level standards is certainly commendable, we have to understand that even *our* food can contain ingredients we would rather avoid, if we could. For instance, that all-American favourite, hamburger meat, has been found to harbour contaminants like rodent hair, insects, unfit meat and mould. But as bad as our food is, pet food is even worse. And any ill effects caused by unwholesome ingredients in pet foods most likely come from those condemned parts and wastes considered unfit for our own consumption.

And just what might these effects be? From his experience as a vet and federal meat inspector, Dr P. F. McGargle concludes that feeding slaughterhouse wastes to animals increases their chance of getting cancer and other degenerative diseases. Those wastes, he says, can include mouldy, rancid or spoiled processed meats, as well as tissues too severely riddled with cancer to be eaten by people.

In addition to disease, this so-called food can also contain large doses of hormones. Similar amounts given to laboratory animals have produced cancer. The high level of hormones in this waste reflects the amount of synthetic hormones fed to animals to stimulate their growth. It also reflects the fact that some of this meat meal comes from glandular wastes and the foetal tissues from pregnant cows. These are naturally high in hormones. Processing and cooking pet food containing these wastes does not inactivate these hormones.

They have the most severe effect on cats, who are extremely sensitive to them. Take, for example, the tissues or pellets that are used to fatten steers and caponize chickens. These are considered toxic to cats, even in *very low* levels.

To support his belief that these waste foods contribute to cancer, Dr McGargle notes which type of farm animals are most likely to develop cancer. Those fed these meat meal wastes are primarily chickens, pigs, cattle and some dairy calves. These animals have a much higher cancer rate than turkeys, ducks and sheep, which eat mostly (or only) plant protein. Furthermore, the increase in cancer rates corresponds to the introduction and increased use of meat meal as an animal food.

It's no wonder that so many pet foods have such an awful smell and appearance – even with the heavy use of artificial additives designed to make them more appealing. According to breeder Lee Edwards Benning, author of *The Pet Profiteers* (Times Books, 1976), one marketing study showed that some children found the smell of dog food so obnoxious they refused to feed their own pets. Poor Mother got stuck with the job. The same study showed that even Mother had qualms. She said she hesitated to use the family's knives, forks and spoons to dig the glop out of the tins.

Perhaps it was this kind of consumer turn-off that led to the development of 'convenience' pet foods. Since they were first introduced, the popularity of 'burgers', soft-moist chunks and dry foods has grown, while the popularity of tinned foods, on the other hand, has diminished.

Unfortunately, this trend means the average pet is eating more 'junk food', because these new foods may be full of sugar and artificial additives to keep them fresh without canning or refrigeration.

The additives in your pet's food

Since I graduated from veterinary school in 1965, I've noticed a general deterioration in pet health. I believe that the chemical additives in pet food play a major part in that decline.

Let's examine the label of a popular American 'burger' product for dogs. The ingredients are listed according to how much of each appears in the product. For example, if the first ingredient is water, then the product contains mostly water. On the soft-moist burger label, the third major ingredient is listed as corn syrup. What is corn syrup doing in a burger? It's providing the soft-moistness! The FDA approved the use of corn syrup in its hydrogenated form as a 'humectant and plasticizer' – that is, an ingredient that can give the product dampness and flexibility. So a pet food is allowed to contain up to *15 per cent* of its total weight in corn syrup.

Chemically derived from cornstarch (in turn derived from maize), this syrup produces the same energy highs and lows as table sugar, and causes the same stress on the pancreas and adrenals, a condition that may result in diabetes.

It's easy to see that corn syrup is hardly a good choice of ingredient, especially when you consider the other shortcomings of such an isolated refined sugar. Not only does it dilute other nutrients in the food by providing 'empty calories' devoid of vitamins, minerals, proteins or fats, but also it can overstimulate the production of insulin and acidic digestive juices. These interfere with a dog's ability to absorb the proteins, calcium and other minerals that *are* in the food.

Moreover, it can inhibit the growth of useful intestinal bacteria. (Food scientists trying to develop similar products for people acknowledge that despite the American sweet tooth, soft-moist dog food is so sweet that 'humans just wouldn't like it'.

Closely following corn syrup on the first part of the long ingredient list we find propylene glycol, also used to maintain the right texture and moisture for such convenience foods. These humectants tie up the water content and thus inhibit the growth of bacteria. A little farther down the menu we find potassium sorbate (a preservative chemically similar to fat), ammoniated glycyrrhizin (a potent sweetener, also considered a potent drug, that should be further tested for safety) and something called ethylenediamine dihydriodide.

After reviewing other brands we can add the following to the list of typical pet food ingredients: sucrose (that's table sugar), propyl gallate (added to retard spoilage, it is suspected of causing liver damage), ethoxyquin (a type of preservative) and glyceryl monostearate. Also add the poorly tested preservative BHT (E 321), which has been suspected by some to cause liver damage, metabolic stress, foetal abnormalities and serum cholesterol increase.

Another class of common ingredients is usually just listed as 'artificial colouring'. This is not required to be labelled any more specifically than that. In pet food, the class typically includes the following coal tar derivative dyes: FD&C Red No. 40 (Allura Red, E129, a possible carcinogen), Red No. 3 (Tartrazine, E102), Yellow No. 5 (Erythrosine, E127) (not fully tested), Yellow No. 6 (Sunset Yellow, E110FCF), Blue No. 1 (Brilliant Blue FCF, 133) and Blue No. 2 (Indigo Carmine or Indigotine, E132) (which has increased dogs' sensitivities to fatal viruses).

Similar dyes previously used widely in pet foods (as well as in our own) and banned by the FDA in the mid-1970s include Red No. 2 (Amaranth, E123, which appears to increase cancer and birth defects) and Violet No. 1 (a suspected carcinogen that can also cause skin lesions). Of the dyes listed above, adequate lifetime feeding studies with animals were performed only on Yellow No. 6 and Red No. 2, but none were studied to see if they caused mutations.

Sodium nitrite is also widely used both as a red colouring and as a preservative in pet foods. People have died from accidental nitrite poisoning. And when it's used in food, it can produce powerful carcinogenic substances known as nitrosamines.

Although people have tried to get the FDA to ban the inclusion of artificial colours in pet foods, their use continues unabated. In a crowded marketplace where all the major competitors use these colourings to make their products seem more like fresh red meat, a company that tries to sell its products in their true colours – various uncomely shades of grey – can put itself at a serious disadvantage. But you can find some products in health food stores that *don't* use artficial colours, preservatives and flavours.

Even more lax are the controls governing the largest class of food additives used in the United States – artificial flavourings. Largely due to a powerful lobby, the manufacturers of these delights can synthesize new flavour-ings, call them safe with little or no testing, and then use them without need for FDA permission under the general term 'artificial flavourings.' Since we have no way at all of trusting or assessing the safety of what is used, anyone seriously concerned about health would be wise completely to avoid using products – for themselves or their pets – that contain this mysterious group of ingredients.

Besides those chemicals intentionally added to pet food, there are others that sneak in on their own. Contamination with lead, for example, can be very severe. A sample of tinned pet foods revealed levels ranging from 0.9 to 7.0 ppm (parts per million) in cat foods and 1.0 to 5.6 ppm in dog foods. Daily intake of six ounces of such foods could exceed the dose of lead considered potentially toxic for children.

Because it comes from a higher rung on the food chain than food from plant sources, meat contains much more pesticide residue, as well as heavy metals and other toxic pollutants. When you also consider that many of the condemned meats used for pet foods probably originated from livestock suffering the ill effects of over-exposure to environmental stress and toxins, you can see that pet food can become a concentrated source of all that we would like to avoid.

CHAPTER THREE
A Natural Diet

We've all heard some veterinary surgeon or pet food manufacturer caution people against feeding an animal table scraps or a home-made diet. Such foods, they contend, have not been scientifically formulated to meet the animal's needs and may ruin a pet's health. Now this might be true if a person just scraped left-over biscuits, white bread, gravy and tinned spinach into a pet's bowl.

But we must remember that do-it-yourself animal feeding is a practice that has been with us since the first dog and person crossed paths at least ten thousand years ago. Generation after generation of healthy animals thrived on the scraps and extras of the whole natural foods eaten by most of our ancestors.

So I wouldn't worry too much about

achieving a 'perfect' balance of nutrients at all times. After all, there is no truly ideal standard that can apply to *all* animals under *all* conditions. On the other hand, we *do* have the benefit of modern dietary analysis and research. Therefore, it makes sense to apply some of that information and experience to what we feed pets because, unlike humans and wild animals with access to adequate food supplies, most pets don't have any say about what they eat. They are rarely able to select the components of their diet by instinct and body wisdom. Instead, they have to take what they can get – or else go 'on strike' until we feed them whatever they *will* accept.

Most people try to feed their pets a food that looks good to the human eye, or a food that has a delicious-sounding name like 'Seafood Dinner with Gourmet Gravy'. But we can be misguided by our own tastes and needs. What's good for us is not necessarily good for dogs or cats. Being carnivores, they have a large need for protein. On a pound-for-pound basis, animals can need as much as 6 times the protein a person does. As for calcium, pound for pound, cats need at least 6 times as much as people, and dogs need at least 17 times more!

To help people feed their pets a good diet, we devised and tested several basic recipes that meet the nutritional needs of pets. Then we tried them out on our 'panel of experts' – dogs and cats that ate the food, and owners who prepared it. All agreed that these meals fill the bill for taste and ease in preparation.

Deciding what nutritional standards to use as our guidelines was not easy. Not only do authorities vary on their recommendations, but there are two types of recommendations: the bare minimum of nutrients for meeting a pet's needs, and the *ideal* amount. For instance, inactive adult cats must have a bare minimum of 21 per cent protein on a solid weight basis. However, an 'ideal' diet like that of cats in the wild state would contain about 47 per cent protein, as well as 33 per cent fat, 17 per cent carbohydrate and 3 per cent ash. By comparison, commercial dry cat foods contain about 34 per cent protein (some of which may be of questionable value, as we have seen) and about 10 per cent fat, whereas canned foods may contain up to 65 per cent protein and 40 per cent fat.

To strike a balance between the ideal and the minimum, the diet I recommend for cats contains an average of 40 per cent protein, 32 per cent fat, 22 per cent carbohydrate and 6 per cent ash. It's a good diet both for adult cats and for growing kittens, which require a bare minimum of 35 per cent protein.

As for dogs, the accepted dietary standards formulated by the National Research Council (NRC) call for minimums of 22 per cent protein and 5 per cent fat. The NRC has not established a recommended amount of carbohydrate in the diet, but other experts in canine nutrition suggest a maximum of 67 per cent. These are average figures meant to cover diets for dogs of all ages and conditions. Commercial dog foods range from lows of about 22 per cent protein and 5 per cent fat in dry food (dry basis) to highs of about 25 per cent protein and 27 per cent fat in meaty canned foods (dry weight basis).

Some authorities would like to see more specific dietary guidelines. For instance, Ben E. Sheffy, Ph.D., of the New York State College of Veterinary Medicine, has proposed an alternative to the NRC guidelines based on research that shows a dog's needs for protein can vary with the amount of fat it eats. The more fat in the food, the more protein the dog needs. That is because fat, carbohydrate and protein metabolism are all interrelated. An increase in fat can create a protein deficiency even though an adequate amount of quality protein is provided. Dr Sheffy also believes a diet should vary according to a dog's age and condition. For instance, pregnant and nursing females, pups and very active dogs need higher proportions of protein in their diets. For the maintenance of average adults, Dr Sheffy suggests optimal percentages ranging from 13 per cent protein in very low-fat diets up to 26 per cent protein in high-fat diets. His guidelines for puppies, mother dogs and others range from 17 per cent to 37 per cent, depending on the fat content of the diet and the dog's specific age and condition.

These more individualized standards make the most sense to me and so we have used them as the basis for our formulations. The six adult maintenance recipes for dogs in this chapter average about 22 per cent protein, 17 per cent fat, 53 per cent carbohydrate and 8 per cent ash. Higher-protein recipes tailored to special needs are found in chapter 5, Special Diets for Special Pets. Now that we've looked at the theory behind the diet, let's get down to the real thing – the food!

What foods to use

Ideally, you should use only organically grown and minimally processed foods. However, it's hard to find (and sometimes to afford) organic sources for everything. Try to use the best whole, fresh foods you can afford. They will be a vast improvement over commercial products, which can be laced with everything from cancerous tissue to sugar, dyes and mouldy grains.

To ensure a good balance of nutrients in your animal's fare, aim for variety. Don't always use the same cut or type of meat or the same grain or vegetable. By using the table of Ingredients Substitutions, on pages 53 and 54–5, you can expand the basic recipes to a repertoire of hundreds of possible combinations. More likely, you will find several that

best fit your lifestyle and your animal's preferences. You can rely primarily on these, with minor variations.

Because some of the new foods may be unfamiliar to your animal friend, the pet may hesitate to eat them. Be patient. *Any* change of diet – even a switch from one commercial brand to another – means the digestive system has to adapt. You also have to consider the peculiar tastes some animals (cats especially) develop. Introduce these new foods gradually over a period of weeks, substituting ever-greater proportions of natural foods for commercial foods. Most people find their dogs and cats love these foods, but if you should encounter any problems with acceptance, refer to chapter 6, Helping Your Pets to Change Their Diet.

Basic food groups

Let's consider the various food groups and how best to buy, store and prepare them.

Meats: Like others who have advocated natural foods for animals, I generally recommend that you feed meat raw. However, fish, rabbit and pork require light cooking to destroy parasites like tapeworms or trichinosis organisms that they can carry. Just don't make a steady diet of these three.

Particularly for small animals, it is convenient to buy a few pounds of meat at a time, chop it up, divide it into daily portions and then freeze the portions individually for future use. While this method has the disadvantage of destroying some of the fresh, live qualities of the meat, it is still far superior to using commercial pet food. I'd recommend this method more for cat food than for dog food. Because dogs are natural scavengers with powerful digestive tracts they can tolerate (and sometimes seem to relish!) raw meat a little too 'gamey' for human consumption. Cats, however, are more truly predators and more highly selective about eating their meat fresh and unspoiled. It's better to freeze excess meat for your cat than to let it age and go uneaten.

Don't feed just one kind of meat. Include some muscle or flesh meats, such as mince, chicken and fish. But also use offal – kidney, heart, liver, brain and tripe. Some people have seen great health benefits from regularly feeding their animals small amounts of raw liver. But I wouldn't go overboard with liver because this organ concentrates and stores many pollutants. I would not give it more than once or twice a week, except in small supplementary amounts. Also, because of the purer diets often fed turkeys, ducks and sheep, as well as the lower cancer rates of those animals, you would do well to draw from these sources when you can.

Bones: Both cats and dogs, but especially dogs, have a high calcium requirement. For that reason bones and bone meal are important foods. Be careful about feeding chicken, turkey, fish or pork bones to your pet, because they can easily splinter and cause injury. Some cats can manage these little bones quite well, but dogs do better with large meaty ones. Use them raw only, because cooked bones can splinter into sharp fragments.

Save the bones you can't give directly to your animal, and simmer them into a mineral-rich stock. Adding a little vinegar and salt to the brew helps to extract the minerals.

Gloria Dodd, D.V.M., a holistic vet of my acquaintance, suggests that one day a week you feed a cat nothing but one small, whole, raw Cornish game hen (this is about the size of a pigeon, or perhaps a poussin). I agree with her. I think cats also can benefit from *occasional* fasting. Dogs can benefit, too. I believe that a dog should eat nothing but water and raw bones one day out of every week or two.

These regular short fasts mimic natural conditions in which predators have both lean and fat times. They give the animal's digestive tract a chance to put aside regular duties and get at some overlooked 'house-cleaning'.

One word of caution about bones. If your dog is not used to eating them, he may go crazy with delight when he is introduced to one. As a result, he may eat too much bone at one time and irritate his digestive tract. The result can then be either constipation or diarrhoea. Also, if your animal's health is not very good, initially he may have some difficulty digesting bones. I believe this problem is related to weak stomach acid that develops because of a nutrient deficiency. So go easy at first. As your pet's health improves, he will be better able to digest bones without difficulty.

Dairy products: Milk, milk products and eggs can form another important part of this diet. I have heard a lot of opinions on both sides of the fence about whether or not adult dogs and cats can properly digest milk and/or raw eggs. As I understand it, the misgivings about these foods are based mostly on some particular research studies that do not duplicate natural conditions. For example, one study says that raw egg whites can cause a biotin deficiency. But this problem occurred when eggs were fed in great excess. Personally, I have never seen such a problem. Remember that in the wild, predators do rely on raw eggs as part of their diets. As a change from raw eggs, you can lightly scramble or boil them occasionally. (The best way to avoid salmonella is to obtain your eggs from a trustworthy organic source.)

As for milk, some people recommend that raw milk and raw cheeses form the bulk of a cat's diet. Others say that cats, especially Siamese cats, do not properly digest lactose (milk sugar), and that drinking milk causes gas and diarrhoea. Based on the feedback I solicit from clients, I have found that milk usually does not cause problems. Pasteurization, however, does alter the chemical structure of protein and can destroy beneficial enzymes and bacteria found in milk, making it less digestible. So if your animal has a problem, try using untreated milk (green top), if you can obtain it. Yogurt and goat's milk are also well digested. If there is still a difficulty, omit milk products from the diet.

Cereals and legumes: This is one group of foods better served cooked than raw. Carnivores usually eat cereal only if it's in the stomach of their prey, and already partially digested. Because dogs and cats have intestinal tracts that are much shorter than those of cereal-eating animals like cows and horses, some pre-digestion (in the form of cooking) is needed.

To save both time and energy, cook enough grains and beans to last for several days. Note that the amounts indicated in the recipes are for *cooked* grains or beans. If you are making a huge batch to feed one or more large animals, you can work out just how much of the raw grains or beans you need to prepare by consulting the table below.

To shorten the cooking time of beans, you can use a pressure cooker. The beans are done if you can blow the skin away from them. If beans give your animal gas, try soaking them in water for at least three hours. After soaking, boil the beans for 30 minutes, then *discard the cooking water*. Finish the cooking process with fresh water. Soya beans are much easier to digest in the form of tofu. Most animals enjoy this bean curd, particularly if you add a favourite flavouring.

You also may include baked goods such as whole grain bread. See pages 54 and 55, Ingredient Substitutions, for interchanging amounts.

EQUIVALENTS FOR DRY AND COOKED CEREALS AND LEGUMES

One Cup Dry Value +	Cups of Cooking Water	Approximate Cooking Time =	Cooked Yield (cups)
Barley	4	1 hour	4
Black beans	4	45–60 minutes	2½
Brown rice	2½	30–45 minutes	3
Buckwheat	5	20 minutes	3
Bulgur	2⅔	10–15 minutes	2⅔
Kidney beans	3	1½ hours	2½
Lima beans	4	45–60 minutes	2½
Maizemeal	4½	30–40 minutes	4½
Millet	4	30 minutes	4
Navy beans	4	45–60 minutes	2½
Pinto beans	2	1½ hours	2½
Rolled oats	2	10 minutes	2
Soya beans	5	3 hours	2¾
Soya flakes	2	15 minutes	2
Split peas	4	30 minutes	2½
Wheat	3½	1 hour	2½

Nuts and seeds: We haven't emphasized nuts and seeds in our recipes because they are often expensive and contain more fat than protein. However, I have heard reports of vigorously healthy dogs who have eaten no form of concentrated protein other than nuts for many years. One of my clients gives his dog peanut butter sandwiches when they go on picnics.

Nuts and seeds are best digested raw, either when made into a nut butter or finely ground. You can include them in your animal's meals by referring to the substitutions list under 'minced beef'. You can also make excellent use of these foods in the form of sprouted seeds and beans.

Vegetables and herbs: Despite their image as exclusive meat-eaters, the wild cousins of dogs and cats do consume plant foods – sometimes they are in the stomach contents of their plant-eating prey (often the first part of the body a wolf eats). Sometimes wild animals eat them directly.

Instead of using vegetables bought in stores, try growing your own. Even flat-dwellers can grow their own vitamin- and energy-filled vegetables in the form of bean sprouts and potted greens. Many dogs and cats relish fresh-grown alfalfa sprouts, wheat grass and oat grass. They'll even 'graze' directly from the pots, if allowed. For those unfamiliar with growing methods, see the instructions listed under 'Cost-Savers' on page 41.

In addition to bean sprouts, dogs and cats generally enjoy carrots (raw and grated, cooked, or even whole), peas, sweet-corn, green beans, potatoes, beets, turnips, spinach, beet and turnip tops, parsley, broccoli, cauliflower, brussels sprouts, kale, green onions, garlic, tomatoes and cucumbers. (I have seen some cats attack a cucumber with more gusto and frenzy than if it were the plumpest of mice, but don't ask me why!) Most of the harder vegetables have to be steamed. But be sure also to serve some raw vegetables – particularly bean sprouts, grated carrots or courgettes, chopped spinach or parsley, fresh corn on the cob or peas.

Some people think their animals have trouble digesting potatoes. Try it and see. But first be sure to cut out all green or sprouting parts, as they contain large amounts of solanine, a toxic substance.

Onions and garlic are good to include occasionally in the diet. They help to purify the system, tone up the digestive tract, and discourage worms and other parasites, including fleas. Garlic is particularly potent when added fresh and raw.

You can use up those old dried herbs that have been sitting in your pantry by adding a pinch of any of the following to your pet's daily food: parsley, thyme, dandelion, red clover, raspberry or blackberry leaves, basil, comfrey, linden flowers, fenugreek and other relatively mild herbs.

Fruits: Many animals like an occasional piece of fruit as a snack. Dogs in particular have a sweet tooth for dried fruits like figs, dates, prunes, raisins and apricots, as well as fresh fruits like apples and berries. Like vegetables, fruits are great storehouses of vitamins, minerals and vital energy. I suggest you feed them apart from the regular meal-time for best digestion.

Dried fruits are especially good natural sources of potassium, an important mineral which can sometimes be in short supply. Other good sources are peanuts, potatoes and tomato sauce.

Flavourings: Daily supplements such as brewer's yeast add their own flavours to the food. In addition, you can experiment with moderate amounts of the following flavourings: tamari (naturally brewed soy sauce), miso, tomato sauce, butter, garlic, chili powder, natural broth powders and herbed sea salt mixtures. Just don't get carried away!

Consult your animal for preferences. It's interesting that dogs, given a choice, usually prefer unsalted food to salted. It seems as if they have some natural sensibilities, doesn't it?

Snacks and treats: Besides bones and fruits you can also offer your pet home-made biscuits for treats. Recipes are on pages 272–5. If you don't have time to make your own, look for the additive-free commercially made biscuits found in health food stores. Read the label carefully and watch out for the ingredients meat meal, sugar (sucrose), and any artificial colours, flavourings and preservatives.

By including some hard foods in the diet, such as biscuits, bones, or even whole carrots, you will give your pet a good way to exercise and clean its teeth and gums.

A good general rule is to give your animal ample amounts of any food it really likes, unless the desire for that one food has become an addiction or unless the food is not of good quality.

Daily supplements

In addition to the basic natural food groups above, I always recommend the inclusion of several nutrition-packed food supplements in the diet. Part of their purpose is to fortify the diet with plenty of important vitamins and minerals. These are often inadequate even in fresh foods today, because of loss during storage and cooking and because of soil depletion and force-growing methods. Moreover, our pets' needs for vitamins and minerals have increased because of the pollution and stress common to modern life. And for animals that are not in the best of health, supplements are essential.

Some supplements have specific purposes. For instance, bone meal provides calcium and other minerals a carnivore needs and would

naturally get by eating the entire body and bones of the prey. The other food groups do not supply enough calcium to meet the required amount. Brewer's yeast, on the other hand, is abundant in B vitamins (especially B_1), which are vital to many basic food functions and which also help to repel fleas. Both yeast and kelp are also important natural sources of many needed minerals.

I include vitamin E or wheat germ oil capsules for several reasons. Not only does vitamin E serve important body functions, such as fighting disease, it also helps fight the effects of pollution. An antioxidant, it also helps to preserve and protect the vitamin A and fatty acids in other supplements and foods.

Here are some brief guidelines for buying and storing supplements.

Yeast: Buy a good-quality brewer's yeast or primary nutritional yeast grown on molasses or grains. I used to recommend calcium-fortified yeast. But I no longer suggest using it because when combined with calcium-rich bone meal, the calcium/phosphorus ratio becomes unbalanced. Unmodified yeast, on the other hand, is high in phosphorus and helps approximate the correct calcium/phosphorus ratio, 1.2:1 for dogs and 1:1 for cats. For the same reason I no longer routinely recommend dolomite as a substitute for bone meal. Dolomite doesn't supply enough dietary phosphorus, either.

Bone meal: Buy this in the powdered form that is sold for human use. Don't feed your animal the type sold for use on gardens, because it may not be sufficiently pure. For those who prefer not to use animal products, substitute dicalcium phosphate (use two-thirds the amount suggested for bone meal). This product is available in pet stores.

Large dogs, especially those with bone problems or signs of hip dysplasia, *may* need more bone meal or bones. There is some confusion about the nutritional needs of large dogs. They require fewer calories per pound of body weight than smaller dogs. So, relative to their weight, they take in less total food and therefore fewer vitamins and minerals. According to our calculations, some large dogs – even those who eat plenty – may not get enough calcium and phosphorus. This lack could be a contributing factor in the bone problems so common in larger breeds. On the other hand, some vets feel these difficulties are caused by too *much* calcium. So I've tried to strike a middle path in my bone meal recommendations for dogs.

Kelp powder: It's simplest and cheapest to buy the powder rather than the fresh or tablet forms. You can usually find this mineral-rich supplement at the best price by buying it by the pound in most natural food stores. But if you live somewhere without one and can't find kelp, substitute a multi-mineral tablet made for human use. Also, if you like, you can try using alfalfa powder in place of the kelp in the supplement group.

Vegetable oil: Vegetable oils provide a good source of unsaturated fatty acids, important for many body functions. Use a cold pressed type, as sold in bulk or in bottles in health food stores, and store it tightly sealed in the refrigerator. Keep it in a brown glass bottle to minimize deterioration caused by light. You can use just about any of the common oils, but safflower and corn oils are the highest in the important unsaturated fatty acid, linoleic acid. They are the best choice for dogs. For cats, which don't metabolize unsaturated fats quite as well as dogs, use olive oil.

Cod-liver oil: This excellent natural source of vitamins A and D is sold in brown bottles. Once open, you should store it in the refrigerator to retard the oxidation process that leads to eventual rancidity. Potencies vary somewhat, so read and compare labels. I

calculate that one teaspoon is usually about 5,000 international units (I.U.) of vitamin A, so if your product is much higher or lower than this figure, adjust the quantity as needed to make it equivalent to the recommended amount.

Vitamin E: Get a natural-source vitamin E containing the d-alpha tocopherols. (The *dl*-alpha tocopherols are a synthetic form.) The gelatin capsule variety provides a good 'storage container.' Open one fresh daily (or else give a double dose every other day, if this is more convenient).

You can also use a natural complex such as wheat germ oil, or use it along with vitamin E. But be careful not to feed your animal rancid wheat germ oil, which is detectable by a slightly bitter or burning aftertaste. Buy it in capsule form for your best bet.

How to use the supplements

The simplest way to use the supplements is to mix the powdered ones and the oils in large quantities at one time. Otherwise, you'll be juggling around so many measuring spoons every day, you won't know what to do! You can mix the three powders – yeast, bone meal and kelp – in one container, preferably a sealed jar, and store it on a dark, cool shelf. The vegetable oil and cod-liver oil can be combined in another jar, preferably a brown bottle with a little vitamin E added to prevent spoilage, then shaken together and stored in the refrigerator. Don't mix the daily dosage of vitamin E in with the other oils, but give it fresh from the capsule for best keeping.

Dogs are less uniform in size than cats, so you can feed your dog supplements in two ways. You can include them with other ingredients when you prepare one of the basic recipes (see chapter 4), or you can measure them directly into the food bowl at mealtime.

Daily supplements for cats

Feed daily:
- 1 teaspoon *Cat Powder Mix*
- 1 teaspoon *Cat Oil Mix*
- 30 to 50 I.U. vitamin E (or 20- to 40-minim capsule or capsules of wheat germ oil)

Note: Supplements for kittens, pregnant and nursing cats, and sick cats are described in chapter 5 and the *Encyclopaedia* section.

CAT POWDER MIX

½ cup brewer's yeast
¼ cup bone meal
¼ cup kelp powder

Mix the ingredients together well and store in a sealed jar on a dark shelf. You can substitute 3 tablespoons dicalcium phosphate for bone meal. If you do, feed a little less – a *scant* teaspoon instead of a whole teaspoon – of the powder mix daily. You also can use alfalfa powder as part of the kelp measure if you want.

CAT OIL MIX

¾ cup vegetable oil
¼ cup cod-liver oil
20–40 I.U. vitamin E (to prevent spoilage)

Shake the ingredients together well in a sealed brown bottle and store in the refrigerator. Olive oil is the preferred vegetable oil.

Daily supplements for dogs

Feed daily:
- *Dog Powder Mix*
- *Dog Oil Mix*
- *Vitamin E supplement*

Amounts vary according to size of dog.

Note: Supplements for puppies, pregnant and nursing dogs and sick dogs are described in chapter 5 and the *Encyclopaedia* section.

DOG POWDER MIX

2 cups nutritional yeast
1½ cups bone meal
½ cup kelp powder

Mix the ingredients together well and store in a sealed jar on a dark shelf. If you substitute dicalcium phosphate for bone meal, use 1 cup of it in the formula and reduce the daily feeding of powder mix by about 10 per cent (use scant measures). You can also use alfalfa powder as part of the kelp measure if you want.

DOG OIL MIX

1¾ cups vegetable oil
¼ cup cod-liver oil
50–100 I.U. vitamin E (to prevent spoilage)

Shake the ingredients together well in a sealed brown bottle and store in the refrigerator. The best vegetable oil for dogs is probably safflower, but soya, corn and sunflower oils are good, too.

Since dogs vary greatly in size, there is no single required amount of supplementation, as there is for cats. Instead, the recommended amount increases with the size of the dog. People who prepare home-made food for their dogs usually find it most convenient simply to add 4 teaspoons *Dog Powder Mix*, 2 teaspoons *Dog Oil Mix* and 100 I.U. of vitamin E to each recipe. If you double the recipe, double the supplements.

The supplement is given in about the right amount for the quantity of food one recipe produces. Therefore, the quantity of supplements your dog consumes will depend on the amount of food it eats. Small dogs, eating small portions, will receive enough of the supplements to meet their needs. Likewise, large dogs that eat large portions also will be sufficiently nourished. This method of adding supplements is convenient if you are feeding two or more dogs of different size.

Do not use this method, however, if you prepare a lot of food in advance. The oils just won't stay fresh. Instead, if you are feeding only one dog, or if you are preparing a lot of food in advance, add the powder mix, oil mix and vitamin E at mealtime. Using the table below, Daily Supplements for Dogs According to Weight, find your dog's weight. Read across the table to find the proper amount of daily supplements to give. For example, if your dog weighs 25 pounds, it should receive 4 teaspoons of *Dog Powder Mix*, 2 teaspoons of *Dog Oil Mix* and 100 I.U. of vitamin E.

If your dog weighs less than 5 pounds or more than 110, you will have to adjust the figures. A 2½-pound dog, for example, should receive one-half the amount recommended for a 5-pound dog. A 150-pound dog should receive the amount recommended for a 110-pound dog plus the amount recommended for a 40-pound dog.

Using supplements with commercial foods

If, despite all you have read on the subject, you decide to go on feeding commercial foods (or feel you must do so at least some of the time), you can improve their nutritional quality significantly by using modified supplements. Since most commercial foods (but not all) are reasonably well fortified with calcium and phosphorus already, you can reduce the bone meal for large animals, and omit it altogether for small ones. You also can

DAILY
SUPPLEMENTS
FOR DOGS
ACCORDING
TO WEIGHT

Weight (pounds)	Dog Powder Mix	Dog Oil Mix	Vitamin E (I.U.)
5 – 15	2 teaspoons	1 teaspoon	50
15 – 30	4 teaspoons	2 teaspoons	100
30 – 50	2 tablespoons	1 tablespoon	150
50 – 80	3 tablespoons	1½ tablespoons	200
80 – 110	¼ cup	2 tablespoons	300
110 +	⅓ + cup	2½ + tablespoons	400

NOTE: If you use wheat germ oil capsules instead of vitamin E capsules, feed about 20 to 40 minims, depending on dog's weight and condition.

use a bit less cod-liver oil, since some vitamin A is added to most brands. But don't skimp on the rest. Use the yeast, kelp, oils and vitamin E as suggested above. You may even want to increase the amount of oils slightly to make up for the low fat content of dry foods.

If you do omit bone meal from the powder mix, adjust the daily amount fed accordingly: ¾ teaspoon *Cat Powder Mix* for cats and two-thirds the amount of *Dog Powder Mix* recommended for your size dog. As for the oils, adapt the *Cat Oil Mix* by putting just 2 tablespoons of cod-liver oil in a measuring cup and then adding enough vegetable oil to equal 1 cup total. Change the *Dog Oil Mix* by combining 2 tablespoons cod-liver oil with enough vegetable oil to total 2 cups. This way you can feed the same amounts of total oil mix already recommended and make the suggested adaptations at the same time.

Also make a point of including some fresh food along with the meals of commercial foods – such as sprouts, raw grated carrots, raw eggs and meat scraps (add more bone meal or bones if you feed much meat in order to keep the calcium/phosphorus ratio in correct balance).

If you use the home-made kibble recipes in the back of this book from time to time, supplements are already included in the recipes, so you need not add more. But do include some fresh foods as just mentioned.

CHAPTER FOUR

Easy Recipes to Make at Home

Cooking for pets . . . is it worth it? How do you do it and how do you keep it simple and affordable?

Nancy Caldwell of Baldwin, New York, is one of many people who have told me in glowing terms how worthwhile it is to feed natural foods to a pet:

'I have an eight-year-old mixed breed (mother pedigree Siberian husky; father Ger-

man shepherd [Alsatian] and Alaskan malamute). He weighs about 90 pounds and is magnificent, both in looks and health. He's never had a bath and yet his coat glistens and has no odour. Also his teeth are strong and pure white.

'His diet since ten weeks has been very varied and all good fresh food. Buck is about the healthiest dog I've ever known. He's playful, happy, loving and, again I must say, gorgeous. He's just bursting with good health.

'His diet is probably no more expensive than commercial food except for the beef, and I guess some pet owners don't want the extra work of preparation. They should know the small investment in time and money is well worth the effort. They have vet's bills – I do not.

'Friends think I'm nuts to cook for a dog. They have younger dogs with loose or missing teeth, severe rashes, heart and breathing problems, overweight, lethargy, etc. They say Buck is so healthy because he's a mongrel. That might help, but I think the diet and care he gets is part of it also. Buck has never had fleas either.

'He has the run of the house at all times and also a fenced large yard. Some folks put dogs in the kitchen, bathroom or cellar when out or at night.'

Once you get used to it, you'll find it very little trouble to prepare the basic recipes in this book, especially if you follow the time- and money-savings tips found in this chapter.

The directions given for preparing the recipes are just suggestions, and you can add some natural flavourings or spices to improve appeal, particularly for bland foods like tofu. You may sometimes want to scramble other ingredients in with eggs and sometimes just serve them raw. Sometimes you may serve raw meat and vegetables, and at other times you may be using cooked left-overs. Occasionally you may need to add a little water or broth to the recipe to achieve the best consistency.

We used the ingredients to calculate the nutritional constituents of each recipe. But don't feel you have to stick with any foods in particular. I encourage you to use substitutions freely for variety, balance and convenience. You will find nutritionally equivalent

substitutions on pages 54 and 55 for all ingredients marked with an asterisk (*) in the recipes.

After you've developed a feel for what your pet needs, you can feed it other things sometimes – a peanut butter sandwich, part of your dinner casserole, cheese and toast, and so forth. But try to stick to the recipes most of the time, so you keep the nutrients in balance. If you are good at estimating volumes, don't worry about making careful measurements every time. With a little experience you will know about how much of each ingredient you need.

In any case, try to serve the meals at about room temperature or slightly warmed, but not too hot, not too cold. Feed the total amount as one or two meals a day and return any uneaten portions to the refrigerator after about half an hour.

Some price comparisons

Perhaps you're wondering how you could ever afford the time and money to cook natural foods for your animal. In this busy and costly world, a lot of people share your concern. It's true that the diet I recommend will be a bit of a bother, particularly compared to the ultimate convenience of scooping a quantity of cheap, mass-produced dried food from a bag in the cupboard. However, consider the hidden costs of the scoop-it-out-of-the-bag approach. One is the very real chance that you will have to spend more time and money on trips to the vet in an often futile attempt to patch up an ailing animal. Other hidden costs include the pain and shorter life of your pet. Also count the nutritionally aggravated behaviour problems that can make both your lives miserable. Looking at it from this larger perspective, I think most people would find that a quality diet is well worth the added time and cost, even in purely pragmatic terms.

But the good news is that some of the high-quality natural foods recipes in this book actually cost *less* than some of the commercial products using inferior ingredients.

Two of our maintenance recipes for dogs (*Meat-Bean-Rice Dish for Dogs*, and the *Bulk Vegetarian Two-Meal Plan*), are comparable to or cheaper than the average price for tinned food. And the average price for all six bulk recipes is less than top-price tinned foods. Now certainly you can cut costs considerably by using the cheapest of the dry foods, but I think you will pay in the long run. (And your pet will pay all along!)

For cats all the maintenance recipes are higher than the average price of tinned food, but most are cheaper than top-price tinned.

Naturally, prices will vary according to inflation, the area where you live, and whether you shop for the best buys. You can cut some costs even more – without sacrificing quality – by making use of the following ideas.

Cost-savers

Buy ingredients in bulk, if possible. You can save money on both foods and supplements by buying them unpackaged, sold in bulk by weight or volume. Many natural food stores sell grains, legumes, seeds, nuts, cheese, oils, seasonings and powdered food supplements (such as nutritional yeast and kelp) this way. Bulk foods are likelier to be found in stores that specilize in food rather than those that mostly carry prepackaged vitamins, food supplements, herbs and other health products. Don't use the bone meal that is sold for gardening, because it may not be pure. Buy vitamin E in sealed capsules to preserve its freshness. Besides, it usually costs less that way and it's pre-measured.

Buy economy sizes and thrift brands. If you're cost-conscious, you probably already know this. But I'll remind you anyway. Many foods such as cottage cheese, cheese, canned fish, packaged grains and beans and milk are cheaper per pound when you buy large packages. You can usually save money by buying a generic or store brand as well, since their marketing costs are less.

Select best-buy protein sources. When deciding what recipes and what substitution/variations you will use, choose foods that cost the least per unit of protein. High-protein foods are the costliest part of the diet, so it pays to compare what you're getting for your money.

We have listed probable best protein buys in the accompanying table for different groups of foods. We have arranged the groups themselves in order of cost, with those we found most economical listed first. Naturally, there is some overlap between the various groups in terms of values.

Use this table for cost comparisons, but don't limit your pet's diet to just the cheap foods. Instead, strive for variety and balance. Remember that the vegetable groups are less concentrated sources of protein, and a dog or cat would find it hard to digest enough volume of food to meet its high-protein needs. Also remember that cats do have a meat requirement. So use foods from the animal-source groups, too, as shown in the recipes.

For those who really need to be cost-conscious, I suggest you use the table, Protein Content of Various Foods, on pages 44–5 to work out the actual cost per gram of protein of various foods. They are grouped according to cost per gram of protein and reflect best buys (bulk and economy sizes, cheapest brands) as recently priced, in our local stores.

Relative values stay fairly constant, but naturally prices and conditions vary. So if you want to check current values in your area, simply divide the price per pound of food by the number of grams of protein it contains. This will give you your present cost per gram of protein – a good way to compare values on one of the costliest nutrients in foods.

Use foods not acceptable to humans. At first, it might sound as if we're suggesting you give worthless scraps to your pet. On the contrary, the idea is to make use of foods that are often very high in nutrition but that we tend to throw away because of our taste preferences or ideas about sanitation. For example, try using free or inexpensive scraps from the butcher and trimmings like fish heads and tails, or chicken necks and gizzards. Use vegetable peelings, cores and ends, which can be cooked or finely grated if they seem tough. Use fine-grind feed store chicken food (which is better suited to dogs than to cats). You also can feed dogs – but not cats – slightly 'gamey' meat. Dogs, being natural scavengers, have digestive tracts that can handle slightly spoiled meat a lot better than humans can. And don't forget about plate scraps.

Feed your unused left-overs. Most animals delight in eating odds and ends of vegetables, meat, salads, casseroles, cereals, sandwiches, gravies, sauces, and so on. Just remember to avoid those with 'junk food' ingredients – sugar, additives, preservatives, white flour and the like. I would also minimize tinned foods. Try to use the scraps in the same proportions indicated for various food groups in the recipes. See page 275 for a tasty recipe that uses a variety of miscellaneous left-overs.

Grow bean sprouts and wheat grass. One of the least expensive and most nutritious ways you can ensure a year-round supply of fresh, live, organic vegetables for your pet (and yourself) is to keep a jar of sprouts or a pot of wheat grass growing continuously in your kitchen. It's much cheaper to grow bean sprouts than to buy them. And it's easy, too.

You also will save money buying your alfalfa seeds, lentils, wheat or other sprouting seeds by the pound (in bulk) in natural food stores. Here are some instructions for the novice:

Bean sprouts: Buy one or two sprouting jars, tubes, or sacks, or else make your own by using elastic to secure a piece of muslin or fine net curtaining over the end of a large jam jar. (We find the commercial units reasonably priced and easiest to keep clean.) For a two-pound jar, soak about two tablespoons of alfalfa seeds or $\frac{1}{2}$ cup lentils or mung beans for eight hours, or overnight. Drain off the excess water through the muslin (save for a soup stock or for watering plants). Rinse well three or four times a day, placing at an angle to allow excess moisture to drain off into a bowl, drainer, or sink. After a couple of days you can, if you wish, flood the jar and wash off the excess seed coats through a coarse sieve. In three to five days, the bean sprouts will be ready to eat. You may need to break them up or chop them (especially larger ones) for some animals.

Wheat grass: Many animals relish an occasional 'graze' off a pot of wheat grass, in much the same way that they may go for your lawn grass. I feel that this habit is part of a natural cleansing instinct, so don't discourage it. Providing wheat grass is a way of ensuring a high-quality suitable grass not contaminated with lawn fertilizer or weed killer.

Soak a handful of grains of wheat overnight. Drain, saving the nutritious rinse water. Sprinkle the grains evenly over the top of a flower pot or plastic planting tray almost filled with potting soil or compost, spacing them about a grain apart. Cover with $\frac{1}{4}$ inch of potting soil and water daily, enough to keep soil slightly moist, until shoots are about 4 inches high. 'Mow' the grass down to about 1 inch tall, chop the trimmings and mix them into your pet's meal. Or encourage your animal friend to graze off the growing greens.

BEST
PROTEIN
BUYS

Food Group (in order of best price value as a group)	Best Protein Values in Each Group (in order of best individual value per gram of protein)
Legumes	Soya beans, split peas, soya protein isolate, lentils, lima beans, chick-peas, peanuts, kidney beans. Tofu is more expensive, but it is still cheaper than many meats.
Grains	Chicken food, rolled oats, rye flakes, maize meal, wheat flakes, barley, bulgur, millet. Brown rice is intermediate and buckwheat and whole wheat bread are high. Differences are not great except when buying in bulk.
Seeds and nut	Sunflower seeds, sesame seeds (bulk prices!). Pumpkin seeds are intermediate. Avoid expensive nuts like almonds, cashews, walnuts, and so forth.
Medium-fatty meats	Chicken necks, canned mackerel, turkey heart, frying chicken backs and wings.
Dairy products and supplements	Non fat dried milk, eggs, brewer's yeast, skim milk, low fat cottage cheese, low fat milk, whole milk. Yogurt and hard cheese are more expensive protein sources in this group.
Lean meats	Chicken hearts, minced turkey (dark meat), beef and chicken liver, chicken gizzard, whole frying chicken, whole turkey, kidney, lean beef heart.
Fatty and very lean meats	*Fatty:* Lamb neck and shoulder, minced beef, fatty beef heart, beef chuck roast. Brain and tongue, if you can find them. Avoid most cuts of pork and lamb. *Very Lean:* Tuna canned in water, turkey breast. Where available at decent prices: lean fish like cod, perch, halibut.

PROTEIN CONTENT
OF VARIOUS FOODS

CHEAP

Food item	Grams of Protein per Pound* (unless otherwise specified)
Soya beans and flakes	154.7
Split peas	109.8
Rolled oats	64.4
Rye flakes	54.9
Soya protein isolate	408.2
Chicken necks	33.7
Lentils	112.0
Mackerel, Pacific, canned	95.7
Cornmeal	41.7
Lima beans	92.5
Turkey heart	73.5
Wheat flakes	44.9
Barley, pearl, pot or scotch	43.5
Chick-peas (garbanzo beans)	93.0
Peanuts, roasted	118.8
Bulgur	46.7
Chicken heart	84.4
Kidney beans	102.1
Milk, non-fat dried	164.0[a]
Millet	44.9
Sunflower seeds	108.9

*Food values, in general, are given for the uncooked form.

SOURCES: Adapted from *Composition of Foods*, Agriculture Handbook No. 8, by Bernice K. Watt and Annabel L. Merrill (Washington, D.C.: Agricultural Research Service, U.S. Department of Agriculture, 1975); and

Nutritive Value of American Foods in Common Units, Agriculture Handbook No. 456, by Catherine F. Adams (Washington, D.C.: Agricultural Research Service, U.S. Department of Agriculture, 1975); except:

MEDIUM

Food Item	Grams of Protein per Pound* (unless otherwise specified)
Minced turkey, dark meat	136.1
Brown rice	34.0
Eggs, large	78.0/dozen
Eggs, medium	68.4/dozen
Sesame seeds	82.6
Beef liver	90.3
Brewer's yeast	176.0
Chicken gizzard	91.2
Chicken liver	89.4
Milk, skim	20/pint (Imp)[a]
Cottage cheese, low-fat	62.3[a]
Lamb neck and shoulder	63.5
Milk, 2% fat	19.5/pint[a]
Whole frying chicken	57.4
Whole turkey	65.9
Buttermilk	19.47/pint[a]
Cottage cheese, creamed	56.7[a]
Frying chicken backs	40.4
Milk, whole	19.2/pint[a]
Buckwheat	53.1
Lamb kidney	76.2
Minced beef	81.2
Tofu	35.4
Tuna, packed in water	127.0
Beef heart, lean	77.6
Red snapper	89.8
Beef chuck roast, choice	71.6
Frying chicken wings	41.1
Tuna, packed in oil	109.8

[a]*Composition of Foods: Dairy and Egg Products*, Agriculture Handbook No. 8–1, by Consumer and Food Economics Institute (Washington, D.C.: Agricultural Research Service, U.S. Department of Agriculture, 1976).

Figures adjusted to Imperial pint.

Food Item	Grams of Protein per Pound* (unless otherwise specified)
Turkey breast	94.8[b]
Cheddar cheese	113.0[a]
Beef mince, lean	93.9
Milk, raw, whole	19.2/pint
Mung bean sprouts	17.2
Potatoes	7.7
Frying chicken drumsticks and thighs	56.4
Whole frying rabbit	75.0
Minced chuck steak	84.8
Pumpkin seeds	131.5
Wholewheat bread	41.3
Salmon, pink, tinned, with bones	93.0
Squid	74.4
Yogurt, low-fat	23.8[a]
Almonds	84.4
Pork chops	61.1
Leg of lamb, choice	67.7
Herring, tinned	90.3[b]
Sirloin steak	74.4
Yogurt, whole	15.7[a]
Walnuts	67.1
Lamb chops	65.0
Sardines, tinned	85.3
Whole lake trout	24.0

EXPENSIVE

[b]*Composition of Foods: Poultry Products*, Agriculture Handbook No. 8–5, by Consumer and Food Economics Institute (Washington, D.C.: Science and Education Administration, U.S. Department of Agriculture, 1979).

Time-saving ideas

For a lot of busy working people, the problem with my suggested diet is not so much its cost but the *time* it can take to prepare it. Often they can barely manage to prepare well-rounded meals for themselves! If this sounds like you, don't give up. There is a way! Once you get the hang of it, you may find it really takes very little extra time, expecially if you make use of the efficiency suggestions that follow:

Prepare large quantities in advance. Particularly for those with small animals, it really makes sense to pre-cook a week's worth of grains and beans, especially if you're cooking them for the rest of the family anyway. If you have a freezer, you can prepare recipes for two weeks or more. Wrap in serving size amounts to freeze. Then just defrost them one at a time, bring to room temperature, and serve. Frozen raw meat is not quite as good as fresh, but it's better than commercial pet food. (If you are feeding your pet a lot of frozen food, it would be a good idea to add fresh ingredients like raw vegetables or raw eggs when the food is served.)

Prepare home-made dried foods and biscuits (see pages 272–5) when you have the time, to help out during more hectic days.

Minimize cooking. The less you cook, the more nutrition you keep in the food. And the more time you save! It's usually not necessary to cook meat, eggs, and certain vegetables. Also, there are many ingredients that are usually served without heating, like milk, cottage cheese, yogurt, tofu (add a little seasoning), bread, nut butters, and cheese. You can modify recipes to use foods that don't need cooking. For instance, you can use tofu instead of soya beans, or bread instead of rice (see pages 54–5). By mixing these ingredients with some bean sprouts and supplements, you can have a meal in no time at all! Think of a few such 'quick' meals you can depend on for busy days.

Work out a few favourite recipes and variations, then stick to them. Take a few minutes to sit down and calculate the needed ingredient amounts for three or four recipes for your size animal, using your preferred substitutions. Write them on recipe cards or fasten them inside a kitchen cupboard for easy reference. Include the amounts needed to prepare several days' worth of food. If you use just three or four basic combinations, preparing meals will soon become so automatic you probably won't even have to bother with exact measurements. But don't use just one recipe all the time, because variety is important.

Share your own meals with your pet, modifying them for its special needs. Once you have used the recipes enough to get the hang of about how much of what goes into a balanced meal for your pet, you can feel confident about occasionally improvising meals using extra portions of whatever you're having for dinner. Just mix your pet's supplements into its portion, and, if it seems appropriate, add a little more protein food (meat, dairy, tofu and so forth) or a little more carbohydrate (bread or grain) to match approximately the proportions found in the recipes. This suggestion is more practical for those with small animals.

Feed commercial animal 'health' foods if necessary. Get a back-up stock of ready-made pet health food. It will be a life-saver on those inevitable 'off' days that happen to us all—the day everyone in the family has the flu and *then* the toilet gets blocked. This back-up supply is also handy if you leave your pet in someone else's care while you're on holiday.

Choose one of the dried, tinned or frozen brands of additive-free pet foods sold in some health food stores. However, I don't recommend this food as a regular diet for several reasons. Despite the good intentions of the manufacturers and the absence of artificial flavours, colours, and preservatives, most of these brands do contain meat meal, the shortcomings of which were discussed earlier. And some of these brands have a very simple formula that appears to me to be inadequately supplied with the needed vitamins and minerals, so be sure to add all the supplements for these. Several of the dried brands I have examined tend to be lower in protein than the usual commercial foods. Some people have told me their cats will not eat dried health food. Perhaps this resistance is a reaction to the food's low protein content. So buy a tinned food (usually high in protein) or else select a dried food that has at least 22 per cent protein (for dogs) or 34 per cent protein (for cats) on a *dry weight basis*. To find out this information, first determine what percentage of the food is dry solids. To do this, subtract the stated percentage of moisture content, or water, from 100 per cent. (Most kibbles are 88 to 90 per cent solids.) Then divide the stated percentage of protein by your result. An example:

$$\frac{18\% \text{ protein (label)}}{90\% \text{ dry solids}} = \frac{20.0\% \text{ protein}}{\text{(dry weight basis)}}$$

If you do use these prepared health foods occasionally, you can greatly enhance their overall quality by adding a small amount of bean sprouts, chopped greens, or grated carrot, along with occasional bits of raw meat or dairy products. The same goes for the home-made dried food recipes found on pages 272–5.

Also, do mix in supplements, perhaps omitting bone meal and cod-liver oil if the package label indicates that these (or comparable sources of calcium and vitamin A) have already been supplied in the formula. The home-made dried food recipes already contain the supplements, but you should also add some fresh vitamin E daily to help counter the deterioration of the oils in the food. If you feed a sizeable amount of meat scraps alongside, then you need to balance the calcium/phosphorus ration by giving a little bone meal (or bones) along with it.

Now that I've dealt with most of the considerations that might prevent you from switching to natural pet foods, it's time to look at the recipes.

Basic Recipes for Cats

The following six recipes will provide about the right daily amount of food for an average nine- to ten-pound adult cat. If your cat is much smaller or larger than this, you can follow the rough guidelines given in the Weight-feeding Guide to work out how much you'll need to feed.

In addition, if your cat is very inactive you will probably need to feed about three quarters of the amount otherwise recommended. Thus, a very inactive six-pound cat (not pregnant or nursing) would need about half the recipe amount ($3/4 \times 2/3 = 1/2$). Naturally, individual needs vary, so use these rations as rough guidelines and adjust them if your cat loses or gains weight.

WEIGHT-FEEDING
GUIDE (CATS)

Your cat's weight (pounds)	Multiply recipes by
5–6	$2/3$
7–8	$3/4$
9–10	1
11–12	$1\,1/3$

CAT OMELET

> *1 tablespoon non-fat dried milk**
>
> *3 medium eggs*
>
> *3 tablespoons dry-curd cottage cheese**
>
> *2 tablespoons bean sprouts or grated or chopped vegetables*
>
> *daily supplements as recommended*

Mix the dried milk with a little water and beat with the eggs. Turn into hot greased frying pan. When the bottom of the egg mixture is cooked, turn it over and place cottage cheese, bean sprouts or vegetables and supplements on top. When firm, fold over (omelet-style) and serve. *Or*, scramble everything together at once.

Yield: about 1 cup

FELINE FATTY MEAT MENU

> *1/4 cup cooked brown rice**
>
> *1/3 cup (2–3 ounces) raw mince or fatty meat**
>
> *2 tablespoons grated or chopped vegetables**
>
> *1/3 cup creamed cottage cheese**
>
> *daily supplements as recommended*

Warm up the rice in a saucepan or steamer, adding the meat and vegetables if they are to be cooked. Mix in the cottage cheese and supplements and serve.

Yield: about 1 cup

Ingredients marked with an asterisk (*) in these recipes may be replaced by equivalent substitutions (see pages 54 and 55). The cup used is a standard American measuring cup, which holds 237 ml – rather less than half a pint.

TASTY TOFU

6 ounces tofu*

3 tablespoons grated cheese*

2 tablespoons sunflower seeds*

1 tablespoon brewer's yeast

1 tablespoon grated or chopped vegetables*

daily supplements as recommended

Mix the ingredients together in a blender, adding a little water, broth, tamari sauce, or tomato sauce as needed for proper consistency. *Or,* if you don't have a blender, chop the seeds as finely as possible and mash everything together well.

Yield: about 1 ½ cups

LEAN MEAT MENU FOR CATS

⅓ cup cooked oatmeal*

½ cup (about ¼ pound) chopped offal or lean meat*

1 tablespoon grated or chopped vegetables*

2 teaspoons butter*

daily supplements as recommended

¼ cup whole milk*

Warm up the oatmeal in a saucepan or steamer, adding the meat and vegetables if they are to be cooked. Mix in the butter and supplements and serve. Give the milk in a separate dish.

Yield: about 1 ⅓ cups

LEAN MEAT AND EGGS FOR CATS

2 medium eggs

daily supplements as recommended

¼ cup (about 2 ounces) offal or lean meat*

⅓ cup cooked brown rice*

1 tablespoon grated or chopped vegetables*

If you cook the eggs, scramble them first lightly with the supplements (and meat, if you cook it). Add the rest of the ingredients and serve.

Yield: about 1 cup

DAIRY DELIGHT FOR CATS

1 teaspoon oil

1 medium egg*

daily supplements as recommended

⅓ cup cooked brown rice*

½ cup creamed cottage cheese*

1 tablespoon grated or chopped vegetables*

Add oil to warm frying pan. Scramble egg and supplements lightly, then mix in the rest of the ingredients. Warm slightly. Serve.

Yield: about 1 cup

DAILY MAINTENANCE
RATIONS FOR CATS

These daily maintenance rations for cats will provide the following amounts of various nutrients (on a dry weight basis).

| Recipe | Percent on a Dry Weight Basis | | | | | Calories |
	Protein	Fat	Carbohydrate	Ash	Calories	per Gram
Cat Omelet	47.2	33.2	13.4	6.2	367	5.5
Feline Fatty Meat Menu	38.3	35.4	21.1	5.2	364	5.6
Tasty Tofu	39.0	35.6	18.8	6.6	357	5.2
Lean Meat Menu for Cats	39.2	28.2	26.5	6.1	363	5.2
Lean Meat and Eggs for Cats	39.4	30.5	24.3	5.8	351	5.4
Dairy Delight for Cats	36.0	30.3	28.0	5.7	354	5.3
Average, all 6	39.9	32.2	22.0	5.9	359	5.4

Recipes average about .9% calcium and .9% phosphorus (1:1 ratio).
One gram = .035 ounce.

Basic Recipes for Dogs

The recipes that follow meet the average daily needs of an adult dog weighing about 25 pounds. To work out what you'll need to feed a smaller or larger dog, use the Weight-feeding Guide. It is based on the average calorie requirements of dogs of various sizes.

Ingredients marked with an asterisk (*) in these recipes may be replaced by equivalent substitutions (see pages 54 and 55). The cup is a standard American measuring cup (237 ml), which holds about as much as a breakfast cup.

WEIGHT-FEEDING
GUIDE (DOGS)

Your dog's weight (pounds)	Multiply recipes by
5	¼
10	½
25	1
40	1½
60	2
85	2½
105	3
125	3½
150	4

CANINE MEAT AND GRAIN MENU

*2 cups cooked brown rice**

⅓ cup fatty meat ⎫ (or use ¼ cup
 ⎬ lean meat and
⅓ cup lean meat ⎭ 2 teaspoons oil)
*¼ cup grated or chopped vegetables**

Mix all ingredients together and serve slightly warm. *Or,* steam meat and vegetables and then add rice and supplements.

Yield: about 3 cups

DAILY DUO FOR DOGS

Morning: Serve as a hot cereal.

*1 ½ cups cooked oatmeal**

1 cup whole milk

1 teaspoon honey

Evening: Combine the ingredients and serve warm.

*1 cup chopped, cooked potatoes**

*½ cup lean meat**

*1 teaspoon oil**

*1 tablespoon grated or chopped vegetables**

daily supplements as recommended

Yield: about 4 cups, total

MEAT–BEAN–RICE DISH FOR DOGS

*1 ¾ cups cooked brown rice**

⅓ cup lean meat

½ cup cooked beans (kidney, black, pinto, navy or lima)

*¼ cup grated or chopped vegetables**

*1 ½ teaspoons oil**

1 tablespoon brewer's yeast

daily supplements as recommended

Heat the rice, meat and beans together. Then mix in the rest of the ingredients and serve moderately warm.

Yield: about 2⅔ cups

VEGETARIAN TWO-MEAL PLAN

Morning: Serve as a hot cereal.

*1 ½ cups cooked oatmeal**

1 cup whole milk

1 teaspoon honey

Evening: Scramble together the eggs, soya protein isolate and supplements. Add the rest of the ingredients and serve.

*2 medium eggs**

2 teaspoons soya protein isolate (found in health food stores)

daily supplements as recommended

*⅔ cup cooked brown rice**

2 tablespoons grated or chopped vegetables

Yield: about 3¾ cups, total

EGGS–SOYA–RICE

*2 ½ ounces tofu (or ¼ cup cooked soya flakes)**

*2 medium eggs**

daily supplements as recommended

2 tablespoons brewer's yeast

*½ teaspoon oil**

2 cups cooked brown rice

*½ cup chopped or grated vegetables**

Scramble together the tofu, eggs, supplements, yeast and oil. Add rice and vegetables, along with any flavouring you have on hand, and serve.

Yield: about 3⅓ cups

POTATOES AU CANINE

*3 cups boiled, sliced potatoes**

*½ cup creamed cottage cheese**

1 tablespoon brewer's yeast

*¼ cup whole milk**

*¼ cup grated cheese**

daily supplements as recommended

*2 tablespoons grated or chopped vegetables**

Layer together the potatoes, cottage cheese, yeast and supplements in a casserole dish. Pour milk over them and top with grated cheese. Grill or bake until cheese is melted and slightly brown (about 15 minutes at 350°F). Let cool. Serve vegetables on the side. *Or,* mix all ingredients together while potatoes are hot after cooking, allowing heat to melt in the cheese, then serve.

Yield: about 4 cups

Naturally, individual needs vary, so watch your dog's weight and adjust the quantity up or down as needed. For puppies, pregnant and nursing females, and dogs subject to hard exercise or extreme temperatures, you will need to use the higher-protein recipes and feeding guidelines in chapter 5. If your dog is particularly inactive, you will probably find that he or she will eat less than the amount suggested.

Bulk versions for large dogs

If you have a large dog or several smaller ones to feed and you have the refrigerator space, you may want to cook a large amount in advance. On the next two pages are the amounts for all six dog recipes, multiplied by six. Each recipe should make enough to feed a 100-pound dog for about two days or a 60-pound dog for three days. Add the recommended supplements fresh daily.

DAILY MAINTENANCE RATIONS FOR DOGS

These daily maintenance rations for dogs will provide the following amounts of various nutrients (on a dry weight basis).

| Recipe | Percent on a Dry Weight Basis | | | | Calories | Calories per Gram |
	Protein	Fat	Carbohydrate	Ash	Calories	per Gram
Canine Meat and Grain Menu	23.1	17.8	51.3	7.8	793	4.6
Daily Duo for Dogs	23.9	17.8	49.3	9.0	778	4.5
Meat–Bean–Rice Dish for Dogs	20.9	12.9	58.2	8.0	783	4.3
Vegetarian Two-Meal Plan	22.1	19.9	49.1	8.9	788	4.6
Eggs–Soya–Rice	21.1	15.9	54.7	8.3	786	4.4
Potatoes au Canine	22.6	13.9	54.9	8.6	798	4.3
Average, all 6	22.3	16.4	52.9	8.4	788	4.5

Recipes average about 1.5% calcium and 1.2% phosphorus (1.25:1 ratio).
One gram = .035 ounce.

BULK VERSION OF POTATOES AU CANINE

18 cups (about 7 pounds) boiled, sliced potatoes (or 13½ cups cooked brown rice)*

3 cups creamed cottage cheese*

⅓ cup nutritional yeast

1½ cups whole milk*

1½ cups grated cheese*

¾ cup grated or chopped vegetables*

Layer potatoes and cottage cheese in a roaster (or other large pan). Pour milk over them and top with grated cheese. Grill or bake until cheese is melted and slightly brown. Let cool. Serve vegetables on the side. *Or,* mix all ingredients together while the potatoes are still hot, allowing this heat to melt the cheese.

Yield: about 24 cups

BULK VEGETARIAN TWO-MEAL PLAN

Morning; Serve the daily ration as a hot cereal with fresh milk and honey in appropriate daily amounts.

9 cups cooked oatmeal*

Evening: Scramble together the eggs and soya protein isolate, then add the rest of the ingredients.

1 dozen medium eggs*

¼ cup soya protein isolate

4 cups cooked brown rice*

¾ cup grated or chopped vegetables

Yield: about 15 cups

BULK MEASURE FOR EGGS–SOYA–RICE

1 pound tofu (or 1½ cups cooked soya flakes)*

1 dozen medium eggs*

¾ cup brewer's yeast

1 tablespoon oil*

12 cups cooked brown rice

3 cups grated or chopped vegetables*

Scramble together the tofu, eggs, yeast and oil. Add rice and vegetables, along with any flavourings you have on hand.

Yield: about 18 cups

CANINE MEAT AND GRAIN BULK MENU

12 cups cooked brown rice*

2 cups fatty meat*

2 cups lean meat*

1½ cups grated or chopped vegetables*

Mix all ingredients together. *Or,* steam meat and vegetables and then add rice. Serve the daily ration slightly warm.

Yield: about 18 cups

Notes: To cook rice, oats, soya flakes and other grains for these bulk recipes, refer to Equivalents for Dry and Cooked Cereals and Legumes on page 32. Ingredients marked with an asterisk (*) in these recipes may be replaced by equivalent substitutions. Refer to pages 54 and 55. The cup contains 237 ml.

BULK MEAT–BEAN–RICE DISH FOR DOGS

10 ½ cups cooked brown rice*

2 cups lean meat*

3 cups cooked beans (kidney, black, pinto, navy or lima)

1 ½ cups grated or chopped vegetables*

3 tablespoons oil*

⅓ cup brewer's yeast

Heat the rice, meat and beans together, then mix in the rest of the ingredient. Serve the daily ration moderately warm.

Yield: about 18 cups

TWO BULK MEALS FOR DOGS

Morning: Serve the daily ration as a hot cereal, with fresh milk and honey in appropriate daily amounts.

9 cups cooked oatmeal*

Evening: Combine the ingredients and serve the daily ration warm.

6 cups chopped, cooked potatoes*

3 cups lean meat*

2 tablespoons oil*

⅓ cup grated or chopped vegetables*

Yield: about 18 cups, total

Ingredient Substitutions

To add nutritional variety and great adaptability to these menus, you can make substitutions as provided by the following tables. The first indicates what foods we include under the terms 'lean' and 'fatty' meats. The substituted ingredients will provide approximately the same amounts of calories, proteins, fats and carbohydrates as those items they replace.

FATTY VS. LEAN MEATS

Fatty meats: minced beef, roasting chicken (whole), lamb (neck, shoulder, leg, chops), pork chops, blade shoulder and chuck steak, brains, tongue, sirloin steak, fatty beef heart.

Medium-fatty meats: frying chicken (necks, backs, wings), turkey heart, mackerel, lean mince, frying rabbit, herring, sardines, silverside.

Lean meats: beef or chicken liver or heart, kidney, tuna canned in oil, frying chicken (gizzard, drumsticks, thighs or whole), turkey (whole, minced, or dark meat), carp, salmon, catfish.

Very lean meats: tuna canned in water, turkey breast, perch, cod, halibut, haddock, bass, sole.

INGREDIENT SUBSTITUTIONS

Ingredient = Equivalent Substitutions	
GRAINS AND LEGUMES	
1 cup cooked oatmeal	⅔ cup cooked brown rice, bulgur, barley or millet, plus 1½ teaspoons brewer's yeast 2 medium slices whole wheat or rye bread 1 cup cooked maize meal plus 1½ teaspoons brewer's yeast
1 cup cooked brown rice	1 cup cooked bulgur, barley or millet 1⅓ cups cooked oatmeal 1½ cups cooked maize meal 3 slices whole wheat or rye bread
½ cup cooked soya flakes	½ cup cooked soya beans ¼ cup full-fat soya flour 5 ounces tofu plus 1 teaspoon honey or ½ teaspoon oil 1½ cups soya milk plus 1 teaspoon honey 2 tablespoons soya protein isolate plus 2 scant teaspoons oil
MEATS	
½ cup raw fatty meat or minced beef	½ cup medium-fatty meat plus 2 teaspoons oil ½ cup lean meat plus 1 tablespoon oil 3 large eggs

Ingredient = Equivalent Substitutions	
MEATS *(continued)*	
½ cup raw lean meat or offal	a little less than ½ cup medium-fatty meat ½ cup very lean meat plus 1 teaspoon oil ⅔ cup creamed cottage cheese 8 ounces tofu
DAIRY AND EGG PRODUCTS	
1 cup whole milk	1 cup whole yogurt 1 cup goat's milk 1 cup soya milk plus 2 teaspoons honey and 1 teaspoon oil ⅓ cup grated cheese ¼ cup dry-curd cottage cheese plus 1 tablespoon butter ⅓ cup creamed cottage cheese plus 2 teaspoons oil 3 tablespoons non-fat dried milk plus 1¾ teaspoons oil
1 medium egg	2½ tablespoons fatty meat 3 tablespoons dry-curd cottage cheese plus 1 teaspoon oil ¼ cup creamed cottage cheese plus ½ teaspoon oil 4 teaspoons soya protein isolate plus 1 teaspoon oil

Ingredient =	Equivalent Substitutions
3 medium eggs	2 tablespoons soya protein isolate plus any one of these: $\frac{1}{4}$ cup peanuts, $\frac{1}{4}$ cup peanut butter, $\frac{1}{4}$ cup tahini, $\frac{1}{3}$ cup ground almonds or $\frac{1}{2}$ cup sunflower seeds
$\frac{1}{2}$ cup creamed cottage cheese	$\frac{1}{3}$ cup dry-curd cottage cheese plus 1 teaspoon oil 6 ounces tofu
1 teaspoon butter	1 scant teaspoon oil or a little less lard or meat drippings
OTHER	
Vegetables	Use vegetables in about the same volumes interchangeably, except for starchy ones like potatoes or yams
1 cup chopped, cooked potatoes	1 cup cooked oatmeal $\frac{3}{4}$ cup cooked brown rice or similar grain
1 teaspoon oil	1 rounded teaspoon butter 1 scant teaspoon lard or meat drippings (**Note:** do not substitute other fats for the vegetable oil in the supplement group.)

Mealtime tips

Here are a few tips for enhancing the mealtime atmosphere and promoting good appetite and digestion.

Serve the food lukewarm or at room temperature – neither too hot nor too cold.

Keep the bowl clean. Don't let uneaten food particles accumulate. Avoid using a harsh or strong-smelling cleanser.

Give each animal its own bowl and keep the feeding routine regular and reliable. In most instances feed one or two meals a day, taking up and refrigerating any uneaten food after about half an hour. Cats may sometimes refuse food because it's natural for them to eat less often.

Provide a reasonably quiet place to feed that is pleasant and protected from intrusions by toddlers, other animals or strangers.

CHAPTER FIVE

Special Diets for Special Pets

Sometimes normal, healthy animals require a special diet – something a bit more supportive than their standard fare. Animals that are pregnant or feeding young fall into this category, as do young animals.

Another special animal is the pet of a vegetarian family. Often, because of ethical or health considerations, some people may choose to live without eating meat. These same people sometimes wonder if such a diet could also be developed for their pets.

The vegetarian diet

Can dogs and cats eat a meatless diet and be healthy?

In a holistic animal-care workshop I gave one Saturday, this topic generated lively discussion. One woman said, 'I am a vegetarian myself and I get along fine without meat. Yet, even though I don't want to, I *have* to feed my dog meat or dog food containing meat. After all, he's a carnivore and *needs* it . . . doesn't he?' She looked around the room and several people immediately smiled in recognition of a common problem.

One responded, 'Well, I've been feeding my dog a vegetarian diet for the last three years and he's in *great* health! He eats mostly bean sprouts, seeds, grains, raw fruits and vegetables and occasional dairy products. He does just fine!'

'But what about the long run?' another interjected. 'Here we've been talking today all about the need for our animals to live and eat as naturally as possible, and a vegetarian diet is nothing like the diet of the dog's wild relatives. After all, wolves don't eat bean sprouts! So if we *really* want to go natural, we should feed them mostly raw meat and bones.'

'But that's impractical,' a fourth broke in. 'It just costs too much. Besides, it has a larger effect. Eating meat contributes to the world hunger problem because it's such a wasteful way to produce protein. To say nothing of the suffering it causes animals!'

There, in that brief exchange, arose most of the basic considerations that occur when people ask if their pets can live as vegetarians. The problem is a complex one with many implications. Until recently, few people ever thought of asking it. We have all been deeply conditioned by our upbringing to think that it's *necessary* to eat a regular and ample amount of meat. (Actually, this degree of meat consumption is a relatively recent development.) Furthermore, it is our social pattern to keep carnivores as pets, which means we have to raise and kill meat for them. Because these cultural patterns are so widespread, we can easily overlook what meat-eating really means, not only for ourselves

and our pets but also for hungry children in Africa or frightened cattle on the slaughterhouse line.

So let's take a look at the major reasons why some people decide to exclude meat (and sometimes eggs and dairy products as well) from their diets, and why they are interested in the same possibility for their pets. The first group of reasons stems from concern about the suffering of others and the second group from concern about personal health.

Ethical concerns about eating meat

The most obvious type of pain that results from eating meat is the pain that falls upon the animals involved. Most of us never see more than the end result of livestock production and slaughtering. We just see a nice, neatly wrapped package of red material in the meat department of the supermarket. Lacking first-hand knowledge, we may imagine the meat came from animals who spent long, peaceful lives lazily scratching or grazing in sunny pastures. At the end of their idyll, we imagine they are terminated quickly and easily by a humane and efficient slaughter.

Unfortunately, the reality is usually quite different.

In my former job as a large animal vet, I was often appalled to witness the crowded, stressful and uncomfortable conditions under which most chickens, pigs and cows actually live and die. Farming has become big business, and most animals are treated more like profit-making units than like living beings capable of feeling pain or unhappiness. Accordingly, most of them are denied decent living environments or normal social relationships in order to minimize costs and maximize profits.

Chickens, for instance, are typically

packed into small wire cages that are stacked together in large buildings housing thousands of birds. They may never in their lives see daylight or stand on the ground, and most are so crowded they can scarcely turn around. Imagine, if you will, the tremendous stress that results. Sickness (for which individuals are not given attention) and cannibalism are common.

An average 'prime' or 'white' veal calf in the United States spends its life separated from its mother, tethered in a stall less than two feet wide in a dark building. It is deliberately made anaemic by excluding iron from its diet. All this for the sake of a certain flavour.

I could go on describing many disturbing conditions, but this is not the place for it. For those interested, there are several worth-while books in print that present the facts about modern livestock production and the ethical case for not eating its products. They have changed the lives of many people.

Another ethical concern is how our high consumption of meat contributes to the problem of world hunger. Undernourishment and starvation plague a large proportion of humanity. Their suffering is largely due to the inefficient use of our crop lands. Protein can be produced on much less land by plants than by meat animals – which yield much less food than they consume.

For instance, an acre of cereal grains can produce 5 times more protein than an acre devoted to meat production. Legumes (beans, peas and peanuts) can produce 10 times more, and leafy vegetables 15 times more. Beef cattle are among the least efficient converters of plant material to meat, taking 16 pounds of grain and soyabeans to produce just 1 pound of meat.

In the developed countries, we have been able to afford the luxury of such wastage (at least up until now) because we have so much land, along with a favourable climate, advan-

ced technologies and economic and political power. However, this inefficient use of crop land has caused a tremendous loss of protein that could have been available for human consumption on the world market. In 1971 this loss amounted to about 118 million tons of grain and soya beans – enough to provide every person then alive with more than a cup of cooked grain daily for a year.

Better health for vegetarians

Many vegetarians throughout history have advocated the health-promoting aspects of their diet and now modern research appears to support their observations. For instance, wartime conditions in this century temporarily required the people of several European countries sharply to reduce their consumption of meat. The result: improvements in national health statistics, including reduced mortality rates from disease in general, as well as improved growth rates and dental health for their children.

Seventh-day Adventists (who usually do not smoke or drink and of whom at least half are reported to eat meatless diets) have intestinal, colonic and rectal cancer rates 50 to 70 per cent lower and heart disease rates 50 per cent lower than those of the general population. Other research indicates that meat fat favours the production of certain carcinogens in the intestines and that vegetarians have lower blood pressure and cholesterol levels, offering a possible explanation for these differences.

Even exercise seems to take second place as compared to the potential benefits of such a diet. A survey of a thousand North Americans found that the healthiest individuals were vegetarians who ran for exercise. The second healthiest group were non-running vegetarians, followed by meat-eating runners and then meat-eating non-runners.

It may just be that we are meant to eat meatless diets, because that's what our ancestors apparently ate before hard times in the Ice Age forced them to begin hunting. Most other primates are basically vegetarians. Our teeth, digestive tracts and even our hands (adapted as they are to picking fruits, nuts and vegetables) seem to be best suited to such foods.

So it's not hard to make the case that a meatless diet makes sense *for people*. But what about for our naturally carnivorous pets? That's another question. As the woman in our workshop suggested, their most natural diet would seem to be fresh meat and bones. But is this completely so?

Actually, a predator's diet usually includes much more than the muscle tissue we call 'meat'. And to try to feed a dog, for example, a diet of mostly meat is to invite nutritional imbalances that can lead to problems like rickets, inadequate calcium absorption and inadequate reproductive capacities. Vegetable matter is a natural part of the varied diet of both the coyote and the wolf. It can include fresh material, like grass and berries, as well as pre-digested food found in the digestive tracts of their herbivorous prey.

So from a strictly health-oriented viewpoint we might speculate that the 'ideal' diet for a dog or cat would consist of fresh raw prey, supplemented with a few vegetables and fruits. But apart from the obvious impracticality of providing such fare, even this diet might not be the best thing for a domesticated pet. Dogs and cats very probably have needs that are rather different from those of hunting animals, who not only get more exercise but who also live in purer environments and often fast between large meals. These wild predators thus have more opportunities for the body to cleanse itself and to eliminate easily uric acid and other waste products of meat metabolism.

We can raise the same objection (and more) to a shop-bought diet of mostly meat. A three-generation test found that dogs fed meat as a sole source of protein, along with other essential elements, had difficulties producing adequate milk for their young, as compared with dogs fed a diet that included milk and vegetables. In addition, meat is the most polluted food source on the market, containing residues of antibiotics, synthetic hormones and toxic materials such as lead, arsenic, mercury, DDT and dioxin. It harbours more pesticide residues than dairy products, grains, vegetables and fruits. Even if it constituted only 10 per cent of a total diet, it would contribute 1.5 times as much pesticide material as dairy products comprising 31 per cent of the diet.

To add insult to injury, market meats are intentionally aged up to two weeks before being cut up, in order to 'tenderize' them via the actions of enzymes and bacteria growing in the tissue.

The long-term effect of all this toxic material – particularly the pesticides and heavy metals – takes its toll in terms of health. The end result, for an animal, could possibly include increased cancer rates, allergies, infections, kidney and liver problems, irritability and hyperactivity.

Nevertheless, dogs and cats *are* natural carnivores and so it makes sense to include some meat in their diets. However, you can greatly reduce the amount by mixing proteins from meat, dairy and vegetable sources, as outlined in the maintenance recipes in chapter 4. The meatless recipes among these have been formulated by combining protein sources in ways that increase their overall biological value. By using food sources that are high in certain amino acids to strengthen others which are low in these same building blocks of proteins, we can increase the nutritional value of plant proteins so that they are comparable to meat.

An all-vegetarian diet?

Is it possible to go all the way? Can you completely exclude meat from a pet's diet without depriving him of his nutritional needs? The answer is a qualified yes.

The experience of many people points to the soundness of a lacto-ovo-vegetarian diet; that is, a diet that includes milk and eggs along with vegetables. Controlled research, for instance, has shown that dogs fed soya protein grow as well as those fed meat. Several meatless pet foods are now marketed through health food stores. One such product, developed by a vet for dogs that are allergic to ingredients in commercial pet foods (including meats of all types), has produced remarkable health improvements in many animals.

The Vegetarian Society of the United Kingdom publishes a pamphlet detailing meatless diets successfully fed to dogs and cats all over Great Britain. Dogs do well, they find, on a breakfast of whole grain cereal and milk, and for dinner, a high-protein food like cheese, eggs, ground nuts, textured vegetable proteins or legumes mixed with raw and/or cooked vegetables. Other foods dogs do well on include wholewheat bread, brown rice, bean sprouts, fruit and some hard foods for exercising the teeth and gums like whole carrots and hard whole grain biscuits.

The same British group reports that vegetarian cats thrive on a varied diet of high-protein sources like textured vegetable proteins, wheat germ, oats, beans, yeast, milk, cheese, eggs, ground nuts, legumes and tinned meat substitutes marketed for vegetarians. They also eat some vegetables (cucumbers, carrots, spinach and the like) as well as occasional melons.

Some people might want to exclude *all* animal food from their pets' diets, including milk products and eggs. While *people* can do well on such a diet when carefully planned, I would not impose it on dogs or cats. First, it would be almost impossible to supply the high-protein needs of carnivores in a palatable form from all-vegetable sources without overloading them with food. Second, several other nutrients would be lacking, like vitamin B_{12}.

Cats, in particular, have certain needs that can be supplied only from animal tissues. For instance, they cannot convert the carotene found in vegetables to vitamin A, as can humans and dogs, and so they require a pre-formed source. They also need a pre-formed source of arachidonic acid. Both of these requirements are well supplied by supplementing the diet with cod-liver oil.

In addition, felines require an amino acid, taurine, in amounts not present in plant sources. One scientific study showed that without a dietary source of this amino acid (which is available in high concentrations in heart tissue and other meat, as well as in milk) a cat would become depleted of taurine and suffer degeneration of the retina in its eyes. These changes were prevented or reversed by using lactalbumin (from milk) or egg albumin as the dietary protein source. So I urge you to include plenty of eggs and milk products in any meatless diet for a cat. I also suggest that you use cod-liver oil in your supplement program. To be on the safe side, consider feeding your cat an occasional bit of heart or some other meat to boost its levels of taurine and any other as-yet-unknown nutrients that may be more amply supplied by these foods.

With these qualifications in mind, I think you will find that a diet consisting of the meatless recipes in chapter 4 (as well as meatless adaptions of the others, see pages 44–5) will keep your pet in good health. You can, if you like, substitute dicalcium phosphate – which is derived from rock – for bone meal (use two—thirds the amount).

For cats, the vegetarian recipes by themselves already provide most or all of their calcium and phosphorus needs in about the right ratio, so you could reduce the bone meal or dicalcium phosphate quantity to about half the usual amount (a full or scant ⅛ teaspoon per day) which would mean 2 tablespoons or slightly less in the *Cat Powder Mix*.

For dogs *only*, you can substitute a vegetarian vitamin A capsule for cod-liver oil (figure about 5,000 I.U. for each teaspoon of cod-liver oil).

Also, do include some hard foods for your pet to chew on to keep its teeth and gums in top shape. Instead of bones you can offer raw carrots, apples, or biscuits made from one of the recipes on pages 272–5.

Even if you are not trying to feed a meatless diet to your animal, you nevertheless can use the vegetarian recipes at least part-time to decrease the amount of pesticides and other toxic residues in your pet's diet, while at the same time lowering your costs.

Besides, it's good to know that by using less meat you can help to allay suffering for both humans and animals around the world.

More special pets

Though most dogs and cats will thrive on the maintenance diets already described, there are some whose needs require individually tailored recipes to meet especially high or low requirements for protein and other nutrients. Animals with special needs include puppies and kittens; pregnant and lactating females; animals in special environmental situations (strenuous exercise, extreme temperatures, and stress); and animals that need to regain strength after surgery, accidents, illness or malnourishment. Diets for dogs and cats with certain health problems – kidney and urinary disorders, diabetes, allergies and obesity – are given in the *Encyclopaedia* section.

Reproduction, stress and convalescence: high-protein, high-energy diets

Both dogs and cats need higher than usual amounts of protein when they must grow a lot of new tissue. Animals need lots of protein when they are young and growing; conceiving, carrying or nursing offspring; recuperating from illness or trauma; or coping with conditions of stress and hard exercise. An elderly animal may also need a higher-protein diet (if there are no kidney problems) because its digestion is less efficient than that of a younger animal.

Animals exposed to very hot weather may need more protein to compensate for the smaller quantity they eat when it's hot. Those exposed to very cold weather or freezing conditions need more calories just to stay warm. Because they can eat only so much, the fat level – which provides about 2½ times as many calories as protein or carbohydrate – will be increased in the recipes to provide these calories. This higher fat level means that a higher amount of protein must also be included for proper metabolism to occur.

Recipes for dogs

As we have seen, your dog's particular needs can vary considerably. To help you decide what these needs are, and to ensure that the amount of protein given is not excessive, we have provided three groups of recipes. Each group is appropriate to different situations.

As you can see from Feeding Dogs with Extra Needs on pages 62–3, the dogs with the greatest needs (nursing females and very young puppies) should be fed only from the highest-protein recipes (Group 1). Pregnant females and older puppies can use either the intermediate recipes (Group 2) or those from Group 1. Animals in the remaining categories

FEEDING
DOGS
WITH
EXTRA
NEEDS

Condition	Feed from Group 1	Feed from Group 2	Multiply Recipes by	Comments
Nursing females	●		1.5–2.0 (peak)	Increase supplements by 1.5–2.0 also. Feed twice daily or more often if needed.
Young puppies* (weaning to 40% adult weight)	●		2.0	Introduce solids when pups start walking. Also double supplements and feed 3 times daily or more often, as needed.
Puppies* (40–80% adult weight)	●	●	1.5	Increase supplements by 1.5 also. Taper feedings down to twice daily.
Pregnant females	●	●	1.0–1.3	Increase supplements by same amount. Feed twice daily or as needed.
Freezing weather or stress	●	●	1.5–2.0	Feed enough to maintain weight, two meals daily. Under stress, increase supplements also.

should do well on the lower-protein recipes from Group 3, but they also can eat from the first two groups for either convenience or variety.

To calculate accurate quantities, first estimate the *normal* needs for your dog's weight (see page 49, chapter 4). Multiply that figure by the *special needs* multiplier factor shown here. This will give you a *combined* multiplier factor that you will use to arrive at accurate recipe amounts. (Multiply the combined factor by the individual ingredient amounts, or by the total recipe yield. That figure tells you how much you should feed your dog daily.)

Here's an example. You have a 60-pound dog at the peak of pregnancy. Look at page 49 and you will see that her weight multiplier

Condition	Feed from Group			Multiply Recipes by	Comments
	1	2	3		
Puppies*	●	●	●	1.2	Increase supplements by 1.2 also. Feed twice daily until full grown (14–18 months for most breeds). Then cut to once daily if desired.
Hard exercise	●	●	●	1.5–2.5	Feed twice daily, increase supplements proportionately.
Hot weather	●	●	●	Feed as needed to maintain weight.	If a dog eats less than usual, be sure it gets the full daily supplement ration.
Old age	●	●	●	Feed as needed to maintain weight.	
Convalescence from injury, surgery, or illness; malnourishment; anaemia	●	●	●	Feed as needed to maintain or regain weight.	Introduce food slowly to allow digestive system to adapt. Supplements may be temporarily increased.

*Do not overfeed puppies in order to attain the maximum possible size for their age. There is some evidence that such practices can contribute to bone problems – especially in larger dogs – including lameness, hip dysplasia and the Wobbler syndrome.

factor is 2. If she weren't pregnant you'd feed her about twice the recipe amounts daily. But since she *is* pregnant, she'll need about 1.3 times her usual amount. This makes for a combined multiplier factor of $2\frac{2}{3}$ ($2 \times 1.3 = 2.6$ or approximately $2\frac{2}{3}$). So feed her about $2\frac{2}{3}$ times the amounts shown in the recipes that are appropriate to use for pregnant dogs (Groups 1 and 2). Since her needs will change after she delivers the pups and starts nursing them, you'll have to readjust what you feed as you go along.

Note that you can use Ingredient Substitutions, pages 54 and 55, for most of the ingredients in these recipes, just as you can with the basic maintenance rations.

GROUP 1 RECIPES
Conditions: Nursing females, young puppies.

CANINE COMBINATION

4 medium eggs
daily supplements as recommended
½ cup lean meat (or 8 ounces tofu or
  ⅔ cup creamed cottage cheese)
1 cup cooked brown rice
¼ cup grated or chopped vegetables

Scramble eggs lightly with supplements and meat. Add rice and vegetables and serve.

Yield: about 2⅔ cups

DOG'S DELIGHT

¾ cup fatty meat (or 5 medium eggs
  and 1 teaspoon oil)
¾ cup cooked brown rice
¼ cup dry-curd cottage cheese
¼ cup grated or chopped vegetables
daily supplements as recommended

Mix ingredients together and serve warm. *Or,* cook meat and/or vegetables first.

Yield: about 2 cups

GROUP 2 RECIPES
Conditions: Pregnant females, half-grown puppies, stress, cold.

CHOICE MIX

1 ½ cups cooked brown rice
½ cup fatty meat (or 3 large eggs)
¼ cup dry-curd cottage cheese
1 tablespoon soya protein isolate
¼ cup grated or chopped vegetables
daily supplements as recommended

Mix ingredients together and serve slightly warm.

Yield: about 2⅔ cups

CEREAL AND EGGS

Morning: Serve as a hot cereal

1 cup cooked oatmeal
1 tablespoon soya protein isolate
  (mixed in oatmeal)
1 cup whole milk
2 teaspoons honey

Evening: Scramble the ingredients together and serve.

4 medium eggs
¼ cup grated or chopped vegetables
daily supplements as recommended

Yield: about 3¼ cups, total

GROUP 3 RECIPES
Conditions: Older puppies, hard exercise, heat, old age, convalescence, malnourishment, anaemia.

ENERGY FOOD FOR DOGS

3 medium eggs (or scant ½ cup of fatty meat)
2 tablespoons brewer's yeast
daily supplements as recommended
1 cup cooked brown rice
⅔ cup cooked soya flakes (or a 7-ounce portion of tofu)
¼ cup grated or chopped vegetables

Scramble the eggs with yeast and supplements. Add the remaining ingredients and serve.

Yield: about 2⅔ cups

Daily Duo for Dogs and *Potatoes au Canine* (both from chapter 4) will also meet the protein and energy needs of Group 3.

Recipes for cats

All of the maintenance recipes in chapter 4 contain enough protein and fat to meet the high needs of cats in special conditions, but *Cat Omelet, Lean Meat and Eggs for Cats* and *Feline Fatty Meat Menu* are the recipes best suited for their needs. Also, you will need to adjust the quantities as outlined in Feeding Cats with Extra Needs on page 66.

Feeding orphaned or rejected kittens and puppies

Mother's milk is the best there is, so use these recipes only if you have no choice. Sometimes a female cannot or will not adequately nurse all her young. Sometimes, unfortunately, the mother dies. In such cases you can keep the baby animals alive with a formula designed to mimic the natural constituents of cat's and dog's milk as closely as possible. There are commercial products which do this (called Cimicat and Whelpi, respectively). But if you want to give fresh foods, here are some formulas you can use.

To boost the protein content of cow's milk to equal that of cat's and dog's milk, we suggest adding protein powders. The best kind of powder to get is one derived from milk and egg (rather than soya) sources. This powder ensures that you meet the special amino acid requirements of your young orphans. Look for the label ingredients: casein, lactalbumin, or egg albumin. Buy a powder that contains at least 80 per cent protein (dry weight basis). Such powders are sold in health food stores.

You can supplement these formulas with a few drops of liquid vitamins made for children.

Kittens: you can use either one of the following formulas. The second is easier to

FEEDING
CATS
WITH
EXTRA
NEEDS

Condition	Multiply recipes by	Comments
Pregnant females	1.3	Also increase supplements by 1.3. Feed twice daily or as needed.
Nursing females	3.1 (peak)	Also increase supplements proportionately. Feed several times daily as needed.
Convalescence, stress, malnourishment, extreme weather	Feed as needed to maintain or regain weight.	Increase supplements proportionately to the recipe increase. But don't feed higher amounts of cod-liver oil for long periods.

Kittens:
  5 weeks (weaning)
  10 weeks
  20 weeks
  30 weeks
	
	0.4
	0.6
	0.7
	0.8
		Introduce solid foods gradually after the kittens start walking. Feed young kittens about ½ the adult supplement quantity, gradually increasing until adulthood. Feed several times a day.

NOTE: If your adult cat is much smaller or larger than the 9- to 10-pound average (or if your kittens are from such stock), you must first adjust the amount of food for the weight difference as described in chapter 4. Multiply by 0.6 to 0.8 for smaller cats, and by 1.3 for larger ones. Thus, an unusually small pregnant cat might need about ¾ of a basic recipe ($0.6 \times 1.3 = 0.78$ or about ¾).

NUTRITIONAL COMPARISON OF NATURAL CAT'S MILK VS. FORMULAS

	Percent on a Dry Weight Basis			
	Protein	Fat	Carbohydrate	Ash
Natural's cat's milk	42.2	25.0	26.1	6.7
Kitten Formula No. 1	43.7	26.3	25.2	4.9
Kitten Formula No. 2	37.8	35.7	22.3	4.2

make, but does not replicate mother's milk quite as well as the first.

Page 66 gives a comparison of the constituents of each formula with natural cat's milk.

KITTEN FORMULA NO. 1
(540 CALORIES)

2 cups whole milk

2 egg yolks

2 tablespoons protein powder

½ teaspoon brewer's yeast

liquid vitamins for children – a few drops

Mix well and warm to body temperature. Feed with a 'pet nurser' or toy feeding bottle. Give the kitten just enough at each nursing to enlarge the abdomen slightly, but not enough to distend or bloat it. The amount will be about 2 to 4 tablespoons per day for a tiny kitten weighing 4 to 8 ounces and about 6 to 10 tablespoons for a larger one weighing 10 to 24 ounces. Feed every 2 hours the first 2 weeks of age, every 3 hours the 3rd week, every 4 hours the 4th and 5th weeks and 3 times a day thereafter. After each feeding, gently swab the genital and anal area with a tissue moistened slightly with warm water (which mimics the mother's licking and is necessary to stimulate proper urination and defaecation). Also massage the belly lightly. Start introducing solids at about 3 to 4 weeks (mixed with the formula to make a gruel). You can wean from the bottle at about 4 to 6 weeks.

KITTEN FORMULA NO. 2
(158 CALORIES)

½ cup cow's milk or goat's milk (preferably unpasteurized)

1 hard-boiled egg

liquid vitamins for children – a few drops

Blend smoothly in an electric blender and feed as recommended for *Kitten Formula No. 1*.

Puppies: The following formula should suffice. Compare it to the constituents of dog's milk as shown on page 68.

PUPPY FORMULA

1 cup half-and-half (milk and cream)

2 medium egg yolks

2 teaspoons protein powder

½ teaspoon bone meal

¼ cup water (boil it first if not of high quality)

liquid vitamins for children – a few drops

Mix well and warm to body temperature. Using a 'pet nurser' bottle, feed enough to slightly enlarge the abdomen but not to distend it. This amount will vary according to age and breed size. If in doubt, consult recommendations for the commercial formula. Feed on the same schedule described for kittens. Clean the puppy after the feeding, as described for kittens. Start introducing solids at about 3 or 4 weeks (mixed with formula to make a gruel) and wean from the bottle at about 4 or 5 weeks.

NUTRITIONAL COMPARISON OF
NATURAL DOG'S MILK VS. FORMULA

| | Percent on a Dry Weight Basis | | | |
	Protein	Fat	Carbohydrate	Ash
Natural dog's milk	33.2	44.1	15.8	6.9
Puppy Formula	33.6	44.0	15.5	6.9

CHAPTER SIX

Helping Your Pets to Change Their Diet

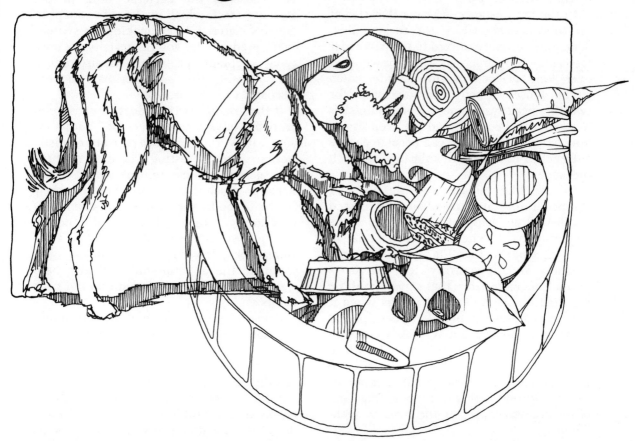

Most pets love their new diet. But some may run into a few snags along the way — snags that can be prevented or alleviated.

For instance, one *Prevention* magazine reader phoned to tell me that her cats would not eat their new food.

'What have you given them?' I inquired.

'You name it! I've tried adding supplements like bone meal, brewer's yeast, wheat germ. I've offered them meats, dairy products, grains, vegetables, everything you can think of! But practically *all* they will touch, especially the older cat, is just tinned tuna and chicken. Not only that, but it has to be one *certain* brand, if you can believe that!'

Another person reported back after a course of natural foods and remedies for a chronic problem: 'Henry was doing well and then suddenly he just stopped eating and acted as though he was ill. He just lay around and didn't seem to have any energy.'

Having started the natural diet, another worried owner phoned to report: 'My dog liked the new food, and he's been on it a few weeks. But yesterday he passed a lot of worms! What do I do?'

In the first instance we have that star of cat food commercials – the fussy feline. Some cats become addicted to the particular foods they were given as kittens, or were fed over long periods of time. Under such circumstances the body's natural instinct for selecting healthy, balanced food diminishes to near-zero. People's food preferences are learned early in life and can become deeply entrenched habits. With animals it is much the same.

In cases like the last two – the dog that stopped eating and the other that passed worms – I am happy to hear about these responses to the switch. It's not that I like to see suffering or that I'm eager for more business. On the contrary. It's just that I know from experience that signs like those reported can be favourable omens when it comes to natural healing. After a brief period on a higher-quality diet, it is fairly common for an animal in less than perfect health to discharge accumulated toxic material or to undergo a brief aggravation of its symptoms. These apparent setbacks are a normal and often necessary part of the road to well-being.

Nearly all the snags your pet might encounter in a change of diet will be of these two types – getting a finicky eater to like what's good for it or helping an animal through the sometimes uncomfortable stages of a natural cleansing process.

In the case of the finicky eater, you can try to introduce new foods gradually, or you can fast your pet until it's hungry enough to try the new diet.

The gradual transition not only allows your animal a little time to get used to the taste of new foods, but also gives its digestive system a chance to adjust. Whenever there is an abrupt change of diet, even from one commercial brand to another, you may see diarrhoea or loss of appetite for a while. The cause is the bacterial flora in the digestive tract, which may need to adapt to the new material. So by making the switch-over a gradual one, you can usually not only avoid acceptance problems, but also reduce the possibility that your pet may undergo discomfort in the process.

If the gradual method doesn't work, you probably have a confirmed food addict on your hands. You'll have to take more drastic measures, such as fasting. Though it might at first seem that some animals would rather starve to death than eat anything but their favourite foods, the instinct for survival is very strong. Sooner or later (usually sooner) your pet will come round. Try fasting your animal for a few days. This will not only stimulate the appetite but will also help cleanse the body and decondition old taste habits.

Some people find such an idea frightening. Somehow we have come to believe that going a day or two without food will take us close to death's door. Not true. In fact, healthy cats have been known to go without any food or water for periods of up to six weeks in favourable environments. Obese dogs have fasted on just water and vitamins for as long as six to eight weeks without ill effect. Wild carnivores fast naturally. So don't worry about trying the fast for a few days.

The fasting method

Briefly, the fasting procedure begins with a break-in period of one to two days, when you feed a smaller quantity of the usual food or (if accepted) a moderate fare of lean meat, cooked grain, and vegetables. For the next two or three days, you give only liquids like pure water, vegetable juices, and vegetable/meat broth. During the fast be sure your pet has plenty of fresh air, quiet, access to the outdoors, and some moderate exercise. Then you break the fast over a day or two by gradually introducing some vegetables, milk or yogurt to the liquid regimen. Next you add lean meat and then a grain, perhaps some tofu or cottage cheese, and so on, until you can get the animal to accept the basic recommended diet with supplements.

In some cases, you may find it necessary to compromise by mixing a small amount of the old food into the new. One woman I know finds that mixing just a spoonful of tinned cat food into the natural recipe makes all the difference. 'As much as anything, it seems to be something about the sight and sound of the old familiar tin-opening process that gets them excited,' she said. But I hope you don't allow your animal to run your life with its habits! Probably you will find that after a period of eating a mixture of both natural and commercial foods, your pet will develop enough interest in the new foods to forget about the old ones.

Other people have found that in stubborn cases it pays to continue fasting the animal a few days more. One client called up to say that her cat wouldn't eat any of the vegetables or other foods in the 'breaking-out' period. I advised her to keep the cat on liquids for a while longer. She did, and in a few days she called back with an enthusiastic report: her formerly finicky cat would now eat all kinds of things it wouldn't touch before – like vegetables, grains, meats, brewer's yeast and soya! In addition to the longer fast, she found it helped to mix a little bit of fish (an old favourite) into the new diet.

So whether your animal responds to the gradual introduction method or whether it requires a fast or two, sooner or later your pet will most likely become a true connoisseur of the good natural foods it needs!

Some animals, particularly those in poor health, may experience some physical difficulties during the transition, despite a period of gradual introduction. If yours is such an animal, a check-up, as described below, will let you know if the problem is one of temperament or physical stress.

How to give your pet a check-up

You may have an animal in poor health without fully realizing it. By making this brief examination you can get a much better idea about its actual state.

1. Does the hair coat feel greasy? Is the skin a normal grey-white or is it pink or red with inflammation? Are there scales of dead skin like dandruff among the hairs?

2. Brush the hair backward, against the grain, using your fingers. Do you see dozens of little black specks? If so, they are the excreta of fleas after they have digested blood.

3. Now, smell your fingers. Is the odour they picked up rancid or rank? Does it smell fishy? If so, things are not good.

4. Examine the eyes. Is there matter in the corners? Are the lids red or irritated on the edges?

5. Look in the ears. Is there a lot of wax? Do they look oily? Do they have an offensive odour?

6. Check the teeth. Are they gleaming white or coated with a brown deposit? Check the back ones, too. How does the breath smell?

The body responds

By making a point of regularly examining your pet, you can easily monitor its overall health. Contrary to popular belief, your dog should *not* have 'doggy odour' nor your cat bad breath. Although these problems are common, they are nevertheless signs of a low level of health, a chronic condition.

If you find your pet is in mediocre condition (or is known to have a disease), then the body may undergo a cleansing process after starting the new diet.

What happens? For years the animal has eaten over-processed food that probably contained harmful ingredients. It has also been exposed to environmental pollutants, and perhaps some strong drugs. So when your pet finally eats really fresh, nutritious food with minimal pollutants, strange things begin to happen. The body responds!

At first the animal usually feels better. Energy and nutrients are flowing through the tissues. The quality and oxygen-carrying capacity of the blood improves. The animal starts to be more active and the added exercise in turn helps to recharge lazy tissues.

After two or three weeks, the body may feel perky enough to tackle some long-neglected house-cleaning and to throw off accumulated debris it's been hauling around for too long. For one thing, it may sweep out a mass of worms that, until now, have been about as happy as worms can expect to be. Suddenly they find themselves being thrust out into a harsh new reality – leaving behind a nice clean intestine.

More often, the cleansing results in a lot of discharge from the kidneys, colon or skin (important excretory organs). Thus, the urine might become dark and strong-smelling, or the faeces might contain mucus or blood, or the skin might secrete noxious-smelling material. Strange as it may look from the outside, the body is getting *cleaner*.

I know that's hard to grasp. Most of us expect that after we effectively treat a physical problem, the disturbance will just go away. Or at least things won't look as if they're getting worse. Of course, that's how antibiotics and other familiar drugs work – at least for a while. The trouble is that such drugs can simply suppress the symptoms rather than correct the underlying disorder or weakness. Eventually, the same or related problems may crop up again.

But it wasn't so long ago that people saw things differently and recognized the stages of healing. One of the stages is a period of crisis when there might be a fever, inflammation, or temporary exaggeration of symptoms. At such a point the patient either began recovering or died. A 'healing crisis', as it has been called, represents the point at which the body's defences are mobilized to their maximum capabilities.

If we interfere with this process by injecting an antibiotic or some cortisone, the defence system doesn't get exercised. And it isn't able to address the underlying weakness that led to the disease in the first place. Like a flabby, unused muscle, the defence system gets weak from lack of use. Soon resistance to future disease is weak, and the body needs even more drugs. Poor nutrition makes things worse by further lowering disease resistance and therefore further necessitating the use of drugs. Weakened by the infection and the toxic aspects of the drug, the body makes even greater demands on the available nutrition. These demands make the nutrition even more inadequate, and we are caught in a vicious cycle.

What will break this cycle? A good diet, for one thing. By supplying optimum nutrients we can not only increase disease resistance but also help the body eliminate the toxic drug effects. So don't be discouraged if you see some signs of detoxification when you improve your pet's diet. You've got things moving!

'But', you may ask, 'how can I know if what I see is due to detoxification or due to a serious disease?' Of course, this is a sticky point. If you feel uncertain, consult your vet for an opinion. If you want to use a conservative approach (minimum drugs, maximum wait-and-see), then tell the vet so. But here are some general clues to help you decide.

If your pet's energy level is high and it generally feels well and has a good appetite, then such symptoms as temporarily passing worms, mucus or a little blood are probably insignificant. (However, it is also common for an animal switching from all-commercial to all-fresh food to undergo a brief cleansing period that may include less energy and appetite and more sleeping. It usually passes in a day or two. This stage may not be seen right away – in fact, it is usually seen two to four weeks after the diet change.) But if your pet's energy level decreases steadily for more than a few days or there are mental/emotional changes like depression, irritability or forgetfulness *which were not present before*, then you may have problems. And, of course, you should always have any severe physical conditions looked at.

Herbs to ease the process

Should your pet have some moderate distress, you can ease it (or try to prevent it from the start) with some herbs that help cleanse the body and rebuild tissue. Use only one, rather than a combination. Pick the one that best matches the problems listed in the brief descriptions below.

Alfalfa (*Medicago sativa)* is an excellent tonic that stimulates digestion and appetite.

It helps animals gain weight and improves physical and mental vigour. It is best used for animals that are underweight, nervous or highly-strung. It can also help those with muscle or joint pains, or animals with urinary problems – especially where there is crystal formation and bladder irritation. Depending again on body size, add 1 teaspoon to 3 tablespoons of ground or dry-blended alfalfa to the daily ration. Or make a tea by steeping 1 to 2 tablespoons of the herb in 1 cup of water for 20 minutes. Mix it with food or give orally with a bulb syringe (or turkey baster), using the dry amounts as guidelines.

Burdock (*Arctium lappa)* cleanses the blood and helps the body detoxify. It's particularly good for skin disorders. Soak 1 teaspoon of the root in 1 cup of spring or distilled water in a glass or enamel pan for 5 hours. Then bring to a boil, remove from heat, and let cool. Give ½ teaspoon to 2 tablespoons per day, depending on the animal's size.

Garlic (*Allium sativum)* helps eliminate worms, strengthens digestion, and beneficially stimulates the intestinal tract. Use it to promote intestinal health. It is also indicated for an animal that has been on a high meat or fish diet, that tends to be overweight, or that suffers hip pain from arthritis or dysplasia. Include fresh grated garlic with each meal, using ½ to 3 cloves, according to the animal's size.

Oats (*Avena sativa)* are also a tonic, particularly for the animal whose main weakness is in the nervous system, as in epilepsy, tremors, twitching and paralysis. Oats also counter the weakening and exhaustive effects of heavy drugging and diseases. They help to cleanse the body and nourish new tissue growth. Use oatmeal as the chief grain in the diet.

Oat straw can provide a healing bath. Boil 1 to 2 pounds of the straw in 3 quarts of water for 30 minutes. Add this to the bath water, or sponge on repeatedly as a rinse after bathing by standing the animal in a bath and reusing the solution. Such treatment is useful for skin problems, muscle and joint pain, paralysis, and liver and kidney problems.

The use of one of these herbs along with the benefits of the new diet should make the road to good health smoother and shorter. After a month or two, give your pet another examination. I bet you'll see a difference. And won't it have been worth it?

If any symptoms – such as loss of appetite, abnormal stools or other problems of elimination – continue despite your precautions, then eliminate the new foods. When the problem clears up, reintroduce vegetables, grains, meats, brewer's yeast and soya flakes one at a time until you find out which one is causing the problem. When you identify the culprit, you permanently eliminate it from the diet.

Some foods that may cause allergic reactions in pets are described along with the allergy diet in the *Encyclopaedia* section under 'Allergies'.

Cats sometimes find it harder to metabolize unsaturated oils than saturated ones. Choosing olive oil as your cat's oil source and adding ample vitamin E to the diet should allay this problem

Most animals that switch to natural foods do not experience the problems described in this chapter. Most enjoy the new diet and digest it well, so do not be needlessly concerned about encountering difficulties. And particularly if you follow the advice here about easing the transition period, you will in all probability simply have a happier and healthier animal as a result.

CHAPTER SEVEN
Exercise and Grooming

If you want to keep your car in top shape, you have to do more than just fill the petrol tank. You also have to provide water for the radiator, air for the tyres, lubrication, tune-ups and parts repairs. Without this attention, even the best car becomes a banger.

Certainly, animals aren't machines. But, like machines, they need more than just the right fuel. They need good water, fresh air,

sunlight, exercise, grooming, space and much more. And, unlike machines, they have special emotional and social needs as well.

So while good nutrition is a very important step to maintaining or improving your pet's health, we can't stop there. Many additional factors affect its well-being. Some are obvious and some are subtle, but they all play a part. What we must do is develop a broad view, a way of seeing the many diverse elements as a whole – a whole that can enhance your pet's life or threaten it.

Stop to consider for a moment how different the lives of our pets are compared to those of their wild ancestors. Let's take a typical dog. Not only does he eat highly processed foods, but he may have never spent a fresh, sunny day investigating the path of a stream or running hard through sweetly scented woods. Instead, he spends most of his life indoors, sleeping or pacing around on linoleum and carpeting made from petroleum products. His time 'outdoors' is often spent waiting in a stuffy parked car while his owner does an errand.

He doesn't socialize much with his own kind, but instead has an intense mutual attachment with one or more humans who often display complex and distressing emotions he doesn't always understand. But most of the time they are at work or school and he is alone in the confines of his house or garden.

Once every week or two comes one of his greatest delights – a walk through the fields. When he gets home, he quenches his thirst with water that is laced with chlorine and other things (as we shall discuss later). Sometimes he's a bit irritable and snappish or depressed and bored – largely due to his lifestyle – but overall he's a good-natured fellow who takes each day as it comes. We have to give him credit for outstanding spirit in the face of luxurious deprivation.

But do our animal friends have to lead lives that are impoverished? Let's look and see what an animal's real needs are, and what steps we can reasonably take to meet them. While the circumstances that affect a pet's health are complex, we can understand them if we remember a basic principle: the less we interfere with nature, the more we allow life processes to flow healthfully and unimpeded.

Some of the factors (besides nutrition) that affect pet health include exercise, grooming, and exposure to environmental pollutants and imbalances.

The importance of exercise

For the wild cousins of domestic dogs and cats, regular exercise is an integral and necessary part of daily life. They have no choice, because they *must* move around to hunt for food. On the other hand, the only exercise many house pets get is a walk to the food bowl. *Yet regular exercise is essential for optimal health.*

Sustained, vigorous use of the muscles stimulates all tissues and increases circulation and the movement of fluids through the body. Blood vessels dilate and blood pressure rises. As a result, tissues become oxygenated, helping to clean the cells of toxins. Digestive system glands more actively secrete their fluids, and the bowels move more easily.

Only a few animals don't benefit from exercise. If your pet is old and weak or has a bad heart, settle for slow walks around the block. But for most, half an hour or more a day of vigorous exercise is a good rule of thumb. Jogging together, playing ball, chasing sticks or other lively activities are all worth while.

Cats, of course, are not inclined to chase balls or go jogging, but they will usually get enough exercise if they are allowed outside part of the time and have a suitable place to 'scratch'.

If your pet is temporarily unable to walk because of a sore foot or even partial paralysis, you can help it exercise by allowing it to swim in place in a bathtub or a large

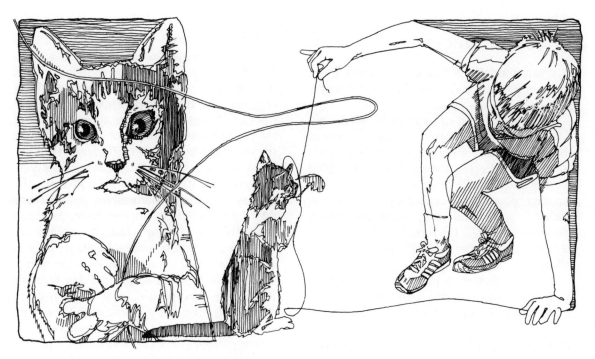

Thing-on-a-string, an irresistible game for cats, provides needed exercise for the 'inside' pet.

trough. Swimming strengthens the body in the same way as running. If your pet tends to sink, hold it up by placing a towel or cloth under the body for support. Dogs with back problems will greatly benefit from this exercise.

Quiet and rest

Every animal needs a clean, quiet, private place to sleep and rest. Smaller animals like cats and little dogs will be happy with a padded basket or even just a clean blanket in a box in a corner. A larger dog needn't necessarily have a bed, per se, but it needs some kind of secure place that is dry,

comfortable, clean and warm – such as a carpeted corner or dog house, an old chair or a special rug of its own in a quiet spot.

A lot of animals – big dogs particularly – seem not to get these things. Many are left out in the elements, but not the way their wild cousins live. Instead of a cosy, rocky den to hide in, they may have a patch of earth next to a street or perhaps a draughty slab of cement beneath a porch roof. There's a difference and it's an important one. So make sure your animal gets what we all need – a place of one's own, safe from the storm, protected from intruders. It needn't be the Ritz, just something quiet, dry and cosy. And take your animal's sensitive ears into consideration when it comes to excess, stress-producing noise.

Cleanliness is next to healthfulness

A clean animal is a beautiful animal. Even more important, a clean animal is a healthy one.

Why is cleaning so important? First, any living organism must constantly break down and eliminate natural metabolic products and old cells (ordinarily about a third of the body's cells are dying and must be broken down and replaced). Second, in today's world, the body must do double duty to counteract the heavy load of synthetic chemicals in the air, soil, water and food chain.

This burden of accumulated toxins, as well as external dirt and secretions, not only encourages the growth of germs and parasites – many of which thrive on such material – but it also decreases general vitality by hampering normal organ and glandular functions. While the build-up of toxins may not in itself produce a specific disease, it can lead to an often unrecognized low-grade susceptibility that sets the stage for sudden severe crises. Thus, a pet can become susceptible to infectious disease or acute inflammation, or succumb to gradual organ degeneration that is punctuated by occasional flare ups. For example, an animal with chronically inflamed skin may develop a sudden moist eczema. Another may get an attack of nephritis (kidney inflammation) that arises from a silent gradual degeneration and loss of kidney tissue over years.

If you doubt that this load of toxins is a heavy one, take a closer look at some animals you know. Give them the quick 'check-up examination' described in chapter 6. I see a lot of animals that show low-grade signs of chronic excessive toxicity. Oily, smelly secretions or deposits on the skin, ears, eyes or teeth are signs that the body is struggling to eliminate toxins.

How can you help your pet's body cleanse itself? One method is regular exercise. Another is occasional fasting. A third is grooming. All of these processes are natural ways to stimulate and assist the hard-working organs – the skin, liver, kidneys, digestive tract and lungs – to carry toxic wastes out of the body. Exercise, as we've seen, stimulates the metabolism and circulation, and thus the removal of wastes. Fasting relieves the digestive tract of its usual duties and frees the organs to devote themselves to breaking down toxins stored in the liver, fats and other tissues. During a fast, the organs are also free to consume excess baggage, such as cysts, scars and growths. A healthy animal will benefit from an occasional day without food. The therapeutic uses of fasting are described more fully in chapter 15, Caring for a Sick Animal. Grooming not only directly removes dirt and secretions, but also stimulates the skin's natural elimination processes. Let's take a closer look at natural and safe ways to groom.

Natural grooming and skin care

Nobody needs to give a wolf or a wild cat a bath, so why should we have to groom our pets? One reason is that a wild animal moves from place to place, which means it can walk away from a colony of parasites such as fleas or lice. But a pet keeps getting reinfested from the eggs they have dropped in its quarters.

A second reason is that a lot of animals have been bred to have abnormally long or curly hair, which becomes an overwhelming challenge for their limited tools of self-grooming – their tongue, paws and teeth. What results is a build-up of matted hair and dirt, which predisposes the skin to irritation.

A third reason is that dust sometimes can carry with it various toxic pollutants. It's better for the pet's health if you remove these poisons than if the animal licks them off and swallows them.

Because we humans have intervened in the natural order and changed the physical structure and environment of these animals, it's up to us to assume responsibility for care of the skin and coat of those pets that need it.

Long-haired pets need daily brushing and combing. It stimulates hair and skin health, brings normal secretions out from oil glands on to the skin and discourages fleas. Short-haired animals may need brushing less often. Regular use of a flea comb, a fine-tooth comb that traps fleas for easy removal and drowning, is an effective weapon in the fight against this common parasite.

Frequent brushing and combing also will keep matted hair from building up and help to remove burrs and other plant debris.

In addition to brushing, you can thin your dog's coat if you live in a hot climate. You can have this done by a professional groomer.

Bathing your pet

Bathing is another important aspect of keeping your pet clean. It is one of the safest and most effective ways to control fleas, which are killed by the soap and water. Don't bathe your pets too often, though, because it can dry the skin. For an adult dog, one bath about every two months is enough, unless it has got unusually dirty. If it has a bad flea infestation, skin problems or discharges, then you may want to bath it about every two weeks. Cats don't need regular bathing, as they generally do a good job of it by themselves. But if your cat has a bad skin or flea problem, you can give it a bath about once a month. Washing an animal can be a useful adjunct to other holistic care for skin problems, but it should not be used as a substitute.

For shampoo, consider one of the follow-

ing: a natural pet shampoo containing flea- and insect-repellent herbs, a good-quality castile soap or a natural shampoo for people.

If fleas are a problem, you can add extra strength to the bath by pouring in a capful of insect-repellent herbal oil, such as penny-royal or eucalyptus. Never rub the un-diluted oil directly on to the skin, because it can cause irritation.

Between baths, help control fleas by frequently laundering the pet's bedding in hot soapy water, and drying it in full sun or in a dryer. Regularly vacuum rugs and furniture every two or three days to pick up flea eggs. Also, remember to supplement the diet with garlic and ample brewer's yeast to help repel fleas. Finally, you can rub brewer's yeast directly into the animal's fur or use a herbal flea powder.

Natural flea powders are typically con-cocted of aromatic herbs like rosemary, rue, wormwood, pennyroyal, eucalyptus or cit-ronella, as well as diatomaceous earth and tobacco powder. When you use the powder, remember to put your pet outside for a while so the parasites don't stay in your house. Some people dust diatomaceous earth on to rugs, furniture and bedding and into all cracks and crevices where dust and flea eggs collect. This product, which resembles chalky rock, is really the fossilized remains of one-celled algae. Though harmless to pets and people, it is fatal to many insects and their larvae, including fleas. The fine particles in the earth kill insects by attacking the wax coating that covers their external skeletons. The insects then dry out and die.

Many health food stores or pet stores also carry natural flea collars which are impreg-nated with insect-repellent herbal oils. Some are made to be 'recharged' with the oils so they can be used again.

For more detailed information concerning both external and internal parasites, as well as skin problems in general, see the topics in

Encyclopaedia section.

Many of my clients have successfully used the following recipe for a general skin toner and parasite repellent.

LEMON SKIN TONIC

1 whole lemon

1 pint near-boiling water

Thinly slice the lemon, including the peel. Add it to the water and let it steep overnight. The next day sponge the solution on to the animal's skin and let it dry. You can use this daily for severe skin problems involving fleas.

The great parasite wars: the dangers of insecticides

No doubt you will notice that I do *not* recommend the use of insecticide-containing pet products commonly employed in the great wars waged against fleas, ticks, lice, mange and mites. It's not that I minimize the great annoyance these pests cause countless pets and people. Rather I see these as dangerous products that *add* to the pest problem by tremendously increasing the load of toxins our animals must bear. Environmental pollution is a serious threat to health. But for pets the greatest chemical threat is that which originates right at home as their well-meaning owners regularly dip, spray, powder, collar and shampoo their flea-bitten companions with every manner of poisonous substance. The labels of some pet products bear such cautions as 'Avoid contact with skin'. I've never been able to work out why something considered toxic if left on human skin for a short time should be applied to and left on a pet's skin over its entire body for weeks or months. Skin is skin, after all. Some flea collars are so potent that they produce extreme skin irritations and permanent hair loss in some animals, particularly if they are too tight.

Just as a lot of people these days are rethinking the wisdom of saturating the land (and food chain) with toxic chemicals in the name of farming, I think it's also time to re-examine our approach to animal parasite control. It's time to stop bombing our pets, lawns and houses with domestic forms of chemical warfare. These poisons ultimately weaken the host as well as the parasite. Instead, let's find out *why* an animal is overrun with fleas, ticks or worms and try a natural way to correct the imbalance.

Parasites do not cause weakness and discomfort in animals so much as they take advantage of it. Have you ever noticed that two animals in the same household can look like pets from two different worlds? One may be lacking in spark and absolutely overrun with fleas and ticks, while the other is perky and has hardly any. It's the same with plants. A healthy living organism attracts far fewer parasites than a weak one. As I see it, part of the role of parasites is to feed on and help finish off weak individuals.

But when we don't address the animal's underlying poor health and instead saturate it – and its environment – with substances so dangerous that their misuse or overuse regularly causes poisonings and fatalities, we are ultimately creating more trouble. We may have succeeded in killing the fleas, but what have we done for the animal's long-term health? These so-called pet aids, along with house and garden products, may contain various classes of insecticides. Sometimes, fatal poisonings have resulted from either improper or excessive use of some of these products, or from simultaneous use of more than one. Here are the health effects of some components in these products:

Organochlorines (examples: DDT, DDE, aldrin, dieldrin and chlordane, which are now banned or restricted; and lindane, toxaphene, paradichlorobenzene and dichlorophene, which are currently still found in consumer products): Though less acutely toxic than other compounds that have largely replaced them, organochlorines persist much longer in body tissues and the environment and thereby lead to the development of insect resistance.

Most pet poisonings have been caused by bathing or dipping pets in excess concentrations. Cats are particularly vulnerable to this group of chemicals, especially to DDT and chlordane. Dogs are more susceptible to toxaphene and DDE.

After excessive exposure to organochlorines, symptoms of poisoning start with exaggerated responces to touch, light and sound. Spasms or tremors appear (usually first in the face), progressing to epilepsy-like seizures, often followed by death.

Carbamates (including carbaryl or Sevin and various methyl carbamate compounds) **and Organophosphates** (such as malathion, ronnel, vapona, diazinon, dichlorvos and parathion): These two groups of compounds are responsible for most pet deaths by insecticide poisoning. They are much more acutely toxic than the slower-acting organochlorines they have largely replaced. You can find carbamates and organophosphates in all types of pet products, from flea dips, collars, powders and sprays to mange and worming medicines and kennel, lawn and house sprays.

Their action is through nerve-paralysing properties. Signs of pesticide poisoning include profuse salivation, muscular twitching, contracted pupils and involuntary defecation, accompanied by slowed heartbeat and laboured breathing, which can result in death. Other signs may include vomiting, diarrhoea, watery eyes, hyperactivity, rigidity, paralysis and bluish discolorations.

Benzyl benzoate: Often used for mange control, this compound can be toxic if applied over too large an area or too often. Cats are more susceptible, but dogs occasionally die, too, from excessive use. Toxic signs include nausea, vomiting, diarrhoea and a slowing of the heartbeat and rate of breathing.

In addition to synthetics, some products derived from natural substances also pose dangers. These include:

Arecoline hydrobromide: Long used in tapeworm control, this is the active compound found in the areca nut, an Oriental folk remedy for worms. Considered unsafe for use with cats, this chemical can cause undesirable responses in dogs, including vomiting, unconsciousness, diarrhoea and depression. It must be considered a potentially toxic substance.

Rotenone and other cube resins: Derived from a poisonous tropical legume, rotenone is considered fairly toxic to mammals. In Sumatra, it's used to poison arrows! However, it loses much of its potency in the presence of light and oxygen and has little residual action. Cube resins are found in shampoos, dips and powders.

Pyrethrins: Considered to be the least toxic of all insecticides used on mammals, pyrethrins are derived from the flower heads of chrysanthemums. This class of insecticide is used mostly in aerosol sprays and sometimes in flea shampoos and sprays. It acts very rapidly on insects, causing convulsion and paralysis of the insect nervous system. Many die, but many also recover. Therefore, frequent applications are necessary.

Note: If you do not achieve results with the natural insect control measures recommended in this book, or if you feel you *must* use an insecticide for some reason, pyrethrins are probably the least dangerous.

CHAPTER EIGHT
The Total Environment

As conscientious and humane people, we can work hard to eliminate the poisons from our pets' diets and home environment. However, no matter how hard we try, our animals will *still* be exposed to poisons – those ubiquitous environmental pollutants that undermine the health of both man and beast.

Unfortunately, one of the most insidious aspects of environmental contamination is that it's so easy to ignore. We don't *feel* as if we're being poisoned. Many of the worst effects, such as cancer, don't show up for 20 or 25 years. And even in the face of public health studies that clearly show the cause-and-effect relationship between poisons and our health, it's easy to miss the connections. Somehow, the facts don't apply to *us*.

Yet toxic substances have been detected in the fatty tissues and critical organs of people, and have no doubt invaded our pets' bodies as well. These include PCBs (poly-chlorinated biphenyls); pesticides such as aldrin, dieldrin, heptachlor, endrin, DDT and lindane; radioactive isotopes such as strontium 90, heavy metals, including lead, mercury and cadmium; asbestos; and a host of other poisons.

Pandora's box has been opened. As a society we must clean up our act as soon as possible. Meanwhile, it is only intelligent to do what we reasonably can to reduce the chemical loads that burden us and our pets. Let's look more closely at the problem – and what we can do about it.

Living close to the ground

Most dogs and cats conduct their affairs in much more intimate contact with the ground than we do. In a relatively natural setting, this intimacy is fine. Unfortunately, though, a lot of dirt is dirtier than it used to be. Therefore, you should take a few precautions to protect your animal friend from possible harm.

Most important, stop using poisonous chemicals in your garden. Pesticides are dangerous, and animals can absorb their residues simply by lying down on treated soil. Animals not only roll around in these chemicals but actually lick them up when they groom themselves. Although several pesticides have already been banned, many more need to be eliminated. A good place to start is at home.

In addition to chemicals, animals are subject to other environmental pollutants such as heavy metals, which settle to the ground. Cases of lead poisoning in animals have been reported – usually among small urban dogs (epilepsy is usually the first symptom).

Asbestos, too, is found all over the urban environment. It comes from brake linings, ceilings, insulations, floor tiles, cement, roofing, paints and fabrics. It is dangerous even at low levels. Other hazardous air pollutants are carbon monoxide, benzene, ozone, nitrogen dioxide, cadmium, arsenic, vinyl chloride and other industrial vapours.

You cannot guard against them all, of course, but there are several reasonable precautions you can take to reduce your animal's (and your family's) intake of pollutants.

Keep your pet away from road fumes and dust as much as you can. Don't place its pen next to the road or driveway. Don't travel with your dog in the back of a pick-up truck, which exposes it not only to un-healthful car exhausts but also to serious potential accidents from falling or leaping out (whether chained or unchained). And don't exercise it vigorously along busy roads.

On smoggy days keep your pet indoors and don't exercise it hard.

Keep toxic house and workshop chemicals away from pets. Thoroughly clean up any spills and dispose of residues in sealed containers in the dust bin. Do not sweep or wash them on to the soil or lawn. When using solvents, paints and volatile cleaners, keep pets away from the work area.

Give up cigarette smoking, not only for your own health but for that of others who breathe the smoke, including your animal. Cigarettes contain more than 3,000 components in the particulate and gas fractions, including cadmium, tar, nitrosamines, pesticide residues and several radioactive elements.

Brush and bath your animal as needed to keep it as free as possible from airborne and soilborne pollutants.

Drinking it in

Another dumping place for environmental pollutants is the water supply. I'm sure we've all seen some poor animal drinking from a filthy puddle. Obviously *that* water is polluted. What many of us don't realize is that our *natural* bodies of waters – rivers and lakes – can be polluted, too. These are most often contaminated by septic tanks, chemicals and landfills. One woman living in the vicinity of a landfill near Niagara Falls, New York (which is estimated to contain as much as a ton of dioxin), has watched six or seven of her pet cats die a few days after going down to the local stream.

Even tap water is less pure than it should be. Much of British drinking water fails to meet E.E.C. standards. Nearly 700 industrial and agricultural chemicals have been found in American drinking water because treatment plants are set up to focus almost entirely on bacteria and sediment, ignoring the ever-increasing load of complex chemicals that find their way into the water supply. Residents of communities that draw their water from particularly polluted sources have unusually high cancer rates of the gastrointestinal and urinary organs.

What to do: You can buy bottled water or purify your home supply with a filter or distiller.

The accompanying illustration shows a home water purification system that was found to be very effective in reducing most chemical water contaminants. The activated carbon granules should be changed about every three weeks, or after about 20 gallons have been filtered. The device produces about a gallon a day, running continuously.

Whether you give your animal purified water or tap water, be sure to change it daily, keep the bowl clean and place it where it's protected from dust and debris. Most of

Home water purification system

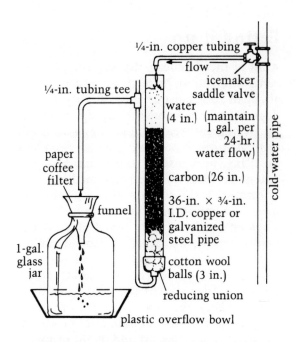

This home-made unit can be installed easily in a cabinet beneath the kitchen sink.

For materials you will need ¼-inch copper tubing, ¼-inch tubing tee, 36-inch by ¾-inch inside diameter copper or galvanized steel pipe, an icemaker saddle valve, reducing union for ¾-inch pipe to ¼-inch tubing, funnel, paper coffee filter, 1-gallon glass bottle, plastic bowl, and cotton wool balls.

1. Construct the filter as illustrated. A shorter column can be used if there are space limitations.
2. Disinfect the empty column with a 5 per cent solution of laundry bleach by filling the column and letting it stand for a couple of minutes.
3. Rinse the column thoroughly.
4. Add the cotton wool plug.
5. Fill the column with water and add previously wetted (two hours), washed carbon to the top to a depth of 26 inches.
6. Maintain the water level above the carbon by placing the ¼-inch tubing tee above the surface of the carbon as illustrated.

Source: *Water Fit to Drink*, by Carol Keough (Emmaus, Pa.: Rodale Press, 1980).

all, make it *available*, so that your pet will not be needlessly thirsty and thus tempted to seek out some unsavoury source.

Eating it up

A lot of the chemicals that are bad for pets come straight in through an eager mouth attached to a curious nose. Both cats and dogs have been known to lap up spilled or uncovered antifreeze, which has a sweetish taste. Antifreeze poisoning, which produces vomiting, nervousness and coma, is a persistent problem in veterinary medicine.

Another is the consumption – usually by dogs – of poison bait put out to kill snails, slugs and rodents. Cats sometimes eat the bait indirectly, by eating a poisoned mouse.

Mischievous pets get into all sorts of trouble. (You know the old saying about what curiosity did to the cat!) Therefore, strive to keep the following out of reach of mouths and paws: automotive products, cleansers, cosmetics, art and photo supplies, solvents, pesticides, paints, disinfectants, medicines and, last but not least, spoiled garbage – a common source of pet poisoning. (See 'Stomach Problems' in the *Encyclopaedia* section for more information.)

Though it is rare, small animals have also been poisoned by eating plants. If you provide your pet with fresh greens such as bean sprouts, parsley or spinach, this occurrence seems very unlikely. In a few geographical areas pets are sometimes poisoned by snakes, toads and the like, but again, this is not common. In any case of suspected poisoning, rush your animal to the nearest vet at once.

In addition to outright poisoning, animals can develop subtle forms of poisoning that result from an accumulation of small amounts of toxic material. For instance, tinned pet foods contain high levels of lead, ranging from 0.9 to 7.0 parts per million (ppm) in those surveyed. A daily intake of six ounces (about what a cat or small dog eats) of these foods could give as much as four times the amount of lead (1.19 milligrams) considered potentially toxic for children (0.3 milligrams). And that figure doesn't take into account the smaller body size of such a pet.

Lead poisoning can produce convulsions, hyperactivity, chronic fatigue, colic, anaemia and psychosis. In addition, it hampers the body's immune response to bacteria and viruses, according to many experimental studies, and it has been correlated with high blood pressure and mental retardation. Sources of lead contamination also include car exhaust fumes, lead water pipes and batteries, coloured newsprint and lead-based paints.

Another hidden poison is fluoride. Its levels in pet food are surprisingly high. A 1971 University of Montana study found that the average measure of fluoride in leading pet foods ranged from 11 to 193 ppm, with the highest values in tinned foods. That means your 100-pound dog could be consuming 21 to 368 milligrams of fluoride daily in its commercial pet food. Compare that figure to the upper daily limit of 2.5 milligrams of fluoride that the U.S. government's National Research Council says is safe for children over three years old.

The Montana researchers also found that fluoride accumulates in pets' bones. They found from 84 to 1,535 ppm in the leg bones of dogs and from 74 to 1,190 ppm in those of cats, the levels increasing with age. Since it's clearly recognized that long-term fluoride intake damages human bones and soft tissues, it's not unlikely that fluoride accumulation is one factor contributing to the increase in bone problems found in pets today.

In addition to tinned meat, pet foods made

of large fish like tuna may also present problems. Tuna has been found to contain high levels of mercury from industrial contamination. Excessive mercury intake can cause blindness, paralysis, convulsions and kidney damage. Fish from polluted waters can also contain high levels of the very toxic carcinogenic substance known as PCBs, which can cause many problems, including skeletal deformities, numbness of the limbs and still-births. Probably the most widespread chemical contaminant known, it concentrates in fatty tissues.

What to do: To minimize the environmental pollutants in your pet's diet, consider the following:

- Feed a natural foods diet that is relatively low in meat content (especially limiting liver) and fat. Many contaminants are stored in fats, so it's better to go with low-fat dairy products or lean meats. For a vegetable oil, corn oil is preferable to soya, due to its generally lower pesticide content.
- If you feed fish to your pet, try to use mostly cod, halibut and pollack. These are usually from less contaminated waters.
- When possible and practical, use organically grown foods.
- Consider extra dietary supplementation. Calcium, for instance, helps protect against some heavy metals and radiation. Vitamin A and selenium also help on the radiation front. Vitamin E counters the effects of many smog pollutants, and kelp helps the body resist radioactive strontium. Some other supplements to consider if you live in a particularly polluted area are vitamin C (for pollutants in general, and specifically for cadmium, lead, copper and DDT); lecithin (for general use); and zinc (for cadmium, lead and copper).

Of rays and radiation

What other factors in your animal's world might make it less healthy than the natural conditions in which we all evolved? The subjects covered so far are ones we hear a lot about. Poor nutrition, insufficient exercise, exposure to chemical contaminants – these are all familiar. Let's explore some dangers that are less obvious.

As modern physics shows us, our seemingly solid world is not really composed so much of solid objects as of a vastly complex interplay of energy fields. For example, the visible light that at present carries the image of this printed page to your eye is a series of wavelengths found in a relatively small range of a huge scale of energies we call the electromagnetic spectrum. And the types of waves that transmit the complex picture on your TV – strange as it seems – are also travelling through your body right now!

These energy fields can play subtle games with health. Ask yourself: is your animal hyperactive? Does it have mange? Is it often irritable? Does it get virus infections? Have tumours? All these things and more may be strongly influenced by various imbalances of natural electromagnetic and other energies that have occurred as side effects of modern life and technology.

Let's start with an energy familiar to us all – light.

The importance of natural light
Maybe because light constantly surrounds us, we haven't paid much attention to it. But light plays a much bigger part in life than simply enabling us to get around without stumbling into the furniture.

Without the natural light of the sun, there would be no life on earth. Yet a lot of companion animals (and people, too) spend practically their entire lives indoors, illuminating their dark corners with incandescent and fluorescent bulbs. Stop for a moment to consider the potentially profound significance of artificial light. What if indoor lighting were missing something found in sunlight? What if artificial light were to natural light as bleached white flour is to whole wheat flour?

That, in fact, appears to be the case.

Researchers have found that visible light can penetrate directly into the body. Surprisingly, it has been detected in the brain of a living sheep. Light acts on the neuroendocrine system, influencing a hormone that induces sleep. It is involved in the regulation of the adrenal, pituitary, thyroid and reproductive glands.

Cycles of light and dark influence the production and release of cortisol, a hormone that is important in the breakdown of protein, resistance to stress, formation of blood sugar, excitation of the nerve tissue, healing of wounds and inflammations, and the functioning of many body processes.

The ultraviolet rays of sunlight act to produce vitamin D in and under our skin. The same applies to pets. Vitamin D is not only essential for the normal growth and maintenance of bones, but also for the proper metabolism of calcium.

What happens when organisms are deprived of natural sunlight? Experiments with animals that lived under different-coloured lights showed they developed problems with both their physical and emotional health. Animals exposed over long periods to pink light, for example, developed difficult behavioural problems. They also had smaller litters, calcium deposits in the heart, tail loss due to skin inflammation and tissue death, and an increase in tumour formation and growth.

Now comes the catch. As compared to natural sunlight, nearly all indoor lighting is much lower in intensity. The light under a shady tree on a sunny day is about ten times stronger than typical indoors levels. Indoor lighting lacks most of the ultraviolet range, filtered out by window glass, quite deficient in fluorescent bulbs and virtually non-existent in incandescent bulbs. Both lights are also markedly weak in the blue and green rays that are the strongest emissions in sunlight. Indoor lighting is also disproportionately high in the red region of the light spectrum, when provided by incandescent bulbs.

Clearly, most indoor lighting is similar to that which caused problems in experimental animals.

It's also my personal observation that a great many of the unhealthy animals I treat spend all or nearly all their time indoors. It often strikes me that this is part of their problem. If your pet has been mostly an indoor animal and has one or more of the following problems, I recommend that you take steps to restore natural light to its life.

- Behavioural problems – aggression, irritability, unfriendliness, hyperactivity
- Endocrine imbalances – of the thyroid (causing obesity, hyperactivity, and skin problems); of the parathyroid (leading to calcium/phosphorus imbalances and bone problems); of the adrenals (producing skin irritation and low stress tolerance); and of the reproductive glands (causing infertility, spontaneous abortions, unusual heat cycles and abnormal sexual activity in neutered animals)
- Also, skin disorders, liver problems,

tumours and malignancies and infections

What to do: Provide natural light for your pet. If you have a fenced garden it should be easy. But what if you don't have such a space or there are unsafe conditions your pet could encounter outside? I've known people with cats who protect them from dogs and cars by building large outdoor wire enclosures connected to open windows. Taking your dog on a daily walk is a great idea for both of you.

If taking the animal out is impossible, you can bring natural light indoors by installing a special light which emits almost the same range and proportions of wavelengths as sunlight. Labelled 'full-spectrum', these lights are available by post.

It's also possible just to let in the natural sunshine. You can install a special plastic window that admits the sun's ultraviolet rays. A southern window would be a good choice since wintertime is when we get outside the least.

Of course, when the weather permits, just open your windows and doors!

The rays we can't see

Important as it is, visible light is just a small part of the vast electromagnetic spectrum. Others parts of the spectrum – radio-frequency and microwave – are invisible to us, but we use them every day. We use them when we turn on a radio, a TV or microwave oven. Radiofrequency is also used in radar.

At sufficient levels of exposure these waves are apparently capable of doing some biological damage. For instance, microwaves not only can cook your dinner but also can exert more subtle influences on the electric or magnetic fields that surround living bodies. Exposure to microwaves has been found to cause the following:

- Genetic problems – chromosomal irregularities, increased mutation rates and birth defects, and lower body weight and brain weight of unborn animals
- Physiological interferences, causing changes in the blood cells, hormonal and biochemical processes, the operation of the normal barrier between the blood and the brain (which filters what may enter the brain tissue), and the electrical signals that regulate the heartbeat
- Physical complaints – headaches, fatigue, reduced sexual capacities, hair loss, loss of appetite, cataracts and eye pain, formation of tumours and (possibly) cancer
- Behavioural and mental disturbances – including loss of coordination and balance, docility, irritability, depression, emotional instability, diminished intellectual capacity, partial memory loss and hypochondria

Some of these effects resulted from exposure to abnormally high levels of radiation, but some were brought about by levels comparable to those frequently encountered by both pets and people in their everyday lives.

Extremely low frequency fields (ELF) surround high power lines. Exposure to these electromagnetic fields, which extend for thousands of feet around the heavy loads of electrical current coursing through power lines, has been found to:

- Influence chemical balances in the blood or rats
- Slow down the heartbeat of salmon and eels
- Interfere with the ability of homing pigeons to find their way home

- Cause changes in hormones, stunted growth and other signs of chronic stress in mice
- Cause bees to cease storing honey and pollen, to kill each other and abandon or seal off their hives (causing death by asphyxiation)

What is the likelihood that these kinds of energy fields are harming your animal? If your animal has one of the following problems, I suggest you consider the possibility that these energy fields are at the very least an aggravating factor (if not the cause): epilepsy, behaviour problems, blood disorders (unresponsive anaemia, clotting deficiency), or any sort of cancer.

What to do: Depending on where you live and what appliances you operate, exposures can be quite high or very low. If possible, stay away from radar installations, microwave towers, TV and radio broadcasting towers and large power lines. For the most part, exposure levels are worse at high locations, such as hilltops or high-rise buildings.

If you use a microwave oven, keep animals (and other family members) out of the room when it is in operation. Look out for cats that like to walk on worktops! The essential fact to know is that microwave exposure decreases rapidly as you move farther away from it.

Another part of the electromagnetic spectrum which is invisible to us includes radioactive energies such as x-rays, cosmic rays and gamma rays. Radioactivity can inflict direct damage to genetic material, causing cellular death, mutation, or cancer. High exposure causes radiation sickness. But the major menace of our times is the constant low-level exposure to which we are all subject, as well as the intermittent accumulation of larger doses from diagnostic x-rays and other sources.

An important rule to remember is this: all radiation exposure is cumulative and harmful. There is *no* dose of radiation, *however small*, that does not increase the risk of getting cancer. This point was driven home to researchers who were trying to establish the safety/danger levels of plutonium 239 (which is a by-product of nuclear power plants). After forcing beagles to inhale various amounts of this potent radioactive isotope, they found to their surprise that even at the very lowest dose given, 100 per cent of the dogs developed lung cancer!

The major sources of radiation are mineral deposits in the earth, cosmic rays from outer space, and medical x-rays. Though only about 3 per cent of the total radiation exposure comes from fallout from nuclear weapons testing, this radiation is particularly dangerous because it causes the greatest biological damage, and the material involved (particularly strontium 90 and plutonium 239) can persist in our bodies all our lives.

What do to: Avoid medical x-rays whenever possible. I believe it is a diagnostic tool overused because animals cannot describe their symptoms. Keep your animal at least several feet away from an operating colour TV set, which emits x-rays. The same rule goes for people. Reduce the radioactivity in your tap water with an activated carbon filter or reverse osmosis filter.

Should you suspect a high exposure to radioactivity from any source, see 'Radiation Toxicity' in the *Encyclopaedia* section for special nutritional treatments to help to counter the effects.

Vitamins of the air: ions

Have you noticed that your animal gets irritable, depressed, 'hyperactive' or just 'under the weather' on hot, dry days 24 to 48 hours before a windy period? Is he disturbed when the moon is full? Or on car trips? Is he absolutely in love with the lawn sprinkler or the seashore? If so, he is probably responding to variations in the quantity and balance of certain electrically charged air molecules, or ions.

The 'ion effect' is another subtle health factor. Yet these little 'vitamins of the air', as they've been called, are an essential part of life on earth. Experimental animals deprived of them all died young. Our modern urban environment is pretty short on them, too.

Created by sunlight, background earth radiation, wind and sprays of water, ions can not only be in short supply, but they can also be imbalanced so as to cause a variety of disturbances among sensitive individuals (around a quarter of the population). Whereas there are usually about five positively charged ions for every four that are negatively charged, certain circumstances can produce an imbalance of either type. An excess of positive air ions can be positively unnerving for many of us, but a negative air ion surplus can be both healing and pleasant.

A natural positive ion overdose occurs in some regions the day before hot, dry winds arrive. Those who suffer their ill effects complain of everything from insomnia, anxiety, depression and violent headaches to dizziness, tremors and heart palpitations. We are all probably affected to some degree.

On the other hand, a negative ion overdose promotes a sense of well-being. Negative ions ease breathing, ward off bacteria and put you in a good mood. A marvellous natural negative ion generator is a simple spray of water. Negative ions are high at the sea's edge, near waterfalls, showers and sprinklers.

Although the balance of positive and negative ions has always fluctuated, modern technology has made unnatural total ion depletion and positive ion imbalances facts of daily life for the average urban dweller and pet. Some of the circumstances, both natural and unnatural, that can create unhealthy shortages or imbalances of ions are: air laden with particles and/or screened from the sun – such as fog, smoke and dust; the friction of moving air masses (e.g., air stratum against air stratum, and ductwork in cars that creates friction between air and metal); a lack of unpaved, open ground; special properties of moving cars and synthetic fabrics and building materials; and the full moon.

What to do: To tell if your pet might be sensitive to ion disturbances, look for nasal and respiratory problems, fatigue, depression, irritability or aggression. If these conditions get worse on dry, hot or smoggy days, in smoke-filled rooms or in a moving car, there's a chance your pet is suffering from the 'ion effect'. See if your pet feels noticeably better outdoors, or near a sprinkler.

Take your pet outdoors frequently, minimize its exposure to smoke and car travel, and let fresh air into the house. Switch from synthetic to natural fibres (cotton or wool) for its bedding. If you suspect it would be of general benefit and you can afford it, there are a number of negative ion generators on the market for home use.

CHAPTER NINE
Choosing a Healthy Animal

One day someone brought a lost dog into a clinic where I work. The poor animal was covered from head to foot with burrs, grass awns and tangled hair. One eye was closed and discharging pus and the areas between his toes were red and swollen.

Plant awns are those sticky little things that attach to your socks when you walk across a field or patch of waste ground. They attach themselves to dogs, too. And because of their pointed shapes, they burrow their way not only into the coat but into the eyes, ears, nose, mouth, vagina, rectum, between the toes and somtimes even right through the skin.

Because our patient was so badly affected, we had to give him a general anaesthetic before we could begin the long and arduous process of removing the stickers from his body. First we clipped and pulled the burrs out of his coat, and then from between his toes. While my assistant worked on the feet, I found and removed two or three awns from deep in the ear canal. Then, carefully pulling back the 'third eyelid', I found another lodged in the eye – the cause of the inflammation and discharge. After extracting it and making sure the cornea was still intact, I applied an antibiotic ointment with the hope that the eye would eventually recover.

Throughout the lengthy procedure of rescuing our patient from the perils of his adventures, my assistant and I began talking about why it is that pets can get into such a state after even a short trek in the fields.

I looked again at the little dog on the table, which had the long curly hair typical of a poodle. 'Here is the cause of the problem,' I said as I held up some of the matted hair we had clipped off. 'An animal with this kind of coat is like walking Velcro. Once the burrs brush against it, it's almost impossible for them to go anywhere else but deeper in.'

I pondered the matter for a moment. 'You know something,' I told my assistant, 'people have actually *created* this type of problem by deliberately breeding dogs to have such hair, as well as these floppy ears. Both are perfect traps for grass awns. Wild animals don't have anywhere near this much problem with plants.'

Later that day someone else showed us a news clipping describing a new breed of cat which was being currently introduced (from Scotland, if I remember correctly).

'Isn't it cute?' she exclaimed.

Sure enough, someone had found a way to breed cats guaranteed to have the same kind of problem as our patient. Instead of having the upright ears typical of felines, the cat in the picture had ears that bent forward in the middle to form a short flap over the earhole. Cats like this couldn't help but be prone to

ear problems. Imagine how it would suffer with ear mites, for instance.

Situations like these have made me do a lot of thinking about the many ways that humans have interfered with the natural reproductive patterns of animals. In the process of selectively breeding creatures in the images we desire, we have not only increased their susceptibility to many health problems (such as ear mites), but have also created a host of congenital defects – abnormal body structures or functions that the animal is born with, including the tendency to develop more problems later in life.

But selective breeding is not the only way humans have caused animal defects. Drugs, man-made chemicals and radiation can damage the foetus and further increase the incidence of inborn defects.

Congenital defects can spell lifelong trouble, despite excellent care and feeding. That's why it is so important to understand how they are caused and how they might be prevented or reduced in number.

Let's start by looking at inheritable problems encouraged by intensive breeding and selection. Then we'll move on to consider the effects of chemicals and other environmental agents, followed by a listing of the common congenital defects of dogs and cats and some guidelines for prevention.

The effects of breeding

As compared to cats, dogs are particularly susceptible to inheritable genetic defects, no doubt because they have been much more extensively and selectively bred. The difference in appearance between most modern dog breeds and that of their wild ancestors is much more striking than is the case with cats. It is no wonder that cats have the lowest risk factor for congenital defects of all domestic animals. (Surely their mating choices are much greater than for those animals that aren't so capable of getting over fences!)

Accordingly, we'll emphasize the inbred genetic problems of dogs, but the same principles apply to cats as well, particularly since they, too, are undergoing more controlled breeding these days.

How is it that deliberate breeding can create special health problems? Isn't it true that breeders select for the best and healthiest individuals, and therefore the offspring should get stronger with time? Before we can answer these questions, we would do well to consider some of the historical and biological factors behind the breeding of pets, particularly canines.

Ever since dogs first associated with people some 10,000 to 20,000 years ago, they have served many purposes, assisting in hunting and herding animals, pulling sledges, providing sport and entertainment (as in fighting matches) and serving as religious and status symbols, watchdogs, guide dogs, personal companions and even as a source of food.

It is believed that all the varieties of domestic dogs were almost certainly derived chiefly from the wolf, whose large and diverse genetic endowment enabled people to select for useful characteristics.

Another important biological factor that allowed so many breeds to be created is something called 'neoteny'. In the field of genetics this term refers to a manifestation that is a throwback to more primitive characteristics – those found either in earlier types historically or else in young animals (in this case, puppies). Typical expressions of neoteny can include short legs and muzzles, silky hair, floppy ears and the tendency to bark (adult wolves do not bark, except very rarely).

Thus, many of the desired features that have been stabilized into various breeds are actually the product of arrested development – either physical or psychological. Two problems result. The first is that the development of a desired trait is often accompanied by a corresponding defect or loss of function. To fix a given characteristic into a breed (so that it will breed 'true'), one must either mate selected brothers and sisters or cross an animal with its parent. Such intensive inbreeding does ensure the desired trait but also can perpetuate weaknesses inherent in the breed. These weaknesses can include poor resistance to disease, low stamina, low intelligence, birth defects and inherited diseases like haemophilia or deafness. For example, miniature poodles extensively bred for colour selection have produced litters in which all the puppies had severely undershot lower jaws.

The second problem is that certain features (for instance, a short muzzle or upper jaw) are controlled by genes that are *separate* from those that determine closely associated anatomical structures (such as the size of the teeth and the length of the soft palate). For a breed like the bulldog, breeding for a single trait spells trouble. Though the breed was developed to have a short muzzle, it still has the same size and number of teeth and the same size soft palate as its ancestors. So the crowded teeth must grow in crooked and sideways and the soft palate hangs so far back into the throat that it threatens the animal with imminent suffocation for most of its life!

The problem of genetic disease is particularly sad because much of it represents unnecessary suffering brought about simply because we humans found one characteristic more attractive than another. We decided to perpetuate it for our own purposes, with little or no regard for the animal's total well-being. Natural forces no longer select which animals are most fit, both physically and psychologically, to survive and repro-

This bulldog's short muzzle barely holds his mouthful of crooked teeth. His misplaced soft palate verges on choking him.

duce. Rather, it is *we* who decide which dogs and cats will carry on the species. And often our decisions are based on something we consider 'cute' or unusual. Rarely if ever do we ask whether or not the animal will have a comfortable, well-adapted, potentially healthy body.

Many people unwittingly may contribute to the problem of genetic manipulation by insisting on owning only pure-bred animals. At the same time, large numbers of mongrels that would make equally good pets often go begging. One study shows that as many as 75 per cent of the dogs and cats born each year are unable to find permanent homes and thus face the threat of accidents, starvation or euthanasia.

Yet, in and of itself, adopting a mongrel from the local animal shelter will not solve

the gene problem either. Often a potential adopter selects a pet which most arouses his or her sense of pity – one with unusually coloured eyes, drooping ears and eyelids which make it look sad, and a short, pushed-in face that most resembles that of a human child, or even one suffering from a health problem. Someone who would like to provide care for a homeless animal would do better to choose one that's healthy, rather than one with inherited problems that can be passed on to future generations.

A case in point: the poodle

To give you a better idea about what problems result from breeding animals to have unnatural appearances, let's consider the poodle.

Besides having floppy ears that encourage infections and grass seeds, as well as a long-haired, curly coat that attracts burrs (traits common to many breeds), the poodle can carry a number of defective genes producing problems such as abnormally shortened leg bones, a defect in the arteries near the heart, degeneration of the retina of the eye, dislocated shoulders, epilepsy, behavioural abnormalities and bladder stones.

Some other problems thought to be hereditary for poodles are collapse of the windpipe, displacement of the kneecap, diabetes, brittle and easily broken bones, skin defects and a loss of the normal insulating coating around nerves in the brain and spinal cord.

In addition to these officially recognized problems, I will add two more. One is hair that grows down into the ear canal and causes unending problems unless it is regularly pulled out. The second is blocked tear ducts that cause eye secretions to run from the corners of the eyes instead of their normal course (into the nose). That's why you so often see dark, moist tracks running from the inner corner of a poodle's eyes.

The poodle's tragic lot in life can include teary eyes, displaced kneecaps, diabetes, brittle bones, skin defects, and more. Poor dog.

Most of the problems I have just mentioned apply to miniature and toy poodles rather than to the standard size. Indeed, it generally seems to be the case that the largest and smallest dogs are those which suffer the most genetic weaknesses.

Some other examples of problems created by our desire for strange shapes and sizes of dogs are those of the bulldog, Chihuahua, and others bred to have a small pelvis. Many of these animals cannot even reproduce themselves effectively and require caesarean deliveries. Giant breeds like Saint Bernards and Great Danes are known for their bone problems and short lives. Brachycephalic breeds (those with abnormally short noses and jaws, like bulldogs, Pekingese, boxers and Boston terriers) are generally afflicted with obstructed breathing as well as pituitary cysts, and it's not too surprising that

dogs bred to have short legs (like the dachshund and basset hound) count themselves among breeds with spinal deformities.

Environmental impacts on congenital problems

In addition to the unwanted qualities that often accompany the traits for which we have selected, there is an additional factor that is playing an increasing role in undermining the quality of the gene pool of animals (and humans as well). Exposure to a number of enviromental toxins can increase the frequency of biological mutations, which can be passed on from generation to generation. A mutation is defined as any inheritable molecular change of genetic material (either of a single gene or of a group of genes in the chromosome). It can produce not only congenital anomalies and genetic disease, but also embryonic death, abortion, lowered disease resistance, decreased life span, infertility, behavioural aberrations and cancer. The effects of mutations of this sort can be exaggerated when the offspring of an affected parent are mated with each other or with the parent (the kind of intensive inbreeding we discussed earlier).

Additionally, some birth defects occur *during* pregnancy as the vulnerable tissues of the developing embryo are exposed to such hazards as radiation, pollutants, drugs, nutritional deficiencies, viruses, traumatic injury, extreme temperatures or stress and certain natural toxins. Depending on when the exposure occurs and its intensity, these agents can produce not only deformed bodies but also embryonic death and miscarriages, retardation of growth, congenital tumours and various functional or behavioural abnormalities after birth.

AGENTS THAT MAY CAUSE INHERITED DISORDERS AND BIRTH DEFECTS

Type of agent or use	Suspected cause of inherited disorders, mutations and birth defects	Suspected cause of inherited disorders and mutations (mutagens)	Suspected cause of birth defects (teratogens)
VETERINARY DRUGS Anaesthetics	urethane		halothane nitrous oxide pentobarbital
Antibiotics and drugs to treat infections		actinomycin D erythromycin streptomycin	chloramphenacol penicillin streptonigrin sulphanilamide tetracyclin
Anti-inflammatory agents to treat arthritis, joint problems			cortisone dexamethasone triamcinolone
Antiseptics, disinfectants, bacteriocidal soaps		hexachlorophene hydrogen peroxide mercury chloride	
Chelating therapy to treat lead poisoning		EDTA	(Table continued overleaf)

SOURCE: Adapted from 'Teratogenesis and Mutagenesis,' by Norman R. Schneider, in *Current Veterinary Therapy VII: Small Animal Practice*, ed. Robert W. Kirk (Philadelphia: W. B. Saunders, 1980), pp. 161–71.

Type of agent or use	Suspected cause of inherited disorders, mutationsand birth defects	Suspected cause of inherited disorders and mutations (mutagens)	Suspected cause of birth defects (teratogens)
VETERINARY DRUGS (Continued) Control of fleas, ticks, worms, parasites	carbaryl dichlorvos dieldrin lindane	ethidium bromide	
Diagnostic dye		methylene blue	
Diuretic			acetazolamide (Diamox)
Muscle relaxant, diuretic myocardial stimulant		theophylline	
Pain relievers		phenylbutazone (Butazolidin)	aspirin
Sedatives anticonvulsants, tranquillizers	chlorpromazine phenobarbital		diazepam (Valium) primidone
Stimulant	caffeine		
Treatment of cancer tumours, leukaemia	cyclophosphamide (Cytoxan)	adriamycin colchicine (also used for gout) cytosine arabinoside vincristine	
Vaccinations, viruses		canine distemper vaccine (measles virus)	feline leukaemia virus parvovirus and feline panleucopaenia vaccines (feline panleucopaenia virus)
AGRICULTURAL CHEMICALS Chemosterilants		apholate hempa metepa TEPA triethylenemelamine	
Fungicides	Captan griseofulvin	ethylene bromide ethylene oxide	methyl mercuric chloride tetrachlorophenol
Herbicides		2,4–D 2,4,5–T ('Agent Orange')	paraquat MCPA

Type of agent or use	Suspected cause of inherited disorders, mutations and birth defects	Suspected cause of inherited disorders and mutations (mutagens)	Suspected cause of birth defects (teratogens)
AGRICULTURAL CHEMICALS (Continued) Insecticides	carbaryl dichlorvos dieldrin lindane	DDT endrin formaldehyde	aldrin diazinon
OTHER FACTORS Environmental stresses			lack of oxygen from air pollution, anaemia, anaesthesia, chemical causes or high altitude overheating from enclosure in hot car, exercise in hot weather or fever traumatic injury
Food additives		EDTA sodium bisulphite sodium cyclamate sodium nitrate	FD&C Red Dye No. 2 (E123)
Industrial effluents, environmental pollutants	compounds containing cadmium, lead or mercury ionizing radiation	1,2-benzanthracene benzyme dimethylnitrosamine methylcholanthrene	compounds containing arsenic, lithium, or nickel microwave radiation ultrasound radiation
Mycotoxins, toxins from food moulds	aflatoxin		cytochalasin B ochratoxin
Nutritional deficiencies and imbalances			deficiencies of copper, iodine, iron, magnesium, manganese, vitamin B complex or zinc deficiencies or extreme overdose of vitamins A and D excessive calcium, iodine, salt, vitamin K general maternal malnutrition
Plants		sweet clover (spoiled)	jimsonweed locoweed skunk cabbage wild pea

Although the largest group of potential teratogens (agents that can cause defects in the developing embryo) consists of man-made chemicals, ionizing radiation is probably the most potent contributor to both mutations and birth defects. Besides receiving general environmental radiation, animals are routinely exposed to ionizing radiation in veterinary medicine in the form of diagnostic x-rays and radioisotopes. This exposure most commonly affects the central nervous system in mammals (which turns out to be one of the most frequent sites of congenital disorders in both dogs and cats, as we will see).

A list of suspected teratogens and mutagens (agents that cause mutations) appears on pages 97–9. Many of these produced effects when they were administered experimentally at unusually high dosages, so they may not necessarily cause congenital problems at common exposures. But while their practical dangers have not all been conclusively proved, neither has their safety. The harm caused by these agents is real enough to be seen in clinical practice, not just experiments. For instance, pups of the brachycephalic breeds (those with short jaws) can become grossly swollen with fluid. The cause of the problem may be related to corticosteroid therapy given the mother dog when she was pregnant. Also, extreme leg and leg joint deformities were observed in an entire litter of cocker spaniel puppies after their mother had been treated with the corticosteroid dexamethasone during the second half of pregnancy.

Now that we have a better understanding of the contributing causes behind congenital defects, let's look at a listing of some of these problems as found in both dogs and cats. Due to space limitations not all could be

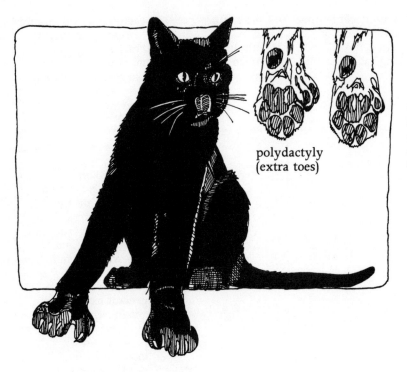

polydactyly
(extra toes)

Certain defects are hereditary, such as developing extra toes or more serious problems like nervous or skeletal disorders.

included, so we emphasize those that occur in more than one breed or those that are considered common.

Congenital defects of dogs

In dogs the parts of the body most frequently affected by congenital problems are the central nervous system, eyes, muscles and bones. For instance, the Alsatian, collie, beagle, miniature poodle and keeshond can inherit epilepsy. A variety of other nervous system disorders are passed through a recessive gene in various breeds. These include paralysis of the front and back legs – Irish setter; a failure of muscle co-ordination – fox terrier; idiocy – German shorthaired pointer and English setter; and abnormal swelling of the brain – Chihuahua, cocker spaniel and English bulldog.

Congenital eye abnormalities – including cataracts, blindness caused by retinal atrophy or maldevelopment, glaucoma and small eyes – are found in *most* of the common breeds. A typical muscular problem is hernia. The basset hound, basenji, cairn terrier, Pekingese and Lhasa apso all have a high risk for inguinal hernias (protrusion of the gut into the groin). Umbilical hernias (protrusion through the navel) are inherited in the cocker spaniel, bull terrier, collie, basenji, Airedale terrier, Pekingese, pointer and weimaraner.

Besides the bone-related problems of the type mentioned earlier (in very small, large or short-legged dogs), many canines suffer lameness from hip dysplasia, considered to be the most common canine congenital defect (see 'Hip Dysplasia' in the *Encyclopaedia* section). It is seen in most purebreds, particularly cocker spaniels, Shetland sheepdogs, Alsatians and many large breeds. Some of the most notable congenital disorders of the more popular dog breeds are shown on page 102–3.

Congenital problems of cats

In cats the most common congenital defects are found in the nervous system. Overall, the problems most frequently reported are:

Cerebellar hypoplasia: a small cerebellum (part of the brain), producing lack of co-ordination, tremors, excessive tension in the limb muscles and retarded reflexes.

Umbilical hernias: protrusion of part of the intestines or fat through the navel. Diaphragmatic hernias are also common.

Eye and lid defects: including absence of the outer half of one or both upper lids (seen in Persians and the domestic shorthair), an unpigmented or multicoloured iris (which is sometimes associated with deafness on the same side, sensitivity to light and unco-ordinated eyes), degeneration of the retina (particularly in Siamese and Persians), strabismus (an inward rotation of one eye when the other is fixed on an object, common in Siamese) and nystagmus (involuntary movements of the eye).

Feet and tail problems: including extra toes (usually in the forepaws), absent tail (typical of the Manx but rare in others; associated defects include spina bifida, hind limb and pelvic deformities and an abnormally small anus) and a kinked tail (a recessive trait, usually seen near the end of the tail).

Palate problems: such as cleft palate, which has been reported as probably hereditary in the Siamese.

Other feline congenital problems which are seen less frequently but not rarely include:

Spina bifida: a closure defect of the vertebral arches, sometimes with spinal cord

COMMON CONGENITAL DEFECTS IN DOGS

	Afghan hound	Airedale terrier	Alaskan malamute	Alsatian	Basenji	Basset hound	Beagle	Boston terrier	Boxer	Chihuahua	Cocker spaniel	Collie
Cataracts	•			•			•	•			•	
Retinal atrophy											•	•
Glaucoma						•	•				•	
Other eye abnormalities			•	•	•		•				•	•
Deafness												•
Epilepsy				•			•					•
Various nervous system defects		•										
Hydrocephalus										•	•	
Kidney disease				•							•	
Bladder stones				•								
Haemophilia and excessive bleeding			•	•			•			•	•	•
Heart valve defects										•		
Other cardiovascular defects				•			•		•	•	•	
Collapsed trachea										•		
Obstructed breathing[1]								•	•			
Diabetes												
Pituitary cysts[2]								•	•			
Cleft lips and palate				•			•				•	
Excess or missing teeth									•			
Jaw too long or short											•	
Spinal deformities						•	•	•		•	•	
Limbs too short						•						
Tail short or missing							•				•	
Elbow dysplasia[3]	(many breeds)											
Hip dysplasia[3]	(many breeds) See the *Encyclopaedia* section											
Dislocation of shoulder										•		
Deformed knee joint								•		•		
Hernia		•			•						•	•
Inherited skin allergy							•					
Nasal sunburn												•
Tumours								•	•			
Demodectic mange	(many breeds) See the *Encyclopaedia* section											
Behaviour abnormalities					•						•	
Testicles don't descend	(many breeds)											

[1]Caused by small nostrils and over-long soft palate, predisposing to collapse of larynx.
[2]Can result in diabetes insipidus, genital atrophy and obesity.
[3]Joints improperly joined, causing lameness.

Dachshund	Doberman pinscher	English bulldog	Fox terrier	German short-haired pointer	Golden retriever	Great Dane	Irish setter	Labrador retriever	Miniature poodle	Pekingese	Saint Bernard	Scottish terrier	Shetland sheepdog	Standard poodle	Weimaraner	Giant breeds, generally	Miniature breeds, generally	Brachycephalic breeds, generally
				•	•			•						•				
					•		•	•	•									
			•															
•				•		•		•	•	•	•			•	•			
			•									•						
									•					•				
			•				•		•			•			•			
	•																	
•								•	•			•		•				
							•	•	•		•		•	•	•			
		•				•												
		•	•	•			•		•				•					
									•								•	
		•								•								•
•									•									
		•								•								•
•		•																
•		•	•															
•																		
•	•					•			•	•							•	
•									•			•						
		•																
			•						•									
									•									
				•						•						•		
			•						•			•		•				
													•					
		•										•						
				•					•					•				

SOURCES: Adapted from *Congenital Defects in Dogs: A Special Reference for Practitioners* by F. Erickson, et al. (Veterinary Practice Publishing Co., 1978). "*A Catalog of Genetic Disorders of the Dog,*" by Donald F. Patterson, in *Current Veterinary Therapy VII: Small Animal Practice*, ed. Robert W. Kirk (Philadelphia: W. B. Saunders, 1980), pp. 82–103.

protrusion. This is common in the Manx, because it is associated with the gene for tail-lessness. Symptoms can include a hopping gait and an inability to control urination and defaecation.

Deafness: particularly in blue-eyed white cats.

Peke face: an unusually short and wide head, seen only in some strains of long-haired Persians.

A cat with problems: This long-haired persian has a peke face – a congenital deformity.

Absence of a kidney: usually the right one. More common in males.

Mammary gland abnormalities: in the formation of the tubular parts (ducts).

Hair abnormalities: such as hairlessness or the 'Rex' mutant, which has curly, short, plushlike hair and missing or abnormal guard hairs.

Circulatory system defects: including narrowing of the aorta or non-closure of the aortic duct (both common conditions that produce murmurs) and various heart and aorta malformations.

Two other common feline problems to note which result from their inbred traits are the chronic build-up of hair masses (hairballs) in the stomachs of long-haired types, and the tendency to ear cancer in white-haired cats (from recurrent sunburn of the ears).

Preventing congenital defects

Once an animal is born with a congenital problem, you can't do much about it. Sometimes corrective surgery will help for a structural malformation and with proper veterinary care, feeding and grooming you can keep other problems under control. But the best treatment of all is prevention.

There are three basic things you can do to minimize the chance of either acquiring or breeding a pet with genetic disorders or birth defects. The first is to avoid selecting or breeding animals either known to carry problems that seem to be genetic in nature or that come from a line that has been intensively inbred. You might even consider avoiding pure-breds altogether, particularly if it is a popular breed that has undergone intensive reproduction in the past few decades (such as poodles, cocker spaniels, collies, dachshunds, beagles, boxers, bull-dogs, Alsatians, Pekingese, or Siamese cats).

The second piece of advice is to select an animal with a conformation and appearance most resembling that of a wild animal like a

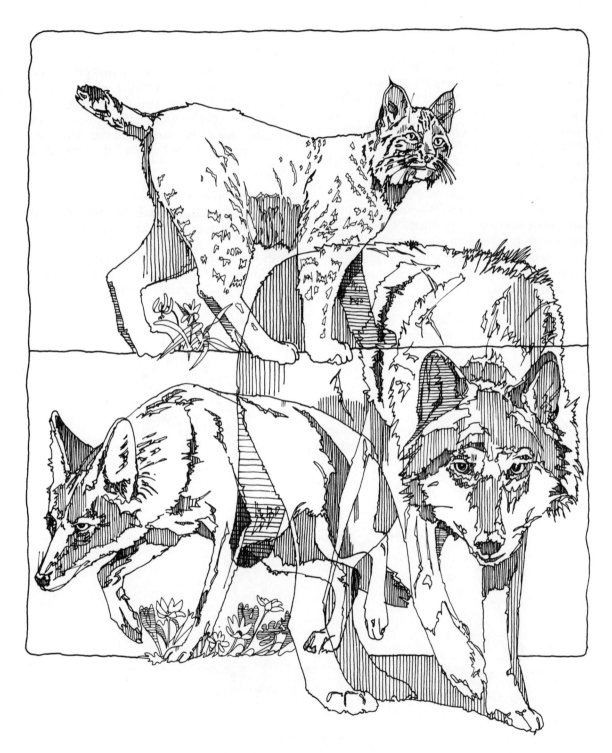

The wolf, coyote and bobcat show the true form of canines and felines, unmanipulated by humans.

coyote, wolf or bobcat. Occasionally I have had the opportunity to examine and treat injured coyotes or foxes and never once have I found one with a grass seed in its ears or anywhere else on its body! Every inch of their bodies reflects the intelligence of millions of years of natural evolution and adaptation. I have been quite impressed with how pefectly their teeth fit together and with their fine haircoats, fastidious cleanliness, natural grace and high intelligence.

You would do well to choose a pet whose natural heritage has been least distorted by inappropriate breeding. (Don't try to adopt a truly wild animal, though. The place for them is in the wild and they do not make good pets anyway.)

How to choose a 'natural' animal

Look for a medium-sized mixed breed (for a dog, 20 to 40 pounds) with short to medium-length hair that is straight and relatively coarse (not silky) and with straight, erect, normal-size ears. See page 108 to help you predict the adult size of a puppy.

See if the upper and lower jaws are the same size and if the teeth fit together well (this particularly applies to dogs).

Does the animal move normally? Or does it swing its hips from side to side as it walks? Swinging is a possible sign of canine hip

The perfect dog

Look for an animal with clean, natural lines, such as this short-haired mixed breed.

dysplasia. Are the legs a normal length and are the front and back legs in the right proportion relative to each other?

Are the eyes normal-looking? Are they the same colour?

Is there normal pigmentation over the nose?

What colour is the coat? Generally it is best to avoid white animals, as they often carry genetic problems.

Look around the navel to see if there is a lump, which could be a sign of a hernia.

Check the scrotum in an adult male to see if both testicles are present.

If the animal is young, observe it carefully to see if it has a normal temperament. Be wary of animals that seem unusually aggressive, clinging, fearful, hyperactive or unaware.

How to predict a puppy's adult size

If you know the present age and weight of a puppy you can get a pretty fair estimate of its eventual adult size by consulting the accompanying table which shows the growth curves for various breeds. The information can also be applied to mixed-breeds, however, simply by finding the curve that most closely matches your data. An 18-pound pup of four months, for instance, will probably attain the adult size of a bulldog, about 42 pounds.

HOW TO
PREDICT
YOUR PUPPY'S
ADULT SIZE

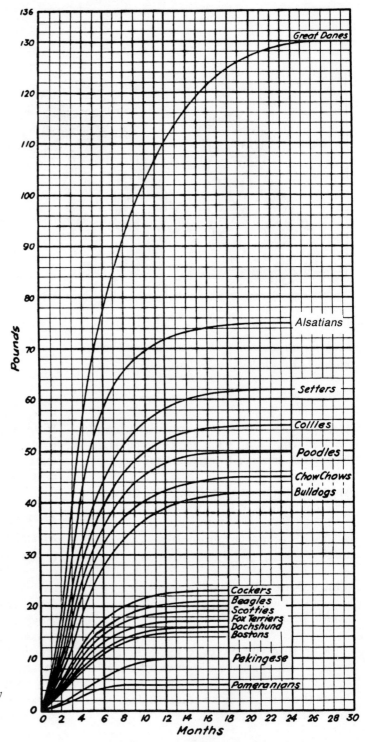

SOURCE: Adapted from *Current Veterinary Therapy V: Small Animal Practice*, ed. Robert W. Kirk (Philadelphia: W. B. Saunders, 1974).

Although inappropriate breeding has rather limited your choices in selecting an animal, it is still possible to find a genetically healthy animal or one with only minor problems. If you don't plan to breed from the animal, and don't mind the extra work of caring for an animal with inherited problems, you could select from a wider variety.

If you are going to breed from your female, there is yet a third step you can take to minimize the risk of congenital problems. Avoid unnecessary exposure to harmful chemicals and other potential mutagens and teratogens as previously discussed. What this translates to in practical terms is to avoid treating a pregnant (or soon-to-be-pregnant) female with antibiotics, flea powders, cortisone, vaccinations, sedatives, anaesthetics and x-rays, unless natural aids fail and medical treatment is demanded.

In addition, you should be sure that she gets good nutrition and does not consume potentially dangerous food additives, mouldy foods, poisonous household chemicals, or lawn grass or other plants treated with toxic herbicides, insecticides or fungicides.

Also, be sure she does not become overheated. Excess heat can retard foetal brain growth. Don't leave her locked in a hot car with the windows closed (a good piece of advice for any animal) or over-exercise her in hot weather. Nor should you take her on an arduous trek into high country or transport her in the baggage compartment of an aeroplane, because the lack of oxygen at high altitudes can induce a variety of foetal abnormalities.

It goes without saying that you should not breed from an unhealthy animal. Even though it may not have a genetically inheritable problem, its overall support system is not a good one for developing healthy offspring.

Although you cannot always foresee or control potential congenital problems, with just a bit of common sense you can actually do a great deal to minimize the risks. In the process, you will be doing a big favour not only for your own animals and yourself but also for those whose time is yet to come!

CHAPTER TEN
The Human Psyche and Animal Health

With the big hulk of a dog glaring at me suspiciously, I carefully examined the foul-smelling, hairless patches that oozed bloody discharges on his back, underside, legs and muzzle. Seldom had I seen a skin case so awful. As if to demonstrate just how bad it was, he jerked around and started chewing violently on the base of his tail.

'Stop that, Bandy!' the man Robert shouted at the dog, which belonged to his wife, Cathy. 'The way I see it,' he explained, 'the biting and chewing only makes things worse, so I always make a point of scolding him when he starts it up.'

'I see,' I replied, resuming the examination, and thinking to myself about discussing the possible effect of such reprimands.

'There are some particularly bad spots

under the tail you should look at,' Cathy interjected. Slowly, I started raising the dog's tail to take a look. All at once he hurled his big jaws around and snapped at me angrily, just missing my hand. Pronouncing the examination complete, I sat down with the distraught couple to try to find out how Bandy had come to such a difficult state.

'It's happened pretty quickly,' Cathy began. 'He had slight mange on his face when I got him as a puppy three years ago, but the real problem started about six months ago, when he began chewing and licking excessively all over his body. The vet said it was a flea allergy, but he didn't seem to have very many fleas.'

As she explained it, the problem had grown steadily worse. They had taken him to a series of vets who had diagnosed 'hot spots', shaved the areas and prescribed antibiotics and cortisone. But all to little or no avail. Finally they'd been advised that he would either have to be put to sleep or else undergo a series of very expensive treatments that might or might not work.

Recalling the scolding pattern, I began to probe further. 'Tell me, did anything significant change in your life or his about the time the problem started?' I asked her. 'For instance, did you move or have a change in the family? Did he start getting less attention for any reason?'

'Well, as a matter of fact,' she related, 'our baby was born just a couple of months before it started, and all my energy started going into him. I didn't want the dog to be around the baby – you know, worms and all that – and he was acting jealous because he wasn't number one any more, so we started keeping him outside all the time.'

Hmm, I thought to myself. That fits.

'Say,' I asked Cathy, 'have you yourself by chance ever had any problems with your skin?'

'Funny you should ask. As a matter of fact, I've had itchy skin for years, and so did my mother. I never have been able to find out the cause.'

Interesting.

As it turned out, this case had nearly every one of the elements I'd noticed ever since I first began to investigate the possibility that owners' psychological attitudes and behaviours could influence their pets' health, particularly in those cases that failed to respond to treatments. First, the dog lost a lot of attention just before the symptoms began. But he did receive some whenever he scratched and bit himself, even if it was only a scolding. Second, he not only mirrored Cathy's own itchy tendencies, but also her attitude (which she later revealed) that she preferred that he be aggressive, because it made her feel safer living in the country. (And dogs that are irritable and aggressive to others often abuse themselves as well.) Furthermore, as we talked together, I noticed an underlying tension between the couple – another source of anxiety that seems to adversely affect many animals.

If you've never before considered that people's thoughts, emotions and behaviour could make their pets ill, such a notion seems pretty improbable. But Bandy's case is only one of many that fits this pattern. I find if I ask the right questions an amazing number of otherwise perplexing cases show at least one of the following patterns.

Pets that have the same health problems as their owners. Itchy dogs with itchy owners (some of whom even scratch their pets for them!) are common, as are overweight pets with overweight owners. Others are more idiosyncratic, such as a cat I saw with a circulatory problem whose owner was troubled by the same difficulty, and a dog with an obstinate sinus infection whose owner 'coincidentally' had the same problem with *his* nose. And then there was the dog that developed an unexplained cough shortly after its mistress had had a bout of asthma. Even more interesting are multiple occurrences in the same household, such as a woman with bursitis on her right side who had a dog *and* a cat with similar problems in the very same location.

Pets that contract the very illnesses their owners dreaded their animal would get. In this pattern the pet seems to 'mirror' the owner's own patterns or expectations. I've seen a number of cases in which people have been worried that their animal would get a certain disease and have even gone to great lengths to try to prevent it. For instance, I have one client who kept her cat inside all the time to keep it from getting exposed to feline leukaemia. Then her mother contracted cancer. About that same time, her cat was accidentally exposed to another cat and soon thereafter he died of feline leukaemia. Another client, whose dog was dying of kidney disease, had lost every pet she had ever had to the same malady, which she had feared would happen once more.

Animals whose problems are aggravated by emotional tensions between family members. Pets can be very sensitive to disturbances in the household and may not understand that they themselves are not part of the problem. Some people may even use their animal in a game of one-upmanship against another person. As John Ihor Basko, D.V.M., of San Jose, California, has noticed, 'The animal is often the centrepost of a relationship.' He told me he can tell how a certain couple he knows is getting along by the way their dog is doing. 'Animals get better when couples settle their differences,' he added.

In the book, *What the Animals Tell Me*, Beatrice Lydecker has cited the case of a dachshund that chewed and scratched at herself every time her owners argued. In addition she was apparently frustrated by being excessively confined. When the people dealt with those problems, her extensive and chronic skin rashes cleared up.

Pets that become ill shortly after an upsetting change in the household. This pattern is one of the most common. The change frequently means a loss of attention for the pet such as may occur when the owner takes a new job, goes on holiday, has a baby or just loses interest in the pet. Or an important companion (either human or animal) may be lost through death, divorce or a move. The animal may lose familiar surroundings or privileges due to a move, or even just because the family bought new carpeting or furniture. Several changes can occur together and compound the problem, as when Bandy found himself not only replaced by the new baby but also banished from his house. (For all *he* knew, this was the beginning of the end!)

Human/animal bonds

Why do we see so many cases where the animal reflects the physical or emotional health of its human companions? Are they more than just coincidental?

To investigate the possible mechanisms at work, we must first put things in their proper context. We need to understand the arena in which the problem exists – the bonds between the animal and the person.

Let's start with the animal's point of view. Pretend for a moment that we are not people, but pets. Here I am, my whole world is this family and maybe a few of the local dogs and cats and children on the street. This family gives me all my food and shelter. I depend on them totally. They pour tons of affection into me and usually I like it. Sometimes they ignore me and I don't always understand why. But it makes me anxious. What would I do if I lost them altogether? I don't know how I could possibly make it on my own. In fact the only food I know comes out of their bowl.

Doesn't this sound familiar somehow? It's very like how it is for all of us as children. And, indeed, pets tend to do just what the dependent young of any species do – to identify the source of security (the parent figures) and to stick to them, obey them, emulate them, and in short, get attached to them.

Biologists call this the bonding or imprinting effect, and it serves a good purpose – it keeps the infant alive. Soon after birth every young animal goes through a critical period in which it learns to 'imprint on' (identify with) its mother, who is its source of nurturance and leadership. If you take the infant away from its natural mother before this critical period, it will imprint on the likeliest substitute around, which can make for some strange twists.

Biologist Konrad Lorenz found, for instance, that by making this switch at just the right time he got a group of young goslings to follow him around as though he were their very own mother goose, even preferring his company to that of their own species! And baby monkeys who were taken from their mothers and placed in cages with 'surrogate mothers' constructed of cloth and wire adopted them as the real thing (as you can imagine, they turned out to be rather neurotic as they grew up).

Along the same lines, it is common knowledge among dog trainers that the best time to acquire a puppy is between the ages of 4 and 14 weeks, which is the critical bonding period in which it will learn to attach primarily to its human master rather than to other dogs. Removing a puppy before this stage produces an insecure and neurotic animal. Removing it too late makes for a dog considered too independent and wild to make a good pet. Also, we must realize that the trait of psychological dependency on humans has actually been genetically bred into dogs, as over thousands of generations we have purposefully selected for survival and breeding those dogs we consider most loyal, affectionate and inclined to bond to humans.

An animal like a dog is also biologically 'pre-programmed' to respond to a natural social structure that revolves around the 'leader of the pack'. In most instances the owner is placed in that role and is treated with the same loyalty, deference and response normally shown to the alpha (lead) animal in the wild. (In some families, though, it appears that the dog considers itself to be the leader and tries to dominate the humans, if he can get away with it.)

It's pretty clear that the natural forces that prompt animals to 'tune in' to their human caretakers are pretty strong. Now what about the other side of the equation? How do people relate to their animals?

Most people have a special reason to acquire an animal, although less often the pet just wanders into their lives and they take it from there. But usually the person wants something out of the relationship, whether it is a watchdog, a substitute child, or perhaps a loyal friend who will always accept and never criticize. Accordingly, some people regard pets as excellent therapists for those who are often neglected by other people, such as the elderly, the young and the handicapped.

Sometimes, people seem to pick pets with which they can identify, a sort of extension of what they think they themselves are. We all know the stereotypes of the squat old gentleman with his squat old English bulldog and the prissy woman with her prissy poodle. Look around and you'll see an element of truth in the stereotype. Elegant, well-groomed people often have elegant, well-groomed pets. Casually dressed, adventuresome types tend to have casual-looking, adventuresome dogs. Obese people have obese pets, and so on. Actually, we humans tend to identify with most of our possessions, but a living animal provides an especially good opportunity to create a sort of alter ego.

Sometimes the phenomenon works in reverse. People pick pets that exemplify the traits they wish that they themselves had. In *Your Pet Isn't Sick (He Just Wants You to Think So)*, veterinary surgeon Herbert Tanzer tells about a very short client of his who consistently picked immense, tall dogs to which he became quite attached. Or often I have noted that people with repressed anger may have an animal that acts out the aggression the owner would like to express but cannot. Acting out incomplete feelings via a pet can seem a lot safer.

Regardless of the reasons, pets have become so important to many people that they feel as much anxiety and concern over an animal's health or death as that of a human friend or relative.

When you take a pet into the family, he often ceases to be 'just an animal'. Instead, he becomes a distinct personality – 'Charlie' – who likes children but not the postman, who loves the old chair in the corner and who always sizes up people correctly. Suddenly, your attitude toward the animal changes. He's no longer a 'dumb beast', but an intelligent, unique individual. And when you begin to hold your animal friend in high regard, and sometimes see life from his point of view, a strange and wonderful form of communication can grow.

Although it may sound odd, I've always believed that animals and humans can develop a psychic or telepathic sensitivity to each other, and I have seen confirmation of this in my own practice. Not only have I met several pet owners who are certain their pets have this ability, but several writers have described this kind of communication in detail.

The sensitivity they describe encompasses not only a responsiveness to cues that can be picked up by the five senses, but also to those that are intangible.

For example, J. Allen Boone, who made human-animal communication his life's work, discovered that by careful and diligent study and attunement, he could create a two-way channel of communication with animals of many species. Boone first became aware of the psychic sensitivities of animals while caring for an intelligent movie star dog named Strongheart, which he described in *Kinship with All Life*. The dog was an expert at detecting dishonesty in people, anticipating Boone's thoughts and plans – and finding ways to transmit and receive complex communications in general.

As Boone's work developed, he concluded that animals often behave the way people expect them to behave. He believed that if you think a certain animal – like a housefly, for example – is a pest, then it will act like a pest. But suppose you were to change your way of thinking. Suppose you could accept and respect the housefly because it comes from the same universal source as people. Suppose you could admire it – say, for its ability to fly, or for the delicacy of its body. How might a common housefly behave under these unusual conditions?

For Boone, the housefly became 'Freddie', who came when silently called, and who, when requested, refrained from walking on Boone's bare skin.

To many people, Boone's experiments may sound quite strange. But there are a number of people who share his findings. One is Beatrice Lydecker, who says that she can communicate telepathically with animals and successfully uses their messages to help vets and owners solve pets' physical and emotional problems. Like Boone, she emphasizes the importance of the mental *images* we project to animals. It's not what we *say* that reaches them so much as what we inwardly feel and visualize. When you consider that there are deep emotional bonds between people and their pets, these mental images can have enormous impact on the animal, impact that may account for some of the 'strange coincidences' of pet health patterns I described earlier.

For instance, it's fairly clear why a pet might be vulnerable to a continuous 'broadcast' by its owner of a strong fear or expectation that it will die of a certain disease (often one that afflicted a previous pet).

Unconscious reinforcement of symptoms

Why animals would tend to mirror people's own health problems is not so clear, unless you realize that animals probably do not readily distinguish where thoughts originate. Rather, they may just soak up whatever is sent their way, including the mental pictures transmitted by the owner as he thinks, 'Oh, my right hip hurts!' or 'My, how my skin itches.'

In the same way, I suspect that animals can be upset by interpersonal conflicts that do not involve them simply because they pick up the emotional energy created by the tensions without necessarily understanding that they are not to blame. Psychologists attribute similar processes to young children, who often blame themselves for their parents' arguments. Before we leave this fascinating subject, I'd like to indulge in a little speculation. I have heard it suggested that a pet can physically or symptomatically

act out its owner's emotional states. For instance, I heard a story about a lady's cat that began a pattern of wandering away at nights and scratching at itself at a time in the woman's life when she was feeling very 'itchy' to move out to explore new things. She felt there was a connection.

Psychosomatic medicine has noted a number of links between various diseases and typical mental patterns or traumatic memories, and perhaps pets also can exhibit their owners' psychological fears and frustrations in a visceral way, becoming a sort of inadvertent testing ground for acting out unexpressed tendencies and incomplete dramas.

Now what about the last type of pattern I mentioned earlier – the pattern of the animal that becomes ill shortly after an upsetting change in the household? Any number of changes can trigger this response. Research has shown that when people experience a large number of lifestyle changes in a short period of time (like a change of job, houses or income, or the loss or gain of a spouse or other family member, or even a switch in recreational activities or eating or sleeping habits), they are more likely to become ill in the near future. I see no reason why changes of lifestyle cannot take a toll on animals as well.

The stress that comes from too many changes, psychological conflict or other factors, tends to manifest itself physically in humans as muscular tension, endocrine imbalance or a change in the rate of metabolism. Stress-induced changes can lead to alterations of organ function, sleep patterns, immune response (and thus the susceptibility to disease) and behavioural response.

Not-so-benign neglect

When a pet becomes ill after a lifestyle change, ask yourself whether the animal is reacting to a loss of attention. Most creatures thrive on a certain amount of social interaction and if a pet suddenly begins receiving less notice it may not always understand the reason. Instead, it may feel threatened, perhaps even fearing that its very survival is endangered. ('They must not love me anymore, so maybe they're planning on getting rid of me.')

A pet often loses attention as a side effect when the owner takes a new job, has a baby, goes on holiday, gets married, when the children in the family leave home, or someone dies (including a playmate animal). The pet may begin to feel that it doesn't count any more, that it has incurred disfavour. The same fear also could arise in an animal that has suddenly (for no reason clear to it) lost a former privilege, such as being allowed on the furniture or in the house or else being given special treats of various types.

So what happens? Perhaps partly as a reaction to the stress of change and partly out of feeling a bit insecure, the animal may develop a minor symptom like excessive licking and scratching (which could remind it of the security of its mother's fondlings when it was an infant), diarrhoea, vomiting or coughing.

The owner immediately gets upset, worrying that the animal may be developing a serious malady. He or she runs over to the animal, strokes it, and, in an anxious voice, lavishes it with concern and anxiety. This response can not only mentally transmit the image of sickness to the pet, but also gives our attention-starved animal a definite reward for acting sick. It's one way the animal can be assured the owner still cares. A small price for survival.

Psychologists who study behavioural conditioning tell us that even negative attention (such as Robert's consistent scoldings of Bandy every time the dog scratched himself) is often regarded as better than none at all.

So whether the owner cuddles the animal and plays 'Poor Baby' (as Dr Tanzer labels this pattern) or else reprimands or punishes the pet, at least it gets some acknowledgement of its existence and continued place in the household.

Moreover, some owners have certain personality traits that unwittingly make things worse. Nearly all of us find it rewarding to nurture and care for another, but sometimes people have such a big need to be needed they feel empty if they don't have somebody to take care of.

For instance, people who felt abandoned or neglected as children will sometimes compulsively adopt every stray animal that comes in sight in an endless attempt to provide the hapless creatures (who represent the self) with the kind of care and attention they wish that *they* had received. One way to distinguish between a compulsive pattern of this sort and simple compassion for another's suffering is whether or not the person would feel empty or lonely if there weren't someone or something to take care of.

With this understanding of how our thinking and behaviour can actually contribute to a pet's health problems, let's examine how to minimize negative input and maximize the positive contributions.

If your pet has a health problem, how can you find out if you are part of it? And if it appears likely that you are, what can you do about it? Even if your pet is healthy at present, how can you create a psychological climate that will help to keep it well for years to come?

A good start is to ask yourself the following questions. Take time to consider them quietly. Discussing them with a friend or partner will probably give you much insight.

The hidden influence quiz

1. Is my pet's health problem similar to one I have had now or in the past?

'Similar' can include problems in the same body area, which can often be on the same side – left or right – as your own.

2. Did I ever worry that my animal would get the very problem it has?

Or if the animal is now healthy, do you entertain such worries now? If you answer no, ask yourself 'What kinds of problems is a dog or cat like mine most likely to get?' and see what comes up.

3. In what ways is my animal similar to me? Why did I choose this particular type of animal?

4. Does my pet seem especially upset when there are emotional tensions or conflicts in the household?

5. With regard to my animal's illness, what mental images, concerns or attitudes typically go through my mind? What messages might I be 'broadcasting' to it?

6. What was happening before this animal first began showing symptoms?

Consider whether anyone entered or left the household, took a job or went on vacation. Did you move, redecorate or start confining the animal more?

7. Whenever this animal shows a symptom, do I give it any special attention, either positive or negative?

8. Do I get anything out of my pet being sick? Do I enjoy looking after it?

If you're not sure about this one, imagine that you no longer have a pet that needs you and see if you would miss it.

If you've answered yes to two or more questions, consider yourself a possible negative health influence.

I see two basic sets of problems. One set reveals a pattern that reinforces the pet's symptoms. If you answered yes to questions 6, 7 or 8, this may be the crux of your problem. Here's my advice: stop giving the animal any special attention for its symptoms (such as coddling it every time it coughs). Yet give it adequate *overall* care and attention. People have found this technique can produce great results.

Dealing with the conditions that may mirror a person's inner thoughts and attitudes is a little more challenging. This set of problems is revealed in questions 1 to 5. If you investigated the questions with some depth and care, then you've already had an inkling of what you need to do. More than anything, simply understand that the way you think and act has its effect in the world, including your pet's world.

There's no need to feel guilty about your thoughts. Thinking things like, 'Oh no, what have I done to my poor little animal?' or 'Stop thinking things like that!' or 'Oh, I wish I could comfort him, he looks so miserable, but Dr Pitcairn says I shouldn't (the nasty fellow)' won't do any good.

What *will* help is to study the problem with your full interest and attention. Study it in a relaxed and exploratory way, the way you'd successfully find out how to fix a broken gizmo. Explore it. Experiment.

Watch what you do during the day and how you think and act with your animal. What things upset it? The symptoms can tell you an interesting story. Perhaps they will even tell you about yourself. When your pet behaves oddly or seems unwell or upset, it may be reflecting something going on inside yourself that you were too busy to notice. Does your pet get anxious when *you* feel that way? Or become ill when you've been stewing around for weeks?

Also, watch and see if your pet's symptoms get worse if you pamper and coddle it or scold and spank it. Is it telling you it feels insecure? Maybe your animal needs a little more of your time and attention in general, not just when it coughs, scratches or throws up. Or maybe it gets too much attention and needs to be more independent!

If you really understand what's going on in your relationship with your animal friend, that insight itself will be your best guide, provided it's part of a continuous exploration and isn't just a one-time thing.

CHAPTER ELEVEN
Responsible Pet Ownership

Living with and getting to know an animal can be a wonderful thing. Creatures of other species – both pets and wildlife – can teach us valuable lessons in living by their daily examples of enthusiasm, grace, affection, forgiveness and many other good qualities. Likewise, an understanding and kind person is very dear to an animal.

But sometimes both people and animals

come up against apparent conflicts of interest that can cause unhappiness and frustration for each other.

Some problems primarily affect animals, because life in an environment tailored to people can be dangerous to four-legged creatures. They can be hit by cars, stolen, abandoned, lost and (if unclaimed) put to death as strays. But more often, the problems are less severe and often stem from just plain frustration. For example, consider the pet that is left all alone most of the time, cooped up in a small apartment or pen. His fate is little better than solitary confinement. Or consider the pet living with a rock 'n' roll enthusiast who keeps the stereo turned up to maximum volume. Or the animal of an upwardly mobile young executive who moves to a new sales region each year. Clearly, human lifestyles can be tough on pets.

On the other hand, some conflicts of interest create problems primarily for people, and not only for the owner, but also for immediate neighbours and the larger community. In fact, a nationwide survey revealed that the number one citizen complaint made to city governments concerned 'dog and other pet control problems'. Surprising? Not when you consider the sum total of befouled lawns, dug-up flower beds, bitten hands, noisy barks and hounded bicyclists.

In this chapter and the next, then, we'll look at these problems in detail and propose some solutions that are fair to everyone, respecting the needs and rights of both animals and people. Solutions that let everyone win are surely the best, because they make for the most harmonious relationships.

Let's say, for instance, that you have a large, aggressive dog that soon becomes a neighbourhood menace if allowed to roam free. You could try to solve the problem (simply from a human viewpoint) by strict control and confinement. Just keep the dog in the house or tied up in the garden.

However, if you go off to work and leave a big dog locked up all by himself every day, you will soon frustrate his normally active nature. Eventually, the dog will act out his frustrations and boredom in destructive ways, such as chewing, digging, whining and barking.

As you can see, total confinement is not a true solution, which must consider the needs of both the person and the pet. In the case just described, the dog's need for attention and exercise were ignored. If he had received lots of affection when his owner was home, and if he had been taken for a long walk or run every day, he might have been able to live in confinement without becoming destructive.

In some situations, unfortunately, a mutually happy solution may be impossible, simply because the basic circumstances are untenable. Take as an example the person who wants a pet but lives in a small flat. Certainly nobody would ever consider keeping a horse in such a cramped space. Yet some people choose to keep a large dog, even though it is nearly the size of a horse, despite living in tiny quarters. Obviously, both human and beast will be frustrated by the impractical arrangement.

Most problems, however, *can* be solved to the satisfaction of both parties. Let's consider some of the dilemmas common to pet owners.

Should pets be allowed to roam?

In some places it is apparently the fashion to allow animals to roam the neighbourhood, doing pretty much as they please. Perhaps this freedom reflects the permissive philosophy of our times or just results from our crowded living conditions. Or maybe it's simply that more people are away during the day and, rather than leave a pet alone for hours, they just let it out to wander and socialize.

However, others I've talked with hold the philosophy that an animal is a free agent deserving its own rights, and should be allowed to move about as it pleases. While the sentiment behind this attitude is commendable in some respects, I think it is based on a fallacy. While it is natural for a *wild* animal to be unconfined, a pet dog or cat is *not* wild. Because these animals have been irreversibly removed from their long-ago origins and now depend completely on humans, we can't treat them as we would treat wild ones. Since *we* chose the arrangement, we must fulfil our part of the bargain to meet all their needs. Moreover, we bear a social responsibility to see that our pets do not endanger or annoy others.

And the fact is, regardless of why they are left to wander, free-roaming pets cause tremendous problems for people, for other animals and for themselves. Consider the following facts:

- More than a million dogs and cats are killed by cars in the United States every year. Besides jeopardizing their own lives, unconfined pets threaten people and property by causing an untold number of car accidents when people swerve or brake to miss them. Data is incomplete, but one report estimated that dogs are involved in about 2,500 personal injury road accidents a year in the United Kingdom (where there are comparatively fewer strays).
- Pets dump a huge load of wastes into the environment, much of it in public places and on neighbours' lawns. The figure for dogs in the United States alone is about 11,000 tons of faeces and 9.5 million gallons of urine daily. These wastes can transmit harmful organisms and disease to humans through such innocent activities as sandbox play and gardening in contaminated soil. And, as we all know, they can ruin a good lawn.
- Dog bites are the second most commonly reported public health problem in the United States. At least one

million people a year are bitten, at a treatment cost of about $50 million. These figures do not include those bites that go unreported. Large dogs are known to harass elderly people carrying groceries and young children with lunch boxes.
- Free-roaming dogs kill or injure both wildlife and livestock. (I've treated my share of small dogs and cats chewed up by such packs, too.) Many of these wild beasts are house pets whose owners have no idea what the family dog really does on an afternoon romp. Cats, too, can threaten wildlife such as birds and small mammals if too many hunt in the same area.
- Not infrequently, pets on the loose hurt themselves. They become victims of intentional or accidental poisoning (sometimes as a side effect of wildlife control programmes), or cruel devices like the steel-jaw trap. Others find new homes – in the research lab – where they are often subjected to trivial and unnecessary experiments that can cause excruciating pain. About 500,000 dogs and 200,000 cats are used yearly in American labs. A great many are supplied by animal pounds, which 'put to sleep' or otherwise dispose of unclaimed animals without licence tags within a short period of time, or by thieves.
- Left on their own, unneutered pets freely follow their instincts to breed. Competition for an available mate can result in a violent and sometimes fatal fight. But because they are so prolific, pets now have their own 'baby boom'. Of the approximately 35 million puppies and 50 million kittens born yearly in the United

States, only about one in six will find a home. The rest will be put to sleep (about 13.5 million pets per year in animal shelters) or abandoned to die a slower and more painful death from disease, starvation, thirst and accidents. In the United Kingdom, at least 1,000 dogs and 4,000 cats *a day* are put to sleep. Every day.

- Government attempts to cope with animal control problems are a major public expense, costing American taxpayers about $500 million a year. That figure doesn't begin to tally up private costs in money, time and psychological stress.

In recognition of some of these problems, many people keep their animals indoors or penned up all the time. But excessive confinement is not fair to animals, particularly large dogs. Continuously frustrated by the suppression of their exploratory nature and deprived of the natural benefits of sunshine, fresh air and exercise, many excessively confined pets are prone to develop both psychological and physical problems.

Let's examine some appropriate ways to control both dogs and cats so they will not become community nuisances or endanger themselves.

Controlling dogs

Proper management of a dog means keeping it on your property or keeping it under control while you are in public. Ideally, your dog should have access to a securely fenced garden or pen big enough for him to run in. His sleeping space – indoors or in a dog-house – should be dry, warm and quiet.

If you can't provide a fenced garden or pen, allow your dog to go outdoors only on a lead, or free under your supervision in a safe, uncrowded area. Tying it to a stake is not an acceptable alternative. The chain tangles, limiting the dog's range. As a result, he's unhappy. He barks to complain. Soon the neighbours are complaining, too.

Because dogs can and do get loose at times, be sure yours wears identification. Should your pet get lost and impounded, the identification is the key to a safe return and the animal's best insurance against being put to death before you can be reunited.

On the identification tag, give whatever information a stranger needs to locate you: your current phone number and/or address. People are more willing to help return a lost pet if they know they can easily reach the owner. A tagged animal also stands a better chance of receiving needed medical care if injured. Besides engraved tags or I.D. barrels, you can make a temporary label by writing your name and phone number on a piece of tape and wrapping it around the dog's collar.

When walking your dog, keep him on a loose lead. (Ideally, he will be trained to walk quietly at heel.) If he is well-behaved, and trained to come on call, you might let him run free in some appropriate areas under your supervision.

On the lead or loose, don't allow your dog to lunge at or jump on passers-by or other animals. Begin his training by not allowing him to jump up on you. To stop him, raise your knee sharply against his chest as he jumps and say, 'No!' Ask friends to do the same. Soon he will understand. With a little bit of initial training aided by a book or an obedience class, your regular walks together can be enjoyable instead of tugs-of-war.

A dog needs to learn and respect some basic rules of human society, just as we need to learn and respect some basic canine codes (such as 'Let a sleeping dog lie'). Teaching him must start with your being clear about what is and isn't socially acceptable. If you don't *consistently* censure him whenever he violates a human code – for instance, the one that gives us all the right to walk peaceably down a public street – then you are condoning anti-social behaviour which will understandably upset others. I say this because I've seen a lot of people stand by and even seem to approve when their dogs threaten strangers who were rightfully going about their business. Perhaps dogs who are so aggressive really are acting out their owners' unspoken attitudes about other people. While it may seem more natural for a dog to snarl at strangers than for the owner to do it himself, it is still unacceptable behaviour.

How can we train a dog to understand and respect those codes we feel he needs to know? In general, successful dog training requires respect, love, praise, gentleness and an attitude of encouraging the animal to co-operate. Since dogs are anxious to please owners they love, they usually respond readily to your clear communications.

Almost always, it's both unnecessary and psychologically damaging to threaten and spank a dog into submission. To encourage *desired* behaviour, use only praise and reward. To discourage *undesired* behaviour, use a firm command such as 'no' or 'bad dog', or slap a rolled-up newspaper against your hand or a table, but only *while he is misbehaving*, never when he is partially behaving. For instance, if you scold him while he comes to you slowly, he can get the message he shouldn't come at all.

Sometimes physical intervention may help you get your message across, as in the training method to keep a dog from barking at or chasing passing pedestrians, bicyclists, cars and other animals. Not only can the 'chase' game be potentially injurious or even fatal, it can create ill will in your neighbourhood. Here's how to train a dog out of this habit.

Attach a long, lightweight cord to his collar. Get someone to tempt him out of your garden by calling him into the street, by walking another dog, or by cycling or driving by. Let the dog take off. But when he reaches the garden limit, pull back hard on the cord and say 'No!' firmly. When he returns, praise and pet him. Tell him how nice it is to stay here in the garden and how much you appreciate it.

Repeat the procedure several times on all open boundaries of the garden until he seems to understand the limits. Then untie the rope and wait for your helper to go by. If your dog rushes outside the garden, follow him, scold him and chase him back. Once he crosses the border, praise him warmly so he will realize that all's well as long as he stays where he belongs.

If your dog is not tired and is learning fairly quickly, have your friend try out another temptation (car, bike and so on). But if the dog's attention begins to wander, save the rest for a later session. In general, always end a training session on a positive note, just after he has done something well. Praise him and give him a special treat.

Controlling cats

We are presently playing hosts to a pair of songbirds nested in one of our backyard bushes. Every day when we walk by and peer through the leaves, we see two pairs of little birdy eyes looking back. It's a delight. But we're a bit concerned about the day when they must learn to fly, because we're not the only ones watching them. Our neighbour's cat is, too.

We aren't alone in our concern. Nice as cats can be, they worry a lot of people who enjoy providing sanctuary for birds and other small wildlife. In addition to their predatory nature, cats have other annoying traits, as well. Their nature causes them to dig to bury their waste. Not only does this habit tear up garden transplants, it also poses the threat of toxoplasmosis (see the *Encyclopaedia* section) to an unborn child. Some bold tom-cats even go so far as to dash through open doors and windows in the neighbourhood, leaving a spray of smelly urine behind.

What can you do to keep your cat from being a friendly nuisance? Fences don't stop a cat. Some people simply keep their cats inside all the time, which may be a necessity if you live in a flat with no garden, or in an area of heavy traffic. If so, try to give your pet some access to sunshine and fresh air. An open screened window will do, or you can provide an outdoor wire enclosure attached to a window. And if you're away a lot, consider getting a second cat for companionship.

Another solution is to allow your cat outdoors *some* of the time, particularly when you can keep an eye on it. But keep it inside at night to give the local wildlife a break, as well as to protect it from cars and dogs. Talk to your neighbours and let them know they should feel free to chase your cat off their property if it's doing something they don't like. Finally, consider attaching a bell to its collar so birds can hear it coming.

Getting lost is always a danger for a cat. You can make a simple, safe cat collar out of sewing elastic; on it, write the needed information or attach an identification tag.

The pet population problem

A male animal – cat or dog – will have much less desire to roam if he is neutered. Moreover, that one simple procedure will spare you years of trying to remove the offensive odour of tom-cat urine from your house. Your pet will also become much less

apt to fight or be over aggresive, something your neighbours will appreciate, too.

Spaying your female will keep packs of males from invading your property every time she comes into heat and will keep her in better health and condition as well. But just as important, it will prevent bringing more kittens and puppies into a world in which there are already far too many. Let's explore the animal birth control issue further.

Why do people allow their pets to breed when there are already too many being born? These are some of the most common reasons given:

- They want their children to see the process.
- They think they can find good homes for the litter or assume the local RSPCA will do so for them.
- They are concerned about the expense, pain and possible adverse health effects of a spaying or neutering operation.
- They want to make a little extra cash selling pure-bred offspring.

Yet when you consider the vast toll of suffering that befalls unwanted, homeless dogs and cats, none of these reasons is very convincing. Surely, for instance, it is more important to teach children responsibility to animals in general than it is to bring more surplus pets into the world. The RSPCA cannot possibly find homes for most of the animals it receives. And even if the owner can find homes, how many animals will still be there a year or two later? And how many offspring will *they* produce? (If she and her descendants are allowed to breed freely, one female dog can produce thousands of animals in just five or six years. Cats are even more prolific.) And assuming you are able to find good, *responsible* owners for each puppy or kitten, consider that these people might have otherwise adopted animals that were destroyed for want of homes.

Furthermore, anyone who can afford to provide decent care for a pet can also afford a spaying or neutering operation, which is far less costly than comparable human surgery. The operation is painlessly performed under anaesthesia by skilled veterinary surgeons and involves very little risk. It not only prevents unwanted births and discourages straying and fighting, but it prevents health problems like cancers of the reproductive organs, stress and complications from breeding, and abscesses and injuries from mating. Contrary to popular belief, neutered pets do not automatically get fat. Because they may be less active, they may burn less energy. So the solution is just to feed less.

See 'Spaying and Neutering' in the *Encyclopaedia* section for procedural details.

Apart from an operation, anyone can afford the time-honoured methods of animal birth control: the door and the lead. Lock up the female securely inside your house during the two- to three-week period of her heat. You should know, however, that an unspayed female cat prevented from mating will often develop hormonal imbalances due to complications caused by not completing the reproductive cycle.

As for the profit incentive behind breeding pets, not only do such ventures often yield little financial return, but also repeated breeding can cost you money because the female's health breaks down. Most 'puppy mills', which add to the glut of dogs born annually, are actually small home businesses run by amateurs whose ignorance and carelessness in breeding is a direct cause of much of the rise in congenital and health problems in many breeds. Surely there must be a better way to earn a living.

Certainly I can understand and appreciate people's desire to see their pets bear young. But, unlike most people, I have had direct exposure to the scope and everyday reality of the pet overpopulation problem. Because I have done a lot of work for a humane society clinic associated with an animal shelter, I see the tragic results of uncontrolled breeding.

If I could take you there and show you what I see every day I work there, I doubt if you would ever want to breed from a pet again. The sheer numbers are staggering. About 17 million animals a year end up in shelters. The reality – in flesh and blood and not just as abstract statistics – is devastating. Each one looks at you, and each is an individual being capable of much love and potential. And most never leave that shelter alive.

Imagine the emotional difficulty shelter personnel experience when they must kill animals by the hundreds, and even by the thousands, many of which the workers have come to know and love. They kill only because they are left with no other humane alternative. A quick, painless death is better than abandonment, better than starvation, better than neglect.

Only when each person who owns an animal takes responsibility for its reproductive function will we ever see an end to the suffering it causes.

Excessive noise: how to keep the peace

Though less dramatic than overpopulation, there is another human/animal problem with which most of us are familiar – noise. Just as a considerate person will not inflict high-volume music or loud noise on the sensitive ears of a pet, a pet should not be allowed to inflict noise on people. Constant barking or feline love songs can drive anyone to his wits' end.

Though cats can split the air with a yowl during mating or fighting, most noise problems are caused by dogs. If you aren't sure whether your dog indulges in endless howling, whining or moaning while you are away, ask your neighbours. *They* know!

A dog that howls when left alone usually is accustomed to extensive attention and pampering. However, in some cases it may live with people who have little time to give and is simply frustrated for want of company. Such a problem might be helped by getting it a companion. But in any case it's a good idea to train your dog (or dogs) to stay quietly alone without you. Here's a good approach:

Begin the training on a day when you'll be at home all day. In the morning, take your dog for a walk, or allow him some other exercise. Then put him in a room alone. So he has something to do, give him some favourite toys. Tell him you want him to stay quietly for a while. Then go out and close the door. If he starts to bark or howl, scold him (through the closed door) and if necessary bang on the door. If that doesn't work, enter the room briefly and give him a light slap under the chin. Don't linger to give him any other attention.

When he's been quiet for about an hour, let him out and praise him warmly for being such a good dog who can stay so nicely and quietly in that safe and comfortable room by himself. Let him have the run of the place for an hour, then put him back into the room. Do the same thing over again, letting him out again after an hour of success at being quiet. Repeat the process all day long and by nighttime your dog should know that it pleases you best if he is quiet when you leave him alone in a room. And dogs do want to co-operate with you.

The next step is teaching him to keep the peace when you leave the house. Again, tell him you are going outside for a while and that you want him to be a nice, quiet dog. (Remember to leave his toys out.) Return in a little while to find out if he's being quiet. If

not, scold or lightly punish him. He will catch on soon enough and you will not only win your neighbours' gratitude but spare your pet the stress and strain of all that yapping.

If your dog barks too much even when you're home, it's usually because he's bored from being left alone too long in a yard or run. Take him for morning and evening walks for his exercise and fresh air, but keep him in the house with you when you're at home. Let him out for brief periods to relieve himself and make sure he stays quiet at those times.

A dog that is encouraged either outwardly or inwardly to be very territorial and to be a 'good watchdog' will, of course, also be a likely candidate for excessive barking. To control his noise you must be clear and consistent about what you teach him. When there are unusual noises or when strangers approach the house, you can thank your dog for giving two or three warning barks, but teach him to be quiet after that and let you handle the situation.

If possible, arrange for your dog and your postman (or other frequent service or delivery people) to get to know each other so that your animal will not bark at or, worse yet, try to bite him. For infrequent visitors like meter readers, call up to find out their usual days to come and keep your dog inside or secured in a separate area so he won't harass the poor person. In one year, for instance, employees at Pacific Gas and Electric Company on the West Coast of the USA suffered 332 dog bites, a record number. As one meter reader testified, 'Every dog owner believes his dog won't bite. If you believe him, you'll be sure to get it from the rear on the way out.'

Dog bites can be extremely serious, though they seldom make headline news unless someone (generally a child) is actually killed. But hospital and medical personnel who treat them know that they range from nips on the ankle to mutilation requiring stitches or reconstructive surgery.

Preventing dog bites

A dog that is teased, frustrated and locked up by itself too much may become a biter. The same is true of many that come out of puppy mills, where they've had minimal human contact early in their lives. And intensive production of some breeds, like the Saint Bernard, has resulted in more aggressive traits.

Vicious bites come mostly from guard dogs and roaming dog packs, but the majority of dog bites come from animals that are known to their victims and that have reputations for 'being nice'. Your own child could be a victim of such a pet.

Besides giving your dog adequate attention, not teasing it, and always reprimanding a puppy or older animal that nips you in play, here are some guidelines to help you prevent bites. Make sure your children understand them. If your dog is left alone in a garden with a fence that a neighbour's child can reach through, talk to other parents to make sure their offspring understand possible dangers. (If necessary, put up a warning sign.)

The first thing to understand is how to avoid provoking a dog. Here are some helpful pointers:

- Never disturb a dog (including your own) while it is sleeping or eating. This is a strong violation of the canine code of respect.
- Do not intrude upon the private territory of a restrained or confined dog. Neutral territory, like a park, is usually much safer.
- Never tease a dog by dangling food or toys over it. A playful nip can easily get out of control. Stop hugging or holding a pet that wants to be free.
- Teach children not to reach out to stroke a strange dog, especially a

large one. It may be a trained watchdog.
- Do not scream and wave your hands and arms around dogs. Children who do this when scared or excited inadvertently provoke many dogs.

It's also helpful to know how to mollify a dog that approaches you in a threatening manner. To determine whether a dog means serious business or just wants to engage in some rough-and-tumble play with you, you need to learn some basic dog body language.

A friendly dog avoids direct eye contact, looks to the side, may expose his throat and even grin. He keeps his ears flat, tail tucked down and body low. If his head is lower than the tail, but he is crouching, pouncing or thrusting about, he's probably just playing and is not a threat.

A potentially dangerous dog, on the other hand, shows these signs: ears raised up and forward, teeth bared in a snarl, hair raised on the shoulders and rump. Even more threatening signs are: becoming stiff-legged, raising a front leg, urinating, growling, staring you in the eye and slowly wagging a high, arched tail. An animal that bites out of fear may give mixed messages, so read the whole animal carefully and avoid threatening any dog that acts wary of you.

If a dog runs at you, stay calm, turn a little sideways, speak in a soothing voice, keep your head slightly lowered and your hands down – all messages that your intentions are peaceable. Do not turn and run away unless you are *certain* of reaching safety. Do not face the dog head on or stare it in the eye. Some vets and animal handlers confound threatening animals they must approach by whistling softly or calling in a friendly tone.

If a dog chases you while you are cycling, slow down, pedal slowly, speak soothingly and get off your bike if you can. Walk at an

A friendly dog (left) avoids eye contact, keeps its ears down, and maybe even grins. You can identify a dangerous dog (below) if its ears are held forward, teeth bared, hair raised across its shoulders. Be extra careful if the dog's legs are stiff, if it stares you down or wags a high, arched tail.

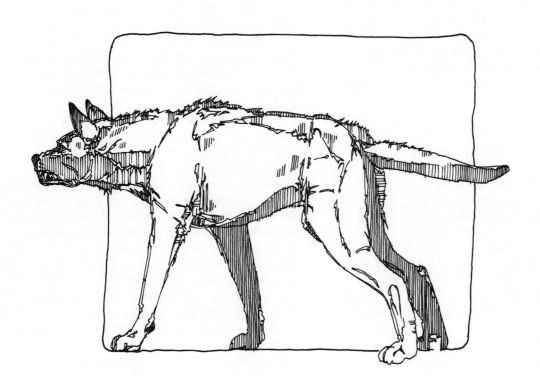

unhurried pace, without turning your back to the dog.

Should a dog bite you, stay as calm as possible. A scream may only scare the dog and provoke it into another bite. Try to put an object near its mouth (such as a bag, newspaper, book or jacket), which will give it something besides you to bite. Report the incident at once to the police and establish the dog's identity if you can. Wash the wound as soon as possible with soap and water. Telephone your doctor for advice if the bite is serious.

Training cats not to scratch and bite

Cats don't inflict much damage to people with their scratches and bites, but their need to exercise and stretch with their claws can be pretty hard on your furnishings.

You can solve the problem by providing a scratching post that beats any piece of furniture. You can make your own by nailing an upright 4 × 4 post (2 to 3 feet tall) to a piece of ½-inch plywood about 1 foot square. Then wrap the post with a piece of carpeting turned inside out to expose the rough side (posts with soft coverings are not sufficiently attractive to most cats). Rubbing a little powdered catnip into it occasionally will make it irresistible.

For maximum stability, place the post butted up against the corner of a room or tilt it on its side. If your cat needs instructions on its use, simply lay it sideways and place the cat on top of it. Then with one hand scratch the post yourself. With the other hand, stroke firmly down your pet's neck and back, which will stimulate the urge to scratch. Don't try to push its feet against the post, as cats only resist force.

Here's another piece of advice about claws. Never let a cat or kitten scratch your bare hands – even in play. If you do, the animal will think it's allowed to bite and scratch you, and won't understand that he can hurt you. So when playing games like 'pounce on the prey', use a toy, or just a piece of cord. Save your hands for stroking and holding.

It's also helpful to trim your cat's claws. Shaped like a scythe, their very tip is the part that does the most damage. A cat will slide that curved tip behind a loop of upholstery fabric and pull its foot straight back – snapping the loop. If the cat makes a practice of this, your sofa will soon look as if it needs a shave. The nail tip is also the part that so easily punctures the skin. It can be removed with ordinary nail clippers. (Be careful to clip only the tip, or you'll hurt the cat.) To extend the cat's claw, press your index finger on the bottom of its foot while pressing with your thumb just behind the base of the nail at the top of the foot. Press *gently*. The claw will slide from its sheath so that you can get at it with the clippers you're holding in your other hand. You may be able to cut only two or three claws in a single sitting, but you can pick up the cat later and continue.

If your cat has developed a clawing or biting habit, you can break it fairly easily by consistently following a method described by Anitra Frazier in her book *The Natural Cat*. If the claws are in you, relax and calmly disengage them by first pushing the feet a bit forward. To get out of a bite grip, relax and press your arm or hand *toward* the teeth (which confuses the cat). Then put the cat away from you with a gentle but firm message of disapproval and disappointment. To underline the message, ignore him for several minutes. Don't even look at him. A few repetitions is usually all that is needed for a cat to learn that if he wants to play with you it's not acceptable to claw and bite. Thereafter he will respect your wishes.

To avoid more serious contact with cat teeth and claws, which are quite sharp, never try to hold on to a cat that wants to be free (unless you are trained in handling them properly). Teach children this point, too. If you must restrain a cat to give it medicine or transport it, wrap it firmly in a towel or blanket or put it in an animal carrier. (I know of more than one serious accident caused by a frightened cat bounding loose in a moving car.)

As for dealing with other undesirable feline habits, like walking on worktops, you don't generally 'train' a cat the same way you would a dog. They have more independent natures. However, it is certainly possible to gently shape its behaviour in desirable directions. But not through yelling, scolding or striking. These responses will only make a cat afraid and cause it to avoid you or your touch. What's needed are affection, understanding and consistency.

When he does something unacceptable, gently but firmly stop his behaviour. Push him off the countertop while saying, 'No!' If the cat disregards you, flick your finger lightly on his nose or perhaps even squirt him with water. However, most cats simply do not misbehave if you provide them with acceptable outlets for their energy (as with the scratching post or the toy for pouncing).

A good way to start cat training is by teaching a cat to come when called. Repeat his name often when you are playing together or feeding him. Call him frequently, offering a titbit of his favourite food. Praise him and give him lots of affection when he responds. Soon he will associate pleasant things with coming when he's called.

Good sanitation: a basic necessity

Animals instinctively seek to relieve themselves away from their usual living area, which is why the neighbour's garden is often a favourite place. You can wean a dog away from this habit and save a good deal of your own lawn, too, by teaching him to use just a certain portion of your garden, such as behind the garage or near certain shrubs.

Place some of his stool there and take him to that spot when it's time for him to answer nature's call. When he uses the spot praise him enthusiastically. Promptly remove droppings from areas you don't want him to soil and if necessary use a dog-repelling deodorant with natural ingredients like citron, lemon oil, eucalyptol, geranium oil, capsicum, and oil of lavender.

For a cat the matter is simpler. Keep a clean litter tray in your garden as well as in your house, and he will have something else to use besides Mrs Jones's flower bed. Keep the trays away from the reach of toddlers and clean them regularly. Wash your hands well afterward, as cat faeces can carry potentially harmful organisms. (A good practice after a dog clean-up, too.)

Dispose of accumulated pet wastes regularly. Though I don't recommend composting them because temperatures are sometimes not high enough (140°F) to kill harmful organisms, you might consider using a small mechanism made especially for dogs and cats. Buried in the ground, it works like a small septic tank.

Both the danger of spreading disease and simple common decency dictate that you clean up any solid wastes your dog may deposit on someone's lawn or in public places. Various types of scoop gadgets make it convenient to pick up and dispose of droppings. Though it may not be the most inviting chore in the world, it certainly isn't any more fun for the person down the street.

Let's consider animal wastes in the same category as human wastes. It makes the responsibily for clean-up much clearer. Then we'd no longer look the other way when an animal defaecates in a public place and its owner fails to clean it up.

For instance, one day I was walking by the seashore when two large dogs bounded by. Soon one delivered a huge bowel movement right at the water's edge, close to where some children were playing. The man and woman walking with the dogs smiled indulgently and made no attempt to clean it up. A lifeguard approached them and reminded them that dogs were not allowed on the beach (as signs clearly stated). The owners protested indignantly and apparently some compromise was reached. The lifeguard left and the people and the dogs continued their stroll. Meanwhile, the faeces were gradually washed about by the tide.

What can we do to prevent the degradation of our parks and careless spread of disease? (And spread it does!) There has been a disturbing rise in such diseases in recent years, largely due to the increased population of dogs and cats. Though some people with pets may underplay the problem, many public health authorities consider diseases that can be transmitted from animals to humans to be a serious problem. The best treatment is prevention – through practicing good sanitation, preventing bites and scratches and keeping your pet healthy. If you take reasonable precautions, diseases won't spread.

Understanding and preventing animal/human diseases

Most diseases picked up from cats and dogs fall into three groups, depending on their means of transmission and, therefore, their means of control. We will consider in turn those spread through (1) faeces or urine, (2) skin and hair contact and (3) bites and scratches.

Diseases spread through faeces or urine

Leptospirosis: This serious bacterial disease is usually acquired from swimming in or otherwise contacting water contaminated with animal urine. Many animals can carry it, particularly rats. Pets can catch it by drinking contaminated surface water (or licking it off their fur) or by eating food on which rats have urinated.

In humans the disease is similar to flu, with fever, headache, chills, tiredness, vomiting and muscular aches. In addition, the eyes and the membranes covering the brain and spinal cord can be inflamed. In some, the liver and the kidneys are damaged. Not many die from this condition, but they can be rather miserable for two or three weeks.

Roundworms *(Toxocara canis, Toxocara cati):* When these common parasites of dogs and cats are swallowed by children, they often will migrate through the body tissues and cause damage, including liver enlargement and fever. These symptoms may last as long as a year. In some children the larvae may enter the eye and cause inflammation. Eye lesions mistaken for early cancer have resulted in unnecessary eye removal by surgeons.

The infectious forms of the worms are their eggs, which incubate for several weeks in the ground where an animal has defaecated. If a child plays there and puts his dirty hands in his mouth, he can swallow the eggs and become infected. Thus, roundworms are most often seen in children aged two to four years. The disease is only rarely fatal. More commonly it is mild and long-lasting.

Tapeworms *(Dipylidium caninum):* Pets can pick up the common tapeworm by biting at and swallowing fleas, which can carry the infective form. Children can get it the same way, either by ingesting fleas while nuzzling the pet's fur or being licked on the mouth by an animal with a flea on its tongue. Actual human infestation is rare, however, compared to other types of tapeworms we can get from eating undercooked infected beef or pork.

Toxoplasmosis: This infectious disease (to which many people are normally exposed and develop natural resistance) can on rare occasions cause death in adults. But more often it causes birth deformities in children born to women infected for the first time during pregnancy (before they have developed immunity). It can be picked up from contact with faeces from an infected cat or with contaminated soil. Or it can come from eating raw or undercooked meat. Because the foetus of a pregnant woman can be very susceptible, this problem is covered in detail under 'Toxoplasmosis' in the *Encyclopaedia* section.

Prevention of diseases transmitted in wastes

Besides cleaning up your pet's droppings, there are a few simple precautions you should take for your own safety. One is to wash your hands after contact with soil where an animal may have relieved itself. Avoid going barefoot in these areas. Teach children the same precautions. Also remind them to wash their hands before eating and not to put their hands in their mouths while playing with animals or on potentially contaminated grounds.

If your dog has gone swimming or wading in a pond, river or rain puddle which could be harbouring leptospirosis, give it a bath.

Diseases from skin and hair contact

Fleas: The common flea will bite people, too. Though fleas prefer pets, they will make a meal of people without qualms. Flea infestation is often at its worst in a house where an animal formerly lived, but which has been vacant. Many young fleas, recently hatched, will be eager to eat.

Ringworm *(Microsporum canis):* Caused by a fungus that eats skin and hair, ringworm often appears in people as circular, scaly, red areas. As the organism grows, it spreads outward in a circle much as a ripple forms around a stone dropped in a pond. In dogs, affected areas tend to be hairless, thickened, scabby and irritated. They are typically disc shaped and about an inch or more in diameter. But most ringworm from pets is transmitted by cats, who often show very few observable symptoms (dogs can also carry the spores without showing visible signs). An infected cat may have hairless grey areas without inflammation or scabbing. Generally they do not itch either.

Children are more susceptible to ringworm than adults, though one can get it at any age.

Scabies *(Sarcoptic mange):* In dogs this form of mange is less common than the demodectic ('red') mange. However, it does occur in both dogs and cats and causes intense itching, irritation and thickening of the skin. People are infected by contact – usually from holding the animal against their body. The result is intense itching, especially at night and in those areas that have been in most contact with the animal (like the inside of the arm, the waist, chest, hands and wrists). Though the animal mange mite can live in human skin, it cannot reproduce there. So eventually the problem ends on its own, if reinfection does not occur. Note that we humans have our own brand of scabies mites, which can cause us prolonged irritation.

Prevention of skin and hair contact diseases

A healthy animal is less likely to harbour parasites like fleas, ringworm and mange mites. Therefore, proper nutrition and overall care are important means of prevention for both of you. In addition, frequent grooming and inspection, along with herbal repellents, will catch most of these problems early. Be especially attentive when your animal has been (1) in contact with other pets (fleas, ringworm, mange); (2) stressed (as a result of disease, emotional upset, or a stay in a kennel); or (3) roaming in the fields (ticks).

Nuzzling and hugging animals can be great fun, but if you like to do a lot of this you take your chances if your animal is carrying these diseases. Wash your hands after prolonged contact. Minimize contact with animals that may have ringworm. Also, since stray hairs can carry active ringworm spores, too, keep the house clean if your animal is infected (or else keep your pet outside until the problem is cured). Avoid or minimize bodily contact with an animal with sarcoptic mange and do not let it sleep on your bedding, clothes or towels.

Diseases caused by bites and scratches

Cat scratch fever: After being scratched by a cat, some people will develop a fever, malaise and enlarged lymph nodes near the area of the scratch (or bite). These symptoms usually occur one or two weeks after the injury. The condition is not serious (that is, fatal), but it is uncomfortable and may be followed by complications. Nobody knows what causes it. A cat bite infected with the bacteria *Pasteurella multocida* looks similar and should be differentiated from cat scratch fever by your doctor.

There is no recognized procedure for preventing cat scratch fever, but common sense will help. What I do after a scratch is to wash the area liberally with soap and water. Several hours later I apply alternating hot and cold soaks. So far I have had no trouble with it.

Rabies: Everyone has heard of this disease and of its high fatality rate (essentially 100 per cent once the clinical signs appear). Caused by a virus transmitted through the saliva of a biting animal, it travels from the bite area to the brain in a matter of days or weeks. There it causes severe tissue inflammation that has symptoms such as convulsions, hysteria and frothing at the mouth.

Fortunately, rabies is not endemic in the United Kingdom, due to strict quarantine laws. If you ever hear of an animal being smuggled into Britain it is essential to report it for the sake of all the other pets and humans who would be at risk.

Prevention of diseases from bites and scratches

In general, reducing your pet's contact with stray and sick wild animals will lessen its chances of picking up all these various parasites and organisms from less healthy creatures. But better yet, feed it a good diet, exercise it daily and keep it in such all-round top shape that most would-be invaders will think twice before making a home out of your animal.

CHAPTER TWELVE

Lifestyle Tips

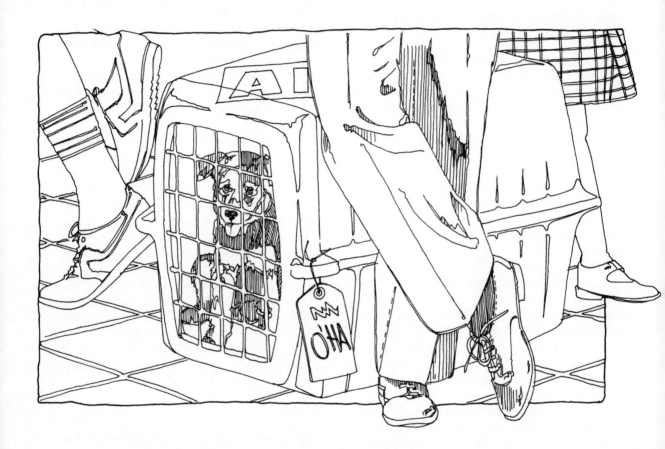

Modern lifestyles often bring with them circumstances that pose special problems for pets and their people. The stress of travel and moving, the ease with which an animal can get lost in the urban maze or the dangers of some common gadgets in the home are representative. Let's look at some ways to make the going smoother for all involved.

Holidays and travel

Ever since the advent of the train and the car ours has been a very mobile society. For most of us, part of modern life involves taking trips, both long and short. Whether your four-legged friend travels with you or stays at home, you'll have to give some thought to its special needs at such times.

For instance, if you journey away for more than a couple of days, your animal could grieve over your absence, unaware that you plan to return soon. A long absence can sometimes lead to such emotional upset – particularly for a dog – that your pet may be unable to respond with complete happiness even when you return, perhaps taking weeks to regain its former vitality.

Or, as some owners fear, it could spell the beginning of the end for a weak animal. Someone wrote me the following letter:

My dog Lassie will soon be 18. We've had family troubles including deaths in the last two years and now my husband and I are planning a ten-day cruise which we feel we must take for our own health. We must leave Lassie in a kennel. I have read that if you leave an old dog in a kennel it might be dead when you return. This has troubled us terribly, as she's so accustomed to our care. Would you have any suggestions for our wonderful dog, who has served us so well?

I can sympathize with their plight. Not only would Lassie miss her companions, but she would be confined in a strange and perhaps uncomfortable run or cage, surrounded by barking and whining animals which might disturb her rest. She might not accept the new food offered her and, while in a stressed and weakened state, she could be susceptible to such diseases as 'kennel cough'. Even younger animals often don't do well during kennel stays. But on the other hand, people do need to get away sometimes and can't always take a pet along.

Though it would not be my own first choice, many an animal may be successfully placed in a kennel, if it is responsibly run and if the stay is not too long. You should look at the premises in person before committing your animal to it. Look for such things as the degree of privacy provided (does each animal have a place to rest quietly?); the sanitation; the noise level; and the availability of sunlight, exercise space, fresh air, water, decent food and medical care, should the need arise.

If your animal is weak, if you plan a long absence or if you simply want to provide a better alternative, there is another possibility which many people and pets find workable. That is to find someone who likes animals and would enjoy caring for your pet – either in your home (coming to feed, groom and exercise it once or twice a day) or in theirs (assuming they have adequate space and do not have pets of their own that might fight yours in defence of their territory). You will have to use your own judgement in deciding where the pet should stay, depending upon its personality and habits. Most cats would probably prefer to stay in their own territory, whereas a friendly and sociable dog might prefer the greater companionship possible at the sitter's residence.

An ideal person would be a close friend, neighbour or relative who already knows and likes the animal and who would not regard the care as an imposition. (This aspect is important.) Also, you could seek out teenagers wanting summer jobs, veterinary students, RSPCA volunteers or retired people, found through senior citizen centres.

Here are some pointers to make the whole process go more smoothly:

- Offer the sitter payment or other forms of exchange sufficient to give him or her a sense of your animal's value to you.
- Introduce the sitter and your pet to each other (if they are not already acquainted) before you leave. The person could take it on a few walks, give it a bath or visit for a few hours. Such preparations will alleviate much of the stress and concern,

particularly for an old or easily excitable pet.

- Ensure that the sitter can and will provide adequate food, water, exercise and attention and that he or she has the money and necessary instructions for taking the animal to the vet in case of an illness or an emergency. You might prepare some natural food meals in advance and freeze them for the sitter's use. Or else you could temporarily use a commercial food (preferably the kind sold in health food stores that is made without artificial additives).

- Start about a week before the trip to eliminate many potential problems by seeing that your pet gets the following supplements, which will help in any situation involving physical or emotional stress: a complete B complex tablet (with B_2, B_6 and pantothenic acid included at the level of 5 to 15 milligrams, depending on the pet's size) and/or a liberal amount of brewer's yeast in the food. Also, give 1 to 2 grams of vitamin C, particularly after the stressful period and preferably spaced throughout the day. Continue to give the supplements for about a week after your return.

Whether you leave your animal with a sitter or in a kennel, when it's time to part, say goodbye with a calm and untroubled mind. Animals readily pick up people's feelings. If you are nervous or upset when you leave, you could start off its stay on the wrong note. If you like, it may even help to look the animal in the eye and visualize a happy reunion scene. Once you are gone don't cause yourself needless worry and anxiety. You did what you could.

Occasional absences, if thoughtfully handled, should not be a problem. However,

I have seen a number of animals that have developed difficult health problems after being passed around from one temporary home to another by an owner with wanderlust or other pursuits that cannot include a pet. In some of these instances I think the animal would be better off if the owner simply placed it in a permanent and supportive home.

Tips for travel

Now what about taking a pet along on holiday?

People have found that both dogs and cats can enjoy the adventure. In fact, they make excellent travelling companions if they are basically well behaved and psychologically and physically healthy. However, certain precautions and considerations should be taken.

Make sure your pet is wearing suitable identification. Should you get parted for any reason, you need a means by which someone can reach you. Many pet shops sell waterproof identification 'barrel' tags in which you can enclose a small piece of paper. On it write or type, 'If lost, please phone . . . and reverse the charges.' Give the phone number of a friend of relative willing to act as a 'message switchboard' to help connect you with someone who might find the pet, or else a temporary number where you are staying.

On long road trips give your pet daily exercise. For dogs, at least half an hour of a vigorous game of fetch or a jog together is important. If you let your dog loose, make sure it's in a safe and appropriate area and that it is trained to return on command.

Because the first few car rides are often upsetting to a cat, keep your pet on a lead during its exercise. Otherwise, your cat might bolt. Once it has relaxed into the journey, and if it will come when called, you might let the cat out a bit. For an added measure of safety, let it out *before* feeding time, so hunger will provide an additional incentive for a prompt return.

Never leave a pet in a sealed car on a hot day. Heat can build up very fast in a closed car, which acts like a solar oven, causing an animal to go into heat prostration. This may lead to serious brain injury and even death. See the *Emergency Guide* for first aid treatment should this problem ever occur.

Take along familiar items. A basket or piece of bedding from home can make animals feel safer and more at ease. You could also take favourite toys to give them something to do.

Supplement the diet. If it is practical, you should endeavour to feed your pet well during travels. Use commercial pet health foods if you must for the sake of convenience, but try to use the recommended supplements as well. Adding vitamin C and the B complex can help travelling animals deal with stress, just as it can help those that are left behind.

Prepare for health problems common while travelling. Constipation can sometimes plague travelling pets. It can be caused by lack of exercise or water, infrequent stops or anxiety about strange new territories. For a cat, a litter tray is basic gear for a road trip. For a dog, take it out when you can (on a lead) and carry disposable bags and a scooper to use in public parks, cities, motel property and beaches. Temporary constipation is not a serious problem and will usually clear up before long. A useful preventative is to feed your pet figs, prunes and raisins, as well as fresh berries or other fruits in season.

A couple of other common problems are motion sickness and eye irritation. Some animals get very nauseated when riding in a car or plane and will either vomit or salivate excessively, or both. The B complex supplementation will help prevent nausea. Also, encourage the animal to lie down on the floor of the vehicle. If motion sickness does occur, give your pet some peppermint tea or capsules to help settle the stomach. Occasionally it may be wise to fast a susceptible pet the day before departure or on the first day of the trip. For an animal going by public transit in a carrier, a 24-hour fast before the trip will generally spare it the problem of becoming soiled with its own excrement as well.

Eye irritation may occur in dogs that like to ride with their heads out of the window, testing all the interesting scents passing by. Sometimes dust and debris enter the eyes at high speeds, scratching the cornea and irritating sensitive membranes. For a mild eye irritation, I have had good luck with a drop of castor oil in each eye (or olive oil or cod-liver oil). If there is serious corneal injury the animal will keep its eye shut most of the time. In such a case, seek veterinary help.

Foreign travel. Don't take your pet abroad. When you want to bring it back into the United Kingdom it will have to spend six months in quarantine – for which you must pay. Other countries besides this one also impose restrictions on animal travel.

Respect hotel and camping site property. Owners as well as guests of overnight facilities will be much more likely to welcome your pet if you state your intention to abide by the following basic rules of consideration, and then stick to your word.

1. Don't leave a dog alone in a hotel room while you're gone (which may lead to barking and chewing) but rather in your car, with the window slightly open to prevent heat build-up

2. Carry a bag and scoop and always clean up any messes, inside or out.

3. Have your pet neutered or spayed. It not only discourages wandering and territory-marking, but also eliminates the sexual scents left on the property by your animal and others that come along later and spray the area in response.

4. Keep the pet on a lead at all times, so it doesn't charge through tender flower beds or interfere with other guests.

These guidelines are worth following when you are visiting friends' homes as well.

Pets on the move

Besides our two-way travels, many people make a significant *one-way* trip – to a new residence. This means quite a lot of animals have to pull up their roots and start all over again the business of becoming used to and claiming a new territory and adjusting to new challenges.

Moves can easily disorient animals, causing them to run off and get lost in their confusion, unable to find their way back. So during a move make sure your pet is under your control at all times and provide it with some familiar items – like its bed, some toys, a favourite rug or its litter tray – for reassurance. Confine the animal to a quiet room (or, if it's a dog, a securely fenced yard or garden) during the hustle and bustle of packing and unpacking.

For some unlucky pets, a move spells the loss of their owners. Many animals are simply abandoned when their owners move, which usually means slow and painful starvation, illness, bewilderment or (if they're lucky) a quicker death by euthanasia in an animal shelter.

Others may be foisted off on to a reluctant recipient, in which case the animal often is neglected, eventually destroyed or given to someone else. Pets that undergo too many changes of owners can develop insecure personalities and behaviour problems that make them undesirable to anyone. For the same psychological reasons, a high turnover of family members (through divorce, marriage, birth, death and children leaving home) can be stressful to an animal's sense of security and may require care to see that it is not neglected. Otherwise, animals can actually become ill as a reaction to such changes.

Finding a new home

Unfortunately, even the most loving owners sometimes find they cannot keep a pet, because of housing problems, allergies, animal incompatibility or other situations. If you are faced with this problem, the following guidelines compiled by a concerned humane society will help you find a good home for your animal friend. Though these guidelines may take a little work, they are worth it, since the only other humane alternative is euthanasia.

You can begin your search for a good adoptive owner by advertising through the local paper and putting up notices. When you find someone, be careful about checking the potential home before releasing your pet. Otherwise, it could be neglected, mistreated, sold to a lab or even used to train fighting dogs. Such things, unfortunately, can and do happen when people give away pets indiscriminately. The same applies, of course, to giving away a litter of puppies or kittens.

Run newspaper advertisements several times to ensure wide coverage. List the animal's qualities (such as 'Loves kids; healthy, quiet, house-trained, affectionate') and state simply that it needs a home. Advertising it 'for free' may attract the wrong people.

Put up photocopied notices (preferably with an appealing picture of the animal) where responsible people might see them, such as in community centres, health food stores, doctors' and veterinary surgeries, churches, senior citizen centres and workplace canteens.

When someone calls, take your pet to *their* home for your meeting rather than inviting them to yours. That way you can check it in person. Does it have a safe fenced garden of adequate size? Is there a dangerous road nearby? Will the pet be left alone too much? Does the interested party appreciate the basics of responsible pet ownership? Does anyone in the family oppose the adoption? Is the person apt to move around a lot? What happened to any former pets? Beware of people who have gone through a series of pets that were lost, hit by cars or given away, as this will likely be the fate of yours as well.

Though it may be difficult and even sad to place your old friend in a new home, you will at least be spared any guilty feelings if you take the time and care to do the job well. Some time later you may return to find everyone pleased with the new relationship.

Lost pets

The danger of losing a pet is not limited to moves and holidays. The possibility exists at all times. By making sure your pet wears proper identification and keeping it under your supervision, you will greatly reduce its chances of being lost or stolen. However, despite the most thoughtful precautions, animals get lost anyway.

What to do if a pet is lost

Visit the local animal shelter(s) in your area. Most such organizations try to find *you*. But if a pet has not got some form of identification, locating an owner is almost impossible. In that case, the burden of responsibility is yours. Go in person to visit all appropriate kennels and rooms, asking to see any quarantine, isolation, holding and receiving rooms. Call out your pet's name as you go.

A brief description over the phone is inadequate, since only you know your pet for sure and there are often many animals there. Check every day for a week or longer after the disappearance, or as advised by shelter personnel. Fill out a lost pet report, providing photos, if possible, as well as noting any unique markings. Also, check any reports of 'found pets'. We reunited a lost dog with its grateful owner this way just last year.

Check with local police. This is particularly important if you have reason to suspect your animal was stolen.

Place an ad in a local daily paper. Put it in the Lost and Found section. Give a description of the animal, note the area where you last saw it and, if possible, offer a reward.

Put up notices in the area where it was lost. The form that follows is a good model. Most photos will reproduce well on a good copy machine. Put the notices on telephone poles, at launderettes and in shop window

LOST

Date _____

This area: _____

HAVE YOU SEEN MY PET?

(photo)

_____ _____ _____
(dog or cat)   *(breed)*   *(colours)*

_____ _____ _____
(sex)   *(age)*   *(collar)*

_____
(special identification or comments)

DON'T WAIT—WE MISS OUR PET

PLEASE CALL: _____ *(name and address)*

_____

_____

OR PHONE _____

notice boards. Remember to remove them when the situation is resolved.

Ask around. Ask postmen, children and housewives in the area if they have seen your animal, as they are the people in the community who are usually most aware of strays.

Hazards in the home

Though some people like to think animals are almost human, clearly they are not. Animals often are unable to understand and avoid certain dangers unique to their human environment. Or sometimes they don't have a choice.

It's hard to anticipate all the unexpected things a pet can get into. We needn't worry excessively about them, of course, but here are a few basic and common things to be aware of.

- Cat can sometimes die from the complications of swallowing knitting wool, string or rubber bands. Because cats' barbed tongues make it difficult to spit objects out, they may be unable to stop the process once it starts. So offer them a ball of wool for play only when you're there to supervise.

- Many poisonous substances are found in most homes, from toxic house plants, antifreeze, insecticides and drugs to caustic cleansers and mothballs (beward of letting a cat sleep in a closet or drawer full of these little buggers – rather, debuggers). Keep on the look out for ways your pet could ingest such material either unintentionally (through skin contact or walking through it) or out of curiosity (through chewing or swallowing). The challenge for you is much the same as that which faces the parents of toddlers. See chapter 8 for more coverage of dangerous substances.
- Always glance in your refrigerator, oven or any drawer or cupboard before you close it. Your curious cat may have jumped inside when you weren't looking. Such oversights have been fatal at times.
- Be careful that your animal does not start chewing on electric cords. Keep them tucked well out of reach, if possible, and don't leave the animal alone in rooms with exposed cords. Reprimand it firmly should you catch it in the act.
- Also take care that your pet doesn't chew up and swallow inedible objects like newspapers, books, plastic toys or bags and other such things that can contain who-knows-what. A rawhide bone makes a good chewing toy instead.
- If you have a toddler, watch carefully to make sure he or she doesn't handle a small animal too roughly, endangering both. Also, the child unintentionally can cause great stress for an animal by making a loud racket near its sensitive ears.
- If your older child is responsible for taking care of the pet, make sure the job gets done the same way you would do it, every day. Don't let the animal become the victim of a 'learning experience'. Make sure your child sticks to any responsibility to which he or she has agreed.
- If you live in a high-rise apartment building, screen your windows. Vets have noted that cats not only can but *do* fall out of windows and off balconies.
- Don't allow pets to lie on or near microwave ovens and colour television sets, both of which emit dangerous and invisible forms of radiation at close range.

By taking these precautions and by adopting an overall attitude of watchfulness and consideration, modern life need not be an undue peril or stress for either your animal or you; instead it can provide unique opportunities for adventure and full living!

CHAPTER THIRTEEN
Saying Goodbye

The evening wore on, the music from the radio drifting out and enveloping us all. And with each moment my wife and I could see that the small black kitten she held in her lap was edging even closer to death. Only a week before we had adopted it from the animal shelter clinic where I had twice saved its life – first from the ravages of parasites, and then from the institutional procedures that required unadopted strays to be put to sleep after a certain period.

But now no more postponing seemed possible. I had done what I knew how to do and yet 'Miracle', as we'd dubbed her on account of her heroic though brief rebound, was surely on her way out.

The signs were clear. Her small body grew steadily weaker and limper and her legs began to stiffen. Her eyes stared, dilated and motionless, fixed upon some awesome eternity. Occasionally she waved her head in small convulsions and feebly licked the inside of her mouth.

We had already discussed the possibilities. We could have struggled to save her all the way up to the end, violating her dignity with needles, tubes and drugs. Or, to spare her – or maybe ourselves – the drawn-out process, we could have injected her with the standard euthanasia solution, a painless passport to a quick end. Yet somehow, in that situation and with that animal, it just seemed right to let her go in her own way.

Without having to talk about it, we both knew it would be best this way. Looking at her, we knew that we didn't really know anything about the mystery of death or of life. We didn't know who or what a cat was, really.

We didn't know from where she had come or to where she would go. But we knew that beneath our surface differences there was a oneness, a bond uniting all living creatures.

We knew that soon this graceful, highly evolved body and its tiny perfect eyes would return to the earth, never to fulfil its promises. We thought of how we would miss her innocence, her playful grace, her courage – and a wave of sadness swept over us.

Yes, what must be must be. And it was all right to be as it was.

Finally the broadcaster announced the arrival of Sunday morning, and shortly after 1 a.m. we turned out the lights and placed her near us on the bed. Her breathing grew weaker and faster. It would soon be over.

Gently and slowly the darkness began to lower us into that unknown into which we all go each night. Through the growing silence there came a few indescribable sounds – long, low half-groans, half-meows.

We reached over and felt Miracle's temperature. It was dropping.

We placed her into her sleeping box on top of some warm hot-water bottles covered with cloth and settled back into bed. Once, in the middle of the night, we awoke to hear another of the strange sounds, this one deeper, longer, with an air of finality.

The sunlight was streaming through the window when we awoke next morning, full of a fresh appreciation for the gift of living. We got up and looked in Miracle's box, knowing what we would find. She was indeed gone now. Her body was rigid and cold. Her eyes and mouth were open, frozen as if in surrender to some great force that had passed through her.

We found the right place to bury her, beneath a towering redwood on the edge of a nearby forest. We dug a small hole at the foot of the tree and then simply sat, silently.

The redwood was magnificent, sparkling and waving in the morning light, surging up from the earth to the sky. Into this great tree something of our small friend would pass. From form to form, life would go on. We laid her body in the soil, covering it over with the tree's roots and the sweet-smelling forest loam. As we tamped down the last of it we heard a small rustling in the bushes. We turned to see.

It was a cat, watching.

Often we think of death as something to be feared, to be put out of mind and avoided at all costs. Yet in the end it comes to all organisms. It will come to your animal, and one day it will surely come to you and me.

But as the passing of Miracle and of others we have known has taught us, death need not be feared. In fact, to be fully with it and let its significance speak to you can make such an experience a thing of beauty. It can remind us, if we have forgotten to notice, just how mysterious and wondrous life truly is.

That is why it saddens me when I see and hear from so many people who are deeply burdened and upset at the anticipation or the memory of a pet's death. Their grief is real – often as great as that felt at the loss of a human friend or relative. But often, because they are unwilling or unable to face their feelings and thus learn from them, people shut themselves off not only from the pain of death but also from its beauty and meaning.

A pet's death can be a complex thing. All sorts of emotions can arise, including sadness, anger, depression, disappointment and fear. With people for whom the relationship is especially important – such as a single person, a childless couple or an only child for whom the animal has been a 'best friend' – the grief may be that much greater. And, too, if the death was sudden and unexpected, or if it seemed preventable (as in an accident) the feelings of loss and disappointment can be particularly intense.

Often a death brings with it memories of past unresolved losses, regrets about things done and not done, resurfacing of a loneliness which the relationship may have covered over and, perhaps deepest of all, the fear of your own death, of becoming nothing. But viewed positively, facing these emotions can provide real opportunities for learning and flowering.

In addition to those psychological hurts common to losing either a human or an animal companion, a pet's death brings its own unique challenges. For one thing, the euthanasia option can burden the owner with a difficult decision. Another problem is that although the grief may be just as real as if you had lost any other family member, it is not socially acceptable to mourn openly over an animal. Often, it's hard to find a sympathetic listener to help you work through the experience. And even the most sympathetic employer doesn't allow absence from work to provide a time of quiet mourning.

Once the death is 'finished', it *is* considered all right to go out and replace the lost pet with a new one immediately. However, if a widower were to wed a new wife the day after his former spouse's funeral, eyebrows would be raised. The effect of an immediate replacement with a new puppy or kitten is to deny the experience of grief, so that the old wound is never healed nor the feelings finished. For a child whose parents rush out to buy him a new pet before he has really said goodbye to the old one, the unspoken message can be that life is cheap, that relationships are disposable.

Handling grief

Of all these considerations, the most important is knowing how to cope with the grief and other emotions that may surface before, during or after the actual death. If you can cope, any choices you must make or actions you must perform will come much more easily.

Lynne De Spelder, a friend who teaches, counsels and writes on the subject of death and dying, emphasized this point in a discussion we had about coping with the death of an animal.

'It's really important to *handle* the grief. Research has shown the costs of mismanaged grief can be great, such as disease in survivors. Hiding makes it worse.'

How can you handle it? The first and most important thing is just to experience it, to give yourself *permission* to grieve. Lynne observed, 'Women often deal with grief better than men simply because they are allowed to cry. It's good to find someone who'll listen. If your spouse won't, find someone who will. If someone laughs at your grief, it's probably his own fear of emotion.'

An essential aspect of healthy coping, we agreed, is the development of a moment-to-moment awareness and insight about what is happening and how one is feeling and thinking. Also, Lynne often encourages people suffering from loss to discover and engage in those activities that are sources of support. For some, such 'survival skills' might include yoga or hiking, for others music or sports. The key is to learn to let go of the past and to live each day fully.

When you must help a child cope with the loss as well, the best thing is first to understand your own feelings. It is important to be honest and open about what happened, without trying to console the child with an instant replacement or with explanations that he or she may misinterpret or take too literally – such as 'he went away' or 'she was taken to Doggie Heaven'. If the child wants to see the dead body before burial, understand that it is a natural curiosity and should be allowed, provided you are emotionally stable about it yourself.

Talk with the child and make sure he is not harbouring needless misunderstandings. Make sure he isn't blaming himself or even you for causing or not adequately preventing the death. If you had the animal put to sleep because it clearly and painfully was going to die anyway, make sure the child understands.

Making a choice

If you are hesitant about having a pet put to sleep, you may be better able to make this decision if you are familiar with the procedure and its alternatives. So I will describe them.

Euthanasia: The idea of 'putting an animal out of its misery' is an old and long-accepted one, even though in most situations people don't have this choice for themselves or their relatives. Technically speaking, vets perform euthanasia in the surgery or hospital by injecting an overdose of a barbiturate anaesthetic into a vein or the heart. The animal loses consciousness within a few seconds, slumps over, and the vital functions cease soon thereafter. It is considered painless, although if the animal is agitated (as it may be if its upset owner is present), the vet may find it harder to inject it properly.

Personally I've always found the whole process rather distressing, and so, I think, do most vets. Mercy killing can make sense, however, in cases where the animal is in great and prolonged pain and the death is slow but inevitable.

Usually it is best not to make a hasty decision for euthanasia in a moment of anguish – before you clearly and rationally understand the animal's chances of survival and any other alternative possibilities. Otherwise, you may be burdened with doubts and regrets, forever wondering if your pet would have survived.

Hospital care: When an animal is seriously ill and you are considering hospitalizing it, ask the vet just what to expect and find out what the realistic chances are for recovery. Special care can often pull an animal through a serious crisis and enable it to live a few years more. However, there are some conditions, such as cancer or major heart or kidney degeneration, for which there is very little or no hope for recovery. Heroic but futile efforts to prolong a pet's life might involve extensive care and expense as well as drawn-out suffering for the animal.

With other conditions, like hind leg paralysis, an animal might live for some years longer but have a permanent handicap that requires the owner to give it a great deal of time and attention. Depending on the total picture and the specific condition, euthanasia might be preferable in the long run.

The typical cost of care for a seriously ill animal in a veterinary hospital ranges from about £10 to £50 a day or even more, depending on the extent of treatment. But the care given is not so intensive as in a human hospital (where a whole team of personnel and special equipment may be continuously used on the patient). Usually the vet or assistants administer fluids and drugs and see that the animal rests quietly. If it becomes apparent that the pet is dying, most vets then put it to sleep (with your prior permission).

Home care: In cases where there is no real hope for a cure and death appears to be relatively close and painless it can make sense to consider a home death. If the family feels willing and able to cope with the death of a pet, both in terms of time and emotional clarity, the experience can be a positive one for all involved, including the dying animal. Unless the pet has been heavily treated with drugs (such as chemotherapy for cancer), death from many serious conditions can be comparatively free of excessive discomfort. Some conditions, however, like kidney failure, can cause a lot of pain (in this instance due to uremic poisoning of the bloodstream) and may warrant euthanasia after a certain point.

As a general guideline, if the animal seems reasonably comfortable and peaceful, you may wish to allow the process to unfold naturally. In terms of physical care, you should not feed a dying animal, but give it only water or vegetable juices, and perhaps aspirin or a pain-easing herbal tea such as camomile or wintergreen. Give it a warm, comfortable, quiet place to rest. Occasionally you may need to help it outside or to the litter box to eliminate. The animal may welcome the gentle and calm presence of those it loves, but do protect your pet from too much noise, activity or disturbance.

When the end is very near, the animal will grow quite weak. The body temperature will drop and breathing may be spasmodic and gasping. The pupils may dilate and the animal may stretch out or perhaps pass urine. This final dying process can last for only a few minutes and rarely for more than an hour or two.

In some cases, of course, an animal dies so quickly or unexpectedly that you have no such choices as these to make at all. But regardless of how the process occurs, I hope that when the time comes, your parting will be a peaceful one.

During the span of years you spent together, there were ups and probably there were downs. Through it all you each learned, loved and did the best you knew how. Life was as it was.

But *now* is the only place life ever is, always new and full of marvellous things. And what more could we ask for?

CHAPTER FOURTEEN

The Holistic Approach and Alternative Therapies

'My dog has arthritis. Can you tell me what vitamin or mineral will help him?'

Often when people come to me seeking an alternative, 'natural' or drugless therapy for a sick animal, they end up thinking in the same old ways – as though there were one simple pill or fix-it treatment applicable to all cases given the same diagnostic label.

Though I am glad that they are interested in a more natural approach, I often feel frustrated because people don't seem to realize that what is really needed is an entirely new understanding, not just the substitution of a vitamin for an antibiotic, or a mineral for a hormone. The fact is, health problems are rarely caused by just one factor. They usually arise from or are aggravated by a broad spectrum of physical, emotional and mental influences and relationships with others. Therefore, in order to respond in a way that can really help, we must take all these realms into account.

We need to look at the *whole picture* of an illness and find therapies that will work with the whole body – not against it – in the healing process. To me, that is what constitutes a true cure. I often use the term 'holistic' to describe this approach to medicine. Unlike many who use the word, I do not equate it with 'natural', for it is certainly possible to use natural methods such as herbs, vitamins and exercise but still fail to see the overall picture of what is happening.

If we don't address health problems in a holistic way, then we are probably suppressing an underlying weakness, which will come out again in one form or another. Let me show you what I mean by describing a typical animal case. We'll call her 'Jessie'. Like so many animals these days, she has chronically itchy and inflamed skin.

Jessie's economy-brand commercial food is deficient in certain nutrients that are essential for good skin and nerve health. In addition, her body is struggling to throw off excess toxins picked up from this poor-quality fare and from frequent rides in the back of a pick-up truck on busy roads. As a result of these physical aggravations, her skin is over-sensitive and reactive to fleas, which are abundant in her quarters and her coat partly because her owner rarely grooms her and vacuums the house only about once a month. Jessie is left alone in the backyard every work day, which also encourages her to bite and scratch herself out of sheer boredom. Between the fleas, the oversensitivity and the boredom, she can get pretty violent about her scratching.

To compound matters, Jessie's endocrine system doesn't function well because her thyroid gland is sluggish from a build-up of toxins and from lack of stimulation from regular exercise. This thyroid disturbance fosters a greasy and inflamed skin appearance. All told, she has a persistent and severe problem.

In response, her owner finally takes her to the vet, and he then prescribes a cortisone-like drug to suppress her itching and a drug that supplies an artificial thyroid hormone. The first drug depresses the adrenal glands, the second discourages the thyroid's natural hormone production and weakens the gland further. He also recommends chemical flea powders, which add to the toxic load, and a daily measure of bacon fat in addition to the usual diet.

Now if the nutritional and environmental factors that contribute to the disease remain the same, but Jessie is given these stop-gap measures, you can see that the problem may be 'controlled' and yet not solved. As the months and years pass by, the accumulated toxicity, poor nutrition, boredom and lack of exercise eventually result in the breakdown of an important body organ – a problem which has been developing for a long time but which was not so visible as the skin inflammation. This 'new' disease is now treated with new drugs. And on it goes. Do you get the picture?

Rather than building up Jessie's health, this conventional treatment has just temporarily covered up her problems, allowing them to get even worse. And when they do, the 'new' disease is mistakenly viewed as being unrelated to the original condition.

The limitations of a partial approach

The conventional approach of diagnosis and treatment, which I learned in veterinary school and practiced for years, has certainly had some remarkable successes, especially in dealing with acute infections and trauma.

Yet it has become so specialized and materialistic as to lose sight of the larger patterns and processes in disease and health. Instead, we have come to rely heavily on the use of drugs and surgery, often to the exclusion of a broader programme of health-building and prevention.

As a result, the major part of medicine today is geared toward controlling and counteracting symptoms and disturbances. It almost ignores the body's innate ability to heal itself, given the right supports. Instead of strengthening the patient, the methods largely just compensate for the body's weaknesses, much as modern farming techniques attempt to substitute chemical warfare on pests for building up the plants' resistance through organic soil enrichment and careful management.

We are so eager for quick and easy solutions that we rather indiscriminately turn to some drug or vitamin. As a result, the undiscovered cause may remain, even though its effects (the original symptoms) have been covered up.

Unfortunately, some modern drugs are very good at such suppression. Some, like the various forms of synthetic cortisone, are so powerful that they can stop a great many widely varying symptoms in their tracks, *but the disturbance goes on.* Time and again we can observe animals treated vigorously with such drugs and apparently recovering, only to fall ill a few weeks or months later, usually with a more serious condition. For instance, a dog with a skin problem like Jessie's that is continually suppressed with a cortisone-like drug can develop a more deep-seated problem, such as calcification of the spine, pancreatitis or kidney failure.

A cat with a chronically inflamed bladder that is treated with drugs will often later show a more internal problem like kidney involvement, arthritis or leukaemia. Though we tend to regard the new conditions as being unrelated to the prior ones, I suggest they are not. The suppressed disorder has simply made a more serious inroad into the body, now involving internal and more critical organs.

A related problem associated with such dependence on powerful drugs is the production of side effects or even iatrogenic ('doctor-caused') diseases. Although iatrogenic disturbances are considered to be a serious problem in human medicine, veterinary researchers have made little study of them. However, in my own opinion and experience, they are common in animal medicine as well. I have seen many pets improve considerably when prolonged drug treatment is ceased.

Some common drug-related complications are a loss of appetite or diarrhoea (from the use of oral antibiotics), as well as skin rashes, convulsions, hysteria or hearing loss (from the use of tranquillizers or antibiotics). If symptoms appear right after therapy begins, they are probably related to the drug.

In many situations drugs are not called for at all, yet they are used to 'appease the client' and to justify the expense of the examination. An example is the use of antibiotics for virus diseases, which they cannot affect. It is not just the vet (or doctor) who is to blame. Many people insist on an injection or some pills to take home and if the doctor doesn't comply, they will go to another who will.

Unfortunately we have all been sold on the necessity for these drugs, an idea I question on the basis of my own success and that of many other people who use more natural methods that work *with* the body's healing forces.

Why have we come to rely so heavily on drugs, as well as on surgery and other compensatory methods? The historical development of Western medicine is a rather complex subject, but I think a lot of it boils down to certain culturally shared ways of thinking that most of us hold, whether doctor or client.

One of these is that we want a 'quick fix'. We don't want to change our lives or habits, or take the time to investigate a health problem deeply. Instead, we just want to get rid of something we dislike, the sooner the better – even if we know the pain may return later on when the drug wears off. If we *do* undertake a change of habits or lifestyle, it is often just to enable us to live with the weakness. Yet if we took the time and care to work a little harder at understanding and treating the disorder, we might be able to do away with it altogether. For instance, some in-depth holistic approaches have enabled patients to recover from food allergies altogether, so that they no longer need to avoid eating certain items.

Another and probably more fundamental stumbling block is that we view both our bodies and our pets' bodies as being primarily or even exclusively physical, material objects – almost machines. Accordingly, when we consider causes of disease we look almost exclusively to physical ones, like germs or parasites 'invading' from outside, a genetic defect or just plain wear and tear from old age. Similarly, when we seek solutions we almost always look only to material means.

Although doctors may pay some lip service to avoiding emotional stress or may notice how often patients fall ill after suffering a psychological upset, the usual 'fix' for a health problem involves drugs or surgery. (Even psychiatrists rely largely on drugs that suppress emotional states.) So while the reality of the mental and emotional world is acknowledged, it is not seriously regarded in the prevention and treatment of most disease.

From this materialistic point of view, which has dominated modern science (and therefore medicine), life is sustained by complex interacting structures of chemicals that originated and presently operate through some sort of happenstance. Because the organism's inner intelligence is mostly disregarded in this viewpoint, it is not surprising that materialistic medicine generally treats symptoms like an enemy which must be controlled and suppressed. Yet in most cases symptoms represent the action of the individual's vital force, which attempts to throw off the disturbance through, say, diarrhoea, vomiting, coughing, sneezing, pus formation and the like. Holistic therapies, by contrast, tend to work *with* the action of the symptoms, gently helping the body in its attempt to restore harmony.

All this is not to deny physical factors. Certainly there are virulent microorganisms and environmental assaults of all kinds. But individuals who are exposed equally to these factors vary tremendously in their resistance. As I see it, the most important factor in susceptibility to disease of any sort is the strength of the defence system. The whole system includes not just the physical responses described by immunologists but also the total state of the individual, including mental and emotional qualities and more subtle fields of energy involved in the makeup of the organism.

Partly because of the materialistic stance, we often view disease as a distinct, separate entity we must affix with the correct label or diagnosis – which is mostly based on interpretation of the results of extensive and costly laboratory testing. Thus we have the illusion of certainty, but also we have put limits on the problem that begin and end with an official definition. Medical researchers often seek ardently for The One Factor behind a given disease – the unknown virus, the missing enzyme, the damaged gene. They take the problem apart in laboratory test tubes and slides and then try to plug their findings back into the whole living organism.

Holistic therapies, by comparison, tend not to seek single causes or cures but rather to understand and treat disorder in the whole individual. Holistic-minded practitioners do not divide diseases into separate entities or components so much as they try to see how various disturbances in a person or animal are linked together.

Basic to the doctrine of materialism is the now outdated Newtonian notion that the world is ultimately composed of minute particles, discrete 'basic building blocks'. Yet, as many modern physicists are now asserting, 'Particles are merely local condensations of the field; concentrations of energy which come and go, thereby losing their individual character and dissolving into the underlying field.' In the words of Albert Einstein, 'There is no place in this new kind of physics both for the field and matter, for the field is the only reality.' To put it differently, it is an illusion to try to analyse things as though they were separate entities or parts, for all phenomena are manifestations of a whole.

One of the important implications of this fundamental breakthrough of understanding in physics is that the fragmented, specialized, particulate approach to knowledge that typifies most of science (including medicine) is erroneous at its very root. We must learn to see problems in relation to the whole and not become lost in the divisions of our artificial labels and definitions.

Evolving into this new way of perceiving is not easy. It has taken me years to get where I am now and I still feel like a beginner. But I do think a holistic attitude is essential if we really want to aim for optimal health and well-being for both ourselves and our animal companions.

Let us say that this theory makes good sense to you. The next question is, 'How do I help my sick pet?' In many simple conditions a supportive environment, some common-sense care and a little time are all that is needed for an animal to get well. Nature does the job, either with us or in spite of us. But if recurrent or chronic disease or weakness afflicts your animal, a return to health will most likely require major lifestyle changes, as well as specific therapeutic measures.

Start with the diet. Is it fresh and natural, or is it highly processed and of inferior quality? Will it support health? Next, consider the environment. Is it peaceful and wholesome or stressful and polluted? Is there adequate sunlight, fresh air and good water? Does the animal have a comfortable, secure and quiet place to rest? Is the sanitation good? Does the animal receive regular and proper grooming and exercise or is it unkempt and sedentary?

Now take a look at relationships. Does the animal have plenty of friendly and happy companionship, either with people or with other animals? Or is it often neglected, bored and frustrated? Are your mental attitudes toward its problem supportive and positive or do you broadcast anxiety, worry and fear? How is it expected to behave? Is it made to be a guard dog, for instance, when its personality rebels at this task? Is there any animal or person in its environment who threatens its well-being or wishes it harm? Did the animal lose someone or something dear to it when the problem began?

Granted, it's not alway easy to unravel the problem or to change some circumstances. If in doubt, start with the natural feeding programme outlined earlier, make sure your pet gets regular affection, exercise and grooming, and then see what problems (if any) remain. If a wholesome physical and emotional environment is not enough to restore it to health, then there are various holistic, drugless therapies which can effectively stimulate healing or a rebalancing of vital body energies.

It would require many volumes adequately to describe all of the possible therapies that could help your animal. However, let's look at the general philosophy and methods of some of the more common holistic therapies that have been used by vets and others to heal animals. Then I'll describe in greater detail the approach to which I personally have gravitated, which emphasizes homeopathic medicine.

The therapies are not as separate as they appear. Most of them overlap to some extent in their methods and their medicines. Their practitioners often advise a combination of methods. For instance, herbal medicine and dietary changes are often used along with acupuncture.

Naturopathy

Defined by a medical dictionary as a 'drugless system of therapy by the use of physical forces, such as air, light, water, heat, massage, etc.', naturopathy is a comprehensive approach which emphasizes supporting the body's physical attempts to eliminate disease. Naturopathic methods follow from the central idea that a major cause of disease is an excessive build-up of toxic materials (often due to improper eating and lack of exercise) which clog the usual avenues of waste disposal.

Various techniques are used to clean out and stimulate the body, a number of which have been used by peoples of various cultures throughout recorded history. One is fasting, which rests the digestive system and allows the body to do some internal house-cleaning. Fasting patients and others are often advised to drink a lot of pure water or juices to flush out the kidneys and to take enemas or colonic irrigations to clean out the lower intestines.

Hot and cold treatments are sometimes used to stimulate the circulation or encourage sweating. They may include baths, saunas, packs, compresses, fomentations, steaming and the like. Other naturopathic methods include exercise, sunbathing, good hygiene and various massage and brushing techniques. Besides the cleansing processes, patients are also put upon supportive programmes of good nutrition (often emphasizing raw foods and juices), combining particular foods (to aid digestion) and judicious use of food supplements, vitamins, minerals and herbs.

Some of these methods are rather difficult or awkward to apply to animals, but others lend themselves well – particularly fasting, exercise, sunbathing and grooming (a form of massage). I encourage their use in many cases.

Donald Ogden, D.V.M., has made extensive and successful use of naturopathic methods for years in animal medicine. He states that nine cases in ten will recover from skin irritations within only two weeks. He attributes his success to thoroughly bathing the animal, then fasting it for seven days on vegetable broths and then for seven additional days on vegetable solids and soups. He advises breaking the fast with raw meat and raw or steamed leafy vegetables, followed by a balanced natural foods diet. Dr Ogden has also found that quiet rest and fasts of three to ten days (until temperature and symptoms are normal) are very beneficial for many conditions, including obesity, rheumatism and arthritis, constipation, chronic cardiac insufficiency, bronchial diseases, heartworm, kidney and bladder stones, gastritis, kidney disease, pyorrhoea, diabetes, liver disorders (unless cirrhosis has developed), open sores, leptospirosis and the febrile (fever) stage of distemper. However, he notes, don't fast an animal with a wasting disease such as cancer, advanced uremia, tuberculosis, prolonged malnutritional practices, severe hookworm disease and advanced distemper. Dr Ogden's writings on the use of naturopathic methods in veterinary care describe this approach as providing impressive results.

Herbalism

Though herbalists often advise methods described under naturopathy as well, the emphasis is placed more strongly upon the specific use of herbal leaves, roots and flowers to stimulate healing. Basic to folk medicine in every culture since ancient times, herbalism is probably the most fundamental system of specific remedies.

Wild animals often instinctively select appropriate herbs when they are ill. In fact, a great many of our modern pharmaceutical drugs are actually compounds considered to be the active principles in herbs. For instance, digitalis derives from foxglove, atropine from belladonna (nightshade), caffeine from coffee, theophylline from tea, arecoline from the areca (betel) nut and reserpine from *Rauwolfia serpentina*. Herbalists contend that the pharmaceutical derivatives and the whole plants from which they come are not the same, however. The strength of herbs is in the unique and complex properties of the original natural substance. Again, the whole is more than the sum of (or one of) its parts.

As compared to their pharmaceutical counterparts, herbs exhibit a slower and deeper action. They assist the healing process by helping the body to eliminate and detoxify, thus taking care of the problem the symptoms are expressing. For instance, they may stimulate physiological processes like the emptying of the bowels or urination. In addition they can serve as tonics and builders that resonate with and strengthen tissues in specific parts of the body (or the whole body, depending on the herb in question). Finally, they can be highly nutritious, containing large amounts of various vitamins and minerals.

Herbal practitioners say that plant medicines, particularly those found locally, bring the healing energy of the environment to the user. Everything, it is said, has a purpose and a use because everything has qualities and properties.

Herbal remedies have been successfully used to treat many illnesses in animals throughout the centuries. In recent years Juliette de Bairacli-Levy has popularized their use for this purpose through her detailed writings (which also emphasize the importance of natural diet and fasting; see page 271). She has reported good results with herbs in the treatment of the following common problems in dogs: worms, fleas, skin problems, mange, distemper, kidney and bladder trouble, arthritis, anaemia, diabetes, leptospirosis, obesity, wounds and fractures, constipation, diarrhoea, jaundice, heart disorders, warts and cataracts.

Levy recommends that whenever possible one should use the freshly gathered herb and that dried herbs should be replaced yearly. I concur with this advice, with the proviso that you must be careful to pick herbs that you know have not been sprayed. In the next chapter I will describe the standard methods of preparing infusions, decoctions and tinctures from herbs. In the *Encyclopaedia* section, I suggest specific herbs for various illnesses.

Besides the difficulty one may encounter in finding fresh material, one disadvantage I find in using internal herbal therapy for animals stems from the fact that the remedies are generally administered in appreciable quantities at fairly frequent intervals over long periods of time (weeks to months). Since they rarely taste good, they usually must be given to animals in capsules or else disguised in food. As you probably know, it is a bit of a bother to force medication down a pet on a frequent and prolonged basis.

For that reason and others I personally

have preferred to emphasize homeopathic medications, which taste good and are given less often. Many of these are derived from plants. Another related system I use with animals is the Bach flower essences, prepared infusions of special flowers. Both are described later.

However, I have seen the power of well-chosen herbs as well and recognize their value. I find them most useful for *external* treatments on animals (as in flea powders and rinses, mite control, skin problems and wounds) or for *minor* upsets (such as motion sickness, indigestion and the like) that do not require prolonged treatment.

For people willing to go through the work of carrying out a complete and thorough programme, herbs can be an excellent way of dealing with intestinal parasites. Anitra Frazier, a professional cat groomer, wrote about her successful experience treating tapeworms with the same programme described in the section on naturopathic and herbal treatment under 'Worms' in the *Encyclopaedia* section. It combines fasting with the use of garlic, rue, wormwood, castor oil and special foods. She explained:

> The hard part was not stuffing powdered herbs and wet, gooey, crushed garlic into empty gelatin capsules. . . . The hardest part was keeping myself from feeding Purr during the fast days. . . .
> I waited a couple of weeks after it was over, examining Purr's stool every morning for signs of wiggly, maggoty things. When everything still remained normal looking, I told [the vet] that the herbal worming seemed to have worked. It's been over four months . . . and so far, so good – it looks like we won.
> Purr was much more playful and jaunty after the experience. I would recommend the herbal worming to any owners who are able to give pills to their

cat. If we can avoid giving poisonous chemicals simply by spending some extra time, I think that is a very small price to pay, because it results in huge dividends in health for the cat.
> —*The Natural Cat: A Holistic Guide for Finicky Owners* (Harbor, 1981).

Chiropractic and other manual therapies

Various types of manipulative therapies have been used throughout the world, since at least the time of Hippocrates. Some of these, like chiropractic and osteopathy, which were founded in the 19th century, view many disease conditions as the result of misaligned or abnormal bodily structures (especially in the spine) that interfere with the normal flow of life forces, nerve impulses or blood circulation.

Of these, chiropractic has become one of the largest drugless healing professions in the world. I first became interested in the potential this therapy holds for animals when I talked with a local chiropractor who told me that many different conditions in pets have been helped by chiropractic, including epilepsy.

Later I met a vet who, with the help of a trained chiropractor and vitamin supplementation, was getting amazing results in one of his canine patients. The dog was afflicted with Wobbler syndrome, an inherited condition in which the neck vertebrae put pressure on the spinal cord and make walking difficult. Before treatment the poor dog could go only about three steps without falling over; now it runs all over and even jumps fences! Also, some clients have reported to me that their dogs were helped by chiropractic adjustments when paralysed by disc problems.

As I understand the original theory, nerve energy flowing through the spinal column, which is essential for the proper functioning of various organs and tissues, can be impeded at certain exit points from the spinal cord due to a subtle misalignment. This irregularity, known as a subluxation, is said to put excessive pressure on the spinal nerves. Treatment consists of careful manipulation of the vertebrae to restore correct alignment and full functioning. To achieve this specialized skill, practitioners must undergo years of training.

The theories of direct pressure on the nerves have been questioned in recent times. My own thinking is that this theory is a somewhat limited explanation. Rather, I feel that the body and mind are one whole, and disturbances in any one local part are felt throughout the entire system and may cause 'resonant' problems in a generalized way.

This viewpoint is supported by the fact that there are many apparently successful methods of diagnosis and manipulative therapy which focus on certain parts of the body with the understanding that they reflect or represent the whole organism. For instance, an iridologist 'reads' disturbances in various organs by a careful examination of the iris of the eye. Practitioners of reflexology pinpoint and treat disturbances elsewhere in the body by manual pressure on certain points of the feet and hands (some people have applied this technique to animals as well). Some acupuncturists diagnose and treat problems solely at points on the ear, which is said to reflect the whole body. (I have met one veterinary acupuncturist who now uses only the ear to treat health problems successfully in horses, even lameness!) Polarity therapy, which includes manual techniques and has also been used on pets, relies upon a method of reading and treating

disturbances by a similarly holistic approach.

In the same way, it may be that body/mind disturbances are reflected in the spinal column, where they may also be associated with irregular muscular tensions and vertebral displacements. Accordingly, they may be helped by corrective manipulation there.

Regardless of the whys and wherefores, chiropractic manipulation has proved to be a real boon for many animal patients, as shown by the following cases.

A *Prevention* magazine reader wrote to me, describing the amazing response of her 18-year-old cat to chiropractic therapy. Twelve years earlier her cat had begun to develop severe attacks of vomiting, loss of appetite and intense itching of the face and shoulders. The poor cat licked and scratched until the skin was bloody. The owner had seen several different vets, but drug therapy had offered only temporary help, if any at all.

By chance, this woman's chiropractor heard of the situation and offered to try to help. After one adjustment there were startling results: the cat stopped vomiting and began to eat! Four adjustments were done in all and the condition has not reappeared in the two years since.

Another case, reported in a veterinary publication, concerned a silky terrier with a back problem. The vet had diagnosed a 'protruding disc' with pain and loss of function. X-rays revealed calcium deposits in the area as well as a deviation of the vertebral joint. Surgery was rejected because of the high cost. Drugs were not helping, even after two weeks of therapy and confinement. At this point a spinal adjustment was made. Though the dog had to be carried in to the chiropractor, 'within a couple of minutes . . . [he] was walking again, painlessly'. The improvement has lasted until this time. The chiropractor, who did not charge for his services, said that he had successfully treated other animals as well. In one case he had restored a cat's sight after pressure on the spinal cord was relieved.

Two equally impressive cases were described to me by a woman whose chiropractor had helped a couple of nine-year-old Alsatians with crippling problems. One was severely dysplastic, with an implanted plastic hip. It had been on cortisone for five or six years and could not go without it for more than a week before becoming almost completely immobile and crying in pain. After only one adjustment and some follow-up dietary changes, the woman reported that the dog had not required any cortisone for the three months since and could manage two flights of stairs with relative ease and no apparent discomfort!

The second Alsatian suffered so badly from degenerative arthritis that he had to be dragged around on a mat. After five adjustments he, too, could tackle stairs.

The use of chiropractic and allied techniques in animals has been slow to develop because only licensed vets are allowed to charge a fee for treating animals and they are not taught such methods in their medical education. Nevertheless, supporters from both the veterinary and chiropractic professions are trying to further this work by coming together to share information.

Though I have not personally learned manual therapies of this sort, I have met one vet and have heard of several others who do use chiropractic techniques on their animal patients. I welcome the introduction of such techniques in veterinary medicine. Certainly an important aspect of a holistic attitude is a willingness to put aside some of the unnecessary ways in which we divide up the healing arts along rigid professional lines, often to the detriment of patients.

Acupuncture and oriental medicine

One traditional holistic approach that does seem to have made fairly significant inroads into the veterinary profession is the use of acupuncture and other aspects of Oriental medicine. One can find texts on the subject and there is even an international veterinary acupuncture society. I am better acquainted with the results of this method than with some other holistic therapies, in part because I know several enthusiastic colleagues who practice it.

The basic theory behind this comprehensive system is that the fundamental energy fields that comprise the body (as well as all aspects of the universe) manifest as two poles, which are actually expressions of one whole. One pole, yang, is described as being constructive, focusing, contracted and positive. The other, yin, is seen as disruptive, distributing, expanded and negative. An individual's state of health depends on the proper balance between these two extremes. A skilled therapist can correct excesses or deficiencies by the manipulation of certain critical points along the body's meridians (channels through which the energy flows). This is accomplished through the use of needles (acupuncture), finger pressure (acupressure or shiatsu), burning the herb mugwort near the point (moxibustion) or, in modern times, electrical stimulation (electroacupuncture). Expressions of the flow of energy (chi) cannot simply be blocked and go nowhere (i.e., be suppressed). Rather, they must be redirected.

Although no one really knows how acupuncture works, in Western terms, it has been empirically observed that white blood cells and general blood circulation are both increased in the area of the point being stimulated. Production of endorphin, a natural brain hormone which regulates pain, also rises. As well, the herb used in moxibustion (mugwart) has been found to emit at least ten different chemicals thought to stimulate the body and special Kirlian photographs of the energy fields emanating from the body show changes after acupuncture treatment.

Though a number of vets have learned basic acupuncture techniques, a *successful* practice requires the vet to upgrade his skills through attendance at seminars and lectures given by experienced practitioners. These are almost the sole source of knowledge in a tradition that is largely oral rather than written.

One such dedicated practitioner of my acquaintance is John Ihor Basko, D.V.M., of San Jose, California. He has told me that as he reaches deeper levels of mastery he often discovers that 'the more you know, the more you know you don't know!' Smiling, he added, 'Oriental medicine comes from [the insight] that ultimately we don't *know* how the body works, and nature cannot be explained by the mind. You can't always go by a recipe. Sometimes I get a hunch to put the needle in a certain point, without knowing why. Then later on, I will read about it and see how it was appropriate.'

What can acupuncture and Oriental medicine accomplish? Some pretty remarkable things, it would seem. Dr Basko reports that results have been generally excellent and that acupuncture is especially effective in dealing with some problems that are often difficult to treat with Western methods – such as spinal disc problems, arthritis, canine hip dysplasia, skin allergies, kidney disorders and metabolic imbalances. He has been able to reduce the use of conventional drugs to about 25 per cent of what he once used in standard practice. Most of these are either injectable vitamins or antibiotics.

Of his successes, spinal disc cases have been especially notable; all the animals he has treated for this condition have improved, some of them quite remarkably. He laughed as he described his initial reaction when he first heard about 'miraculous' results using acupuncture on cases of back problems: 'You must be joking!'

He described as 'amazing' acupuncture's effectiveness in some cases of uraemia (a toxic kidney condition) that he handled while working in a veterinary hospital. Though he also administered standard fluid therapy, these were cases he would not ordinarily have expected to survive.

Even advanced canine distemper and feline leukaemia (diseases for which modern veterinary methods can do little) have yielded to this holistic approach. And in a case when the animal does reach its end, Basko has noticed that its death is usually more peaceful and involves less suffering than otherwise would be typical.

In addition to these encouraging results, Dr Basko also has seen a remarkable overall improvement in his patients, who often emerge from a series of treatments with more energy, playfulness and general well-being than they've had for years. He attributes the improvement to a rebalancing of the whole body and mind. Although acupuncture, like Western medicine, *can* be used to treat symptoms alone, the best approach is to correct the underlying imbalances in the organism as a whole, which create the conditions that foster specific diseases.

As you might guess, such a holistic approach can also be used to *prevent* disease, much like getting a 'tune-up' for the body. In fact, the ancient Chinese, who developed the system over thousands of years of practice and observation, emphasized prevention above all else. They resorted to acupuncture or herbs only when the preferred methods (meditation, exercise, massage) failed to cure. Most contemporary acupuncturists emphasize a total approach to health and include advice on the use of food, herbs and the like in their methods as well.

Another colleague, Gloria Dodd, D.V.M., has been equally impressed with the results of acupuncture therapy. In a discussion we had about ways to deal with several outstanding medical challenges – including severe anaemias, difficult labour, serious infectious disease, shock and collapse, and a distressing skin irritation called 'lick granuloma' – Dr Dodd told me that acupuncture has succeeded with all of these conditions. She then described several cases in detail and added, 'I could go on and on into cases. I've got a whole box full of them.'

One dramatic story involved a puppy at death's door with severe pneumonia. Having been unsuccessfully treated by several other vets, it was brought to her as a last resort. Heavy discharge ran from its nose and it gasped for air. The signs of impending death seemed clear.

'It had a temperature of 105°F,' she explained. 'I turned to my needles and within 20 minutes the thick buttery discharge from the nose had changed to a clear liquid! The dog lifted its head (it had been carried in) and began to breathe easier and the temperature dropped to 104°F. After completing the initial treatment, excess fluid had almost disappeared from the lungs. It was like a miracle. The owner, who was a doctor, also listened to the lungs and could not believe the change.'

Dr Dodd then administered appropriate antibiotics and acupunctured the dog about four days in a row ('You have to get the momentum of energy going and keep it going'). Within two weeks the dog was entirely normal and showed no lung damage. Surely an amazing case!

As Dr Dodd learned, she expanded her method to include other holistic therapies as well, such as vitamin and mineral supplementation, dietary recommendations and, most recently, various homeopathic preparations she has found effective for reactions to vaccinations and insecticides and even for feline leukaemia. (Of six cats who had suffered from this usually fatal condition, all are now clinically normal and four have high enough antibodies to be resistant to the disease, she said.)

Because Dr Dodd is a very busy woman, our exchange took place in her treatment room and was sandwiched between successive electroacupuncture treatments on a large Alsatian with severe hip dysplasia.

'This is the second treatment and already he is better,' his smiling owner explained.

I learned that the dog had become so immobilized by his defect that he had been unable to raise himself with his rear legs and was forced to drag them along to get around. I watched Dr Dodd apply an electrical treatment plate to the dog's hindquarters and show the owner how to hold it in place for the duration of the treatment. By the time we finished our discussion the therapy was over and the big animal was released from the restraining sling. Ecstatic at escaping his confines and eager to taste the sunny day outside, the once-crippled dog lunged out of the office, dragging his pleased owner at the other end of the lead.

Not bad at all!

Homeopathy

We now come to my own particular love, the science of homeopathy. In my search for effective holistic therapies I started using nutrition and herbs (and I still do, along with naturopathic methods). But by themselves they didn't always seem sufficient. (Or the underlying principles that surely governed their best application were not always apparent to me.) As a result, I kept my eyes and ears open for a system that might be more effective. Here and there I kept hearing praise for homeopathy, particularly from individuals whose sense of judgement I most respected. Finally, I decided to examine it for myself. That decision was a turning point that opened my horizons to a medical approach of unique elegance, order and effectiveness.

Homeopathy is practised in most of the world. To my way of thinking, it deserves far more attention than it presently receives in this country. Because of its many virtues, I hope it will become a prominent medical art of the future.

The real beauty of the homeopathic system lies in the simplicity of its basic principles, and the exhaustively researched criteria that determine the practitioner's choice of remedies. Whereas conventional medicine seems to be a composite of various hypotheses and changing fads, homeopathy was founded on one basic unifying principle that has held true ever since the system was originated in the early 1800s by the German physician Samuel Hahnemann. That principle, recognized as early as the 10th century B.C. by Hindu sages, as well as by Hippocrates and many others, is that Like Will Be Cured by Like (*Similia Similibus Curentur*).

Hahnemann noted certain similarities between symptoms produced by some diseases and by the drugs used to treat them. From that relationship he formed this theory: a disease can be cured by whatever medicine produces similar symptoms when given to a healthy person. Called the Law of Similars, its beauty is that the treatment provided goes *with* rather than *against* the body's own efforts to regain health.

A good practitioner can read a set of signals flashed by a disease. Rather than prescribing a medication for a headache, another for an upset stomach, and a third for depression, the doctor will offer a single remedy for the whole set of symptoms. He will choose the one medication that would produce all three symptoms if given repeatedly to a healthy person.

How homeopathic medications are prepared

Most preparations can be purchased in a specific strength. Therefore, if treatment for, say, nausea requires Ipecac 3X, *you simply purchase the* Ipecac *at that strength.*

The number following the name of the preparation indicates how many times the tincture has been diluted. For example, 1X indicates that one drop of medication has been added to nine drops of alcohol. The medication is now at 1/10 of its original strength. If you add one drop of this 1X mixture to nine drops of alcohol, the solution would be labelled 2X, at 1/100th of its original strength.

Thus:

$$1X = 1/10 \text{ strength}$$
$$2X = 1/100$$
$$3X = 1/1,000$$
$$4X = 1/10,000$$
$$5X = 1/100,000$$
$$6X = 1/1,000,000$$
$$12X = 1/10^{12}$$

These numerical indications of strength also apply to powders, which are diluted with powdered milk sugar.

Rarely, the Encyclopaedia *section directs you to dilute certain medications on your own. For example, you may be asked to dilute goldenseal by adding 2 teaspoons of powdered root to 1 or 2 ounces of vodka or brandy and later adding 120 drops of distilled water. Simply follow the directions in the* Encyclopaedia *section as you would a recipe.*

The specially prepared substances used as remedies in homeopathy contain minute doses of herbs, minerals, animal products such as bee venom and cuttlefish ink, and various other products. These substances are diluted so that only minuscule amounts actually enter a patient's body. Sometimes dilution is so extreme that it goes far beyond the point where the substance could act through molecular strength. While there is much debate about how these greatly diluted substances actually do work, many homeopaths believe that they carry information derived from the original material, while others believe magnetic forces come into play.

From my own experience, I can testify that homeopathic remedies really work. When I am able clearly to recognize the unique symptom picture – taking into account the mental, emotional and physical levels – and match it to the right remedy, I can be certain the patient will respond. Though it's not always easy to make such a match, when I do, I can count on this principle just as I can count on gravity.

Here's a simplified example of how homeopathy works.

We know that a bee's sting will cause a certain typical reaction, including swelling, fluid accumulation, redness of the skin, pain and soreness, that is accentuated by the application of heat or pressure. Some sensitive people also will experience mental symptoms such as apathy, stupor, listlessness, *or* the opposite, whining and tearfulness. If a homeopathically prepared dilute solution of bee venom is given to a person with these symptoms – even if they are caused by something other than a bee sting – the condition will begin to clear up. The essential feature is that there be close similarity between the remedy and the condition for it to work properly.

To know what conditions a remedy can cure, it is first empirically 'proven' by a group of human volunteers who take the substance in a diluted form for several days or weeks. Each day they note their symptoms – mental, emotional and physical – in a diary that is used to provide a 'symptom picture' characteristic of the substance under study. As this substance is investigated in this way, it is added to the *Materia Medica*, a reference work that catalogues several hundred remedies and their provings. Almost all of the medicinal herbs have been studied in these testings, providing consistently accurate guidelines for their use.

These studies also provide some interesting sidelights. One is the discovery that some remedies have many applications that were not previously known. For example, one of the symptoms noted by those testing bee venom was a urinary disturbance characterized by concentrated, dark urine that burned during urination. It was later found that some forms of cystitis (bladder inflammation) that are associated with burning and soreness during urination can be cured by administering homeopathically prepared bee venom (*Apis mellifica*). While bee venom will not work in *every* case of cystitis, it will work in those cases showing similar characteristics. (See my suggestion for using *Apis* for cats, under 'Bladder Problems' in the *Encyclopaedia* section.)

Strange as it may seem, the most effective remedies are diluted substances, which work better than the crude form, or physiological dose. Their effectiveness seems to follow from two things: (1) the diluted remedy introduces less 'drug' substance into the body, so that toxic or chemical effects are eliminated; and (2) the dilution is 'potentized' or prepared in such a way (shaking or grinding) that it apparently releases its inherent electromagnetic pattern, and so makes the resultant remedy more effective than the untreated substance.

The medicinal effect is thought to be like this: when the body is disturbed (diseased), the symptoms manifested *are its attempt to heal* and restore balance. We know, for instance, that inflammation with redness, pain and swelling are primary defence tactics of the body. Therefore the affected part is particularly sensitive to the action of a matching remedy, which acts like a *catalyst* or booster to the self-healing process.

Standard drugs, by comparison, are generally used either to take the place of normal body processes (hormonal drugs), inhibit body responses (painkillers, anti-inflammatory drugs, antihistamines) or weaken or kill bacteria or cancer cells (antibodies, chemotherapy, radiation therapy). Therefore they are frequently used in combinations to treat different conditions in the same patient, like arthritis, pyorrhea and migraine headaches.

Homeopaths, on the other hand, consider that the individual has only *one* disorder, which can create many symptoms and idiosyncratic characteristics. Therefore, only one remedy is administered at a time – the one thought to be the best catalyst for the body's total defence response.

The contributions of homeopathy to our general understanding of health and disease have been enormous. *The Science of Homeopathy*, by George Vithoulkas, is an important modern discussion of the principles involved and is invaluable for a person interested in any form of holistic therapy.

Theory aside, homeopathy does work exceedingly well in both animals and people, as clinicians will testify. A double-blind study of 46 human patients with rheumatoid arthritis underscores its effectiveness. Half were given homeopathic treatment and half placebos (unmedicated tablets of the same appearance). Though neither the attending doctors nor the patients knew whether a remedy or a placebo was being taken (to rule out the effect of suggestion), the results clearly showed that the treated group had significant improvement in subjective pain, joint tenderness, grip strength and morning stiffness. All without any toxic reactions of side effects (*British Journal of Clinical Pharmacology*, May, 1980).

An interesting sidelight about homeopathic medicine is the way remedies are tested. They are tried on *people*, not animals.

Because important mental and emotional symptoms must be studied before the action of a substance is fully grasped, only astute human observers can note and report these internal events. They are volunteers, and any unpleasant symptoms they develop during the provings go away after they cease taking the substance.

Homeopathic studies are a world apart from conventional laboratory studies, where an animal is given a 'human' disease. This approach ignores the real subject of the illness, the human being. From a holistic viewpoint, such animal research will never solve the problem of human disease. We must do that ourselves, by using the tremendous potential for direct learning about the process in ourselves.

Let me tell you about a few animal cases. I once treated a cat that was suffering from a rare, post-surgical reaction – septicaemia (bacterial spread in the bloodstream) and a general breakdown of her blood-clotting mechanism. She was in pitiable condition, with a high fever and vomiting. Dark blood leaked from her back, stomach, legs, feet, mouth and vagina. I also detected bleeding under the skin (dark blue swellings under the eyelids and ears). Though antibiotics seemed indicated, I was not sure they would act quickly enough in this crisis situation. She seemed to get worse even while I was examining her!

As a temporary measure I decided to

administer fluids under her skin, to help counter her moderate dehydration. While doing so I immediately noticed that she was very hypersensitive to pain and could not bear being touched at all. Perhaps that may not sound unusual, but the extent of her reaction was greater than one would expect. At this point, I recognized the similarity between her unique symptoms and the provings of the remedy *Arnica* (from the plant *Arnica montana*). Among the characteristics of *Arnica* are fever, haemorrhage, black and blue spots under the skin from bleeding, septic conditions, hypersensitivity to pain and an aversion to touch!

So I immediately gave her a tablet of *Arnica* and repeated it every few hours. Later in the day she was much improved. By the next morning, her temperature had dropped and she was no longer bleeding. The cat was obviously calmer – eating for the first time since becoming ill. Within 48 hours, the only remaining evidence of what had so recently been a life-threatening condition were a few dry scabs where the haemorrhage had been. A week later I called to check on her and she was in good health. Rather impressive results! I never did need to use antibiotics.

I'm often amazed to see how *rapidly* homeopathic medications can work. I usually find that in acute problems, they restore health much more quickly than drugs. But they also excel in many chronic conditions. Some of the problems I've treated successfully with these remedies include demodectic mange and other severe skin problems, cystitis, parvovirus, punctures and gunshot wounds, distemper, concussion and a host of general and vague complaints including such symptoms as diarrhoea, depression, loss of appetite, itchiness and the like.

A recent case that comes to mind involved an older cat whose lab tests had confirmed that he had feline infectious peritonitis – a terminal condition not curable with drugs.

His symptoms included repeated vomiting, diarrhoea, loss of appetite and swelling of the abdomen. Over a period of several days my client and I gradually changed his diet to a home-prepared one (as outlined in this book) and increased his vitality through the use of herbs and thymus gland supplements. I then recognized an appropriate homeopathic remedy, which for this particular fellow was *Arsenicum album* (white oxide of arsenic).

I gave him one dose, which was followed by a short aggravation of symptoms for a couple of days and then a continued improvement for a long period. One more dose of remedy was given two months later when the vomiting began to recur. He quickly returned to normal health and has remained stable ever since. On top of it all, his personality improved, so that he is now considerably calmer and steadier, and his weight increased from 6 to 11 pounds!

Favourable personality changes often accompany successful physical treatment, as in this case reported by Dorothy Shepherd, an English homeopath who returned home one day to find her puppy lying in its basket almost unconscious, pale, barely breathing and dribbling saliva. Though his nose was warm, the rest of his body was icy cold. His pulse was scarcely detectable. I rather doubt that this puppy could have been saved by any amount of drug treatment. Our undaunted doctor, however, gave a homeopathic preparation made from camphor (which matched his symptoms) and brought a quick response.

In a remarkably short time he opened his eyes and feebly tried to lick my fingers, which I had dipped in warm milk dosed with a drop of brandy. Joyfully he was fed with a little more milk and brandy, the first nourishment he had deigned to take for hours. Next morning, quite a different spectacle met me; he had

crawled out of his basket and was lying in front of the fire, gaily wagging his tail as usual in the morning.
> —*Magic of the Minimum Dose* (Health Science Press, 1979).

That was the end of the puppy's illness, after only one treatment. Thereafter his personality changed and he went from being rather slovenly to being 'quite house-clean and quite an exemplary dog'.

Indeed, homeopathic remedies *can* be used to treat personality problems. For instance, I treated one client's cat that had spontaneously developed a drastic personality change for the worse. Where she had once been friendly, she was now irritable, resistant to being held and generally stand-offish. Homeopathic treatment with *Nux vomica* restored her to her normal affectionate self.

Tissue salts

In the *Encyclopaedia* section I often recommend tissue salts as well as homeopathic preparations. The system of therapy using these salts was devised by Wilhelm Heinrich Schuessler in the 19th century. Schuessler, a medical doctor, physiological chemist and physicist, based his treatment on the fact that the human body is composed of an enormous number of cells that contain a perfect balance of water, organic substances and inorganic substances. While the inorganic substances are present only in very small quantities, they are vital to living tissue – helping cells build or heal.

These substances, generally called tissue salts, are prepared homeopathically. That is, they are divided into 12 separate salts – each serving to stimulate the body in certain ways. They are usually known by their abbreviated names, and often by a number as well. They are:

1. *Calcarea fluorica* (Calc. fluor. or calcium fluoride). Its basic function is to preserve the ability of elastic tissue to contract.

2. *Calcarea phosphorica* (Calc. phos. or calcium phosphate). Generally, it is used to aid growth and development, for rickets, to aid digestion, to boost circulation and to speed recovery.

3. *Calcarea sulphurica* (Calc. Sulph. or calcium sulphate). It is generally used to purify blood of non-functional organic matter.

4. *Ferrum phosphoricum* (Ferr. phos. or iron phosphate). This tissue salt is like the cavalry – it comes to the rescue by carrying oxygen into the bloodstream and to all parts of the body. It is useful where there is inflammation, pain or fever.

5. *Kali muriaticum* (Kali mur. or potassium chloride). It is often used as the remedy for sluggish conditions and often used in conjunction with other tissue salts.

6. *Kali phosphoricum* (Kali phos. or potassium phosphate). A tissue salt that serves as a nerve nutrient.

7. *Kali sulphuricum* (Kali sulph. or potassium sulphate). It is often used in cases where there is a sticky, yellow discharge from the skin or mucous membrane.

8. *Magnesia phosphorica* (Mag. phos. or magnesium phosphate). Known as the antispasmodic tissue salt, its main function is to treat the nervous system and muscle cramps.

9. *Natrum muriaticum* (Nat. mur. or sodium chloride). Often called the water-disturbing tissue salt, it controls the ebb and flow of body fluids. Excessive wetness or dryness in any part of the body can indicate a deficiency of this tissue salt.

10. *Natrum phosphoricum* (Nat. phos. or sodium phosphate). This tissue salt is an acid neutralizer that is important for the proper functioning of the digestive tract.

11. *Natrum sulphuricum* (Nat. sulph. or sodium sulphate). This salt removes excess water from the fluids that bathe tissue cells, and is a tonic to the liver.

12. *Silicea* (silicic oxide). This tissue salt is a cleanser capable of breaking up accumulations of pus, as in the case of abscesses or sties. It is also used to eliminate foreign material such as plant seeds or splinters.

Flower essences

In addition to homeopathic remedies, I also use something similar – the Bach flower essences – to treat both behavioural and physical problems. Though these dilute infusions of flowers and tree buds are said to act primarily upon the mental state, a psychological improvement often brings a physical one as well. These extracts are given orally several times a day, often for several weeks.

One case in which I used a flower essence concerned a dog with a host of distressing symptoms. These included a loss of appetite, lack of energy, unusual behaviour, vomiting, collapse, fever, damp body hair, a tense abdomen, and enlarged spleen. In addition, laboratory tests showed that the animal was anaemic, with abnormally shaped red blood cells, an above-normal number of white blood cells, elevated liver enzymes (showing liver damage), elevated cholesterol and bile pigments, high blood sugar, and so on. The x-rays taken were normal.

All these symptoms were threatening ones and seemed to indicate a serious physical disturbance. Yet previous treatment with a synthetic cortisone preparation, antibiotics, and vitamin B_{12} injections had had no effect on the dog.

Because I knew the family was under stress, I suspected a disturbance on the psychological or mental level. Accordingly I prescribed one of the Bach flower essences, Larch, to be used 4 times a day for a week. For the first few hours after starting the treatment the symptoms became exaggerated, but marked improvement was seen by the next day. A week later, the symptoms were gone and have not returned for over a year. In addition, this dog's personality changed. She became more playful and outgoing with the other animals in the family, something not seen before. This change has persisted even though the original treatment was only for a few weeks.

I've also found the Bach flowers useful in some conditions that developed shortly after a traumatic or upsetting experience. For instance, a woman brought in a cat a couple of weeks after it had been violently shaken by a large dog. The animal was uncomfortable, irritable and constipated. It had a fever, weight loss, fluid accumulation in the lungs, and a painful abdomen. The most severe injury seemed to be a displaced vertebra in the lower back, which I could feel was out of place. It hurt the cat very much when I touched it.

I prescribed the Bach flower, Star of Bethlehem, 2 drops to be given every 2 hours. Three days later, the cat's owner called to say that her cat was quite recovered. The drops had noticeably relaxed her. After a couple of days' treatment, she began stretching by hooking her claws in a piece of firewood and pulling from side to side. Apparently the stretching corrected the back problem. Soon it was difficult to medicate the cat – she was too busy leaping tall fences in a single bound!

As you can see, some pretty remarkable things can happen when we adopt a new view of the wholeness of the body and mind, and treat from there. The success of the holistic therapies described in this chapter depends on the skill of the practitioner, the strength and will of the patient, the degree of support in the environment and the appropriateness of the selected method.

This brief survey was meant to introduce you to the many exciting approaches that can help to relieve the suffering of animals. And if we are but willing to extend our mental horizons, how much more is possible?

CHAPTER FIFTEEN

Caring for a Sick Animal

Should your animal become ill, there are several advantages to caring for it at home, if possible. First of all, home is familiar and safe, free of the stress inherent in being placed in a busy veterinary surgery with animals and people who are strangers to your pet. Second, if you have the time you can provide some really useful nursing care at home. Treatments such as fasting, special nutrition and meticulous cleaning may not be done in a surgery, either because they are time-consuming or because the philosophy of disease treatment is different. Third, at home *you* are in charge, so that alternative or natural forms of treatment can be used without conflict.

On the other hand, a vet is a skilled professional. Years of training and experience enable him or her to assess the seriousness of a condition and employ the proper diagnostic techniques. For conditions that are either very messy to take care of (like vomiting and diarrhoea) or life-threatening (such as a car accident or severe infection) the veterinary surgery offers support that is impossible at home, such as anti-shock therapy, intravenous fluids or surgery.

Whether at home or not, your pet can recover faster and more completely if you make use of the general health care principles in this book (good nutrition and supplements, exercise, a supportive relationship and so on) and some of the nursing care methods in this chapter. However, if you are giving your animal a prescription drug recommended by your vet, do *not* use the homeopathic remedies suggested in the *Encyclopaedia* section, since they tend to work against each other. However, you can use some of the herbal recommendations, particularly those that are suggested for external use or those whose primary purpose is to help rebuild the tissues.

A seriously ill animal has certain basic needs. When wild animals are sick or injured they go off by themselves to rest in a secure, peaceful place and to allow nature to heal the condition. We need to provide our pets with a comparable opportunity. Most sick animals want to be quiet, safe and warm and to have access to fresh air and sunlight. Also, they will often fast instinctively. The loss of appetite seen in most disease is part of the healing response rather than a symptom to be forcibly overridden.

So provide comfortable bedding in a cosy spot that is free of draughts, disturbances and loud noise, where your dog or cat can rest peacefully and feel protected. Keep the area clean, changing the blankets or towels as necessary. If your pet desires it, allow it some access to fresh air and sunlight (but don't impose it).

Fasting

Generally, it's good to encourage fasting the first day or two of an illness, especially if there is a fever. A good rule of thumb is to fast your pet until its temperature returns to normal – one or two days, or as long as four or five (if necessary and if the animal is in reasonable condition).

Fasting is one of the oldest and most natural methods of healing. Normally the body constantly eliminates waste products, along with any tainted or toxic materials that have been eaten. Fasting greatly reduces the body's usual assimilation and elimination load, allowing it to break down and expel older wastes that may have accumulated in the liver and fatty tissues. The body also gets a chance to unload the products of inflammation, tumours and abscesses. Once the body has cleansed itself, the overworked glands, organs and cells have a chance to repair and restore themselves.

Dogs and cats have been fasted for periods ranging from one to 50 days with excellent results and amazing recoveries. Of course, you should not attempt a long fast without professional experience and training. See the section on naturopathy in chapter 14 for conditions that generally benefit from fasting, as well as for those for which fasting should not be used.

The following programme is a good basic guideline for fasting your animal. It can be used during illnesses, but it also can help your pet make the change from its old eating habits to a new natural foods diet.

The break-in period: Begin by easing the animal into the fast for one or two days. Feed it a lighter, simpler diet that includes a moderate or small amount of lean meat or tofu, along with some vegetables and oatmeal. (Of course, if your animal is suddenly ill and loses its appetite, this step is not necessary or appropriate.)

Use vegetables that are considered to be beneficial to the kidneys and the liver, organs that will be playing major roles during the fast. They include broccoli, kale, cauliflower, cabbage, beets and turnips (with tops), dandelion greens, spinach, sweetcorn, potatoes, cucumbers, parsley and tomatoes. Serve them either raw and finely grated (which is preferable) or lightly steamed.

The liquid fast: Next proceed with the main part of the fast, a liquid diet. In acute problems, continue the fast until the temperature is normal and the animal is well on its way to recovery. In more chronic or degenerative conditions, the length of the fast may vary from about three to seven days – until there is substantial improvement and a hearty appetite returns. If you begin reintroducing solids and your animal doesn't seem hungry for them, then stay with the liquid fast a little longer.

During this period offer plenty of the following:

Water: Use a pure source, such as bottled, spring, filtered or distilled water. Do *not* use tap water, which may contain chlorine, fluoride and other unwholesome chemicals.

Vegetable juices: Use fresh, not tinned, juices only. Do not use juice more than 48 hours old. If you cannot give your pet fresh juice, offer it chopped or grated raw vegetables (especially greens and juicy ones) mixed in a blender with pure water and strained through a sieve. If you can't come up with either of these alternatives, then just feed water and the broth below.

Vegetable broth: Using the vegetables listed for the break-in period, make a soup stock by chopping and then simmering them 20 to 30 minutes. You may add a small amount of meat or a bone to flavour the stock, but no spices or salt. Pour off the liquid for the animal and save the solids for a soup or casserole for yourself.

If your animal is young or run down and seems to need a little extra energy you can occasionally offer it a bit of honey (a teaspoon or so).

If you notice that your pet is having strained or constipated bowel movements early in the liquid fast stage, you can help get things going by slowly (over 1 to 2 minutes) administering an enema (see the instructions in the section on special care, which follows). Though an enema usually is not needed during a short fast if the animal is in fairly good shape, a pet with a chronic disease or an acute infection will benefit from several enemas during the fast.

Breaking the fast: When it's time to end the fast, give your pet a simple diet for several days. This transition diet should last two or three days for every seven days the animal was on liquids. Offer water, juice, broth and a moderate amount of raw or steamed vegetables (the same group used before) plus a little raw milk or plain yogurt. After this period, begin adding other natural foods, starting with oatmeal or flaked barley cereal, milk, honey and figs or prunes. Then, after a day or two of that fare, offer some raw lean meat (or tofu or cottage cheese), some other grains or dairy products and some brewer's yeast until you have worked into the standard natural diet with supplements.

It is very important that you break the animal out of the fast gradually and that you avoid any temptation to feed commercial foods or highly processed titbits at this point, or else you may undo the beneficial effects of the fast and cause serious digestive upsets by overtaxing the system before it has fully reestablished peristalsis, contractions that aid in digestion.

Carried out properly, a fast of this sort can be a great boon for your animal's health. I hope that you understand the *spirit* of the fasting instructions and do not misinterpret them. I am *not* saying that you can just put a sick dog in the back porch with no food and a little water to drink! I am not suggesting neglect by any means, but rather an attitude of support, which includes doing the right things at the right time. Though outwardly the two approaches may appear similar, your inner intent and concern is the decisive factor that makes the difference.

Special care

Depending on the animal's condition and symptoms, you may need to provide other kinds of nursing care as well.

Enemas

Animals can benefit from the use of enemas in some conditions, particularly in fasting, constipation, irritation of the bowel (from bone fragments or the presence of toxic material like garbage or spoiled food in the digestive tract), dehydration or excessive vomiting.

Use pure water that is warm but not hot (test it on your wrist). A large volume is not needed, only about 2 tablespoons for a cat up to a pint for a large dog. Even a small amount of fluid will stimulate the bowel to empty itself. Add a few drops of freshly squeezed lemon juice to the water and administer the solution with a plastic or rubber syringe (or enema bag and nozzle) over a 2- to 3-minute period. First, lubricate the end of the syringe with Vaseline and, while someone else calmly and gently holds the animal standing on the ground or in a tub, insert the nozzle carefully into the rectum and with gentle, consistent pressure slowly fill the colon. If the solution does not flow in readily, it's probably because the syringe is up against a faecal mass, in which case you'll need to adjust the angle a bit. Administer an enema in this fashion once or twice a day for a couple of days. That's usually enough.

Dehydrated animals may simply retain the fluid. I have seen this many times. What happens is that the colon absorbs the fluid, which the body desperately needs. Thus, enemas are an excellent way to administer fluid therapy at home! Give them about every 4 hours under these circumstances, or until fluid is no longer retained.

If your animal has been doing a lot of vomiting and can't keep water in its stomach, an enema can introduce fluid as well as salts needed to replace those lost through vomiting. To the enema water add a pinch of sea salt plus a pinch of potassium chloride (KCl, a salt substitute sold in supermarkets especially for people on low-sodium diets). This same salt replacement fluid therapy will help a dog or cat with prolonged diarrhoea. Again, administer every 4 hours or until fluid is no longer retained.

Bathing and cleaning

In some cases an animal is so fouled by vomiting, diarrhoea or skin discharges that a cleansing bath seems needed. However, you should take on this task only at the end of an illness, when the animal is well on the way to recovery and the temperature is normal. Otherwise, rely upon the cleaning methods described below. Even then, be sure the animal does not become chilled. Dry him quickly by giving him a good towelling, followed by a warm sunbath or a blow-dry with the dryer set on low. The only exception to the rule of waiting is when the dog or cat, particularly a young one, is so heavily infested with fleas and lice that its strength is being sapped. A soapy bath that removes and drowns these parasites is then called for.

Care of the body openings: Very often, a disease will cause discharges from various body orifices, especially the nose, eyes, ears and anus. Sick animals, especially cats, are made miserable by accumulations they can not remove, which can irritate underlying tissues. A few simple cleansing techniques will offer great relief.

The nose: If plugs and secretions have formed, carefully clean the nose with a cloth or gauze saturated with warm water. Sometimes patience is needed in order to soften the material so that you can gradually remove it. Two or three short sessions may be better than one long one.

Once the nose is clean and dry, smear the area with one of the following: Vaseline; Vaseline mixed with powdered goldenseal root; almond oil; or calendulated oil (add 2 drops calendula tincture to an ounce of olive oil; mix well). Apply two or three times a day.

The eyes: To clean crusts and secretions from the eyes and eyelids, make up a soothing, non-irritating salt solution by mixing a rounded ½ teaspoon of sea salt in a pint of distilled water. Stir well and use this mixture to clean the eyes in the way described for the nose. After the eyes are clean, apply 1 drop in each eye of one of the following soothing treatments: olive oil (for mild irritation); castor oil (for more irritated and inflamed eyes); or cod-liver oil (for eyes that are dry or ulcerated).

Alternatively, bathe the eyes frequently with one of the following herbal infusions. First, make up a basic salt solution by stirring a rounded ½ teaspoon of sea salt to 1 pint of distilled water. Bring this basic solution to a boil. For an infusion of red eye-bright (*Euphrasia officinalis*) mix 1 heaped teaspoon of the herb to 1 cup of the basic salt solution. For an infusion of powdered goldenseal root, mix 1 teaspoon powder to 1 pint of the basic salt solution. Allow the brew to cool down before using. Use one of these solutions to clean and treat the eyes 3 times a day, or as needed. Make them up fresh daily.

The ears: If the ears contain much oily or waxy secretion, trickle about a teaspoon of olive oil into the ear hole, preferably using a dropper or squeeze bottle. First, pre-warm the oil in a cup or glass that is partly immersed in a sink or bowl of hot water. Firmly lift up the ear flap or tip. You may need someone to help you hold the animal's head in place, because if you let go or the animal pulls away before you finish the job you're going to get oil shaken all over you! Let the olive oil run down into the ear for a few seconds. Then, while still holding the ear flap, reach down with your other hand and massage the ear canal at the bottom of the ear. It feels like a firm plastic tube that you can compress as you massage. If you do it right, you'll hear a 'squishy' sound. This treatment loosens up and dissolves the lodged wax and helps bring it up. Use a tissue to remove any excess oil and material that work their way out. Don't use a cotton swab except around the opening.

If the ear is very red and inflamed, use calendulated oil (see the directions for cleaning the nose) instead of the olive oil. It's usually adequate to treat the ear this way once every day or two.

On the other hand, if the ear is painful when touched at the massage point but shows no discharge (in other words, your animal has an earache!), put a few drops of mullein oil (*Verbascum thapsus*) in each ear. Let it run down the ear canal and very gently massage it, if possible.

The anus: Often the anus will get very inflamed as a result of excessive diarrhoea, causing the surrounding tissue to get irritated and infected with bacteria. To keep this area clean during the diarrhoea stage of an illness, sponge it gently with a damp cloth (rubbing can further irritate it). When dry, apply some calendula ointment, a soothing preparation described under the list of remedies which follows. Apply 2 or 3 times a day or as needed.

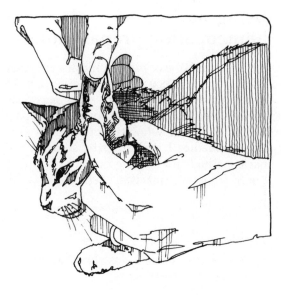

To remove a waxy or oily build-up in the ears, trickle a small amount of pre-warmed olive oil into the ear. Then massage the ear canal until you hear a squishing sound. Use a tissue to remove the material that has worked its way out.

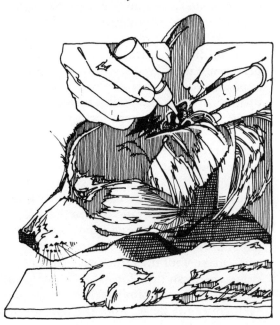

Using herbs and homeopathic preparations

In the description of the specific diseases that follows in the *Encyclopaedia* section I have noted many places where you may use various herbs and/or homeopathic preparations. For those who are not familiar with these remedies I will describe some of the basic methods for making them or obtaining them from pharmacists. Let's start with herbs.

Herbs

There are three basic forms of herbal preparations used in treatments.

The fresh herb: When possible, it is ideal to use an herb that has been freshly harvested right before use. In some areas of the country useful medicinal herbs can easily be located in waste ground, along roadsides (be careful of busy areas, because of car exhaust contamination), in country fields or woods or perhaps in your own herb garden. Those familiar with the identification of herbs can collect them as needed (or there are many useful books to help you identify them). Do not gather herbs from an area you think might have been sprayed with weedkiller or insecticide.

For optimal effectiveness, you should gather a herb when its essential oils are at their peak. In general, you should collect any aboveground parts in the morning, after the dew has dried but before the hot sun has evaporated some of the oils. Leaves are best collected at the time of year just before the plant is about to begin its flowering stage, whereas flowers are best taken just before they reach full bloom (they have much less value after that). If you're going for the *whole* aboveground part (leaves, stems and all), pick it just before the flowering stage. Roots

and rhizomes are best when they are collected in the autumn, when the sap returns to the ground and the leaves are just beginning to change their colour and the berries or seeds are mature.

Because most of us find it hard to use fresh herbs, the instructions in this book usually refer to the dried herb. Generally speaking, then, if you are able to find the fresh plant you should use about three times the volume (or weight) I have indicated for dried herbs in the listings.

Dried herbs: Most herbs you buy will be dried, cut or powdered, and sometimes put into gelatin capsules. Or you can dry your own fresh herbs for later use by washing them and then hanging them upside down in bunches in a well-ventilated, dry, shaded area. If you've gathered roots and barks, scrub them well and then chop them up and dry them on screening (you can use chicken wire or similar wire netting) in direct sunlight. Properly cured herbs retain most of their medicinal quality. Since these properties are destroyed by heat, sunlight and exposure to air, store the dried product in opaque, or brown, capped jars in a cool, dark place. They can be kept for a year.

Herbal tinctures: The best form of tincture is one made from the freshly collected plant. Herbal tinctures are a very potent form of medicine and must be used carefully at low dosages, as the specific instructions in the *Encyclopaedia* section will indicate. Tightly capped, they will keep for three years.

To make your own tincture, macerate and grind the fresh herb (or use a blender) with enough vodka or brandy (at least 80 proof) to well cover the herb. Store the mixture in a clean, tightly capped jar and shake it once or twice a day for two weeks. Then strain off the solids with a fine cloth or paper, collecting the liquid, which is your tincture. Store it in tightly capped glass bottles in a cool, dark area. (If you used dried herbs instead of fresh, use 2 ounces of the cut or powdered herb for each scant half pint of alcohol.)

Administering herbs to animals

The fresh or dried forms of herbs are used either as infusions, in which boiling water is added to the herb and steeped (like making tea), or else decoctions, in which the roots or barks are simmered in boiling water for periods ranging from a few minutes to an hour. Infusions should be steeped in a covered, non-metallic container like pottery or glass (to keep in the volatile substances). Decoctions should be simmered in an open non-metallic pan (to concentrate the product). Always use purified water (distilled or filtered) for these preparations. More specific instructions are given in the *Encyclopaedia* section.

An alternative way of using herbs is by mixing the powdered form with cold water to make a 'slurry', which is then given by mouth. Another, more expensive, route is to buy powdered herbs pre-packed in gelatin capsules (or buy empty capsules from a pharmacy and pack your own). One '00' capsule contains about ½ teaspoon of the powder.

Tinctures are administered either by placing a drop or two directly in the mouth or else adding the drops to a larger amount of water. To administer the diluted tincture, a herbal slurry or any other liquid medication, use the following technique.

How to give liquid medication

First, pry open the mouth by firmly grasping the animal's upper jaw with one hand and inserting your thumb and fingers in the gaps between the teeth. (For a cat or tiny dog, just

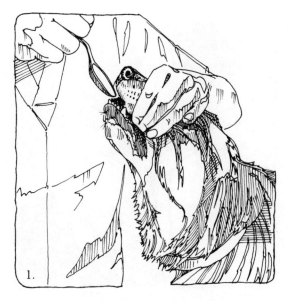

Giving liquid medication: Step 1: Hold the mouth open with your fingers while you pour the medicine between the front teeth.

Step 2: Tilt the head back and stroke the throat to make the animal swallow.

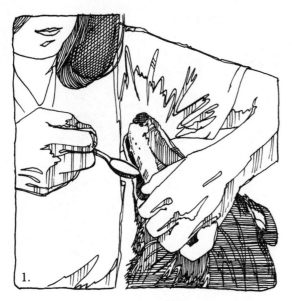

If your pet resists: Step 1: Pull out the lower lip, forming a pocket to hold the medicine.

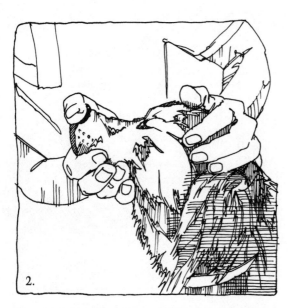

Step 2: Make the animal swallow by gently and briefly putting your thumb over the nostrils.

one finger is needed in addition to the thumb.) Most animals will then relax their mouths slightly so that you can pour the liquid with a spoon or dropper between the front teeth. Tilt the head back when you do this so that the liquid will run down to the throat.

As an alternative method, use one hand to pull out the lower lip to make a little pouch, and, keeping the head tilted back, pour the liquid into it with the other hand.

In either instance, if the liquid doesn't go in, it's because the teeth are clenched too tightly. If so, pry them open slightly with your finger. If your animal backs away, put it in a corner so it can't move away from you during the process, or else get someone to help hold it. For a cat you may need someone to gently but firmly hold its feet, or you can do the job alone by wrapping it quickly and snugly in a towel. Be gentle and positive so your animal doesn't have reason to feel afraid and put up a struggle.

After the medicine is in, induce swallowing by gently holding the mouth closed and massaging the throat. Or you can briefly put your thumb over the nostrils to achieve the same purpose. When the animal has swallowed, the tongue will usually come out between the front teeth.

How to give pills and capsules

To give most solid medications like herbal capsules or vitamin pills, open the mouth by grasping around the upper jaw, as described for liquids. Hold the capsule or pill between your thumb and the first finger or else between the first and second fingers. Use the remaining fingers to press down the lower front teeth and thus pry the jaw open.

Insert the medication into the throat, pushing it as far back as you can. Then induce swallowing as described above.

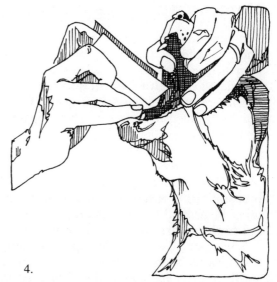

Giving pills and powders: Pry the mouth open (1), place the pill on the back of the tongue (2) and quickly push it as far back into the throat as you can (3). Then, hold the muzzle shut and massage the throat to induce swallowing. For powders and crushed pills (4), slide the contents from a folded paper directly on to the tongue.

To give a homeopathic or tissue salt tablet, use a slightly different method. Make a crisp fold in a small clean sheet of paper. Pour the tablet(s) from the bottle on to the open fold. Crush the pill(s) between the paper to a powder (they're soft). With a word of encouragement, invite your animal to lick it off the paper (it tastes sweet). If he is not interested, use the same holding and prying technique described for other pills and pour the powder from the paper on to the animal's tongue. This method both eliminates the possibility of your pet spitting the medicine out and also keeps it from being contaminated.

Alternatively, give the homeopathic tablet whole, using the method described for other pills.

Homeopathic preparation

The remedies that I will mention in the *Encyclopaedia* section either can be ordered by mail (see pages 269–70) or, in some cases, purchased in health food stores. The latter applies mostly to the tissue salts (12 in number), a special subgroup of homeopathic remedies made from the basic mineral salts found in the body, such as sodium phosphate (*Natrum phosphoricum*) or potassium sulphate (*Kali sulphuricum*). Since this group of preparations is easier to obtain than many other homeopathic preparations, I've referred to them fairly often for treatment.

There are distinct advantages to using homeopathic drops or tablets. Because only a small number are given, they are easy to administer.

You will notice that references to the strength of the medication use such terms as 3X or 6X. These terms are based on the decimal system. Thus, a 1X potency is what is made by diluting one part of a tincture of the medicinal substance in nine parts of alcohol.

The mixture is then shaken vigorously to help to transfer the special properties of the substance to the liquid (potentization). (See the box *How Homeopathic Medications Are Prepared* in chapter 14.) This process can be repeated many times to produce high-potency remedies that should be used only by skilled homeopathic doctors. The action of these special preparations seems to be enhanced, so that their effect is actually greater than that of the starting herb or tincture. Yet they are free of discomforting side effects because such a small amount is used, which is one of the reasons I like to use them.

Dilutions made from herbs and similar substances are often then added to preformed tablets made of a milk sugar base for greater ease of administration. Thus the tablets of different preparations are often indistinguishable in appearance. In the case of certain substances that can't be dissolved in alcohol (such as metals and the tissue mineral salts), dilutions are made directly into powdered milk sugar. Special machines grind the substance and the milk sugar powder together for a couple of hours to produce the 1X level. A further dilution of 1X to nine parts of milk powder produces the 2X and so on, as for the liquid method.

A home remedy kit

Don't wait until your animal needs treatment to track down basic supplies. Like the Boy Scouts, be prepared. Preparations can be ordered by post from the suppliers listed on pages 269 and 270. Others can be obtained at your local health food store, herb shop or even grocer's. And of course you can grow or collect many herbs yourself. But in all cases, it's best to have a group of commonly useful substances on hand. Most are really quite inexpensive. Here are those that I would recommend, followed by indications for the most likely sources.

Tissue salts: Ferr. phos. (*Ferrum phosphoricum*) 6X for fever, inflammations; Kali. phos (*Kali phosphoricum*) for nervousness, sleeplessness; *Silicea* 6X to promote discharge from wounds, and abscesses; Nat. phos. (*Natrum phosphoricum*) 6X for tendency to have worms; Nat. mur. (*Natrum muriaticum*) 6X for itchy greasy skin – all found in most health food shops, or available by post from homeopathic pharmacies (see page 269).

Homeopathic remedies: *Arnica* 6X for injuries, bruises, pain relief; *Ledum* 6X for animal and insect bites; *Nux vomica* 3X for indigestion, constipation; *Ipecac* 3X for nausea and vomiting; *Podophyllum* 3X for diarrhoea; calendula tincture, for wounds and haemorrhages; calendula-hypericum ointment for wounds – all available by post from homeopathic pharmacies (see page 269). The ingredients for calendula-hypericum ointment can be purchased separately.

Goldenseal root powder or tincture, from a herb or health food shop.

Household supplies: olive oil, garlic, lemons.

Of course, if the case calls for it, you'll need other substances, too. See the *Encyclopaedia* to find out what preparations are necessary to treat any specific disease.

PART TWO

The Encyclopaedia of Common Pet Ailments and Their Treatments

How to Use the Encyclopaedia

Many health problems common to dogs and cats are discussed in this section, with specific treatments suggested. Some can be used in conjunction with professional treatment, if necessary. Homeopathic medicines, however, should not be used with drugs. If possible, work with a co-operative, holistically oriented vet.

If you have read the first part of the book, you already know that the road to health requires a total approach. Any causative factors in the lifestyle, environment or diet must be understood and changed so that there are no external obstacles to your animal's recovery. Then, as much as possible, select from the treatment choices the one that best fits your pet's unique situation and most accurately corresponds to its symptom complex. To do so requires careful observation on your part.

I've tried to suggest remedies that are easily obtained and safe for home use.

Those who are interested in learning more about the holistic approach will profit greatly from reading some of the relevant books recommended on page 271. Naturally, the more you understand the action of particular herbs or other remedies, the more successfully you will be able to use them.

Finding a particular disease: You may have to look under a larger grouping. For example, canine distemper, chorea (a common after-effect of distemper) and feline panleucopenia (often called feline distemper) are all listed together under 'Distemper'. Many conditions are grouped according to the body part or organ they affect, such as 'Stomach Problems', 'Skin Problems' or 'Ear Problems'. The cross-references should help to lead you to the right category with a minimum of difficulty.

Assessing the results: Except in some acute conditions that may clear up rapidly, healing is a process that takes time. It took time for the body to get out of balance and it takes time to restore it. Of course, if we give a suppressive drug, such as cortisone or a painkiller, we may see some rapid relief but not a true cure. Take away the drug and, sooner or later, the symptoms are likely to return, often worse than before. But since our aim is to address the underlying weakness, we must learn to recognize the progressive stages of healing. Then, as symptoms change, we can tell whether the animal is getting better or worse, and can thus tell if our approach really is helping.

For instance, many natural therapies include the notion of the 'healing crisis', a brief aggravation of symptoms that occurs just before the patient really starts to recover. Without understanding the significance of this favourable sign, one might jump to the conclusion that things are getting worse and therefore load the body down with a host of heavy-duty drugs that could interfere with the cure.

Many physicians and healers have noticed certain specific symptom patterns the body expresses in its attempt to cope with health imbalances. Homeopaths have formalized it as 'Hering's Law of Cure'. Here is the way I understand the process:

There is an underlying intelligence in the body that corrects health disturbances. To do so it utilizes a few basic strategies to limit the problem and protect the most vital and governing aspects of the organism. Thus it attempts to: (1) keep disturbances from spreading (for instance, by localizing the problem with inflammation and thickening of tissue); (2) keep the responses on the surface of the body rather than within vital organs; (3) keep responses around the limbs, rather than on the trunk; (4) keep responses at the lower end of the body, away from the head, and therefore the brain and sensory organs; and (5) keep the problem at the physical level rather than the emotional or mental level, which would interfere more seriously with the overall functioning of an individual.

Do you understand the pattern? Common sense tells us that a disease is taking a wrong turn if it starts to spread or begins to involve deep-seated organs. The more the condition disturbs the functioning of parts of the body that are most crucial to its survival and governing capacities, the worse it is.

Recognizing *improvement* requires careful reading of more subtle indications. It is a favourable sign, for instance, if an animal with a chronic degenerative disease affecting vital organs begins to develop a bit of a skin rash or discharge. Overall improvement takes place and generally the surface problem will pass away before long.

By studying the strategy outlined above you can tell if the *whole individual* that is your

animal is actually getting better or worse. Let's say your dog has a tendency to get fungus infections around the feet and lower legs. After months of strenuous treatment, the feet have cleared up but now little bald patches and irritation are appearing on the skin of the abdomen and between the front legs (on the trunk and nearer the head). Though the problem may be given a different diagnosis, the original problem has just been suppressed in that the progression of symptoms has moved from the periphery closer to the vital parts of the body.

A more subtle indication of a worsening condition is this: your dog's chronically inflamed ears have finally cleared up after lots of treatment and surgery. But now, several weeks later, you notice he isn't as friendly as he used to be. He prefers to go off by himself and may even growl or bite. The seat of the disturbance has moved inward, from the physical to the *emotional* level. Though various drugs could be tried as a means to control the personality changes, the problem will only get worse. He may become easier to live with (friendly in a passive way) but he may become affected now at the *mental* level, perhaps acting sluggish and disoriented. He may have spells of confusion. The disturbance now has interfered with his core processes of information organizing and orientation. Though this may sound like a far-fetched example, I assure you it is not. Cases like this happen all too often!

If the dog had been effectively treated in a *curative* way at the point when his problem became emotional, you probably would have seen a return of a *physical* symptom – perhaps a brief re-emergence of the ear inflammation – after his moods improved. Then the ear or other surface problem might be treated in a non-suppressive manner if so indicated. (It might even go away on its own, since the direction of cure has been established.)

Let's say you have a cat who had an

Parts of a dog

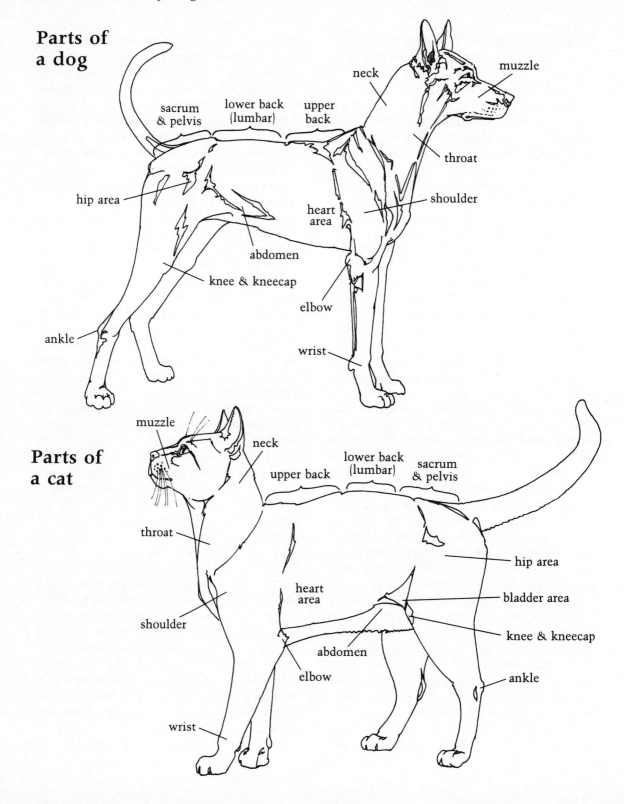

neck

muzzle

sacrum & pelvis

lower back (lumbar)

upper back

throat

hip area

shoulder

heart area

abdomen

knee & kneecap

elbow

ankle

wrist

Parts of a cat

muzzle

neck

upper back

lower back (lumbar)

sacrum & pelvis

throat

hip area

heart area

bladder area

shoulder

abdomen

knee & kneecap

elbow

ankle

wrist

abscess, and *also* was showing emotional signs – depression and lethargy. However, it has recently begun running about and being frisky. Even though there may still be a discharge from the abscess, the psychological improvement is a very favourable sign and it should be followed by physical healing.

Here's another example. The mange on your dog's face has cleared up, but now new spots appear on his rear legs. Do you despair? No! Because the condition is moving away from the head and toward the rear, you have it 'on the run'; your treatment is working.

In general, these signs during therapy also indicate good progress:

- An increase in energy and overall playfulness
- A calm, good-natured manner
- Self-grooming (especially true of cats)
- A return of appetite
- Normal bowel movements and urination
- Sound and restful sleep

Let's also look carefully at some of the *methods* the body uses to heal itself. Generally, when a disease is being eliminated you will see signs of discharge. It signals that build-ups of toxic materials are leaving the body. The most common ways this elimination occurs are through: (1) the formation of a pus-pocket and drainage out of the body; (2) the development of skin eruptions (a very common route); (3) the urine, which may become dark or strong-smelling; (4)

the colon, in the form of dark, smelly faeces or diarrhoea; and (5) vomiting (especially during acute conditions).

Therefore, when using the holistic methods discussed in this book you will see one or more of these forms of discharge (usually to a mild degree) – particularly if the problem is well established in the body.

For example, I saw a dog that had just recovered from a severe attack of distemper. His owner had used herbs and fasting with satisfying success. However, now the animal was covered with red, itchy skin that oozed sticky fluid – clearly a discharge phenomenon. A few more days of supportive treatments were followed by full recovery. Once the recovery is complete, an animal will be much stronger and better able to withstand future diseases.

Let's summarize the ways to evaluate progress. Supportive and non-suppressive therapies both exhibit two processes: (1) a movement of symptoms in a favourable direction and (2) some form of discharge. If you see these signs, chances are very strong that the animal is getting better, irrespective of which form of therapy you are using.

I should add as a cautionary note that treatment with some drugs, particularly with cortisone, can create a *false* sense of well-being that disappears when the drug is discontinued. So keep in mind that the response we are looking for is the one that comes *from* the animal, *assisted by* the treatment. Such a response will lead to recovery and real healing, not a dependence on a drug.

Common Pet Ailments and Their Treatments

ABSCESSES

Abscesses, which are a common complication of puncture wounds from fights, plague cats much more than dogs. That's because their needle-like teeth and claws inflict small but deep wounds. Feline skin seals over very quickly, trapping inside bacteria, hair or other contaminated material. Cat abscesses usually occur around the head, front legs and base of the tail.

In dogs, abscesses are often the result of plant awns that get trapped in the hair and work their way through the skin (especially between the toes, around the ears and between the hind legs). An abscess that keeps on draining and does not heal up (a fistula) usually indicates the presence of a foreign object somewhere in the tissue, sometimes several inches from the place of drainage.

Prevention and Treatment
Cats

I have had several very healthy, well-fed cats that seldom, if ever, developed abscesses after injuries. My impression is that excellent nutrition is the best preventive. Neutering also reduces the problem or else eliminates it altogether. The close proximity of several male cats leads to continual warfare as each animal tries to establish a territory and compete for females. In such circumstances, fights and resultant abscesses are a continuous problem.

In an early case, where there is swelling, pain and a raised temperature (locally or of the whole body), restrict solid food and fast the cat for 24 hours on liquids only – meat and vegetable broth and spring water. Give 250 milligrams of vitamin C 3 times a day for 3 days to promote the activity of the animal's immune system. In addition, choose the *one* remedy from the following list that best fits:

Tissue Salt – *Ferrum phosphoricum* (Ferr. phos.) 3X: Give 1 tablet every 2 hours until pain and heat are gone. Most useful for the 'average' situation, which is not severe and where pain and heat are predominant. Best given early.

Homeopathic – *Ledum* 3X (Labrador tea): Give 1 tablet every 2 hours the first day, then 3 times a day for 2 more days. Useful early on, especially where there is not much inflammation around the puncture wound itself.

Herbal or Homeopathic – *Echinacea angustifolia* (purple cone flower): Use the tincture. Give it by mouth, 1 drop every 2 hours until there is improvement. Indicated for the animal that is in poor condition, thin, develops abscesses easily (a recurring problem) and is very weak. It functions primarily to purify the system, especially the blood, and also restores health to the skin.

Later stages of the condition are marked by pus formation. The abscess may feel like a water balloon under the skin, or, if open, be draining pus.

Tissue Salt – *Silicea* 6X: Give 1 tablet every 3 hours until the wound is obviously healing and no longer draining. Prevent the opening from closing prematurely by cleaning away any discharge or scab once or twice a day with hydrogen peroxide (or use calendula lotion as described below).

In all cases, relief and improvement will follow the application of very warm calendula tincture (diluted $\frac{1}{4}$ teaspoon to a cup of distilled or spring water). Sponge on repeatedly over a container to catch run-off (or apply a washcloth saturated with the solution) twice a day as needed.

Treatment
Dogs

If the abscess is the result of an animal bite, use the treatment indicated for cats. Adjust the amount of vitamin C to the size of the dog. Three times a day give about 250 milligrams (small dog), 500 milligrams (medium dog), or 1,000 milligrams (large dog).

However, if the abscess has been caused by plant material, splinters or other embedded foreign matter, the discharge will not cease permanently until the object is eliminated. Since the tissues cannot 'digest' it, it must either be expelled or removed surgically.

The natural 'expelling process' can be aided by using the tissue salt *Silicea* 6X. Give 1 or 2 tablets 3 times a day. Also, apply hot compresses of a solution made up of 2 of the *Silicea* tablets dissolved in spring water (once a day for 5 to 10 minutes should do). If the

affected area is a foot, then the whole foot can be soaked in a jar of the hot solution.

In natural healing the tendency is for drainage of pus of fluid to occur at a point *lower* than the site of the foreign body (so that gravity will help out). Therefore, apply the poultice not only at the opening but also several inches higher so you cover the probable location of the foreign body. The hot solution will promote the flow of blood into the affected area and keep the process moving. When enough pus has formed around the foreign body to loosen it, it may flow out, right along with the pus. At that point, drainage will stop.

Note: Because of the structure of plant awns, they tend to migrate deeply into the tissues. If you don't get results within a short time you will probably need to have the culprit tracked down surgically.

ACCIDENTS
See the *Emergency Guide*

AGGRESSION
See 'Behaviour Problems'

ALLERGIES

An allergy is regarded as an abnormally intense reaction to some substance, often something not obviously harmful to the body (like wheat or plant pollen). I am afraid that in many cases the diagnosis 'allergy' has become something of a catch-all term to obscure our ignorance. To say that my animal has an extraordinarily severe reaction to flea bites, for instance, doesn't really explain very much, nor does it tell me why this apparent abnormal sensitivity has developed.

I view the allergic condition as one more

symptom, like any other symptom, that is indicative of a disturbance in the body's order. Also, I see no reason why this symptom can't be eliminated like any other. In my own approach, I generally have ignored the significance of the allergy diagnosis in regard to flea bites, for example, and have seen this hypersensitivity clear up along with the rest of the skin problem under treatment.

However, many researchers have implicated allergic conditions (whether secondary to other problems or not) as contributors to a variety of disturbances, including gastroenteritis, dermatitis, chronic bronchitis, hepatitis, pancreatitis, nephritis, epilepsy and personality changes. Some research suggests that about a third of all allergies are caused by foods.

Treatment

If you suspect your animal has a food allergy, try the diet below, which omits the common allergens implicated in both animal and human conditions: beef, wheat, milk, eggs, nuts, fruits, tomatoes, carrots, yeast and various spices and additives. If the problem clears up during the diet, then slowly reintroduce the omitted foods one at a time to find out which one or ones are causing the problem.

To give this diet an adequate chance, keep your animal on it for at least two months. If your pet's condition has not improved by then, the cause of its problem may not be an allergy. Or there is still an offending substance in the food. In most cases it is the meat. Therefore, try the vegetarian diet I suggested in chapter 5. There are also commercial pet foods used with success in many food-aggravated conditions considered to be allergies.

Realize that only some of the offending substances may be in the food. Other possible sources are chemicals used in cleaning floors or carpets, synthetic carpets, plastic food

---

CAT ALLERGY
DIET

⅓ cup lamb, mutton, or chicken

4 ounces tofu

¼ cup cooked brown rice, buckwheat, millet or oats

2 tablespoons grated or chopped vegetables

daily supplements as recommended (but substitute a B complex tablet for the yeast)

Simply combine the ingredients and serve.

Yield: about 1 ⅓ cups

DOG ALLERGY
DIET

½ cup lamb, mutton or chicken

6 ounces tofu

1 ½ cups cooked brown rice, buckwheat, millet or oats

¼ cup grated or chopped vegetables

daily supplements as recommended (but substitute a B complex tablet for the yeast)

Simply combine the ingredients and serve.

Yield: about 3 cups

bowls, vaccinations, certain plants or grasses, regularly administered drugs or flea chemicals and, of course, fleas.

Determining exactly what substances are causing an allergic reaction can be difficult. I find it easiest to put the animal on a natural diet (which by itself clears up a lot of problems) and to try to eradicate the allergic tendency through appropriate holistic therapy. Most of you will not have this option, however. Instead, I suggest you carefully follow the diet advice given here and in chapter 3 and do what you can to eliminate toxic and possibly offending substances. Give special attention to chapter 7 and secondarily to chapters 8 and 10.

Vitamin C when given in high doses acts like a natural antihistamine, and the B complex is also very useful. Be sure to include these as regular dietary supplements. Following this overall plan, you will find the condition much easier to control with drugs (at lower dosages) if they are still needed.

ANAL GLAND PROBLEMS

Difficulties with the anal glands are primarily canine problems. Dogs have a pair of small scent glands on either side of the anus, under the tail. Similar in structure to the scent gland of the skunk, they contain a strong-smelling material which is apparently used to mark territory or to express extreme fear.

Problems manifest either as *abscesses* that form within the glands themselves or as what is called *impaction*, in which the glands become torpid and overfull of secretion. In the latter case the dog will often 'slide' along the floor or ground in an attempt to empty these glands, which have exceeded their normal capacity. My sense is that the follow-ing factors play a major role in the development of such problems:

- Frustration in trying to establish a territory, perhaps from being crowded with other animals or from having inadequate space for exercise and exploration
- Constipation or infrequent bowel movements, especially as a result of not being frequently allowed outside. Many an indoor animal will hold its urine or faeces to the very limit rather than soil the house and displease its people
- Toxicity due to poor food and inadequate exercise. In such a case, a disorder of the skin or ears frequently occurs as well

Prevention

Make sure your animal has adequate exercise, the opportunity to go outside and have frequent bowel movements, and psychological 'space'. Good nutrition is important also, as it is in most conditions. Especially useful would be those nutrients that help promote healthy skin; zinc, the B complex, vitamin A, lecithin and unsaturated vegetable oil. Olive oil is a good source of unsaturated fatty acids and has the advantage of being a slight laxative by promoting muscular contraction of the bowels.

ANAL GLAND ABSCESS

Treatment

Treat as specified under 'Abscesses' (for cats), using *Ferrum phosphoricum* (Ferr. phos.) 3X during the acute (early) inflammatory stage and following with *Silicea* 6X to promote the discharge of pus and encourage healing. Also apply warm or hot calendula solution (see 'Abscesses') twice a day for at least 5 minutes each time. Usually the calendula treatment will run about 3 days, though a longer period is permissible if necessary.

IMPACTED ANAL GLANDS

Treatment

Since this condition is associated with sluggishness of the tissue and often with toxicity and obesity as well (see 'Weight Problems'), regular vigorous exercise is an important part of the treatment. Adding vegetables, bran and olive oil to the food will help to regulate the intestines and encourage bulky bowel movements. Copious evacuation will stimulate the natural emptying of the glands.

In addition, a hot poultice of either calendula solution or an infusion of red clover blossoms will stimulate the glands and soften their contents. Immediately after the application, use gentle pressure with a 'milking' action to help to empty them manually. I look at the manual emptying as a temporary measure, not something to do continually. It's much better (I'm sure you would agree!) if the glands empty naturally.

A useful adjunct to the above measures is to give the tissue salt *Calcarea phosphorica* (Calc. phos.) 6X (1 tablet 3 times a day for 10 days) followed by *Natrum muriaticum* (Nat. mur.) 6X (1 tablet 3 times a day for 10 days).

ANAEMIA

Anaemia is often caused by blood loss from either wounds or parasites like fleas and worms. The problem is characterized by white gums and a fast pulse. Occasionally it indicates more serious diseases like leukaemia or a toxicity resulting from drug treatment. However, here we'll consider only the more common and simple blood loss anaemia, with a view toward promoting the growth of new red blood cells.

Treatment

A diet rich in iron, protein and vitamin B_{12} is important. These foods will be particularly helpful:

- Beef liver (for protein, B complex, B_{12} and iron)
- Brewer's yeast supplemented with B_{12} (same benefits as liver)
- Green vegetables (for iron and other minerals)
- Kelp powder (for iodine and other trace minerals)
- Vitamin C – 500 to 2,000 milligrams a day, depending on the animal's size (promotes the absorption of iron)

In addition to the nutritional supports, give daily:

Tissue Salt – *Calcarea phosphorica* (Calc. phos.) 6X: 1 tablet 3 times a day for 2 weeks, to serve as a tonic and to stimulate the formation of new blood cells.

Tissue Salt – *Natrum muriaticum* (Nat. mur.) 6X: 1 tablet 3 times a day for 3 weeks, to help an animal that is depressed and low in energy, or constipated.

Generally, select one or the other of these two tissue salts. But if both seem indicated because the animal is pretty run down, then alternate them, giving one tablet and then the other, treating every 4 hours.

If the anaemia is caused by parasites, of course these must also be controlled (see

'Skin Parasites' or 'Worms'). In such a case use the nutritional advice given for anaemia, but instead of using the tissue salts suggested, follow the nutritional and specific treatment guidelines under either 'Skin Parasites' or 'Worms'. (But *do not* use the fasting programme for an anaemic animal.)

Fleas are best controlled (most safely) by frequent bathing with a non-toxic soap, use of the lemon skin tonic described under 'Bathing your pet' on page 80 of chapter 7 and control of fleas in the environment. the animal is stronger you can use more strenuous flea control methods if required, but I do discourage the use of poisonous chemicals, because they are not really effective in a long-term way and are very toxic to both human and animal.

Sometimes very young kittens or puppies will become so besieged by fleas that they are almost drained of their blood. In such cases, it is essential not to use flea powders or sprays, even though the temptation is great. The young animals are much too small and weak to handle such an assault. Instead, bathe them often and use the lemon rinse. To prevent them from getting chilled, dry them thoroughly afterward with a dryer set on low or else in the warm sun. Keep them warm and quiet in general and, if the weather allows, give them some fresh air and sunlight. Feed only natural foods – no commercial fare – and follow the treatment programme as suggested. You will be amazed at how quickly these little creatures can respond!

ARTHRITIS

Arthritis is much more common in dogs than in cats and usually takes one of several forms.

Hip dysplasia: a malformation of the hip sockets that allows excessive movement in the joint, causing chronic inflammation and

thus further breakdown and the deposition of calcium. Common to larger breeds (see 'Hip Dysplasia').

Dislocation of the kneecap: a malformation of the leg bones such that the kneecap is repeatedly pulled out of position, thus slipping back and forth and causing continuous low-grade inflammation. A condition seen in small breeds that owes much to poor breeding and low-quality food.

Degeneration of the shoulder joint: the breakdown of cartilage in this joint, leading to inflammation and pain on movement. A condition seen most in medium to large breeds.

Arthritis of the elbow: a condition that is caused by improper bone formation and is considered to be hereditary. It is generally seen in Alsatians. I believe that nutrition is a more significant factor.

Swelling and pain in the leg joints: a condition seen in young dogs (a few months of age) of the large breeds that is apparently due to inadequate formation of vitamin C and is the result of poor nutrition and heredity.

Prevention

Most of these conditions could be prevented if the female were properly fed throughout her pregnancy. The time of growth in the uterus is critical in terms of the formation of structure and essential tissues. Inadequate nutrition is most detrimental at this time (see 'Pregnancy, Birth and Care of Newborns'). Avoiding commercial foods and feeding a natural, wholesome diet is the best and only real preventive.

In addition, the regular use of vitamin C will minimize or prevent most of these problems. Depending on the size of the animal and its age, give 250 to 2,000 milligrams a day. For instance, a small puppy would get 250 milligrams, a large puppy (like an Alsatian) 500 milligrams. As the dog matures, increase the dose from 500 to 1,000 milligrams for most sizes and perhaps up to 2,000 milligrams for a giant breed like the Great Dane or Saint Bernard.

Prevention is very important in arthritic conditions, because once the joints are distorted, the damage has been done.

Treatment

Assuming you are feeding a natural diet (otherwise the suggestions that follow will not be effective), you can do several things to minimize your animal's discomfort.

Use as little meat and yeast as possible. Emphasize the vegetarian diet in chapter 5 and substitute a B complex tablet for brewer's yeast in the supplement programme. Use a complete, natural B complex made for human use, giving about 10 milligrams of the major B vitamins for smaller animals and about 20 milligrams for larger ones. This dietary restriction is designed to minimize the production of uric acid and urea, waste products that may aggravate an established condition. Since you have reduced the volume of the *Dog Powder Mix* supplement by omitting yeast, allow about half of the daily quantities recommended in chapter 3 for various sizes of dogs. Be sure to include the recommended amounts of bone meal (or even increase them somewhat), as calcium is very important for arthritic conditions.

In addition to the regular supplements, add vitamin C to the diet, using 500 to 3,000 milligrams a day, depending on the animal's size. It's better to divide the daily amount and give it twice a day. Other vitamins and supplements that are especially important are the vitamin E and cod-liver oil (for A and D) already covered in the normal feeding programme.

Be sure to include raw grated vegetables in the diet, particularly carrots, beets and celery.

In addition to these nutritional guidelines you may find one of the following remedies to be helpful. Choose the one which best fits your situation.

Herbal – alfalfa (*Medicago sativa*): Indicated for the thin, nervous animal with a tendency toward digestive problems as well as arthritis. Depending on its size, add 1 teaspoon to 3 tablespoons of ground or dry-blended alfalfa to the daily ration. Or you can administer alfalfa as a tea, which can be made by steeping 1 to 2 tablespoons of the herb in a cup of water for 20 minutes. A third choice is to give your pet 2 to 6 alfalfa tablets a day.

Herbal – garlic (*Allium sativum*): Garlic is suited for the overweight animal with hip pain and is especially useful for one that has been on a high-meat diet. Include fresh grated garlic with each meal, using $\frac{1}{2}$ to 3 cloves, depending on the body size.

Homeopathic – *Rhus toxicodendron* (Rhus tox.) 6X (poison ivy): Do not use the herbal form, of course, but the safe homeopathic preparation, which you buy from chemists in tablet form (see page 269). Rhus tox. is indicated for a dog or cat with chronic arthritis, pain or stiffness which is most apparent after a long rest (like overnight). The animal shows discomfort or stiffness when first beginning to move, but after a few minutes it seems to loosen up and feel better. If the pet also has a tendency toward red, swollen, itchy skin, Rhus tox. will work on both problems (see 'Skin Problems').

Give 1 tablet twice a day for 10 to 14 days. As soon as the condition improves, stop the treatment at once. Give another tablet only if and when any symptoms return. This is important. It's not that the dilute preparation is toxic, but rather that the method works better if done this way.

Homeopathic – *Bryonia alba* 6X: This is

another herb that is powerful in its crude state but nicely tamed by homeopathic preparation. Order the tablets and give 1 every night and every morning for a week or two. As with the *Rhus toxicodendron* (Rhus tox.), if improvement occurs, cease treatment, thereafter giving 1 tablet at a time as symptoms demand it.

Bryonia (white bryony) is best suited for the animal with lameness of one or more legs which (in contrast to *Rhus toxicodendron*) does *not* get better with exercise. Rather, the animal is reluctant to move. If it does, the condition tends to get worse. It may not show much obvious pain and often such an animal is young rather than old.

Tissue Salts – *Natrum phosphoricum* (Nat. phos.) 6X and *Natrum sulphuricum* (Nat. sulph.) 6X: These are useful for a mild condition without any clear symptoms that indicate use of the above remedies. They will help to normalize the blood acidity and strengthen the liver function and elimination, especially in those animals that have been overfed with rich or fatty foods. Give 1 tablet of each (used in combination) 3 times a day for several weeks.

BEHAVIOUR PROBLEMS
See also chapters 9, 10 and 11

Behavioural abnormalities are often complex and difficult to eradicate, but often you can help considerably. One problem is that poor breeding, especially of pure-bred dogs, has fostered the development of many such disturbances, including viciousness, epilepsy, repetitive habits and other signs of nervous system imbalances (chapter 9). It is also my impression that many behaviour problems have their roots in one or more of the following: poor nutrition and associated toxicity; inadequate exercise; insufficient psychological stimulation and attention; and the influence of the owner's personality patterns, expectations or conditioning (chapters 10 and 11). For instance, family conflict, excessive attachment to a pet as an attempt to escape loneliness or the desire to have an aggressive animal in order to feel safer from other people can all have a strong adverse influence on an animal's personality.

Treatment

In this brief discussion we'll focus on general measures that can be very helpful and in some cases may be sufficient to treat the disturbance, provided that the contributing environmental factors are understood and eliminated. Start with nutrition.

Take the animal off commercial food, if you have not already done so. Any food that contains artificial preservatives, colouring agents or other additives may harbour chemicals that can irritate the brain tissue and cause abnormal responses.

Provide a complete vitamin supplement, one that is especially rich in the B complex. I would use a multivitamin tablet with the major B vitamins at the 20- to 50-milligram level for a trial period of at least 2 months. If you already are using the natural supplements I recommend, particularly the cod-liver oil, then use a B complex tablet without any vitamin A or D in it (to avoid overdose of these vitamins).

If you suspect a build-up of toxic material, use the following supplements to help eliminate and counteract the effect of substances that may be irritating the brain cells: zinc (5 to 30 milligrams a day, depending on the animal's size); vitamin C (250 to 2,000 milligrams a day); lecithin (1 teaspoon to 1 tablespoon of granules in the food daily); and calcium (as already provided in the bone meal supplement described in chapter 3). Also useful is algin (sodium alginate), a natural substance which removes heavy metals like lead from the body. Depending on the animal's size, use from one-quarter of the full dose to the full amount recommended on the label for human adults. Adding ½ to 2 teaspoons of ground sesame or sunflower seeds to the food will increase both calcium and magnesium content.

The zinc and the vitamin C work together as a team to eliminate toxic heavy metals, while lecithin protects the nerve cells against irritation. This group as a whole helps to detoxify the body and to protect the nerves.

Minimize exposure to toxic substances. Make sure the animal is protected from accidental poisoning by various household chemicals. Just as important, minimize its exposure to such pollutants as cigarette smoke, car exhaust and antiflea chemicals (which affect the nervous system).

In addition to these measures, one or more of the following may be useful:

Tissue Salts – *Calcarea sulphurica* (Calc. sulph.) 3X and *Natrum sulphuricum* (Nat. sulph.) 3X: Indicated for the animal thought to be toxic from poor-quality food or exposure to environmental pollutants. Give 1 or 2 tablets of each substance twice a day for several weeks.

Tissue Salt – *Kali phosphoricum* (Kali phos.) 6X: Indicated for the hyperactive, over-sensitive animal whose problem seems to stem from psychological or hereditary factors rather than toxic exposures.

Directions for tissue salts: Use either the first two salts together *or* the Kali phos. by deciding which best fits your situation. Or you could use the Kali phos. *after* the programme of cleansing with the other two remedies.

Alternatively, if you find it more convenient or preferable to use herbs instead of the tissue salts, select one of the following herbs that best fits your animal's problem.

Herbal – common oat (*Avena sativa*): Oats are well suited as a general nerve tonic and are particularly useful where nerve weakness or irritability may have appeared after other stressful diseases. This remedy is good for animals that have received a lot of drugs, are old or have a tendency to epilepsy. It is also helpful for the animal with weak legs, muscle twitching, or a trembling associated with weakness. All of this, of course will be *in addition to* any particular behaviour problems exhibited (this applies to all of the herbs to be described).

Though feeding rolled oats as a cooked grain in the diet is helpful, a more potent preparation is the tincture. You can order this as the tincture of *Avena sativa* from a homeopathic supplier (see page 269) or, if you have access to a field of oats, you can make your own. Gather some fresh, ripe grain and straw and make it according to the tincture directions in chapter 15. In either case, administer the tincture twice daily in these quantities: 1 to 3 drops for a cat or small dog; 2 to 4 drops for a medium-small dog; 4 to 6 drops for a medium dog; 6 to 8 drops for a large one; 10 drops for a giant-sized one.

Herbal – blue vervain (*Verbena hastata*): vervain is suited for animals that are depressed and have weak nervous systems. It's also for those with irritated nerves and muscle spasms and is especially appropriate for those whose abnormal behaviour is associated with epilepsy; in such cases it will strengthen the brain function.

To use vervain, pour a cup of boiling water over 2 teaspoons of the rootstock (chopped or powdered), letting it steep until cold. Pour off the liquid and give it in drop form 3 times a day, using double the dosages indicated previously for the oat tincture. (It has a bitter, disagreeable taste.)

Herbal – skullcap (*Scutellaria lateriflora*):

This herb is useful for behaviour disturbances that centre around nervous fear. The animal may also show one or more of the following signs: intestinal gas; colic; diarrhoea; muscle twitching; and restless sleep. Make an infusion by steeping 1 teaspoon of the dried herb in a cup of hot water for 30 minutes. Use the same dosage schedule as given for camomile (below).

Herbal – valerian (*Valeriana officinalis*): Valerian suits the animal that tends to get hysterical, associated with a hypersensitivity. It shows a changeable mental disposition and an irritable temperament. Like skullcap, valerian may be most successfully used for animals that have digestive disturbances like gas and diarrhoea, due to nervous derangement, and those that may also have a history of leg pains or joint inflammation.

Make an infusion of the *fresh* rootstock using 1 teaspoon to a pint of boiling water. Remove from heat, allowing the mixture to steep. When cool, strain it and use it on the following dosage schedule indicated for camomile. Since valerian is one of those herbs that can cause a toxic reaction if given in *large* doses over a *long* period of time, I advise that you try it for a few days, no more than a week. If you don't see beneficial results by then, discontinue use and try one of the other suggested remedies, such as the oat tincture (see the general directions for herbs, which follow).

Herbal – German camomile (*Matricaria chamomilla*): Animals that will benefit from this herb are noisy, whining, moaning and complaining. They will let you know about their pains or discomforts. They are sensitive, irritable and thirsty and may snap or try to bite. Such animals don't like to be hot and are often mollified or quiet only when being carried or constantly stroked.

Make an infusion by steeping 2 teaspoons of the dried or fresh flowers in $\frac{1}{2}$ cup of boiling water. When cold, strain and give the following amounts 3 times a day: 1 teaspoon for a cat or small dog; 2 teaspoons for a small or medium-small dog; 1 tablespoon for a medium dog; 2 tablespoons for a large dog; 3 tablespoons for a giant dog.

General directions for herbs: Use the suggested schedule for the herb you have chosen for a week. If you see an improvement in that time, even a slight one, continue the treatment as long as the improvement goes on, up to a maximum of 2 or 3 weeks. Then discontinue the *regular* use of the herb, but give one dose of it whenever symptoms return or worsen. Also, the herb can be used preventively. Give it to the animal before an event you know will trigger the problem behaviour – for example, before leaving your pet alone for long periods. In this way it can be used as needed over several weeks of months.

What if you don't see a good response over the seven-day trial period? Then discontinue the selected herb and either try it again after a few weeks on a better diet or else use one of the alternative herbs suggested. The one exception to the seven-day trial period is with the use of the oat tincture. Try it for several weeks, if necessary, until results are forthcoming.

I would like to suggest one additional alternative for those who are willing to go a little further. In my own work I find that the best herbal system for behaviour problems definitely centred in the *psychological* area is the use of flower essences. These were originally developed for human use by Dr Edward Bach in England in the 1930s. I have found them just as effective in animals. They are dilute extracts of selected flowers given by mouth over a long period (weeks to months), often with remarkable improvements, both mental and physical.

To adequately cover this extraordinary system is beyond the scope of this book, but interested readers will find relevant suppliers and books on pages 270 and 271. For those who want to explore the system or who are already acquainted with it I would point especially to the following flower essences (not to exclude the others):

Chicory: for the over-attached, possessive animal.

Holly: for the vicious, aggressive, suspicious or jealous animal.

Impatiens: for the 'uptight', impatient or irritable pet.

Mimulus: for the animal afraid of specific things, like the dog afraid of men or thunder.

Rock rose: for use where attacks of terror or panic are part of the disturbance.

Star of Bethlehem: for use where physical or emotional shock seems to have been what initiated the imbalance.

Walnut: for the animal that is excessively influenced by a strong personality (human or animal) or apparently under the influence of bad heredity.

General directions for flower essences. Depending on the size of the animal, give it 1 to 3 drops by mouth (preferably directly, or else mixed with a little food or milk if necessary) 4 times a day until the desired results are obtained. Limit the number of essences used to three or four. See page 270 for sources and further instructions. There is no unfavourable side effect or possible toxicity with this system.

BIRTH

See 'Pregnancy, Birth and Care of Newborns'

BLADDER PROBLEMS

Inflammation of the lining of the bladder and urethra or the formation of urinary mineral deposits and stones have become common problems for pets, particularly for cats. Symptoms usually manifest as increased frequency of urination, the appearance of blood in the urine and – in severe cases – extreme discomfort, straining and partial or complete blockage of the bladder.

Though orthodox veterinary treatment assumes that the causative factors are bacterial infection or excessive ash (mineral) in the diet, I am not convinced that these are significant to any degree. Though bacteria are often found, I feel that they are secondary to the disorder – that they are just taking advantage of a weakened state. In a male cat with severe inflammation and blockage of the urethra, the usual treatment is to insert a catheter and give fluids, antibiotics, antispasmodics and other drugs. Such methods *can* be life-saving when uremia threatens to poison the animal, but they do not really cure the condition, as it tends to recur again and again, regardless of preventive measures. Often the owner is advised to moisten the food and add salt (in order to encourage the consumption of more water) and to feed a low-ash diet, but I have not found these measures to be preventive to a significant degree.

It is clear to me that most of this problem originates in the feeding of poor-quality food with a resulting toxicity and excessive elimination load on the linings of the urinary system. Almost invariably the first attack follows a history of feeding dry commercial foods for a long period of time. I've found that the condition is very responsive to diet changes and natural therapies, resulting in a stable cure rather than a temporary alleviation.

Treatment

First and foremost, change the diet. If commercial foods continue to be used as a major part of the nutrition, the condition almost always will recur. During the acute phase of the condition (see the following section), put the animal on a liquid fast, offering a broth (made from such vegetables as potatoes, broccoli, carrots and others, with a little meat or bones added) several times a day. You may add a small amount of natural tamari soya sauce as a seasoning and to supply easily digested amino acids. In addition, provide your pet with pure water at all times.

After improvement or recovery, feed the natural diet as advised in chapters 3 and 4, with these modifications:

For one month, feed no offal or yeast, in order to reduce the purines (which create excessive uric acid) in the system.

Use a B complex tablet daily, with the major B vitamins at the 10-milligram level.

Give vitamin C, 250 to 500 milligrams twice daily, in order to control bacterial infection and maintain an acid urine, which makes mineral salts more soluble and counters the formation of crystals.

Increase the amount of vitamin E to minimize or prevent scarring of healing tissues. For a cat this would amount to 60 to 100 I.U. daily.

We will now consider more specific treatments, in addition to diet. First we'll look at the cat (usually a male), which is most prone to these problems, considering in turn different treatments for different phases of the problem. Then we'll discuss what to do for the dog.

Cats *(acute cases)*

If the urethra becomes thoroughly plugged up, the cat cannot pass urine and the bladder becomes enlarged and hard. It feels like a stone in the abdomen. The condition is quite serious, because urine and poisonous waste products are backing up into the blood-stream. Either make an emergency visit to your vet to have a catheter put in, or – *if* there

is time and you have prepared in advance – try the following remedies:

Homeophathic – *Thlaspi bursa pastoris* (shepherd's purse): Put 2 drops of the tincture on the tongue every 30 minutes until urination is achieved. Because you haven't got much time when a case has gone this far, don't try this alternative for more than 2 or 3 hours. Or use it en route to the vet. The cat that seems alert though uncomfortable is not in as much danger as the cat that is becoming weak and lethargic.

Either order the tincture in advance from a homeopathic supplier (see page 269) or make your own from the fresh, flowering plant as described in chapter 15. If it brings improvement and the urine begins to pass freely, decrease the treatment frequency to every 2 hours. If progress continues, decrease to every 4 hours and stay on this schedule for 3 days or until recovery is obvious.

If improvement occurs but then 'plateaus' for 12 to 24 hours, use one of the following medications as recommended for subacute cases.

Cats *(subacute cases)*

Here the problem is not obstruction but *inflammation*. The cat feels a frequent urge to urinate, but the flow is scanty or blood-tinged. This misery can go on for days, with perhaps temporary improvement (especially with antibiotics). However, the problem recurs every few weeks. For these cases I am going to suggest some specific homeopathic medications which are quite effective, though not easily prepared at home. So if your cat is prone to bladder problems, you may want to order these for future use. Choose from the three remedies below the *one* that best suits the condition. Consider ordering all three in advance; they are inexpensive. Don't mix them.

Homeopathic – *Urtica urens* 6X (stinging nettle): *Urtica urens* is well indicated for the cat that, in addition to the bladder problems, *wants to be warm* (it may huddle next to a stove or other warm place) and *is reluctant to move*. The cat will stay in one spot without changing position except to go to the litter pan to urinate. Bloody drops of urine may come from the penis. In addition, the cat will not want to be touched or handled, *preferring to be left alone*. *Urtica urens* is often the first remedy to try in these cases, as it seems to be effective in a great number of them.

Give 1 tablet of the 6X potency every 4 hours for 2 or 3 days until improvement is marked. Then use 1 tablet every time the symptoms begin to return. Cure is usually evident in a few days.

Homeopathic – *Apis mellifica* 3X (bee venom): Homeopathically prepared from the venom obtained from a bee's sting, this remedy is useful for the cat which, in contrast to the one above, *does not like heat* in any form. Here is how you can tell. Put out a hot water bottle or heating pad wrapped with a towel. If your cat is not interested in huddling next to it and prefers to lie on something cool like cement, tiles, linoleum or even the bath or sink, then you will know its fondness is for cold and not heat! Such an animal will not like to be held because it gets too warm. Usually the urine is passed in small amounts and does not contain blood, but is extremely concentrated and offensive.

Give 1 tablet every 2 hours until improvement is noted, then every 4 hours for a day or two (or whenever symptoms are apparent). It is seldom necessary to treat more than 2 or 3 days.

Homeopathic – *Rhus toxicodendron* (Rhus tox.) 6X (poison ivy): This remedy is indicated for the cat that likes to sit around on cold cement, stones or steps when it is well. But then it may get chilled and have an attack of cystitis (bladder inflammation). So the problem often crops up after cold, wet, rainy weather. *When sick*, this cat will *prefer to be warm*, will like a hot water bottle and to be *touched or rubbed*. However, rather than being passive when resting, a cat with this problem will always be *getting up or changing position* or stretching the limbs. Its urine will be dark and scanty and may contain blood. Urination is difficult and painful.

Give 1 tablet every 4 hours until improvement is obvious. Then give 1 tablet as needed when symptoms return. Recovery usually takes 2 or 3 days.

Note: If you do not see any improvement after 24 hours of using one of these homeopathic preparations, discontinue the treatment and reassess the situation. If antibiotics and other drugs were used at any time, they may have altered the sympton picture. Think back to the symptoms that were present before treatment was started. Use these as your guidelines in choosing a remedy. When in doubt, try *Urtica urens*. Also note that the female cat will have the same symptoms as given above (typical of male cats), but she is not liable to the plugging of the bladder seen in male cats, which have a longer, narrower urethra.

Cats *(chronic cases)*

Where conditions are never severe but there is a weakness and a tendency toward inflammation in the urinary tract, try the following herbal treatment. Or use any *one* of the medications as recommended for subacute cases in cats, if the symptoms displayed match those described for the particular medication.

Herbal – shave grass (horsetail grass, scouring rush – *Equisetum arvense*): Steep 2 teaspoon of the dried herb in ½ cup hot water. Give ¼ teaspoon of this infusion 3 times a day for a week or two, if needed that long. After a week's rest you can repeat it again if appropriate.

Dogs

Though bladder problems are generally more common in cats, dogs do get them, too. Their most common disturbances are either cystitis (as in cats) or stone formation. In cases of cystitis, if symptoms are noted which are similar to those in cats – increased frequency of urination, discomfort, blood in the urine – use the same treatment programme outlined for cats, adjusting nutritional amounts to your dog's body size. Use the same remedies (with the same indications) but give large dogs 2 tablets instead of 1. If you use the herb shave grass, then increase the amounts stated up to 1 teaspoon 3 times daily.

What about stone problems? They occur in two forms – small, pellet-sized stones that form in the bladder but move to block the urethra, and very large stones that fill the bladder.

Small stones are most troublesome to the male dog. They pass down into the urethra and get caught at the point where it passes through the bone in the penis. When this happens, the unfortunate animal will attempt to urinate frequently, without success, or will give off little spurts of urine instead of a full flow. In such cases, immediately use the *Thlaspi bursa pastoris* tincture advised for cats. However, it may be necessary to have the stone removed surgically if relief does not follow. The tissue salt *Magnesia phosphorica* (Mag. phos.) 6X given with the herb will help reduce urethral spasms. Give 1 to 2 tablets every 2 hours.

Large stones are another matter. Numerous large stones (known as calculi) can grow to fill the bladder and eventually irritate the lining, causing bleeding and recurrent bacterial infection. This disease is more common in dogs than in cats. The stones can be surgically removed. However, they usually recur at shorter and shorter intervals, necessitating repeated surgery.

It's hard to know if the stones have formed as a result of bacterial infection, or vice versa. In any case, improving the diet will help the animal by strengthening the urinary tract, normalizing liver function and adjusting its metabolism.

For both large and small stones, give special attention to the following supplements. Use them in conjunction with the low-ash diet recommended under 'Kidney Failure'.

Vitamin A: The cod-liver oil supplement in chapter 3 will suffice, or you can give it as natural vitamin A capsules, allowing 5,000 I.U. for cats and small dogs, 5,000 to 10,000 I.U. for medium dogs and 10,000 to 12,000 I.U. for large dogs.

Vitamin C: Give it to aid detoxification and to acidify the urine, which helps control bacterial infection. Twice daily give 250 milligrams to cats or small dogs and 500 milligrams to medium dogs. Large dogs get 500 milligrams 3 times daily.

B complex: The most important B vitamins for this condition are B_2 (riboflavin) and B_6 (pyridoxine). However, don't give them alone. Always use a complete natural formula so no imbalances of the B complex occur. Give cats or small dogs a daily tablet with the major B vitamins (including B_2 and B_6) at the 10-milligram level; for medium and large dogs make it the 20-milligram level.

Magnesium: This mineral helps prevent re-formation of stones. Magnesium chloride or other magnesium chelates are good forms, given at levels of 50 to 300 milligrams a day, depending on the animal's size.

In addition to these dietary measures, I would use *one* of the following treatment programmes for the tendency to form stones, either small or large:

Tissue Salts – *Calcarea phosphorica* (Calc. phos.) 6X and *Magnesia phosphorica* (Mag. phos.) 6X: The first helps prevent recurrence and normalize calcium and phosphorus metabolism (give 1 to 2 tablets 3 times daily).

The second regulates magnesium metabolism (use it at the same time, giving 1 to 2 tablets morning and night). Administer the tissue salts for a month, then discontinue. You can repeat this treatment later, if necessary, or as indicated by urine analysis. It is *not* a substitute for nutritional therapy.

Herbal – barberry (*Berberis vulgaris*): This herb is good for an animal with arthritic or rheumatic tendencies in addition to forming bladder or kidney stones. Briefly boil 1 teaspoon of the fresh or dried root bark in 1 cup of water; let it steep 5 minues and strain. Three times a day, dose as follows: 1 teaspoon for a cat or small dog; 2 teaspoons for a medium-small dog; 1 tablespoon for a medium dog; 2 tablespoons for a large dog; 3 tablespoons for a giant dog.

Herbal – sarsaparilla (*Smilax officinalis*): Useful where 'gravel' and small stones are in the urine, accompanied by bladder inflammation and pain. Urination may be painful and blood may be passed. Often the animal suited to this herb will also have dry, itchy skin that flares up most in the springtime. Make an infusion by steeping 1 teaspoon of the rootstock in a cup of near-boiling water until cool. Strain and give it 3 times a day as follows: 2 teaspoons to a cat or small dog; 4 teaspoons to a medium-small dog; 2 tablespoons to a medium dog; 4 tablespoons to a large dog; 6 tablespoons to a giant dog.

BRONCHITIS
See 'Upper Respiratory Infection'

CANCER

The dreaded disease, cancer, is becoming increasingly common in our time. Research has shown that environmental pollutants are really the major factor in the development and support of this group of diseases. The way I see it, there are many factors that seem to 'cause' cancer, but for them to best take effect the animal must be in a weakened, susceptible condition. The condition of the thymus gland and its associated lymphatic tissues and immunological functions is very important. If the animal can be kept in *excellent* health with good food, adequate exercise, access to the elements and a stable emotional environment, then this immune system will be strong. Whereas a weaker animal might succumb to the effects of carcinogens, the strong one will more likely resist and detoxify them. Prevention is really the most we can do and it is very important. No drug or vaccine can ever take the place of good health!

Prevention

Certain influences in animals' lives increase their exposure to carcinogens, and you should help your pet avoid them as much as possible. They include chronic exposure to cigarette smoke, riding in the back of a pick-up truck (and inhaling car fumes), resting close to a colour TV set (x-rays), drinking water from street puddles (which can contain hydrocarbons and asbestos dust from brakes), frequent diagnostic work with x-rays (all irradiation is accumulative), use of strong toxic chemicals over long periods (as with flea and tick control) and consuming pet foods high in offal and meat meal (concentrators of pesticides, and hormones, which can promote cancer growth), as well as in preservatives and artificial colours known to cause cancer in lab animals. (Unfortunately, for a pet that already has cancer, the time for prevention has passed. However, by avoiding these toxins the animal will not add stress to an already burdened body.)

In addition to these precautions, a fresh

natural diet is imperative. Supplement it with vitamins C, A and E, as well as yeast and fresh raw vegetables (particularly green sprouts and grasses, notable for their B vitamin and trace mineral contents), which are particularly helpful.

Treatment

Successful treatment of cancer, as you can imagine, is difficult and time-consuming in most cases. The complexity of the condition also makes home care problematic. However, I do think it is possible for some animals to improve or recover under natural treatment, if they have not been treated with anti-cancer drugs or cortisone, and if the condition is not too far advanced. But the likelihood is not as good as in most other diseases.

I do not advise the use of x-rays, anti-cancer drugs or cortisone. These methods invariably suppress the very immune system that is so vitally needed to fight off the malignant cells. In my experience they also reduce the animals's quality of life and make for a prolonged and difficult end.

Unfortunately, however, skilled alternatives to orthodox treatment are not available to most people. So if you do opt for the orthodox approach, I suggest the following measures to help support the body during therapy:

- Totally avoid commercial foods; give only fresh, unprocessed foods, including as much raw fare as the animal will accept.
- Give high levels of vitamin C (2 to 6 grams daily), vitamin A (double the recommended amount of cod-liver oil) and vitamin E (give 4 times the usual level).
- Use *Bioplasma*, a preparation com-

bining all 12 tissue salts, 2 to 6 tablets 3 times a day.
- Give oat tincture as described under 'Behaviour Problems'.

If you *don't* want to put your animal on the orthodox treatment I suggest these measures:

- Avoid all commercial foods, feeding the natural diet with an emphasis on additional high-quality protein. Organic raw beef liver is often accepted and is excellent, nutritionally speaking, for cancer. So is raw thymus (sweetbread). If you can't get organic meat, you have to weigh the advantages (liver has been an important part of some cancer cures, such as the Max Gerson approach) against the possible disadvantages (the liver accumulates toxic chemicals). My own sense is that by feeding it raw the nutritional advantages outweigh the shortcomings in most cases.
- Use higher levels of vitamins as indicated above.
- Give *Bioplasma*, or study the individual tissue salts from books suggested on page 271. Use the two or three salts that seem to best apply.
- Use only spring, distilled or other pure water, *not* tap water.
- Give a dilution of the tincture of goldenseal (available in some herb stores or as *Hydrastis canadensis* from homeopathic suppliers). Use the 1:100 dilution method described for *Phytolacca* (pokeweed) under 'Mammary Tumours'. Be sure to shake it thoroughly! Twice a day, give it as follows: 1 drop to cats and small dogs; 2 drops to medium dogs; 3 drops to large or giant dogs. Because the animal is in a weakened and

fragile condition, be sure to follow the instructions *carefully*, just as I describe. As soon as *any* reaction seems evident (the animal gets weaker, symptoms worsen or the appetite is lost), temporarily discontinue the treatment. Usually the animal will improve, only to have some of its previous symptoms return. At that point begin the goldenseal treatment again, but as soon as an aggravation of symptoms is seen (even after one dose), discontinue again. On the other hand, if the animal shows only improvement after the initial dosages (as is more common), continue the treatment as long as improvement goes on. When a plateau is reached, in which things get neither better nor worse, then make a 1:100 dilution *of the first dilution* (following all of the initial instructions) and continue from there.

Feline leukaemia is a particular form of cancer that has reached epidemic proportions among cats. However, if you can catch it early, it is easier to treat than many other forms of cancer. A strict adherence to fresh, unprocessed foods (preferably with many of them raw) is essential, as are the basic vitamin and mineral supplements recommended in chapter 3. In addition, the following measures are very helpful.

Give large doses of vitamin C (as sodium ascorbate powder). Use about 3 to 5 grams a day (around a teaspoon), divided into doses.

Feed foods high in calcium or administer a liquid calcium supplement from a gelatin capsule (400 milligrams daily).

Use the tissue salts Natrum muriaticum (Nat. mur.) 6X and *Calcarea phosphorica* (Calc. phos.) 6X. Use Nat. mur. as the primary remedy, 1 tablet 3 times daily (especially useful for a weak cat with severe anaemia and dehydration). Give Calc. phos. as the secondary remedy, 1 tablet twice a day, before the Nat. mur. in the morning and after it at night.

If the condition does not progress favourably (don't neglect the diet!), try the goldenseal dilution as described previously for cancer in general.

Good nursing care is important. If your cat seems more comfortable with a towel-wrapped hot water bottle, keep one filled with hot water all the time for him to huddle near. If you don't have a hot water bottle, a large jar will do. If possible, brush and comb your pet. Maintain a positive and relaxed attitude to ensure a supportive emotional environment for your animal.

Even if the treatment is not successful in leading to a cure, all the cats I have worked with in this way have died quietly and without excessive discomfort. Such a peaceful end is not, unfortunately, always true for the animal treated extensively with drugs.

CATARACTS
See 'Eye Problems'

CHOREA
See 'Distemper, Chorea and Feline Panleucopenia'

CORNEAL ULCERS
See 'Eye Problems'

CONSTIPATION

Constipation sometimes occurs when animals don't get enough bulk in their diet, or don't get enough exercise. If a dog or cat is not allowed to evacuate when the urge is there, it may develop the habit of holding its stool. A dog that is not let out often enough, or a housebound cat with a dirty litter tray, is most likely to develop this habit. In relatively simple cases like this, the following treatments generally will suffice.

Treatment

Feed a natural diet that includes fresh vegetables for adequate bulk. Raw meat seems to be a natural laxative for dogs and cats. Milk sometimes is the same for cats.

If the animal's stools seem dry, add ½ teaspoon to 1 tablespoon of bran to each meal. It will help the stools hold additional moisture.

Liquid paraffin can be used temporarily where there is discomfort. Depending on the animal's size, add 1 teaspoon to 1 tablespoon to the food twice a day, for no more than a week. Continued use is inadvisable because it will draw off reserves of vitamin A from the body and may also create a dependency on its use for normal evacuation.

Make sure the animal gets plenty of exercise, which is very important for massaging the internal organs and increasing blood flow throughout the body, often stimulating a sluggish metabolism. Long walks or runs or a game of fetch are excellent. For a cat, try games involving pouncing, such as 'thing-on-a-string'.

Dogs *(chronic cases)*
For the dog with chronic constipation try the best suited one of the following *additional* methods:

Homeopathic – *Nux vomica* 6X (poison nut): This is safe in homeopathic form, despite the name. It is very effective for constipation caused by poor-quality food in the diet, eating too many bones, or emotional upset (frustration, grief, scolding). It is best suited to a dog that has repeated but ineffectual straining, that may show irritability, pain and a tendency to hide or be alone. Give 1 tablet 15 minutes after each meal or 3 times daily. As soon as you see a positive response, give the tablets only if straining or discomfort returns, and then only 1 at a time.

Tissue Salt – *Silicea* 6X: *Silicea* best suits the constipated animal that seems to have a weak rectum. With this weakness, the stool, though partly expelled, slips back in again. It's also good for a dog that has trouble getting the whole bowel movement out, and for the poorly nourished animal. Give 1 to 2 tablets 3 times daily for a week. You can use the treatment on alternate weeks, allowing a week of rest in between.

Tissue Salt – *Natrum muriaticum* (Nat. mur.) 6X: When the stool seems very dry and thus hard to expel, yet the dog otherwise has tendencies toward watery discharges (teary eyes, watery vomiting, excess salivation, for example), use this remedy as outlined for *Silicea*.

Constipation resulting from aluminium sensitivity: If your dog has a chronic constipation problem and straining, and his stools are not hard but are sticky and messy, his problem may be aluminium poisoning. In such a case weakness of the rectum makes passage difficult even though the stool is soft. Consider this possibility in all recurrent cases, even though the symptoms may be different from those given. Appropriate treatment of such a case is first to curtail aluminium ingestion as much as possible. Stop using aluminium cooking pots or dishes for your animal. Also, avoid processed cheese (which may contain sodium aluminium phosphate as an emulsifier), table salt (which often contains sodium silicoaluminate or aluminium calcium silicate to prevent caking), white flour (which may be bleached with an aluminium compound, potassium alum) and tap water (aluminium sulphate may be used as a precipitant to remove water impurities).

To help remove the aluminium from the body, use high levels of vitamin C (500 milligrams to 3 grams daily), along with a zinc supplement (5 milligrams for cats and small dogs, 10 milligrams for medium and 20 milligrams for large dogs). A chelated form of zinc is best.

Please understand that not all animals are adversely affected by aluminium, only some individuals that are very sensitive to it.

Cats (chronic cases)

For the cat with chronic constipation use the basic treatment described earlier and choose the *one* remedy below that best suits your cat's condition.

Homeopathic – *Nux vomica* 6X (poison nut): For the cat that strains ineffectually or passes only small amounts without relief. It may be irritable, withdraw or avoid your touch. Constipation may follow emotional upset, stress or too much rich food. There may be a history of nausea and vomiting. Give 1 tablet after every attempt to strain or eliminate, though not more often than every 2 hours. You should see relief within 24 hours. (If not, try another treatment or get professional help.) Once you see noticeable improvement, discontinue the tablets. If the symptoms return, resume giving the tablets 1 at a time.

Herbal – garlic (*Allium sativum*): For the cat with a big appetite that likes a lot of meat and tends to constipation with discomfort, add ½ to 1 clove of freshly grated raw garlic to its daily food. Most animals like the taste.

Herbal – olive oil (*Olea europaea*): This oil serves as a tonic for the intestinal tract and stimulates the flow of liver bile and contraction of intestinal muscles. Any excess oil will also lubricate the faecal mass and soothe mucous membrane linings of the intestine and rectum. Give 1 to 2 teaspoons twice daily until the movements are regular. (You also can give it once a week as a tonic.)

Tissue Salts: If so indicated, try those listed for dogs.

Consider the possibility of aluminium sensitivity, as described for dogs.

CYSTITIS
See 'Bladder Problems'

DEMODECTIC MANGE
See 'Skin Parasites'

DENTAL PROBLEMS

The mouth and its associated structures are very important to animals, not only for eating but also for grooming and carrying things. The area contains many nerves and is served by a plentiful blood supply, making dental problems more serious than you might expect. Mouth pain can keep an animal from eating enough or grooming properly. Three problems are most common: accidents that damage the teeth or gums, congenital or developmental disorders and periodontitis (calculus on the teeth and associated gum disease). Let's look at each in turn.

Accidents: If an animal is hit by a car, it's common to have its teeth broken off or knocked out. In most cases, after the initial inflammation has subsided, the animal feels no real discomfort. Since dogs and cats only very rarely get cavities, even the broken teeth don't decay. However, sometimes the root will become abscessed and require removal. Generally, a broken tooth can be left in place at least until a convenient occasion for removal occurs, such as another need for surgical anaesthesia.

As for injured gums, an excellent immediate treatment to stop bleeding and promote rapid healing is calendula tincture. With a saturated cotton swab, apply it directly to the bleeding gum, or dilute the tincture with

10 parts water and use it as a flushing mouthwash, applied with a syringe or turkey baster.

Congenital or developmental disorders: Problems of this sort are so common in some breeds of dogs, they seem to be standard equipment. Cats, however, have very few congenital mouth problems, probably because they've been less modified by intentional breeding.

Some dogs, especially toy breeds, have teeth that are simply too crowded, often overlapping in position. Sometimes the jaw is too long or too short. Worst of all is the fate of breeds like the bulldog and Boston bull terrier, who have very short jaws with teeth that are crammed together, turned sideways and malpositioned. They really have a mouthful of problems.

What can you do about it? I recommend extracting some of the permanent teeth as they develop, preferably while the dog is still young. Left untreated, the crowding and poor fit may lead to gum disease and loose teeth. Some dogs have relatively straight, uncrowded teeth, but one jaw is longer or shorter than the other. As a result the teeth don't meet properly, causing discomfort and premature breakdown of both teeth and gums. If the difference between the jaws is $\frac{1}{4}$ inch or less, removal of some of the deciduous (baby) teeth before the arrival of the permanent set may restore proper alignment. But if the difference is greater, little can be done preventively.

Other structural problems include 'supernumerary' (extra) teeth, which should be removed to prevent accumulation of food and debris, and retained baby teeth, which force the permanent teeth to grow beside or in front of them (trapping debris and perhaps distorting the jaw formation). They, too, should be removed.

Periodontal disease: This is the most common tooth and gum problem. It results from a build-up on the teeth of calcium salts, food, hair and bacteria that put pressure on the gums, causing inflammation, swelling, pulling away and receding. A pocket opens up between gums and teeth, collecting still more debris, further worsening the problem. Eventually the process can loosen the teeth and cause them to fall out.

Of course, periodontal disease doesn't destroy teeth overnight. It may take months or years. A very serious complication is that bacteria growing around the teeth may enter the bloodstream and reach other parts of the body. I have noted (as have other vets) that many dogs with heart problems have had infected gums and teeth for long periods. Perhaps the bacteria play a role. One veterinary specialist also noted that many digestive, urinary or genital diseases are caused by such teeth and gum problems.

If your pet has periodontal disease, it will show these symptoms: bleeding gums; foul breath; excessive salivation; painful chewing; and possible loss of appetite or weight. You can see heavy brown deposits (calculus) on the teeth, particularly on the back ones. And the teeth may be loose. The usual causes for the build-up of this calculus are misaligned teeth, overfeeding, poor-quality food, no hard, chewable things to exercise the teeth and gums, and frequent nibbling. Once the deposits have formed, they are rock-hard and can only be adequately removed (under anaesthesia) by an ultrasonic cleaner. Often the infected and loose teeth must also be extracted and haemorrhage controlled.

After any dental work at the surgery, you can do a lot with follow-up care both to promote rapid healing and to prevent recurrence. The gums will be very sore and inflamed. Certain herbs will be very helpful. Choose *one* of the following that seems best suited (or, if indicated, you may use both the goldenseal and the myrrh).

Herbal – *Echinacea* (purple cone flower – *Echinacea angustifolia*): Useful where the teeth were found to be infected and the animal is thin and run down. Boil 1 teaspoon of fresh-smelling rootstock in 1 cup of water for 10 minutes. Cover, remove from stove and let steep for an hour. Strain and apply this decoction directly to the gums with a swab (or use it as a mouthwash). It promotes saliva flow, so don't worry if your pet begins to drool.

Herbal – goldenseal (*Hydrastis canadensis*): This herb is antiseptic and helpful for gum tissue growth. Steep 1 teaspoon of powdered rootstock in a pint of boiling-hot water until cool. Pour off the clear liquid and use it to flush out the mouth and gums.

Herbal – myrrh (*Commiphora myrrha*): Myrrh is indicated for loose teeth. Steep 1 teaspoon of the resin in a pint of boiling-hot water for a few minutes. Strain it and paint the infusion on the gums or flush them using a syringe or turkey baster.

Herbal – plantain (*Plantago major*): This herb helps when the condition is not serious enough to require major cleaning but where there are minor deposits on the teeth and inflamed gums. Steep 1 tablespoon of the leaves in $\frac{1}{2}$ cup of boiling-hot water for 5 minutes. Strain and use as a mouthwash.

General directions for herbs: Whichever herb you choose, use it twice a day for 10 to 14 days. Alternatively, use the herb in the morning and apply vitamin E (fresh out of the capsule) to the gums with your fingers at night. (This treatment is very soothing.)

Diet is also extremely important in the period after teeth cleaning. Without proper nutrition, the gums can't repair themselves or maintain necessary resilience. Emphasize those vegetables rich in niacin, folate and minerals – leafy greens, broccoli, asparagus, lima beans, potatoes and lettuce. Also, serve fresh liver twice weekly for its folate,

vitamin A, protein and other richly supplied nutrients. Other good folate sources are eggs or plain peanuts.

To the basic supplements recommended in chapter 3, also add $\frac{1}{8}$ to $\frac{1}{2}$ teaspoon of dolomite powder (for extra calcium and magnesium), 100 to 1,000 milligrams of vitamin C twice daily and a B complex tablet or capsule with the major vitamins at the 10- to 20-milligram level (amounts depend on the animal's size). Use these extra supplements for a few weeks.

These foods will help to prevent or minimize future recurrences. Also give your pet its own natural 'toothbrush' – either bones or a hard raw vegetable like a carrot. For dogs I advise that one day a week you feed nothing but one large *raw* bone. There is no better natural teeth cleaner. But avoid cooked bones, small or easily splintered bones from chickens and turkeys. These can be dangerous. Some dogs that have trouble digesting bone fragments get irritation and constipation, usually a result of weak stomach acid from improper feeding. Good diet and a B complex supplement will likely clear the problem up. For the first few weeks limit bone chewing to 30 minutes a day.

One last thing: If you're about to get a new pet, look for one with properly formed teeth and jaws (and parents with the same). See chapter 9 for hereditary defects.

DERMATITIS
See 'Skin Problems'

DIABETES

Seen usually in dogs but occasionally in cats, the diabetes animals get is similar in most ways to the sugar diabetes seen in humans. Because a failure of insulin secretion from the pancreas does not allow proper use of blood sugar, problems ensue. Instead of reaching the body tissues, the increasing levels of blood sugar spill over into the urine and are lost from the body. Thus, despite adequate caloric intake, the tissues are in a condition of semi-starvation all the time.

Some of the resulting symptoms are not hard to understand. The animal eats a lot, but nevertheless gets thinner and thinner. The continuous presence of sugar in the urine causes fluid loss, as the sugar has to be dissolved in water to be eliminated (so it carries the water out with it). Thus, the animal is abnormally thirsty and passes large volumes of urine.

Apparently there is more to this condition than just lack of insulin, however, because even if insulin needs are carefully supplied with injections of this hormone, there are still progressive changes and weakness that may persist. These include sometimes recurrent pancreatic inflammation, formation of eye cataracts and an increased susceptibility to infection (particularly of the urinary tract).

The usual treatment consists of strictly regulating food intake and using daily injections of insulin (derived from the glands of other animals). Feeding is usually restricted to tinned food fed once a day, about 12 hours after the insulin is given (when its activity is the highest).

My feeling is that a major causative factor underlying the condition is the feeding of processed foods that are devoid of sufficient vitamins, minerals and trace elements. I particularly suspect the soft-moist burger-type dog foods that come in cellophane bags and don't need refrigeration. These products are very high in carbohydrates, like sugar, that are used as preservatives, as well as artificial colours and other preservatives. The principle is the same one used in setting jam by adding a lot of sugar to the fruit.

Treatment

The diabetic dogs I have treated have generally done well on the basic natural food diet (with a few modifications) given as several small meals during the day rather than one large one. Their insulin needs seem to stabilize, rather than going through erratic ups and downs from day to day. You may need to experiment with your animal to find the best frequency of feeding, also taking into account the advice of your vet.

In addition to the nutritional advice given here, see that your animal gets lots of exercise, which has the effect of decreasing insulin needs. *Erratic* exercise could destabilize the insulin needs, though, so a regular, sustained programme of exercise is best. You may also find help with the use of the tissue salts *Natrum muriaticum* (Nat. mur.) 6X and *Natrum sulphuricum* (Nat. sulph.) 6X, giving 1 to 2 tablets of each (together) 3 times a day. They can be used for a long period of time, if necessary.

Dietary guidelines: The main goal of a special diet to control diabetes is to reduce the stress placed on the pancreas. That means

---

CATS: DIABETES DIET No. 1

 ½ cup offal or lean meat
 ½ cup cooked brown rice or other grain
 1 tablespoon grated or chopped
   vegetables
 daily supplements as recommended
 ⅓ cup milk (serve separately)

Combine all ingredients except milk. Serve.

Yield: about 1 cup

CATS: DIABETES DIET No. 2

1 large egg
½ cup creamed cottage cheese
½ cup brown rice or other grain
1 tablespoon grated or chopped
  vegetables
daily supplements as recommended

Combine all ingredients and serve.

Yield: about 1 cup

DOGS: DIABETES DIET

1 medium egg
½ cup offal or lean meat
2¾ cups cooked brown rice or other
  grain
¼ cup grated or chopped vegetables
daily supplements as recommended

Combine all ingredients and serve.

Yield: about 3½ cups

---

strict avoidance of sugar-containing foods, as well as a low fat intake (because the pancreas produces a number of enzymes particularly involved in the breakdown of fat). The recipes which follow will provide a good low-fat programme.

Certain foods are particularly beneficial for diabetes, so emphasize them in your selections. Good *grains* to use are millet, rice, oats, cornmeal and rye bread. Excellent *vegetables* are green beans (the pods of which contain certain hormonal substances closely related to insulin), dandelion greens, alfalfa sprouts, corn, parsley, onion, Jerusalem artichoke and garlic (which reduces blood sugar in diabetes). Garlic also stimulates the abdominal viscera and increases digestive organ function. Use it regularly in some form (fresh or in capsules). *Milk* and milk products are helpful because they are alkalizing (as are vegetables and most fruits), which helps to counter overacidity due to a disordered metabolism in diabetes. They are best fed raw, as are meat, eggs, fruits, and some vegetables, because uncooked foods are much more stimulating to the pancreas. *Fruits* in season are fine, if acceptable to your animal; the natural fruit sugar (fructose) can

be used by the diabetic animal. Feed them separately from other foods.

Note: You can also feed diabetic dogs *Potatoes au Canine* or *Meat – Bean – Rice Dish for Dogs* (see chapter 4), as both are low in fat. For both dogs and cats, use all the regular supplements as indicated in chapter 3, however:

Reduce the fat intake by using just ¼ cup vegetable oil and ¼ cup cod-liver oil in the oil mix, serving only ½ teaspoon of the mix daily. Include the usual (or an increased) amount of vitamin E, which helps to detoxify and to prevent pancreatic scarring.

Give a trace mineral tablet containing manganese and zinc.

Use vitamin C, 500 milligrams to 3 grams daily (depending on the animal's size), divided into 2 or more doses. It apparently lowers insulin needs.

Feed lecithin in granular or liquid form to stimulate liver function: ½ teaspoon to 1 tablespoon a day.

Don't neglect the other standard supplements, particularly the brewer's yeast which is important for its chromium content (important to sugar metabolism).

DIARRHOEA AND DYSENTERY

Diarrhoea, though common, is not a very specific condition. That is, many things can be said to be the *cause* of diarrhoea and yet the clinical appearance (frequent, soft or fluid movements) is about the same. It helps to understand the general purpose of it, which is that the gastrointestinal tract has one major defence against irritants of many sorts – to move its contents along more quickly than usual. The cause of the irritation may include worms, bacteria, viruses, spoiled or toxic food, food sensitivities (see 'Allergies'), bone fragments or indigestible material like hair, cloth or plastic. The primary response to this material is to increase contraction (peristalsis) in order to flush out the system. Because the intestinal contents move along so quickly, the colon does not absorb the amount of water it usually does. Thus, the bowel movement is abnormally fluid.

Depending on what part of the tract is irritated, you may see certain additional symptoms. If there is inflammation and bleeding in the upper part of the small intestine, near the stomach, then the bowel movement will be very dark or black, due to digested blood. You also may notice a build-up of excess gas that causes belching, a bloated stomach or flatulence. This pattern usually shows no particular straining during evacuation.

A different picture appears when the inflammation is lower down in the colon. Generally, there is no problem with gas build-up. The diarrhoea tends to 'shoot' out of the rectum with force and obvious straining. If there has been bleeding in the colon, the blood will appear as a fresh red colour mixed with the stool. The bowel movements tend to be more frequent than when the disturbance centres in the small intestine.

Often you may notice excessive mucus that looks like clear jelly.

Because diarrhoea can be associated with so many causes and other disorders, I really can't suggest a few treatments that will cover all situations. However, most of the time, diarrhoea is caused by eating the wrong kind of food or spoiled food, overeating, parasites (in young animals especially) or virus infections. The following guidelines are useful for treating simple or mild conditions that fall in the above categories. If they don't clear it up or if conditions are severe or otherwise seem to warrant it, seek professional help.

Treatment

Most important, stop the use of solid food entirely for the first 24 to 48 hours. A liquid fast will give the intestinal tract a chance to rest and do its job of flushing things out. Make plenty of pure water available at all times and encourage drinking. A danger of excessive diarrhoea is that the body can get dehydrated from the loss of water, sodium and potassium. So provide these in the form of a broth made from vegetables, rice and some meat or a bone. You may also add a small amount of naturally brewed soya sauce to enhance flavour and provide easily assimilated amino acids and sodium. Use just the liquid part of the soup, serving it at room temperature several times a day during the fast period.

If the condition is mild or is a sudden attack following consumption of spoiled food, this treatment alone may suffice. However, in more severe cases it will be wise to use *one* of the following as well:

Kaopectate solution: Made from finely powdered earth and pectin from plants, this over-the-counter pharmaceutical absorbs irritating substances and soothes inflamed tissue without slowing down the intestinal activity. Depending on body size, give 1 teaspoon to 3 tablespoons every 4 hours for a couple of days.

Activated charcoal: Sold in chemists as a powder or in tablets, this type of charcoal prepared from plant matter has the ability to absorb toxins, drugs, poisons and other irritating material. It's especially useful for treating diarrhoea caused by eating spoiled food or toxic substances. Mix it with water and give it by mouth every 2 or 3 hours for a 24-hour period (except during sleep). Because over-use of charcoal could interfere with digestive enzymes, a short course is best. Depending on the animal's size, use ½ to 1 teaspoon powder or 1 to 3 tablets.

Roasted carob powder: Available in health food stores, this plant substance commonly used as a chocolate substitute is also a popular and soothing aid to diarrhoea. Mix it with water and perhaps a little honey and give it by mouth 3 times a day for 3 days, using ½ to 2 teaspoons.

Herbal – garlic (*Allium sativum*): Garlic stimulates the digestive organs, regularizes the action of the liver and gallbladder, and is especially useful where infection, parasites or overeating may be a factor underlying the diarrhoea. Give ¼ to ½ teaspoon of fresh juice of crushed bulbs, thinned with water, 2 or 3 times a day for 3 days. Alternatively, you can use a deodorized extract (like Kyolic liquid garlic, tablets or capsules) that may be more acceptable to some animals – or to you! Deodorized or not, if you use a prepared form, give a liquid preparation in the same amount as above. Give 1 to 3 tablets or capsules 2 or 3 times a day for 3 days.

Homeopathic – *Hyland's Homeopathic Combination Tablet No. 16:* Available in many health food stores (and by post; see pages 269–70), this particular formulation of herbs and substances is particularly useful for diarrhoea, especially the type in which fresh blood and mucus is passed with much straining. Give 1 to 2 tablets every hour until you see improvement; then reduce the frequency to every 3 hours, then every 4 hours, so that there is a tapering off in treatment. If there is a clear positive response in a day or two then use the tablets only when the symptoms worsen or return.

Tissue Salts – You can use the following remedies either alone or with either the kaopectate or garlic treatments described earlier. They can be very effective in severe cases. Pick the best-suited *one* or, if indicated, use two of them together, alternating them every 2 hours. Give 1 to 3 crushed tablets by mouth every 2 hours the first day in acute cases or 4 times a day in chronic cases for several days or until improvement is noted. Then decrease frequency to twice daily for a few days. The indications are as follows:

Ferrum phosphoricum (Ferr. phos.) 6X: Helpful in most cases of diarrhoea because it soothes inflammation. It's especially good for young animals and those with a fever.

Natrum phosphoricum (Nat. phos.) 6X: Good for diarrhoea associated with worms in young animals or where there is constipation punctuated with attacks of diarrhoea. This condition is associated with excess acidity in the blood, so give attention to proper diet.

Natrum muriaticum (Nat. mur.) 6X: Appropriate for longer-lasting diarrhoea of the watery, frothy, mucousy type. The affected individual tends to be dehydrated (doesn't retain fluid in the tissues). Nat. mur. helps to regulate water balance in the body.

Tissue Salt Combination C (made up of *Magnesia phosphorica* [Mag. phos] *Natrum phosphoricum* [Nat. phos.] *Natrum sulphuricum* [Nat. sulph.] and *Silicea*): Useful for the chronic or longer-lasting diarrhoea with stomach upset, sluggish liver and gas build-up.

General advice: It is important to be watchful during the treatment for the possibility that some causative factor remains, for instance an irritating chemical (a new flea collar?), the use of milk (which bothers some animals), polluted water, access to spoiled food in somebody's rubbish bin or a compost pile and so on. Lack of response to treatment can sometimes be traced to persistence of such a cause. Also, consider worms and infectious diseases and treat either at home or with your vet's help, as is appropriate.

Once recovery seems on its way, feed small amounts of plain yogurt to help replenish the intestinal tract with friendly bacteria. Always provide yogurt when antibiotics are being used, as they kill off normal bowel inhabitants and leave a space for the growth of nasty things like yeast and fungus. Yogurt or acidophilus milk will provide protection.

When you are breaking the animal out of the fast (after a couple of days) start with the broth, mixed with the solid vegetables used to make it. After 24 hours, you can introduce the yogurt and begin to re-establish a regular diet, using rice as the grain, because it is generally good for diarrhoea.

DISTEMPER, CHOREA AND FELINE PANLEUCOPENIA

We will consider all three of these diseases together, as they are related. (Chorea is a common result of distemper and panleucopenia is often called cat distemper.) Let's discuss each in turn.

CANINE DISTEMPER

Distemper is so common that few dogs, if any, escape exposure to it. The chief factor is thought to be a virus that is spread among animals through the air (from exhaling or sneezing) or by contact with contaminated objects (like bowls, toys, bones and such).

Distemper progresses in stages. After a six- to nine-day incubation (which is not usually noticed), there appears an initial fever and malaise for a brief time. Afterward, the dog is apparently normal for a few days or a week and then it will suddenly show the typical distemper symptoms: fever; loss of appetite and energy; and perhaps a clear discharge from the nose. Within a short time the condition advances and the dog develops one or more of the additional symptoms: severe conjunctivitis (eye inflammation) with a thick discharge that sticks the lids together; heavy mucus or yellow discharge from the nose; diarrhoea; and skin eruption on the belly or between the hind legs.

Though I have treated many distemper cases with the orthodox approach of anti-biotics, fluids and other drugs, I have not seen it do much good. Indeed it sometimes seemed to be harmful. I say that because a typical complication of distemper is apparent improvement or recovery, later followed by severe inflammation of the brain (encephalit-is) or of smaller areas in the spinal cord. At this stage, these animals are usually put to sleep because any orthodox treatment is almost always ineffective. I am convinced that drug treatment increases the likelihood of encephalitis, while natural methods make it less probable. I have witnessed many successful recoveries in distemper cases treated by a variety of alternative methods. The suggestions that follow are gleaned from this experience.

Treatment

In order to prevent the complications noted, it is crucial to withhold solid food while the dog is in the acute phase of the disease with a fever. The normal rectal temperature should not exceed 102.5°F. Fast the dog on vegetable broth and pure water as described in chapter 15, until at least one day after the temperature has become normal. Should the fever return, fast again. Record the temperature morning and night, so you will be aware of the trend and can tell when it is really ending.

In case you are wondering how long the dog can go without solid food before starving, the normal *healthy* animal can get along all right for several weeks. A dog that is *sick* with distemper and is of normal weight and general condition (and is not a puppy) can profitably fast for seven days. However, few will need to fast this long. Make sure you have fresh pure water available at all times.

Vitamin C provides a supplementary treatment of much importance. I've seen many distemper cases recover without ill effects by using vitamin C and fasting alone. Dose as follows: 250 milligrams every 2 hours for puppies and small dogs; 500 milligrams every 2 hours for medium dogs; 1,000 milligrams every 3 hours for large or giant dogs. Don't continue the dosing through the night, because rest is also important. Once the acute phase and fever have passed, you can reduce the frequency, doubling the time interval between doses. Continue until recovery is complete.

Care of the eyes may be necessary, because the lids can get severely inflamed. As described in chapter 15, bathe the eyes in a saline solution and then put a drop of castor, cod-liver or olive oil in each eye to help heal and provide protection.

During the early stages of distemper, treatment with *one* of the following remedies should help considerably:

Homeopathic – *Distemperinum* 30X: Specially prepared from the distemper virus, this is the most effective remedy I have used in the early stages (available by post; see page 269). I've seen it produce recoveries in just a day or two. Give 1 tablet morning and evening until improvement is evident. Then give only if symptoms flare up again.

Tissue Salts – *Ferrum phosphoricum* (Ferr. phos.) 3X or *Natrum muriaticum* (Nat. mur.) 6X: These are more convenient to obtain than *Distemperinum*, therefore you may want to use them instead. Use Ferr. phos. for the early stage that shows fever. Nat. mur. is for the early stage with a lot of sneezing.

Homeopathic – *Hyland's Homeopathic Combination Tablet No. 11:* Another alternative available in many health food stores, this particular product contains 3 herbs and a tissue salt in homeopathic form that are useful for the early stages where fever is dominant. Dose: 1 to 2 tablets, following the instructions on the label.

During the later stages of distemper, select one of the following treatments (if you did not treat earlier or if it has progressed to this point despite treatment):

Herbal – goldenseal (*Hydrastis canadensis*): Indicated for an animal with more advanced distemper where there is yellow discharge of mucus from the nose, depression and skin eruptions, goldenseal can be used in one of two ways.

1. The first form is made by thoroughly mixing 7 parts powdered goldenseal root, 2 parts powdered licorice root and 1 part powdered ginger root. You can put it in capsules, but usually it's easier to give as a 'slurry' by stirring the powder into a little water. Dose as follows: a scant $\frac{1}{8}$ teaspoon of the powder twice a day for puppies and very small dogs; $\frac{1}{8}$ teaspoon 3 times daily for small dogs; $\frac{1}{4}$ teaspoon 2 times daily for medium dogs; $\frac{1}{8}$ teaspoon 3 times a day for large dogs.

2. The other way is to obtain a tincture of goldenseal (available also as *Hydrastis canadensis*). Make a homeopathic dilution by putting 2 drops of the tincture, 60 drops (1 teaspoon full to the brim) of brandy or vodka and 120 drops (2 teaspoons) of distilled water into a clean new dropper bottle. Mix the capped mixture very thoroughly by striking it briskly against your hand at least 20 times (so bubbles form). Depending on the animal's size, give 1 to 3 drops by mouth every 2 hours. Discontinue treatment if there is an adverse reaction (such as increase of lethargy or hiding in a corner or dark place); otherwise continue it for several days, as long as it seems to help.

Tissue Salts – *Kali muriaticum* (Kali mur.) 6X and *Calcarea sulphurica* (Calc. sulph.) 6X: Useful at the stage showing a lot of coloured mucous discharge and inflammation of the nose and throat, these remedies should be alternated with each other every 2 hours (1 to 2 tablets with each dose).

Homeopathic – *Hyland's Homeopathic Combination Tablet No. 14:* Useful for the case that has advanced beyond fever to a lot of head symptoms like irritated eyes and runny nose, this product contains three herbs and a salt of iodine in homeopathic form. Dose: 1 or 2 tablets, following the instructions on the label. It is available in many health food stores.

Recovery

With proper treatment distemper is really not too severe and you can generally expect recovery in a few days to a week. The *initial* state of health of the animal and the degree of immunity acquired from the mother (in the case of puppies) seem to be important factors in the severity of individual cases.

If recovery is not easy or complete or leaves the animal in a weakened condition, the following measures should help. Feed the high-protein convalescence diet found in chapter 5, emphasizing oats (to strengthen the nervous system) and B vitamins (give a natural B complex tablet in the 10- to 50-milligram range for a few weeks).

For the animal weakened by this disease and as a nerve tonic give a tincture of the common oat (*Avena sativa*). Twice daily give 2 to 4 drops for small dogs or puppies, 4 to 8 drops for medium dogs and 8 to 12 drops for large ones.

If the animal is left with a weakened digestive system, residual diarrhoea or chest complications, give fresh grated garlic (*Allium sativum*) 3 times daily. Use ½ small clove for small dogs or puppies, ½ large clove for medium dogs and 1 clove for large ones. Add the garlic to the food or mix it with honey and flour to make 'pills.'

CHOREA

Usually an after-effect of the distemper virus infection as a result of damage to a part of the spinal cord or brain, chorea is a condition in which some muscle in the body (usually a leg, hip or shoulder) twitches every few seconds. Sometimes this contraction will go on even during sleep. It is not considered curable and most such animals are put to sleep, but sometimes (rarely) spontaneous recovery occurs. I think it is worth giving alternative therapy a try, as it may be successful. Read over the section on 'Behaviour Problems', since some of the information there about diet and herbs will apply. In addition, try this specific treatment:

Three times daily for several weeks, give 1 to 3 tablets of one of the following: Hyland's Nerve Tonic Tablets, Hyland's Biochemic Phosphates or Luyties' Tissue E Biochemic tablets. They are often found in health food stores.

FELINE PANLEUCOPENIA
Feline distemper; infectious enteritis

This disease of cats comes on very suddenly and severely, without apparent warning. A kitten less than four months old will commonly die from it in 24 to 48 hours. The associated virus is thought to be spread by contact with urine, faeces, saliva or the vomit of an infected cat. Epidemics are prevalent.

After an incubation period of two to nine days (usually six), the first signs appear as a high fever (up to 105°F), *severe* depression and severe dehydration. Most often, vomiting follows soon after. At first the vomit appears as a clear fluid; later it is yellowish (tinged with bile). Typically, the cat will lie with its head hanging over the edge of its water dish, not moving except to lap water or vomit.

Apparently it's not the virus itself that produces such severe symptoms, but a secondary infection. As part of the virus's growth, certain tissues are rapidly destroyed, particularly the white cells that protect the body against infection. In many cases they are almost eliminated, which opens the door to the growth of other bacteria or viruses.

Treatment

The most crucial factor in successful treatment is to catch the disorder in its earliest stages. Since young animals can die very quickly, there often isn't enough time to get a home treatment under way. Clinical methods like whole blood transfusion, fluid therapy and antibiotics can be successful in some cases if started early, so I recommend getting professional care if possible.

If you aren't able to get such care right away and you are prepared with supplies, here is a regimen I suggest: give no solid food while fever or vomiting is present. Use the liquid fast instead. Administer high doses of vitamin C, mixing sodium ascorbate powder (4 grams per teaspoon) in water and giving orally. Give about 100 milligrams per hour to very small kittens and 250 milligrams per hour to young and adult cats.

If vomiting causes both the loss of essential fluids and the vitamin C, focus on using the following homeopathic treatment alone, until symptoms are improved. Then go back to giving vitamin C, along with the homeopathic treatment.

Homeopathic – *Veratrum album* 6X (white hellebore): This is indicated for the weak, depressed and cold animal. There will also be vomiting and diarrhoea, aggravated by the drinking of water. Place 1 crushed tablet in the mouth every hour until some relief is apparent. Then give 1 every 2 hours. You can gradually decrease the frequency of administration over a couple of days if there is improvement. Eventually, give 1 tablet only when there is need, as indicated by recurrent symptoms of nausea or lethargy.

If the condition is different from that described above – and there is fever and less depression – then try *Hyland's Homeopathic Combination Tablet No. 11*. Use it on the same time schedule as *Veratrum album*. If you find that despite either treatment the vomiting is very severe and life-threatening, then follow the advice under 'Vomiting'.

For those who can prepare it in advance, consider this alternative herbal treatment: mix 1 teaspoon of the tincture or decoction of purple cone flower (*Echinacea angustifolia*) with 1 teaspoon of the tincture or decoction of boneset (*Eupatorium perfoliatum*). Give 2 drops of the mixture every hour until you see improvement, then reduce to every 2 hours until recovery.

For the animal already very ill and close to death, a different approach is needed. Such a cat will lie in a comatose state, hardly moving. Its ears and feet will feel very cold to the touch. Its nose may have a bluish look. As an emergency measure, administer camphor. Use an ointment containing camphor, such as Tiger Balm. Hold a small dab in front of the cat's nose so that a few breaths will carry in the odour. Repeat every 15 minutes until there is response.

Once you see improvement you can go to one of the other treatments outlined. *Veratrum album* is the remedy to try first. Be sure to discontinue the camphor and remove it from the vicinity when homeopathic or herbal remedies are used, or it will counter their effects.

Recovery

Once the cat is obviously getting well and the fever is gone (the normal temperature should be 101.5° to 102.5°F rectally), you can offer solid food once again. The instructions in the section on canine distemper apply here, too. Raw beef liver is a good 'tonic' for cats and can be used to advantage for a few days.

Take care to minimize stress and avoid chilling for several days after the initial recovery, as a relapse is possible. Continue the vitamin C at reduced levels (250 to 500 milligrams twice daily) for 2 weeks to prevent complications or residual effects.

DYSENTERY
See 'Diarrhoea and Dysentery'

EAR MITES
See 'Ear Problems'

EAR PROBLEMS

In my experience there is one major cause of ear problems, particularly for dogs, and three minor or complicating causes. The major factor is anatomical and is found in many canine breeds. The minor and associated difficulties are (1) water in the ear canal, which predisposes the animal to infections, (2) trapped plant awns and (3) ear mites (a parasite). The latter is the most common feline problem. Let's examine each of these in turn.

ANATOMICAL PROBLEMS

The ears of wolves and coyotes stand upright from the head. This naturally evolved shape has proved to be highly functional in terms of maintaining health and, or course, for hearing very effectively. As you can see in the illustration, the upper ear acts as a funnel to capture sounds and pass them directly into the ear canal. A natural upright ear also allows air exchange between the ear canal and the outside atmosphere and thus enables regulation of moisture. If water should get in the ear, head-shaking and the free flow of air will soon reduce the humidity to the proper level.

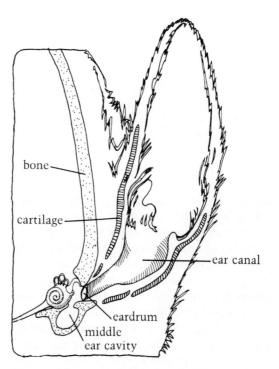

The upright ear is shaped to catch sound. Its openness allows moisture to escape.

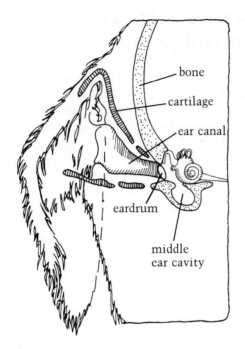

The floppy ear traps moisture and shuts out sound.

But somewhere along the line of domestic canine evolution a mutation developed that caused the ear to hang straight down. This probably did not occur as a single mutation, but rather as a series of intentional human selections for ears that folded over and hung down. These ears also are larger, heavier and hairier. (In the case of the poodle, the hair even grows *inside* the ear canal itself!) From a health standpoint, these mutations that result from selective breeding are unfortunate. Though the resultant features may be appealing to some people (such as the rounded head which may resemble that of a child), nonetheless the development of floppy ears has resulted in a great deal of unnecessary suffering for animals. And expense for people.

Looking at the illustration, you can see what an effective 'trap' the hanging ear creates. The canal is effectively closed off,

moisture cannot be discharged, and free air exchange is nil. With this underlying anatomical problem in mind (of course, not all dogs have ears like this), let's look at the other three factors in ear problems.

WATER IN THE EAR CANAL

Many dogs enjoy running through and swimming in streams, ponds and other bodies of water. Invariably they get some of the water down their ears, and sometimes it's not very clean stuff. This excess moisture can lead to a condition much like 'swimmer's ear' in people, a low-grade irritation which can occasionally develop into more serious infections.

If your dog has this tendency you can help prevent it by the use of a slightly acidic wash that will diminish the chance of bacterial or fungal infection and that is healing to the ear tissue. Whenever your pet returns from swimming, flush out the ears with a warm solution of water and lemon juice (use about half a small fresh-squeezed lemon to a cup of water). Alternatively, use water and white vinegar (about a tablespoon of vinegar to a cup of water). If either preparation seems to 'burn,' dilute the mixture further with warm water. With the help of a dropper or small cup fill and then massage the ear canal from the outside (see the instructions for ear care in chapter 15). Afterward, allow the animal to shake its head well (it's hard to *keep* them from it!) Blot off all the excess moisture from the inside ear with a tissue and gently swab out just inside the ear opening with a cotton swab. Remember, you are just taking up moisture; do not rub against the skin.

As a further precaution you may clothes-peg or tie the ears up behind the head to allow them to dry out further. Do not peg or tie the ear itself, only the hair at the end. Also, if hair grows inside your dog's ears, ask your vet or groomer to show you how to pull it out every so often.

TRAPPED GRASS SEEDS

These and other plant burrs are much more likely to get stuck in the ear canal of a dog with hanging ears. The flaps act like hinged trapdoors that direct the seeds right into the ear canal. Though you can do little to prevent this (other than cutting down your weeds and controlling where your animal runs), here is how to deal with them if they get trapped in your dog's ears.

After an excursion in the fields or tall grasses, immediately check the ears and between the toes as well. If you *see* grass seeds, pull them out. If you can't see any but *think* there is one deep down in the ear, *don't* try to remove it yourself. The ear can easily be damaged or the seed pushed right through the eardrum. Try pressing gently on the ear canal, which feels like a small plastic tube and is under the ear as shown in the illustrations. If the dog cries out in pain, there is a good chance something is trapped inside.

In such a case, if you cannot immediately get veterinary care, put some warm olive oil into the ear. It will soften the plant material and make it less irritating. Very rarely, a dog can shake a seed out after it has been saturated with oil, but don't count on it. As soon as possible, take your dog to a vet. The seed must be removed with the proper instruments (sometimes under anaesthesia) or very severe damage can be done. And if you leave it in, terrible infections can result.

EAR MITES

These are very common in cats, and dogs usually get them from cats. Because a general condition of low vitality invites infestation, improved nutrition will indirectly aid in both prevention and recovery (see the diet guidelines in chapter 3). Garlic and brewer's yeast are especially helpful. An infested cat will have brownish-black deposits in its ear canals, which you can see easily. It will scratch like mad whenever you rub its ears. In dogs, ear mite infestation is characterized by a lot of head-shaking and ear-scratching. There is usually not a bad smell or discharge, but when a vet examines the ear canal, it appears quite red and inflamed. You'll probably need a professional diagnosis, because the mites are almost microscopic and very hard to see with the unaided eye. However, if you have a cat with ear mites *and* your dog shows these symptoms, there's a good chance he has them, too.

A mild healing treatment for both animals starts with ½ ounce olive oil and 400 I.U. vitamin E (from a capsule). Combine them in a ½-ounce dropper bottle and bring the mixture to body temperature by immersion in warm water. Holding the ear flap up, put a dropper or two in each ear. Massage the ear canal well so that you hear a fluid sound. After a few minutes, let the animal shake its head. Then gently clean out the opening (not deep into the ear) with cotton wool to remove debris and excess oil. The olive oil mixture will smother many of the mites. It also starts a healing process inside the ear that will make it less hospitable for the little parasites. Use this method once a day for 3 days; keep the unused olive oil and vitamin E mixture tightly capped in the refrigerator between uses.

After the last olive oil treatment, let the ear rest for 3 more days. Meanwhile, prepare the next medicine, a herbal extract which is used to directly inhibit or kill the mites. Use one or more of the following herbs: thyme (*Thymus vulgaris*), rosemary (*Rosmarinus officinalis*) and rue (*Ruta graveolens*). Grind about 1 ounce dried or 2 ounces fresh herb(s) in a mortar and pestle, food processor or blender. Combine with ½ cup of olive oil in a clean jar. Leave it in a warm place, like a sunny windowsill or on top of a water heater, during the 3-day rest between treatments. Stir or shake the mixture several times a day to help extract the essential oils.

When complete, strain the mixture through cloth. Put it in a 1-ounce dropper bottle and add 400 I.U. vitamin E to preserve the mixture and to increase its healing properties. Resume treatment for the next 3 days: Once a day put 1 to 2 droppers of the pre-warmed herbal oil in each ear. Massage well and remove the excess. Then for the following 10 days cease treatment. Afterward, repeat the 3-day treatment with the herbal mixture (store it in the refrigerator). This repeat procedure is to catch the mites that hatched from any eggs that remained in the ear canal or in the hair at the edge of the ear. Between these treatments a good cleansing shampoo of the head and ears is also helpful.

If necessary, you can repeat this herbal treatment again after a 10-day rest period. However, if the condition persists and recurs, it may point to a general condition of poor health that makes the animal susceptible. In such cases fleas and worms usually will be problems, too.

Since mites tend to be more persistent in cats (and thus are a source of reinfestation for other pets, too), you may need to repeat the treatments. Toning up the skin with a nutritious diet is absolutely necessary for the cat with a stubborn mite problem. Also, in persistent conditions, try shampooing the tip of the cat's tail, because the mites can get on it when the tail is curled around the head. Use a tea (infusion) of thyme, rosemary or rue as a final rinse.

ECLAMPSIA
See 'Pregnancy, Birth and Care of Newborns'

ECZEMA
See 'Skin Problems'

EMERGENCIES
See the *Emergency Guide*

ENCEPHALITIS
See 'Distemper, Chorea and Feline Panleucopenia'

EPILEPSY

Epilepsy has become almost common in dogs, though it is rather unusual in cats. Often it's very difficult to know for sure what causes it. Epilepsy seems to be transmitted as a predisposition from generation to generation in some cases; thus, intensive inbreeding is probably one factor.

In general, we can say that the health of the nervous system and brain is influenced by heredity, nutrition during the mother's pregnancy, and the nutrition of the affected individual from birth on. Also, a particular brain disease or a severe injury can lead to epilepsy as its aftermath. But for most animals, it's hard to point to an obvious cause. The convulsions may start without warning and continue with increasing frequency. An epileptic animal may be either young or old at the time of the first attack. My thought is that the younger ones have probably inherited the problem and the older ones are more likely affected by accumulated toxins or brain irritants.

The diagnosis of epilepsy is usually made only after other possibilities have been eliminated – like worms, hypoglycaemia and poisons. Thus, it is a sort of diagnosis by default, and the epilepsy may actually be caused by a mixture of things.

Treatment

My own approach is to use a natural diet to promote optimal nutrition for the brain tissues, to detoxify or eliminate possible toxins in the environment, and (if possible) to use natural herbs or other substances to control the seizures.

Nutrition should be geared toward preventing the intake of substances that may irritate the brain tissue. Work with hyperactive children has pointed to the probability that additives in food could affect the brain in this way. Thus I recommend that you put your animal on a strict regimen that excludes all commercial foods, snacks or foods containing additives or colouring agents.

Use the basic diet described in chapters 3 and 4, with some modifications I will describe. Use offal (especially liver and kidney) only once a week, because they are more likely to be contaminated by pesticides, antibiotics, heavy metals and hormonal substances. Also, since many human epileptics can be significantly helped by avoiding meat, consider feeding the vegetarian recipes to your dog. Give it a trial of at least two months to see if it helps.

Certain supplements are noteworthy. Since the B vitamins are very important to nerve tissue, use a natural, complete B complex containing the full spectrum of the B group, with the major ones at the 20- to 50-milligram level (depending on body size). Niacin or niacinamide should be at the 25-milligram level. Also supplement with $\frac{1}{4}$ to 2 teaspoons of lecithin and 10 to 30 milligrams of zinc (the chelated form is best). Give about 250 to 1,000 milligrams of vitamin C daily to assist detoxification and try using dolomite (which contains magnesium) as a substitute for about half the bone meal recommended in the standard guidelines.

Environmental considerations are to avoid exposure to cigarette smoke, car exhaust (rides in the back of pick-up trucks), chemicals (especially flea sprays, dips and collars, which affect the nervous system) and excessive stress or exertion (but moderate regular exercise is beneficial). Don't let your animal lie right in front of an operating colour TV, which emits x-rays, or extremely close to an operating microwave oven.

Remedies focus on strengthening the nervous system. See the herbs suggested under 'Behaviour Problems', giving special attention to common oat, blue vervain and skullcap. An alternative measure is to use the tissue salt *Kali muriaticum* (Kali mur.) 6X. Depending on the animal's weight, give 1 to 3 tablets 4 times daily for several weeks. If you don't see results, try one of the following, whichever seems best suited:

Tissue Salt – *Kali phosphoricum* (Kali phos.) 6X: Consider it where there are other nervous disturbances, like insomnia, irritability or excessive nervousness. Very strengthening to the nervous system. Give 1 to 3 tablets 4 times a day.

Tissue Salt – *Ferrum phosphoricum* (Ferr. phos.) 6X: Best for the type of seizures accompanied by head congestion (that is, the head feels hot and the whites of the eyes look bloodshot). Use 1 to 3 tablets every hour until the seizure and its effects have passed; then for longer-term use switch to one of the other remedies.

Tissue Salt – *Natrum sulphuricum* (Nat. sulph.) 3X or 6X: Use it if the epilepsy began after an injury to the head. Give 1 to 3 tablets 4 times daily for a long period.

Tissue Salt – *Silicea* 6X: Indicated for attack that occurs during sleep or at night. Give 1 to 3 tablets 4 times daily for several weeks.

If one of these measures is not completely effective in controlling the condition, consider going to homeopathic treatment. To be really effective, you'll have to pick carefully the right medication for the individual animal. However, the following may be tried and may be successful in limiting frequency or severity of the seizures. Pick the one that's best suited for your pet:

Homeopathic – *Artemisia vulgaris* 3X (mugwort): Suitable for petit mal (mild) seizures which may take the form of trembling, stumbling and falling, or standing as if dazed for a few seconds. There may be a pattern of several convulsions close together. Before onset, the animal may be irritable and excited. The seizure may have been brought on by extreme fright or a blow on the head. Give 1 to 2 tablets every 8 hours until relief is obtained, then discontinue.

Homeopathic – *Bufo rana* 6X (toad secretion): Appropriate for the nervous, impatient animal. Symptoms associated with epilepsy may include agitation, howling or the tendency to bite. The animal may also like to hide or be alone. Useful for epilepsy that has persisted for a long time. Give 1 to 2 tablets once immediately *after* each seizure ends. This may prevent recurrence.

Homeopathic – *Cicuta virosa* 6X (cowbane): Symptoms include delirium and acting stupid after the attacks. Convulsions are violent, with distortion of the limbs and backward arching of the head and neck. Give 1 to 2 tablets *after* a seizure.

Homeopathic – *Oenanthe crocata* 3X (hemlock water dropwort): Indicated for violent convulsions with a *rigid* body, locked jaws, foaming at the mouth. The head may be drawn back. Dose as for *Bufo rana*.

General directions for homeopathic treatments: These are just a few possible remedies. If you find they slow the frequency of attacks, be heartened! Treat the next seizure with the *same* medication as before. You may see increasing periods of time between attacks. Eventually, they may cease altogether.

However, sometimes a new attack occurs (or several in a row) sooner than expected – perhaps in just a few hours or days. It so, it is a sign that the medicine was probably right. After the initial stimulation of the symptoms, improvement will follow over the next few weeks. Do *not* repeat the medicine during these sooner-than-expected reactions. If after a period of improvement (days or weeks) the attacks return again, then give one treatment after each attack as described previously.

If you are able to tell when an attack is coming on, treatment at that time may avert it. It is a good way to use these medicines if they are effective only temporarily.

EYE PROBLEMS

Three major problems can affect animals' eyes: cataracts, corneal ulcers and ingrowing eyelids (entropion). We will consider each of these in turn.

CATARACTS

In this condition the round, clear lens in the interior of the eye which transmits and focuses light becomes cloudy or white (milky). Cataracts are more common in older animals and in dogs; they also are common in animals that have diabetes mellitus, even with insulin treatment. The cause is often unknown and treatment (if any is appropriate) usually consists of surgical removal of the lens. But natural methods have had considerable success in some cases.

Treatment

In response to a column I wrote for *Prevention* magazine, a reader wrote to me that she had had a marvellous response after treating her dog's cataracts with eucalyptus honey, of all things. I later suggested this treatment to others, who also had excellent results. The cataracts cleared so they were only about 15 per cent of what they had been. The technique is simple enough. Carefully apply a small dab of eucalyptus honey (see pages 269–70 for supplier) inside the lower lid with the blunt end of a toothpick once a day for several weeks; or use a dropper bottle and apply 1 drop in each eye. If you prefer or need another approach, try the following treatments.

In the early stage, when the cataract is just starting to form, give 1 to 2 tablets of *Natrum muriaticum* (Nat. mur.) 6X 4 times a day for several weeks. If the eye surface or lids are inflamed, use a tea made from the herb eyebright (*Euphrasia officinalis*) as an external eyewash. Pour a pint of boiling water over 1 ounce of the herb and steep 20 minutes; strain, add ½ teaspoon sea salt and use when cool. Also, increase the vitamin E supplement recommended in chapter 3 by four times.

In the later stages, when the cataract has existed for a while, give 1 to 2 tablets of *Silicea* 6X 4 times a day for several weeks. Also use high doses of vitamin E as in the early stage of treatment.

CORNEAL ULCERS

These are usually the result of an injury such as a scratch. When the surface of the eye is broken, it hurts and tears. The injury itself can be so small you can't even see it unless a light is cast upon it from the side or a special dye is used. Bacteria may infect the scratch but in the healthy animal an uncomplicated recovery is common.

Treatment

If the injury is deep or there is debris or a splinter stuck there, the condition will re-quire careful professional treatment under anaesthesia. Superficial injuries do not bleed. If you see blood, suspect penetration into and damage of delicate internal structures. This kind of injury can be very serious.

The following recommendations are for treating slight irritations, shallow ulcers or uninfected scratches.

Increase the cod-liver oil in the diet to twice the usual amount until the eye is healed. Also, double the daily amount of vitamin E. Every 4 hours, apply a drop of cod-liver oil directly on to the eye or into the lower lid. The oil has protective functions and the vitamin A in it will stimulate healing. *Or*, instead of dropping the oil into the eye, you can use an infusion of the herb eyebright. Prepare the tea as described for cataracts (remember to add the salt); when cool put 1 or 2 drops in the eye and gently wipe around the lid area with a tissue or cloth dampened with the infusion. Treat 3 times a day.

INGROWING EYELIDS
Entropion

In this condition the lids turn in and press the eyelashes against the corneal surface. The constant rubbing of the hairs causes a large (sometimes white), long-lasting ulcer to appear. This problem is not as easy to see as you might suppose. Gently pull the lids away from the eye and let them fall back several times. In the process you should be able to see the curling in of the lids as they are released. Some dogs are born with this condition so you can see it when they are quite young. Others develop it after a long period of low-grade conjunctivitis (eyelid inflammation). The repeated inflammation and contraction cause the lids to turn in. Entropion is less common in cats than in dogs.

Treatment

The usual correction is surgery, which is quite easy to perform and usually successful. Of course, if the underlying cause is chronic inflammation, then you must deal with that. In such a case, try the tissue salt *Magnesia phosphorica* (Mag. phos.) 3X (1 to 2 tablets every 4 hours), alternated with *Calcarea phosphorica* (Calc. phos.) 6X (1 to 2 tablets every 4 hours). Thus, tablets of one or the other will be given every 2 hours. Continue for several days, until improvement is noted.

Or, if the lids have become hardened through scarring, use the tissue salt *Silicea* 6X, 1 to 2 tablets 4 times a day for several weeks.

Also, double the amount of vitamin E in the basic diet for the same period of time.

FELINE LEUKAEMIA
See 'Cancer'

FELINE PANLEUCOPENIA
See 'Distemper, Chorea and Feline Panleukopenia'

FELINE UROLOGICAL SYNDROME
See 'Bladder Problems'

FLEAS
See 'Skin Parasites'

GASTRITIS
See 'Stomach Problems'

GRASS SEEDS
See also 'Ear Problems'

One enemy of dogs and cats is the army of plant awns and wild oat seeds that get caught in the hair and crevices of their bodies. Because of the way these are constructed, they will not easily dislodge. Instead, they tend to migrate through the skin or into body openings (eyes, ears, nose, mouth, anus, vagina, sheath) where they cause tremendous problems. If a grass seed works through the skin, the body cannot digest it; even years later it will look fresh on removal.

Thus, although the body makes every effort to eliminate the awn or seed, it clings tenaciously to the tissue. The result is a constantly inflamed tract that drains puslike fluid and never heals completely. The plant material can migrate a foot or more into the body, making it difficult, if not impossible, to find. Toes are a favourite lodging place, as are the ears (see 'Ear Problems') and eyes – where they can get behind the 'third eyelid' and cause a lot of irritation.

Prevention

Always check your animal over after it has run in fields, waste ground or other weedy places. Check all the body openings, and run a comb or brush through the hair. Be sure to check between the toes, too. If you keep the hair there clipped during the summer, your job will be much easier and your animal's life much more comfortable. Also, have the hair coat trimmed to a short length, an inch or less, and trim away any hair growing around the ear hole or inside the ear flap. Seeds are much likelier to get into the ears of dogs with hanging ears. See 'Ear Problems' for a discussion of that as well as of specific treatment for grass seeds stuck there. Also, see 'Abscesses'.

Treatment

If your animal already has a seed or awn under the skin with chronic discharge from a small opening, and your vet is not able to find and remove it, the following treatment may help:

Tissue Salt – *Silicea* 6X: Give 1 to 3 tablets twice a day for 2 or 3 weeks. If the seed sticker does not work its way out, your vet must keep trying to remove it surgically. (Always have him or her try to remove seeds as soon as possible; the above treatment is a last resort to try when surgical intervention has failed.)

HAIR LOSS
See 'Skin Problems'

HEART PROBLEMS

Disorders of the heart are relatively common in the later years of life for both dogs and cats. They do not have atherosclerosis and 'heart attacks' like those people get, however. Rather, the problem is usually a weakness of the heart muscle and dilation of one or both sides of the heart. Sometimes there is inadequate heart valve action or a rhythm that is too quick or too slow.

Typical signs of a heart problem include one or more of the following: becoming easily tired by exercise; bluish discolouration of the tongue and gums upon exercise; sudden collapse or prostration; difficult breathing or wheezing; a persistent dry cough that produces little expectoration; and an accumulation of fluid in the legs or abdomen (a pot-bellied look).

Treatment

The usual approach includes digitalis, a diuretic and a low-sodium diet. The method implies that the condition is progressive and the treatment is to control symptoms rather than to cure.

I prefer an alternative approach emphasizing nutrition and homeopathic herbal or mineral remedies. Though complete recovery may not be possible, these measures do more than just counteract symptoms; they can strengthen the affected tissues. The chance of help from any treatment, of course, depends on the amount of tissue damage that has occurred and the age of the animal. Prevention, in the form of a healthy lifestyle with nutritious food and regular exercise, is the best route. However, if symptoms have already developed, here is what I suggest.

Nutrition should emphasize the basic natural foods diet (chapters 3 and 4) with certain modifications. Feed only a small amount of meat, perhaps $\frac{1}{2}$ to 1 ounce raw beef, turkey or chicken heart daily or several times a week. For protein, depend on eggs, dairy products and tofu (see the vegetarian diet in chapter 5). Give plenty of grains and vegetables. Do not add any salt, soya sauce, bacon or other salty foods or flavourings to the food. Use spring water or other water that is unchlorinated and unfluoridated.

If the animal is overweight, use the diet under 'Weight Problems' to help it slim down. Weight reduction is important because more heart energy is required to push blood through all that fat.

In terms of supplements, give a complete B complex tablet that has all the B vitamins, especially niacin and pyridoxine. Major components should be at the 20- to 50-milligram level (depending on the animal's size). Use dolomite powder instead of the bone meal (feed a little more than the recommended amount of the latter), a trace mineral supplement containing chromium and selenium (scale the recommended human dose on the label down to your animal's size) and chelated zinc (5 to 20 milligrams daily).

Other important measures are regular daily exercise that is not too strenuous or exciting (walking is good) and the avoidance of cigarette smoke. In the sensitive animal, many of the symptoms of heart disease can be caused by exposure to cigarette smoke, including irregular pulse, pain in the heart region, difficult breathing, cough, dizziness and prostration.

Specific remedies may be helpful. Where the condition is not too severe, try one of the following two tissue salts:

Tissue Salt – *Calcarea fluorica* (Calc. fluor.) 6X: Helps to restore strength to the heart muscle, especially when it is dilated and the action is weak. Give 1 to 2 tablets 4 times daily.

Tissue Salt – *Kali phosphoricum* (Kali phos.) 6X: Suited for the problem that seems more functional (rather than the result of tissue changes or pathology). That is, such things as nervousness and physical or emotional excitement seem to lead to symptoms. Give 1 to 2 tablets 4 times daily.

For more severe or persistent symptoms that are not controlled by the nutritional programme and other measures, pick out one of the following treatments, whichever seems best indicated. (Don't skip the other measures and expect good results, however!)

Homeopathic – *Crataegus oxyacanthoides* (hawthorn berries): Indicated for the animal with a dilated heart, weak heart muscle, difficult breathing, fluid retention and (often) a nervous or irritable temperament. Use the homeopathic tincture (or make your own if you can get fresh berries). Give 1 to 3 drops 2 to 3 times a day.

Homeopathic – *Strophanthus hispidus* (kombe seed): For the weak heart with valvular problems. The pulse is weak, frequent and irregular and breathing is difficult. There may also be fluid retention, loss of appetite and vomiting. Obesity and chronic itching of the skin also point to this medicine. Use the tincture or the homeopathic 3X preparation. Give 1 to 2 drops (or tablets) twice a day.

Homeopathic – *Digitalis purpurea* 6X (foxglove): Give one tablet of the 6X potency after an 'attack' characterized by faintness or prostration after exertion, in which the tongue turns blue or the animal collapses. Often the pulse or heart rate is abnormally *slow*. There may be heart dilation and fluid retention. Liver disturbances may be evidenced by a white, pasty stool. If you give a tablet *after* each attack, attacks will become less frequent if the herb is helping.

Homeopathic – *Spongia tosta* (roasted sponge): For the animal with a rapid pulse, difficult breathing and evidence of fear during crises. It may have difficulty lying down and may breathe easier sitting up. A dry, persistent cough or asthma is often associated. Use the tincture, giving 1 to 2 drops 2 to 3 times daily.

General directions for the homeopathic remedies are that if any of these preparations seems to help and there is obvious improvement, stop the treatment. Later, if improvement ceases or symptoms return, continue the same treatment that helped before.

HEPATITIS
See 'Liver Problems'

HIP DYSPLASIA

This term describes a poorly formed hip joint. The veterinary profession generally regards it as a genetic problem complicated by a variety of environmental influences. Unfortunately, it is common among dogs. Hip dysplasia is not present as a deformity at birth but appears during growth. The hip joint forms in a loose or 'sloppy' way, allowing too much movement of the leg bone in and out of the socket. Irritation and scarring occur because the weak ligaments and surrounding joint tissues aren't able to adequately stabilize the joint. After years, severe arthritis may result.

Prevention and Treatment

Orthodox treatment centres on a number of surgical procedures that involve cutting certain muscles, repositioning the joint, removing the head of the leg bone or completely replacing the hip joint with an artificial device. But there are other avenues of greater promise.

A good starting place lies in prevention by good nutrition. As I understand it, hip dysplasia is a degenerative condition brought about by generations of poor feeding practices. The effects of poor nutrition are always magnified with succeeding generations. If you can avoid it, don't adopt an affected dog in the first place (see guidelines for choosing a healthy animal in chapter 9). Apart from that, good prevention begins with feeding the pregnant female or newly acquired puppy a wholesome, fresh, well-supplemented diet as outlined in this book. Be sure to include plenty of bone meal. As a preventive, also give lots of vitamin C (ascorbate), particularly if either parent had the condition or the pup comes from a commonly affected breed, especially Alsatians and other large pure-breds.

Indeed, there is some good evidence that hip dysplasia is caused by chronic subclinical scurvy (a lack of adequate vitamin C), which results in a hip malformation that is *secondary* to weak ligaments and muscles around the joints (ascorbate is essential to these tissues). Wendell Belfield, D.V.M., reported in *Veterinary Medicine/Small Animal Clinician* (October, 1976) the complete (100 per cent) prevention of hip dysplasia in eight litters of Alsatian pups coming from parents that either had the condition themselves or had previously produced offspring with it.

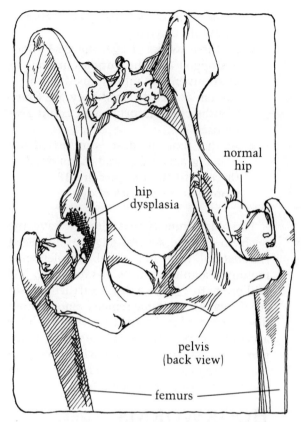

Hip dysplasia is a condition in which the hip's ball and socket joint does not form properly. Severe arthritis may result.

The programme he used was this:

Four steps to prevent hip dysplasia

- The pregnant female is given 2 to 4 grams of sodium ascorbate crystals in the ration daily ($\frac{1}{2}$ to 1 teaspoon of the pure powder).
- At birth, the puppies are given 50 to 100 milligrams of Ce-Vi-Sol (by Mead Johnson) orally every day. (This is a

liquid form of ascorbate; any other would do as well.)

- At three weeks of age, the Ce-Vi-Sol is stopped and the puppies are instead given 500 milligrams daily of sodium ascorbate until they are four months old. (Ascorbic acid could also be used.)
- At that time the dose is increased to 1 or 2 grams a day and maintained there until the puppies are 18 months to two years of age.

For older animals that already have the problem, I have several suggestions. Feed the natural diet and usual supplements, including ample amounts of vitamin C, 500 milligrams to 2 grams a day. In arthritic cases see if there is a suitable remedy among those described under 'Arthritis'. If you have access to acupuncture or chiropractic treatment, you may find your dog will experience marked improvement. See chapter 14 for some interesting case examples.

HOOKWORMS
See 'Worms'

HYPERACTIVITY
See 'Behaviour Problems'

INGROWING EYELIDS
See 'Eye Problems'

INJURIES
See the *Emergency Guide*

INTERVERTEBRAL DISC DISEASE
See 'Paralysis'

ITCHING
See 'Skin Problems'

KENNEL COUGH
See 'Upper Respiratory Infections'

KIDNEY FAILURE
For stones, see 'Bladder Problems'

Because the kidneys have the essential task of cleaning the blood, anything added to the body which is unusable and must be eliminated simply adds to the work they must do. Thus chemicals in food (like preservatives, colouring agents and artificial flavouring agents) and in the environment (contaminated water, air and soil) are directly stressful to the kidneys and probably play a role in the development of the condition. In addition, lack of adequate exercise and diminished exposure to natural environments compound the problem of inadequate elimination and a sluggish metabolism. During exercise, for instance, the lungs and skin play a bigger role in elimination.

The skin, which is another important eliminative organ, seems to be linked to the kidneys in that long-term skin irritation and eruption often seem to precede eventual kidney failure in old age. If the skin disorder is repeatedly suppressed with doses of cortisone or related corticosteroid drugs, the relationship seems especially true.

If you are observant, you can detect the signs of kidney failure early. They are thirst, much drinking of water, frequent urination with large quantities of pale urine, inability to hold the urine all night long, and occasional periods of low energy, lack of appetite and nausea that last for a few days. By identifying the problem early, you stand a much better chance of prolonging your animal's life with a special diet and other natural treatments than if you wait until an emergency.

If untreated, the early symptoms progress

into a more severe form of failure that is characterized by lethargy (low energy), frequent vomiting, dehydration, complete loss of appetite, foul breath and perhaps an inflammation of the mouth or presence of mouth ulcers. At this point the animal needs an emergency intravenous infusion of large quantities of fluids to save its life. The fluids are given to replace essential salts that are lost by the damaged kidneys and to flush toxic metabolic wastes out of the bloodstream. This more serious stage of the condition is called uraemia.

If this intensive treatment is successful, your animal will be returned to you in more or less normal condition. But it is a fragile normality, for in many cases 80 to 90 per cent of the kidney tissue has been destroyed, and cannot be regained.

Ordinarily, healthy kidneys have plenty of time to filter all the blood that flows through. In addition, they return needed salts to the bloodstream and remove excess water from the urine. But with so little functional tissue left, the fluids are pushed through much more rapidly, resulting in a loss of essential salts and water. The end result is dehydration, loss of the water-soluble vitamins and the back-up of metabolic waste – most of which is in the form of urea, a by-product of protein digestion.

Treatment

At any point in the disease you can spare the kidneys much of their workload by carefully monitoring the diet and environmental conditions.

Since the main goal is to reduce the load on the kidneys and since most of the metabolic waste results from protein, what we must do is to feed protein that is of high quality but that is the bare minimum needed in the diet. That way the body can use it efficiently and

have little left over as waste. The kidney diet is also low in ash content, which makes it suitable for use in animals prone to stone formation and urinary obstruction.

The recipes that follow provide such a low-protein, low-ash diet. Use them as your basis.

FELINE KIDNEY DIET No. 1

1 large egg
¼ cup lean or organ meat
½ cup cooked barley or brown rice
1 tablespoon grated parsnip, parsley or other vegetable
1 teaspoon oil
daily supplements as recommended

Simply combine the ingredients and serve.

Yield: about 1 cup

FELINE KIDNEY DIET No. 2

¼ cup medium-fat mince or other fatty meat
¼ cup cooked kidney beans
¼ cup booked barley or brown rice
2 tablespoons creamed cottage cheese
1 tablespoon chopped parsley or other vegetable
daily supplements as recommended

Simply combine the ingredients and serve.

Yield: about 1 cup

CANINE KIDNEY DIET No. 1

> *2 medium eggs*
> *½ cup lean meat or offal*
> *2 cups cooked barley or brown rice*
> *daily supplements as recommended*
> *2 tablespoons grated parsnip or other vegetable*
> *1 tablespoon honey*

Mix the first four ingredients as the main ration. Roll the parsnip and honey into balls and feed as a treat.

> *Yield: about 2 ½ cups.*

CANINE KIDNEY DIET No. 2

> *⅓ cup medium-fat mince or other fatty meat*
> *⅓ cup cooked kidney beans*
> *1 ¾ cup cooked barley or brown rice*
> *1 tablespoon non-fat powdered milk (or ⅓ cup skimmed milk)*
> *¼ cup chopped parsley or other vegetable*
> *daily supplements as recommended*

Simply combine the ingredients and serve.

> *Yield: about 3 cups*

Supplements should be modified by cutting the usual amont of *Powder Mix* (yeast, kelp, bone meal) in half. Vitamin A (found in the standard cod-liver oil recommendation) and the water-soluble vitamins (B and C) are particularly needed. Also add a natural B complex preparation to the diet. The major B vitamins in it should be at about the 10-milligram level for small dogs and cats, 20 milligrams for medium dogs and 20 to 50 milligrams for large dogs. Also, give vitamin C twice a day in these amounts: 250 milligrams for cats and small dogs; 500 milligrams for medium dogs; and 1,000 milligrams for large dogs.

Certain foods are considered especially good for kidney problems, so work these into the recipes: parsnips, parsley, cabbage, kidney beans, barley, carrots, leafy greens, watercress, onions, bone marrow and red meat. Don't feed meat in excess. However, once a week a small amount of raw beef liver or kidney is advisable. For treats try strawberries, apples and honey.

Other therapeutic measures are to avoid cigarette smoke, chemicalized or chlorinated water, highly processed, overcooked, spoiled or commercial foods, stress, extreme heat and unnecessary exposure to chemical products, car fumes and polluted environments in general.

It also helps to vigorously brush the coat and skin regularly and to give a weekly bath with a mild, non-drying shampoo. Provide regular mild outdoor exercise and exposure to fresh air and sun. Always allow easy access to a place for urination and defaecation. Make lots of pure water available for drinking at all times and feed the daily rations as two meals instead of one.

Herbs and tissue salts that may strengthen your animal's kidney tissue are listed below; pick one of them.

Herbal – alfalfa (*Medicago sativa*): Use the tincture; 3 times daily give 1 or 2 drops to cats or small dogs, 2 to 4 drops to medium dogs and 4 to 6 drops to large dogs. Continue this use until you see benefit, then reduce to once a day or as needed. As an alternative, use alfalfa tablets, giving 1 to 4 twice a day (depending on the animal's size). They can be crushed and mixed with the food.

Herbal – marsh mallow (*Althaea officinalis*): Prepare an infusion by adding 2 tablespoons of the flowers or leaves to 1 cup of boiling water. Let steep 5 minutes. Or, make a decoction (which is more potent) by simmering 1 teaspoon of the root in a cup of boiling water for 20 to 30 minutes. Twice a day give $\frac{1}{2}$ teaspoon to cats or small dogs, 1 teaspoon to medium dogs and 1 tablespoon to large dogs. Try mixing it in the food. Continue for several weeks and then taper off to twice a week.

Tissue Salts – *Calcarea phosphorica* (Calc. phos.) 6X and *Natrum muriaticum* (Nat. mur.) 6X: Give 1 tablet of each of these together morning and evening. Continue for several weeks, then taper off to twice a week. As an alternative, use *Tissue Salt Combination G*, 2 tablets, morning and evening.

Crisis therapy

A severe crisis in an animal with weak or failed kidneys is best handled by your vet. Often the technique of intravenous fluid administration is critical to survival, because anything given by mouth is immediately vomited. However, if you can't get to a vet, I would suggest the following treatment adapted from that used by herbalist Juliette de Bairacli-Levy.

Until the crisis passes, withhold all solid food. Instead give:

Cool parsley tea: Steep a tablespoon of fresh parsley in a cup of hot water for 20 minutes. Give 1 teaspoon to 2 tablespoons 3 times a day.

Barley water: To make this, pour 3 cups of boiling water over a cup of whole barley. Cover and let steep overnight. In the morning strain and squeeze out the liquid through muslin or cloth. Add to it 2 teaspoons each of honey and pure lemon juice. Feed your animal $\frac{1}{4}$ to 2 cups of this liquid twice a day. (Make a bigger batch if necessary.)

Parsnip balls: Roll raw, grated parsnips, which help to detoxify the kidneys, with some thick honey (an energy source) into balls. Give as desired.

Pure water: Make it available at all times. Your pet may have trouble keeping fluids down. If so, to rehydrate and help detoxify the animal give 1 to 3 enemas per day, until vomiting stops. For each 20 pounds of weight, combine $\frac{1}{2}$ teaspoon sea salt, $\frac{1}{2}$ teaspoon potassium chloride (a salt substitute), 1 teaspoon lemon juice and 500 milligrams vitamin C, well dissolved in a pint of lukewarm water. See instructions for administration in chapter 15. When an animal is dehydrated it will retain the enema.

After the crisis stage, you can return the animal to food slowly, utilizing the maintenance program already described. Remember, the single most important thing is to give large volumes of fluids (with salts added) to rehydrate the tissues and to flush the kidneys. Without adequate fluid, treatment will not be successful. If vomiting is severe and continuous, use the suggestions under 'Vomiting'. Particularly try the homeopathic remedy, *Ipecac* 3X.

LEUKAEMIA
See 'Cancer'

LIVER PROBLEMS

The liver may be the most important organ of the body. It is involved in innumerable events, including the manufacture of blood proteins, fats and the proteins responsible for blood clotting; storage of energy (as glycogen) for production of blood sugar as needed by the body; storage of the fat-soluble vitamins and iron; the detoxification of drugs, chemicals and other unusable substances; the inactivation of hormones no longer needed; and the secretion of bile and other factors necessary for proper digestion. As if these tasks were not enough to keep it busy, the liver also must filter blood coming from the digestive tract to keep potentially harmful bacteria from reaching other parts of the body. It is the organ that prepares toxic material and waste products for subsequent elimination by the kidneys.

Therefore, as you can imagine, inflammation of the liver (hepatitis) and other disturbances of this vital organ are very serious conditions. Symptoms of liver trouble include nausea, vomiting, loss of appetite, jaundice (yellowing of the tissues, best seen at the whites of the eyes in animals) and perhaps the passing of light-coloured or 'fatty'-looking bowel movements (from insufficient bile and poor digestion) or the swelling of the abdomen from fluid accumulation.

Liver malfunction is caused by many conditions. Common factors are virus infections or swallowing poisonous substances. But in most cases it's hard to tell just what initiated the problem.

Treatment

Because the liver is so central to the whole process of breaking down and using food, treatment includes minimizing the work it must do by fasting or feeding small, frequent, easily digested meals. In the early acute stage of liver inflammation fasting is best, especially if a fever is present. Follow the directions for fasting given in chapter 15. Keep your dog on a liquid diet for a few days until the temperature returns to normal or there is some improvement. During this period give the following treatments.

Vitamin C: 500 to 2,000 milligrams 4 times a day. This is most easily given as sodium ascorbate powder dissolved in a small amount of water. ($\frac{1}{4}$ teaspoon is about 1,000 milligrams.)

Tissue Salt – *Natrum sulphuricum* (Nat. sulph.) 3X or 6X: Give 1 to 3 tablets every 2 hours. Give the vitamin C first, followed by the Nat. sulph. in a few minutes. If the ascorbate causes increased vomiting, discontinue it for a day and try again. (Or use *Ipecac* 3X; see 'Vomiting'.) As soon as the vomiting is controlled, try the vitamin C again.

If the Nat. sulph. doesn't help after 24 hours, try the homeopathic remedy *Bryonia* 6X, giving 1 to 2 tablets every 2 hours. *Bryonia* is indicated when the animal is very thirsty, is reluctant to move (because of pain) and vomits after drinking warm liquids.

As the animal improves and the symptoms subside, ease it on to a diet similar to that given for kidney failure. However, reduce the fat content of the diet by substituting uncreamed cottage cheese for creamed, lean meat for fatty and eliminating the added oil. Cottage cheese and eggs usually are well tolerated by the liver patient, as are grains. Feed small amounts, giving about one-quarter of the recipe serving 4 times a day, with food warmed to room temperature. Use the supplements indicated in chapter 3, but hold back on the vegetable oil until the condition is quite normal. Then reintroduce it, starting in small amounts.

After a month or two of recovery, you can gradually and carefully switch to the more extended recipes outlined in chapter 4. During this time of healing, emphasize raw foods as much as possible (cottage cheese, eggs, meat and finely grated vegetables). Some foods, of course, must be well cooked for digestion (like grains and beans). Combine the foods only after the cooked ingredients have cooled. This precaution will provide optimal amounts of unaltered nutrients needed for the quickest possible recovery. If these foods are accepted, try including raw grated beets (about 1 to 3 tablespoons) every day as a liver stimulant. One to 2 tablespoons of fresh minced parsley is also useful.

During recovery also continue the ascorbate. As you see improvement, gradually taper off use of the Nat. sulph. or *Bryonia* to twice a day, then to once a day. Finally, use it only when there seems to be a flare-up of the problem indicated by loss of appetite or nausea).

JAUNDICE

Jaundice, seen as a yellowing of the tissues, can occur without liver inflammation. If there is a rapid breakdown of red blood cells, the liver can't process all the released haemoglobin quickly enough. The result is a back-up of this pigment which stains the tissues yellow. Causes of such a rapid red blood cell breakdown include blood parasites, certain chemicals or drugs, various infections and poisonous snakebites. Your vet will have to distinguish between jaundice caused by factors like these and the type associated with liver disease. Where the liver is ailing the stool is often light coloured or pale. However, if the jaundice has been caused by red blood cell breakdowns, the stool is typically very dark, from extra bile flow.

The sudden loss of intact red blood cells results in a form of anaemia, even though no blood was lost to the outside. To enhance red blood cell replacement, follow the nutritional and other advice under 'Anemia'. Apart from underlying causes (which may need to be dealt with, too), a non-inflammatory simple jaundice of this sort can be treated very simply by exposing the animal to direct sunlight (or indirect if it's too

hot) for several hours a day for a few days. Sunlight stimulates the elimination of the pigments responsible for the jaundice. See the discussion of natural light in chapter 8. In addition, it may help to use the *Natrum sulphuricum* (Nat. sulph.) as indicated for liver inflammation for a few days to stimulate liver function and enhance a return to normal.

MAMMARY TUMOURS

Mammary tumours are seen mostly in older bitches that have not been spayed. Generally, the spaying process (in which the ovaries and uterus are removed) acts as a preventive of this disease. Perhaps the unnatural situation of repeatedly coming into heat without being bred leads to a sort of cellular frustration and the beginning of abnormal growth. My recommendation is that you have your bitch spayed, both for this reason and to prevent the birth of puppies in a world that cannot provide homes for those it has already.

Treatment

In many cases mammary tumours are malignant and radical surgery involving removal of associated lymph nodes is performed. If your pet develops such tumours, have her examined by your vet. If the tumours are not thought to be malignant, one of the following treatments can be tried:

Homeopathic – *Phytolacca decandra* (pokeweed): This herb is known for its use in disorders of the mammary glands, especially enlargements and tumours. Obtain the tincture from a homeopathic supplier. Make a

1:100 potentized dilution by first putting 2 drops of the tincture into a new, clean 1-ounce dropper bottle. Then mix 60 drops (1 teaspoon filled to the brim) of brandy and 120 drops (2 teaspoons) of distilled water in a clean glass. Pour this into the bottle containing the 2 drops of tincture and shake the mixture vigorously by hitting it hard against the palm of the hand 20 to 30 times until it foams up well. Used in large undiluted quantities, this herb can be poisonous; by following these directions it is safe. Give cats and small and medium dogs 1 drop twice daily; use 2 drops for large dogs.

As an alternative to that treatment (which is easier than it sounds!), you can use tissue salts. You can use two of them together, if so indicated. Pick the one that is best suited as your primary treatment and use it as indicated. The second choice can be given morning and night, on either side of the sleep period.

Tissue Salt – *Kali muriaticum* (Kali mur.) 3X: Use where the tumours are sensitive to pressure and feel soft. Give 1 to 2 tablets 3 times daily.

Tissue Salt – *Kali phosphoricum* (Kali phos.) 6X: Use where the tumours discharge a smelly secretion and the animal is nervous, tired, highly-strung or exhausted. Give 1 to 2 tablets 3 times daily.

Tissue Salt – *Silicea* 6X: Use where there tends to be pustular discharge or the indication it may happen (tenderness, pain, heat). Also good for *hard* swellings. Give 1 to 2 tablets 3 times daily.

Note: Remember, nutrition is important, as it is in all diseases. Besides the natural diet, offer large amounts of vitamin C (500 milligrams to 5 grams daily), as well as vitamin E (double the usual amount) and vitamin A (as obtained in the recommended amount of cod-liver oil). All three vitamins are useful for detoxification.

MANGE
See 'Skin Parasites'

METRITIS
See 'Reproductive Organ Problems'

MITES
See 'Ear Problems' and 'Skin Parasites'

NEPHRITIS
See 'Kidney Failure'

NEUTERING
See 'Spaying and Neutering'

NOSE PROBLEMS
See 'Grass Seeds', 'Upper Respiratory Infections'

OBESITY
See 'Weight Problems'

PANCREATITIS

Pancreatitis is a sudden severe condition usually seen in the overweight middle-aged dog that has long overindulged in fatty food or in rubbish bin raiding. Symptoms can include a complete loss of appetite, severe and frequent vomiting, diarrhoea that may contain blood, reluctance to walk, weakness and pain (crying and restlessness).

The severity of the attack can vary from a mild, almost unnoticed condition to a severe shocklike collapse that can end in death. The problem centres in the digestive tract, particularly in the pancreas. It results from long-term poor nutrition high in fat and sugar, which assaults the pancreas with an excessive demand for digestive enzymes and insulin.

Prevention and Treatment

Prevention consists simply of a properly balanced natural diet *coupled with regular and adequate exercise*. The exercise is important because it improves digestion and peristaltic movements of the intestinal tract, thus regularizing the bowels. It also keeps weight under control. Do not overfeed your dog, because obesity is a predisposing factor. Many people end up with fat dogs because they enjoy watching the animal eat heartily. If this describes you, see chapter 10 and 'Weight Problems'.

Treatment usually requires hospitalization, with fluid replacement therapy for the animal suffering with extreme vomiting and diarrhoea. If the condition is mild but recurrent, the following measures should help to restore a balance of health.

Feed the basic natural diet and supplements (chapters 3 and 4), *except* omit vegetable oils or butter, as well as other fatty food that may irritate the pancreas. But do use cod-liver oil or a vitamin A and D capsule to take its place. Be sure to use the vitamin E (preferably raw), but include a variety of others as well. Avoid fruits.

Feed small, frequent meals instead of one large one. Offer all food at room temperature for best digestive action.

Use vitamin C and bioflavonoids regularly, 3 times a day if possible. Depending on the dog's size, give 250 to 1,000 milligrams vitamin C with each dose. Sodium ascorbate powder may be better tolerated than ascorbic acid, which is sometimes a bit irritating to the digestive tract. (A teaspoon of ascorbate powder has about 4,000 milligrams.) Give 25 to 50 milligrams of bioflavonoids (vitamin P) to enhance the action of the ascorbate.

Eliminate any food or supplement which seems to upset the digestive tract or aggravates the symptoms. Find a substitute form for any supplement you discontinue.

In addition to the nutritional advice above, try one of the following as a supportive treatment, whichever you prefer:

Herbal – yarrow (*Achillea millefolium*): Make a tea from the whole plant. Add an ounce of the fresh, clean plant to a pint of boiling water (or a teaspoon of the dried plant to a cup of water). Steep 10 minutes and strain. Give 1 teaspoon to 2 tablespoons (depending on the animal's size) 3 times a day. Yarrow strengthens the pancreas and helps to control internal haemorrhages. It is indicated where there is dark, chocolate-coloured diarrhoea that changes to black (perhaps containing blood) and is foul smelling.

Homeopathic – *Iris versicolor* 3X (blue flag): This remedy is particularly suited to the pancreas and may be more effective than yarrow, though not as easily obtained. Give 1 tablet every 3 hours during an attack. Taper off (treat 3 times a day, then twice a day) as symptoms diminish.

Tissue Salts – *Natrum phosphoricum* (Nat. phos.) 3X or 6X and *Ferrum phosphoricum* (Ferr. phos.) 6X: As needed, alternate 1 or 2 tablets of the Nat. phos. with 1 or 2 tablets of the Ferr. phos., dosing every 2 hours. This treatment is most useful during the inflammatory stage. Later, for long-term use, Nat. phos. can be given alone for a long period to strengthen the digestive system. Give 1 to 2 tablets 3 times a day.

PANLEUCOPENIA (See

See 'Distemper, Chorea and Feline Panleucopenia'

PARALYSIS

Causes of paralysis can range from accidents that damage the spine to blood clots that form in brain arteries to intervertebral disc disease ('slipped disc'), as well as many others. Here we will consider the two most common causes, which are intervertebral disc disease and spondylosis (a built-up of calcium on the spine).

To some extent we can consider these two conditions together because both are degenerative processes involving the spine. In intervertebral disc disease, the soft gelatinous material between the vertebrae (bones that enclose the spinal cord) escapes its normal position and puts pressure on the spinal cord. The apparent cause is a breakdown of the ligaments that keep this material in place. The condition is worse in breeds that have long backs in relation to their legs, such as dachshunds.

Spondylosis is seen more often in large dogs like Alsatians. It is associated with a long-term inflammation of the vertebrae, which the body attempts to heal by immobilizing spinal movements with calcium deposits. These deposits eventually encroach on the nerves that branch out from the spinal cord, interfering with their functions. Symptoms are not obvious to the untrained eye. Be on the lookout for some rigidity of the back and some difficulty or pain on getting up. Usually a diagnosis is made only after an x-ray is taken. Spondylosis often is associated with hip dysplasia as well, so look at that entry, too.

Prevention

My opinion is that both of these conditions have common underlying causes – poor nutrition, inadequate exercise and stress. They are better prevented than treated. Your best insurance is to follow the natural diet recommendations and the advice in chapter 7. See also chapter 9; avoid selecting a breed that is more prone to intervertebral disc disease and other spinal problems because of an altered anatomy.

Treatment

If your animal (usually a dog) already has intervertebral disc problems that flare up occasionally, here is what you can do.

Nutrition should be emphasized. Avoid commercial foods and treats, using only the natural diet and supplements advised in this book. Be sure to include the brewer's yeast regularly, because it is helpful for this problem. The vitamin E will help reduce inflammation.

In addition to the usual supplements, give 500 to 1,000 milligrams of vitamin C twice a day to strengthen the connective tissue involved and to counteract stress.

For specific treatment you can try the homeopathic remedy *Nux vomica* 3X (poison nut). It is most effective where there is pain in the back, muscle tightness or spasms along the lower back and weakness or paralysis of the rear legs. Give it 3 times daily, especially at first or during attacks, tapering off when improvement occurs. If constipation develops after using this treatment for a couple of weeks, discontinue it until needed again.

If you catch the problem early, *Nux vomica* may help to prevent the pain, tightness and rear leg symptoms for which it is indicated. The dog that has been paralysed a long time may not easily respond. In such a case try the tissue salts *Kali phosphoricum* (Kali phos.) 6X or *Magnesia phosphorica* (Mag. phos.) 6X, either alone or in alternation. Give 1 to 2 tablets, 3 times a day for several weeks. You can use these instead of *Nux vomica*, or after trying it.

A paralysed animal will benefit from massage of the back and legs and passive movement of the limbs to keep the muscles from shrinking away. If there is slight voluntary movement of the legs, exercise the animal by helping it to 'swim' in a bathtub or pool. Support most of its weight with a towel.

Other approaches that have helped this

problem include acupuncture and chiropractic adjustment.

If your animal has spondylosis I must say that it can be difficult to treat once it has developed. The chance of improvement is less for a dog already paralysed than for one that is only weakened. A short fast (see chapter 15) may be helpful, followed by the basic natural diet and supplements given in this book. Cod-liver oil (for vitamins A and D), bone meal (for calcium), vitamin E (or wheat germ oil) and vitamin C (see 'Arthritis') will be especially important.

Besides exercise and massage, try a course of treatment with the tissue salts *Kali phosphoricum* (Kali phos.) 6X (2 to 4 tablets every evening) and *Silicea* 6X (2 to 4 tablets every morning).

Continue this course for several weeks or until there is improvement. If you see encouraging signs, gradually increase the amount of exercise to encourage redevelopment of the muscles.

POISONING
See the *Emergency Guide*

PREGNANCY, BIRTH AND CARE OF NEWBORNS
See also 'Reproductive Organ Problems'

The key to a successful and easy pregnancy and delivery is good nutrition. During gestation (63 to 65 days for cats, 58 to 63 days for dogs) tremendous demands are made on the mother's tissues to supply all the nutrients needed to build several new bodies. The general rule is that kittens or puppies come first. That is, they get whatever is available nutritionally and the mother gets what's left. If she doesn't consume enough food to supply complete nutrition, her body provides whatever is lacking.

A female that is not adequately fed, or that is bred from again and again, accumulates a nutritional deficiency that becomes greater with each pregnancy. Eventually the mother will become diseased or the young will be weak and susceptible to disease – perhaps during their entire lives. The special recipes in chapter 5 for pregnant and nursing females and for young animals are designed to meet their special needs and prevent this nutritional depletion. Let's look at the two most common problems – eclampsia and dystocia (difficult delivery).

ECLAMPSIA

Eclampsia is a term for a severe disturbance induced by a lack of calcium. As new skeletons are being formed or milk is being produced, the demand for calcium from the mother's body increases very much above normal. Therefore, this condition is usually seen at the end of pregnancy, right after birth or during nursing. Symptoms include loss of appetite, a high fever (sometimes dangerously so) and convulsions. During convulsions the muscles become rigid and the animal falls over with the head back; more typically, you may see a series of rapid contractions and relaxations of the muscles that looks like uncontrollable shaking. Strenuous treatment is necessary, including intravenous injections of calcium by your vet and ice baths (to bring down the temperature). Such treatment is usually successful but the condition can recur if the young continue to nurse.

It is *much* better to prevent this problem in the first place by proper and bountiful nutrition rather than to try to patch up the animal once it has occurred. However, in the event that your female already suffers from eclampsia, put her on the diet in chapter 5 that is appropriate for her stage of pregnancy or lactation. Be sure to include all the supplements advised there, particularly bone meal. In addition, use the tissue salts *Magnesia phosphorica* (Mag. phos.) 6X (1 to 2 tablets 3 times a day for 3 weeks). The Mag. phos. helps control muscle spasms and the Calc. phos. aids in the assimilation of calcium.

DYSTOCIA (difficult birth)

Cats and dogs with normal anatomy rarely have problems giving birth, particularly if they are adequately fed during pregnancy. However, lack of certain essential nutrients like calcium may weaken the uterine muscles and cause weak or short contractions. This problem is uncommon, but has been increasing in incidence. In addition, some foetal deformities can cause obstruction of the birth canal during labour. But the biggest problem occurs in female dogs that do not have a normal anatomy. Generally, these are dogs deformed by breeding trends so that the pelvis is too small in relation to the size of the puppy. Other than the use of caesarean sections, little can be done about this problem except the obvious: avoid breeding such animals or selecting them as pets (which creates a market for them).

If your female's trouble is that contractions are not producing results, use the tissue salt *Kali phosphoricum* (Kali phos.) 6X (get it beforehand just in case). Give 1 to 2 tablets every 15 minutes for 3 doses. If there is improvement, don't repeat the dose unless things slow down again. Remember that often the mother will naturally rest between deliveries, even taking a nap for as long as an hour or two. So don't rush things too much.

If a puppy or kitten is part way out and seems stuck, pulling on it *very gently* may help. Anything more vigorous than an extremely gentle touch can cause damage to either the mother or the unborn. Kali phos. may help. Get professional help if the baby has been trapped in the birth canal for more than half an hour (it will be dead by then) or if labour has been long but without result. A caesarean section will probably have to be performed. If your vet thinks it advisable, this is also a good time to have the animal spayed.

If all goes well at home and the delivery is complete, use the tissue salt *Ferrum phosphoricum* (Ferr. phos.) 6X (1 to 2 tablets 3 times a day for 3 days) to strengthen the mother and prevent infection.

I should add that it is a good idea to count the afterbirths, one for each newborn, so you know they have all come out. Look fast, because the mother will generally eat them. If an afterbirth stays inside, serious problems can result. If one is retained, use the Kali phos. every hour for a few doses to stimulate explusion. If this is ineffective, take the mother to your vet for more extensive treatment.

CARE OF THE NEWBORN

Fortunately for you, the mother generally will do everything necessary to care for the newborn. It is best not to interfere unless there is a problem. Right after birth she will clean the little ones. Part of the cleanliness programme is to lick up and swallow all the urine and faeces voided by the growing young. This is nature's way of keeping a clean nest. A possible problem is that if the offspring develop diarrhoea, the mother's meticulous cleaning may never let the evidence collect to warn you.

Diarrhoea is one of the more common problems at this stage of life, so let's discuss it briefly. Causes can include getting too much milk (sometimes a problem with hand-raised puppies or kittens), infection in the uterus or mammary glands of the mother (check her temperature; normal is 102.5°F or below) or the administration of antibiotics to the mother (they can get into the milk).

The puppy or kitten with diarrhoea will get dehydrated (the skin will be wrinkled and look too big for the body) and cold. It may crawl away from the nest and will usually 'cry' (even when returned to the mother). What you need to do is to feed it by hand with a pet nurser bottle (sold at pet stores). See chapter 5; use the formulas there, or a commercial milk preparation made for kittens or puppies. However, until the diarrhoea is under control, feed the formula diluted half and half with pure water. After a few feedings the problem should correct itself, but if more treatment is needed try one of the following two methods.

Use a mixture consisting of half formula (regular strength) and half warm camomile tea. Feed on a regular schedule until the problem is controlled, usually by two or three feedings.

Use the half formula/half water mixture, but add to it a crushed tablet of the homeopathic preparation *Podophyllum* 3X or 6X (may-apple). Mix well. One such therapeutic feeding should be enough, but repeat this formula every 4 hours if necessary.

After the diarrhoea is under control you can return the puppy or kitten to the nest, but be watchful in case the diarrhoea returns.

RADIATION TOXICITY

The most common sources of radiation exposure for the average animal are diagnostic x-rays or radiation therapy (I do not recommend the latter). Other possible sources are less obvious – such as the leakage from a nuclear power plant.

In either of these situations, the body is challenged to repair a lot of damage at the cellular level. And to do so it must use repair mechanisms that also may be affected. Fortunately there are some constructive steps one can take to enhance the healing process after radiation exposure. Use them after any unusual radiation exposure. (Also, if there is leakage from a power plant or other atmospheric leakage, it would be best to keep your animal and yourself indoors for a while.)

Nutrition is the main precaution. Emphasize the use of rolled oats as the grain for several weeks. It helps counteract nausea and other side effects. Helpful supplements already included in the standard recommendations are brewer's yeast, cold-pressed unsaturated vegetable oil (for vitamin F) and kelp (which contains alginate, a substance that helps remove strontium 90 from the body and also protects against absorption of radioactive iodine).

Additional supplements to use while needed are rutin (vitamin P or bioflavonoids), which has reduced the death rate in irradiated animals by 800 per cent; vitamin C, which works with rutin to strengthen the circulatory system and counteract stress; and pantothenic acid, which helps to prevent radiation injuries and has increased the survival rate in irradiated animals by 200 per cent. Depending on the animal's size, give daily: 100 to 400 milligrams rutin; 250 to

2,000 milligrams vitamin C; and 5 to 20 milligrams pantothenic acid.

In addition, use *Bioplasma*, a combination of all 12 of the tissue salts, as a general tonic which will also help counteract radiation effects. Use 1 to 4 tablets 3 times a day until there is recovery (or a minimum of 2 weeks).

If your animal (or anyone else) is more than mildly affected by radiation so as to need more strenuous treatment, there are several homeopathic medicines that may be helpful when carefully prescribed on an individual basis. Contact a homeopathic physician for assistance, if possible.

REPRODUCTIVE ORGAN PROBLEMS

The two most common problems in the reproductive tract, pyometra and metritis, affect the female animal. In both cases the uterus is the seat of the disorder and prompt treatment is needed before the condition progresses too far. We'll look at each of these, and then mastitis (mammary gland infection).

PYOMETRA

Coming on slowly over a period of months or years, pyometra can be recognized by the development of irregular heat periods and a discharge of reddish mucus from the vagina. This discharge will occur *between* heat periods. If unrecognized and untreated (especially in bitches), it will progress to the point where these symptoms are seen: severe depression; loss of appetite; vomiting; diarrhoea; discoloured vaginal discharge (not always present); excessive drinking of water; and excessive urination. The large intake of

fluids will mimic kidney failure, but the other symptoms – particularly vaginal discharge, and its occurrence in unspayed females several years old – will differentiate pyometra from kidney problems.

The susceptible animal is the unspayed female (either bitch or cat) that comes into heat season after season without breeding. A probable secondary cause is a diet containing hormones used to fatten cattle or natural gland hormones. These are concentrated in meat meal and other pet food, and may predispose the uterus to malfunction. Prevention, therefore, is simple – the spay operation for the young female.

Treatment

Treatment usually consists of surgical removal of the uterus, which has probably become quite large and distended with fluid. The operation is basically the same as the spaying process but it is much more serious and complex. In bitches and sometimes in cats the condition suddenly develops into a crisis that requires this kind of professional intervention.

Those animals not so severely affected may be helped by the homeopathic remedy *Helonias* 3X (unicorn root), given as 1 or 2 tablets every 2 hours for several days. The animal most likely to benefit from it is the middle-aged female that is depressed and want to lie still. She will have vaginal discharge associated with excessive drinking and urination and pain in the back (over the kidneys) when this area is pressed.

METRITIS

Right after giving birth and once in a while right after breeding, the uterus is susceptible to bacterial infection. Should infection occur, symptoms can be severe. They include fever, depression, not caring for the young and a foul-smelling vaginal discharge. The normal colour of the vaginal discharge that follows an uncomplicated delivery is dark green to brown and it is odourless. If all the young and all the afterbirths have come out properly, within 12 hours it becomes more like clear mucus (though possibly tinged with blood). But if a dark green to reddish-brown, thick and unusually foul-smelling discharge continues for 12 to 24 hours after the delivery, the uterus is probably infected.

Prevention and Treatment

Once metritis has developed, it can be severe. You should seek professional help. However, you may be able to prevent it by using *Ferrum phosphoricum* (Ferr. phos.) 6X, as discussed under 'Pregnancy, Birth and Care of Newborns' in the section on dystocia, at the time of delivery and afterward to help expel all material and prevent inflammation.

If the animal has had a difficult labour, metritis may follow. As a preventive, use *Echinacea* (*Echinacea angustifolia* or *E. purpurea*). Start it after using the Ferr. phos. every 4 hours for 3 treatments. Give 2 or 6 drops of the herbal tincture (or, as a second choice, the decoction) every 2 hours. You can try this same treatment in early cases of metritis.

MASTITIS

When the mammary glands are actively secreting milk, they are more susceptible to infection than at other times. An infected mammary gland will be hard, sensitive, painful and discoloured (reddish-purple). There may be abscesses and drainage as well. Your vet will usually prescribe antibiotics. A

successful homeopathic treatment I have used is *Phytolacca* 3X (1 to 2 tablets every 4 hours, continued in that dose until the glands return to normal appearance and then used twice a day for a couple of days).

RINGWORM
See 'Skin Parasites'

ROUNDWORMS
See 'Worms'

SINUSITIS
See 'Upper Respiratory Infections'

SKIN PARASITES

External parasites seem to be most attracted to those animals in a poor state of health. I have seen many pets with fleas on the outside, worms on the inside, and some other problem like chronic skin disease. I've also observed that when an animal starts eating a natural diet, along with experiencing other environmental changes as discussed in this book, the number of fleas and other parasites often will markedly decrease. That is not to say that they will *completely* disappear, but rather that they no longer constitute a problem. Other measures of control, if needed, are then much easier and more effective.

When I'm trying to evaluate an animals's overall health I find it useful to consider the nature of any skin parasites it has. Ticks seem to be the least serious, then fleas, followed by lice, and then mange mites or ringworm – in that order. Thus, I consider a cat with lice to be more seriously ill than one with fleas, and a dog with mange worse off than one with ticks, and so on.

Now let's take each of these in turn and discuss some alternatives to the use of chemicals for control. Realize that these suggested measures *by themselves* are not effective in the long term. Neither is the use of chemical insecticides. The *best* results occur when an animal is on a natural diet, lives in a good environment, gets enough sunlight and is exercised and groomed regularly. All these factors are discussed elsewhere in the book.

Note: Ear mites are discussed under 'Ear Problems'.

TICKS

Ticks are not permanent residents. Rather they attach themselves, suck some blood and later fall off to lay eggs. The young ticks that hatch out crawl up to the ends of branches and grasses and patiently wait (for weeks, if necessary) for something warm-blooded and good-tasting to come along and brush against the vegetation. Then they drop on and find a nicy cosy place to attach.

Prevention

Before you take your animal out to run in an area likely to contain ticks, like woods or fields, groom its coat thoroughly. Remove loose hair and mats, and dust the coat with herbal repellent powder (see page 269 for suppliers, or make your own by combining equal amounts of powdered rosemary, rue and wormwood). Avoid getting it in the eyes or nose, but otherwise thoroughly work the powder in with your fingers, particularly over the neck, back and legs and under the tail and ear flaps.

Treatment

After the adventures are over and you've returned home, check your animal for any stalwart ticks that may have made it aboard despite precautions. A fine-tooth flea comb may help to capture those not yet attached. (This is a good time to remove burrs, too.) Look especially around the neck and head and under the ears. If you find a tick already attached, remove it like this: with the nail of your thumb and forefinger (or a pair of tweezers), reach around the tick and grasp it as close to the skin as possible; don't worry, it won't bite! You want to remove the whole thing, not just pull off the tick's body and leave the head still embedded. Use a slow, steady pull (10 to 20 seconds) and with a slight twist pull out the tick – head, body and all! You will have to pull strongly but not quickly. If you are successful, a careful examination will show you the tick's tiny head with a little shred of tissue still attached to it. A method sometimes used to make the tick loosen its grip is to light a match, blow it out, and while it is still hot place the head of it on the tick's back (be careful not to singe your animal). Wash your hands when you're done.

If, despite your care, the head is left behind, the area may fester for a while just as if a splinter were under the skin. But this problem is minor and can be treated with calendula lotion or tincture until healed. This remedy is described under 'Abscesses'.

Sometimes small ticks crawl down inside the ear. If your dog is shaking its head a lot after a trip through tick land, have your vet look down the ear canal with an instrument to check for this or for some other intrusion.

FLEAS

Fleas – the bane of dog and cat alike. I find the best solution is to change the total lifestyle! By lifestyle I mean a natural diet, lots of sunlight, regular exercise, frequent grooming (including use of a flea comb), herbal repellent powders and conscientious cleaning (vacuuming, washing and so on; see chapter 7) of the animal's hangouts. Some additional specific measures that help are to add plenty of brewer's yeast to the daily ration; double the recommended amount if you have a problem. Also, try adding fresh, raw, grated or minced garlic to each feeding. Where necessary, wash the skin daily with a lemon rinse (see chapter 7) to make it less attractive to the fleas.

If, in spite of all this commendable effort, your animal still has a serious problem with fleas (not just a few but tens or twenties or more), a specific remedy just for this problem is needed. (You should also check to see if your pet has tapeworms, because fleas carry their larval form and the worms could be sapping energy; see 'Worms'.) I have used homeopathic preparations with success, sometimes made from the flea itself and sometimes from certain minerals. This method is discussed under 'Skin Problems'. Perhaps acupuncture would be as effective. In any case, it is my impression that these particularly susceptible animals need a treatment that improves their entire constitution, not just something to kill the fleas.

A word about flea collars: they don't work. They are toxic. Some cats even hang themselves on them or get the collars caught between their jaws, causing serious damage. Others get permanent hair loss around the neck due to 'allergic' reactions, particularly when the collar is too tight.

Chemical insecticides in shampoos, soaps, powders and sprays also are dangerous, as discussed in chapter 7. Notice the label warnings about wearing gloves or avoiding contact with your skin and so forth. How can it be so dangerous to you and so safe for your pet? Think about it.

LICE

These are rather uncommon, but occasionally infest a run-down dog or cat. They are somewhat hard to see, but careful looking reveals their presence and their eggs (sticking to hairs). They don't move qcukly or jump like fleas, but they're about the same size. Start treatment with a good shampoo containing a herb like pennyroyal or rosemary (see chapter 7). Also use the herbal repellent powder or lemon rinse described in chapter 7 – every day. An important part of lice treatment is to build up the health with a natural diet. So don't delay. Start right off with some home-prepared food and emphasize brewer's yeast and garlic as previously prescribed for fleas.

Basically you'll use the flea programme (including grooming) and in doing so will eliminate the young lice as they hatch. Building up your pet's health will make its skin less desirable to lice.

Note: We are very used to *immediate* results such as we get when we use chemicals. Though the lice are killed almost immediately by pesticides, the state of the animal that engendered the problem in the first place is not altered by this external treatment. Indeed, the toxic effect may weaken the animal even further.

To work with nature is to be patient.

MANGE

The most common form of mange is *demodectic mange*, which is caused by a microscopic mite that lives in hair follicles. The other type is called *sarcoptic mange*, caused by a mite that burrows into the skin, making both pets and people itch (see the discussion in chapter 11).

Demodectic mange is found in dogs. It usually first appears as a small hairless patch near an eye or the chin. Generally it doesn't itch much and may pass unnoticed. The mite that causes it is very widespread and is actually found on most 'normal' dogs and also on the faces of people. However, it causes a problem for some dogs. Even then, the mange clears up spontaneously without treatment by the time a dog is 12 to 14 months old.

But in a small percentage of those affected, the mite continues to spread and can eventually cover much of the body – resulting in hair loss and skin irritation and thickening. Bacteria (staphylococcus) also can get established, causing further complications such as 'pimples' and a pustular discharge, particularly around the feet. These abnormally susceptible animals apparently have a defect in the immune system so that they cannot properly eliminate the mite.

Treatment

The orthodox treatment is harsh, poisonous and generally futile. (Mild cases clear up on their own anyway.) Strong insecticide dips are 'painted' on the skin after all the hair has been clipped off. They are so toxic that only a part of the body can be done at a time. Unfortunately, no antitoxic nutrition or vitamin supplements are usually recommended, so the dog's condition goes from bad to worse. Even those dogs that apparently recover after weeks or months of treatment can have recurrences or another more serious, 'unrelated' problem will develop.

Under no circumstances should cortisone-type drugs be used. They depress the immune system further and therefore just about guarantee non-recovery (in the true sense) by any methods!

I have had good results using just nutrition and homeopathic remedies, though treatment must be individualized and requires close attention to progress. Here are some general guidelines for a natural approach.

Fast the dog (if its weight and health are good) for 5 to 7 days as outlined in chapter 15. Afterward, use the natural diet and supplements (chapters 3 and 4), doubling the amount of cod-liver oil and brewer's yeast. Also add zinc (feed ground pumpkin seeds or give a 20- to 30-milligram tablet of chelated zinc daily), vitamin C (250 to 1,000 milligrams of ascorbate twice a day) and lecithin ($\frac{1}{2}$ to 3 teaspoons a day). Don't neglect the vitamin E already included in the regular programme. Temporarily minimize the use of vegetable oils and milk, however, until the condition has cleared.

Rub fresh lemon juice on the sore spots every day, or use the lemon rinse recipe in chapter 7.

A homeopathic preparation that suits many cases of mange is *Sulphur* 6X. Give 1 tablet each morning and each night (give no food 20 minutes before or after). I would use this treatment for 10 days. If there is no adverse reaction, continue giving *Sulphur* for up to a month. During this treatment you will probably see some ups and some downs. Over a period of weeks, however, you should be able to see gradual improvement. When the condition is obviously clearing, use the *Sulphur* less frequently on a tapering-off programme.

The dog with a staphylococcal infection of the skin on top of the mange condition will benefit from the use of *Echinacea* tincture (purple cone flower). Depending on the animal's size, give 3 to 10 drops 3 times a day. You also can add the tincture or decoction of *Echinacea* to water and sponge it on the affected skin every day. After the skin has been cleared of bacterial infection or is considerably improved, switch to using *Sulphur* as described.

RINGWORM

Though this disease sounds as if it's caused by some kind of curly worm, it is actually caused by a fungus (similar to athlete's foot). The growth starts at a centre point and spreads out in a ring shape, much as a ripple forms around a stone tossed in a pond. As the fungus grows in the skin cells and hair, the skin may become irritated, thickened and reddened, and the hairs may break off and leave a coarse stubble behind.

In cats, which are more commonly affected, the condition often looks like circular grey patches of thin hair without much sign of itching or irritation. Ringworm is contagious to people (especially children) and other animals; see the precautions in chapter 11. Like mange, widespread ringworm indicates the animal's health is not good, as it is usually the stressed, sick or weakened ones that get severe infestations.

Treatment

First, clip the hair around the bare spot and about ½ inch beyond it, being careful not to injure the skin. Clipping discourages the spread of ringworm and makes the local treatment easier to apply. Burn or carefully dispose of infected hair that you remove. (Always be sure to vacuum carefully and frequently if you have a pet with ringworm, in order to catch loose hairs. Also wash bedding and utensils often with *hot* water and soap.)

Treating the sore spot will speed healing and help protect others from getting ringworm. Choose *one* of these three herbs:

Herbal – great plantain (*Plantago major*): Make a decoction of the whole plant by putting about ¼ cup of the plant (a common weed) to every cup of spring or distilled water in a glass or enamelled pot. Boil for about 4 minutes, then let the brew stand for 3 minutes, covered. Strain and cool. Massage on to the skin once or twice a day until the condition clears.

Herbal – goldenseal (*Hydrastis canadensis*): Make a strong infusion by adding 2 heaped teaspoons of the powdered rootstock to three quarters of a pint of boiling water. Let stand till cold. Carefully pour off the clear fluid and massage it in once or twice a day.

Herbal – lavender (*Lavendula vera or L. officinalis*): Paint on oil of lavender once a day until the hair begins to grow back.

For the overall treatment, start with a fast of 2 or 3 days (see chapter 15); follow with the basic natural diet and supplement programme in this book. Until the condition is clearly improved (for about a month) double the usual amounts of cod-liver oil and brewer's yeast. Also add 5 to 20 milligrams of zinc chelate and ½ to 2 teaspoons of granular lecithin to the food (depending on body size).

In addition to the local herbal treatment and the nutritional programme, use the *Sulphur* 6X treatment programme described previously for mange for 10 days. Repeat in a month if necessary.

SKIN PROBLEMS
Mange and ringworm are discussed under 'Skin Parasites'

The poor skin gets assaulted from two sides. The rest of the body uses it as a place to eliminate toxic material, especially if the kidneys aren't able to cope, while at the same time, environmental pollutants or applied chemical products assault it from the other direction.

One thing is certain – skin disorders are the main problem in dogs and cats. On the positive side, if a skin disorder is your animal's only health problem, you might consider yourself lucky. It's when skin eruptions are suppressed with repeated drug treatment and are no longer seen that a more serious condition may arise. (The problem of suppression is discussed further in the section on treatment, and in chapter 14.)

The symptoms of skin disorder are among the easiest to detect. They usually include one or more of the following: very dry skin; flakiness or white scales resembling dandruff; large brown flakes, redness and irritation; itching (ranging from slight to so severe that blood is drawn); greasy hair; a foul odour to the skin and its secretions (mistaken for normal by many people); pimples, blisters that form between the toes and discharge blood and pus; skin discolouration (brown, black or grey); formation of scabs or crusts; and hair loss. I also include chronic ear inflammation (inside the ear canal and under the flap), anal gland problems and thyroid gland depression as related symptoms.

Modern medicine has taken the approach of dividing these many symptoms into different categories and considering them as separate disease entities. I feel this approach only confuses the picture and doesn't lead to understanding the problem in a holistic sense. From a wider view, these symptoms seem to be one basic problem that manifests differently in individual animals, depending on such conditions as heredity, the environment, food, parasites and so on. Thus, one dog may have severely inflamed, moist, itchy areas at the lower back near the base of the tail, while another may have thick, itchy skin along the back, with greasy, smelly secretions.

What is the major underlying problem? Toxicity – probably most of it from poor-quality food and some of it from other sources, like environmental pollutants, ap-

plied pest-control chemicals, vaccinations and the remains of inadequately treated, suppressed disease. Psychological factors and frustrations also play a part (probably in a more secondary way) in many cases.

Thus, much of the problem can be reduced or eliminated altogether simply by fasting, proper food and the total health plan suggested in this book. While homeopathic medicines can work, they require an individual diagnosis that is beyond the scope of this book.

The most difficult cases to treat are those previously dosed with a lot of cortisone or its synthetic forms (prednisone or prednisolone). These suppress symptoms such as inflammation and itching, but are in no sense curative. You may not know if your animal has received cortisone, because your vet may have used terms like 'anti-itch shots' or 'flea allergy pills'. They usually look like water-clear or milky-white injections or little pink or white tablets. If possible, ask your vet if he is giving your pet cortisone. Generally, a natural approach will not work well if you also continue cortisone therapy.

Treatment

For the animal with acutely inflamed, irritated skin ('hot spots'), but otherwise in good condition, start with a fast. See the directions in chapter 15; continue the fast from 5 to 7 days for dogs, and 3 to 5 days for cats. This fasting mimics the natural wild situation that allows the body to clean out between hunts (as with wolves) and removes the pressure on the system both to digest food *and* deal with the disorder at the same time.

Afterward, carefully introduce natural foods, as described in chapters 3 and 4, in order to supply needed nutrients and to rebuild damaged tissue. Be sure all your ingredients are fresh and of high quality; emphasize raw foods as much as possible.

Of the standard supplements, these are particularly useful for skin problems: brewer's yeast, cod-liver oil, cold-pressed unsaturated vegetable oil and vitamin E (or wheat germ capsules). Also valuable are chelated zinc (5 to 20 milligrams a day) and granular lecithin ($\frac{1}{2}$ teaspoon to 1 table-spoon a day).

It helps to clip away the hair on severely inflamed areas, and give a bath with non-irritating soap (*not* flea soap). When the skin is dry, apply a poultice or frequently wash the area with a very strong black or green tea. It supplies tannic acid, which helps to dry up the moist places. Alternatively, use a strong infusion of goldenseal root (*Hydrastis canadensis*). Allow three quarters of 2 tea-spoons of the powder to three quarters of a pint of water. You also can apply vitamin E oil and fresh aloe vera gel (from the living plant).

In addition to these measures use the following:

Tissue Salt – *Ferrum phosphoricum* (Ferr. phos.) 6X: Give 1 to 2 tablets every 4 hours during the acute phase for the inflammation, pain and redness.

Tissue Salt – *Natrum phosphoricum* (Nat. phos.) 3X: Alternate with the Ferr. phos., giving it every 2 hours after the above treatment. Thus, you'll give 1 to 2 tablets every 4 hours.

If the animal is very irritable and nervous and seems quite bothered by the condition, substitute *Kali phosphoricum* (Kali phos.) 6X for the Nat. phos., using it in the same way.

For the animal with a long-term, low-grade condition of itchy, greasy or dry and scaly skin (who may also have low thyroid activity), fast it 1 day every week, offering only broth (see fasting, in chapter 15.) On the 6 days when your pet is not fasting, give it only natural foods and supplements. Give no commercial foods or commercial supple-ments containing questionable ingredients,

because hypersensitivity or allergy to pro-cessed components or artificial additives may be part of the problem.

Make sure that constipation or sluggish bowels are not contributing to the problem. If they are, use one of the following two remedies:

Herbal – garlic (*Allium sativum*): Give $\frac{1}{4}$ to 1 fresh grated or minced clove or 1 to 3 small garlic capsules daily (can be continued for months – discourages fleas as well).

Homeopathic – *Nux vomica* 3X: Give 1 tablet before each meal, as needed until bowels are regular.

If the skin is greasy and foul, bathe your pet as often as once a week, as described in chapter 7. If the skin is dry, bathe less often. Also be sure to control fleas (see 'Skin Parasites'), using the lemon rinse described in chapter 7.

When it isn't necessary to treat for consti-pation first, use one of the following treat-ments, whichever fits best:

Tissue Salt – *Kali phosphoricum* (Kali phos.) 6X: Especially indicated for the ner-vous animal or one with greasy hair, offen-sive smell and itching. Give 1 or 2 tablets twice a day for a couple of weeks (or until improvement is noted).

Tissue Salt – *Natrum muriaticum* (Nat. mur.) 6X: Suited for the animal with greasy, oily skin with much irritation and itching. There may be a tendency toward thyroid imbalance as well. Dose as for the Kali phos.

Tissue Salt – *Silicea* 6X: Indicated for the animal that gets little pimples, puslike dis-charges or inflammations around the nails. Dose as for the Kali phos. and Nat. mur.

Homeopathic – *Sulphur* 6X: Good for a dog with dry, flaky skin that itches, and that has a lot of fleas. Give 1 tablet once a day for 10 days; see the directions in the section on mange under 'Skin Parasites'.

Note: In general, these deeply ingrained skin conditions require patience and persistence. Usually the beneficial effects of the programme will be apparent within six to eight weeks, or sooner. However, a small number of obstinate cases will not completely recover, though they will improve. These need more individualized treatment with one of the holistic approaches described in chapter 14. Find a skilled professional to help if you can.

For the animal suffering hair loss, try a somewhat different programme. Often a pet will just begin to lose hair without any other apparent problem, or the hair loss may be secondary to skin inflammation where a lot of chewing and scratching removes the hair. Or the hair loss could be the result of poisoning – not necessarily the intentional kind, but rather the accumulation of toxic substances that may affect sensitive individuals. Common agents to consider include fluoride (in some drinking water and commercial pet foods; see chapter 8) and aluminium (from use of aluminium bowls or cooking utensils). Sensitivity to aluminium seems to vary and not all animals show this reaction.

In addition, hair loss can reflect a disturbance in the endocrine glands or a deficiency of a certain nutrient. In any case use the same treatment.

Feed only the natural diet and supplements; kelp powder is particularly important, because its iodine content will help to stimulate the thyroid. In addition, give vitamin C (250 to 1,000 milligrams, depending on the animal's size) twice a day to aid detoxification, and chelated zinc (5 to 30 milligrams a day) to enhance the elimination of heavy metals. Discontinue use of aluminium utensils and fluoridated water (call your water company to find out if your tap water is so treated; if it is, use bottled water).

Try one of these two remedies as well, whichever fits best:

Tissue Salt – *Calcarea phosphorica* (Calc.

phos.) 6X: Indicated for the animal that has not had good nutrition in the past. Use 1 or 2 tablets twice a day for a month.

Tissue Salt – *Silicea* 6X: For the oversensitive, irritable animal that has a tendency to skin infections or for the problem that came on soon after vaccinations. Dose as for the Calc. phos.

SPAYING AND NEUTERING

These operations remove the glands of reproduction. Spaying is an ovario-hysterectomy, a removal of the ovaries and uterus of the female; it prevents her from conceiving and giving birth and eliminates her periods of heat as well. Neutering, or castration, is the removal of the testes of the male (the scrotum is left). It prevents him from impregnating the female and also reduces aggression, wandering and territorial behaviours. Both operations are performed painlessly under anaesthesia, with rapid subsequent recovery.

Some people who want to provide a natural lifestyle for their pets are concerned about such seemingly major surgical alteration. But the beneficial effects for both the animal and society far outweigh any negative consequences (mostly, a tendency to gain weight if overfed). Coming into heat two or more times a year is demanding and frustrating for the female prevented from breeding and may cause health problems too (see the section on pyometra, under 'Reproductive Organ Problems'). Breeding not only adds to the tremendous animal overpopulation problem, which results in the killing of thousands of dogs and cats every year (see chapter 11), but it can be draining to health, too – particularly if done repeatedly. See 'Pregnancy, Birth and Care of Newborns' and 'Reproductive Organ Problems' for some examples. Spaying also prevents the development of mammary cancer, which affects many intact females.

Neutering has obvious benefits. The havoc wreaked by intact males allowed to roam about looking for action is considerable – property damage, fights, the smell and stain of territorial marking, accidents caused when they wander on to public roadways, packs that attack or threaten wildlife, other domestic animals or even people. Neutered males, on the other hand, are typically more affectionate and gentle animals and make better companions.

The general recommendation is that animals be sterilized after reaching six months of age (females) or nine months (males). If you want to be *sure* the animal has reached sexual maturity (thus ensuring least effect on the neuro-endocrine system) you may want to wait until the signs are clear, as some animals mature later than others. For a female this means after going through the first heat (keep her carefully confined to prevent pregnancy). For a male cat it's when the urine changes odour and becomes strong smelling. Consult your vet.

Though nearly all animals bounce back to normal within a day or two after surgery (often sooner), you can enhance recovery and help counter the effects of anaesthesia by giving some vitamin E, a B complex tablet and plenty of vitamin C for a few days before and after.

If you are vacillating over having your animal altered, do so no longer. If you're worried about money, contact your local RSPCA for information about special reduced-fee programmes arranged with area vets.

STOMACH PROBLEMS

The stomach comes in for its share of upsets quite often. Usually the upset is caused by eating either the wrong *kind* of food (spoiled, tainted, indigestible) or too *much* food. Beward the greedy eater! However, stomach problems also can indicate a wide variety of other disorders – such as infectious diseases, kidney failure, hepatitis and a host of others. Because problems in other areas of the body can cause symptoms like vomiting, nausea and lack of appetite, you may be fooled into thinking that only the stomach is involved. Ask your vet to make a diagnosis, especially if vomiting is persistent or severe.

Here we will discuss three common conditions that centre in the stomach itself: acute gastritis (sudden upset), chronic gastritis (low-grade persistent upset) and gastric dilation (swelling with gas, sometimes causing the stomach to twist shut). The suggestions offered are alternative treatments for those animals diagnosed as having these problems, and having them repeatedly.

ACUTE GASTRITIS

Gastritis is a term that means inflammation of the stomach. *Acute* signifies that the attack is sudden, appearing in a few minutes or hours. The most common sufferer is the dog that likes to raid rubbish bins (cats, being more finicky, rarely have this sort of problem). Dogs, often rather indiscriminate in their eating habits, may scrounge about in someone's refuse and consume an extraordinary mixture of foods (often spoiled) that don't react well in the stomach. Compost heaps are another common source of spoiled food.

The vomiting (and possible diarrhoea) that

follows is the body's attempt to right the wrong by getting rid of the noxious material. Some dogs will overeat and instinctively remedy things by eating grass, which stimulates vomiting. You will also see this response in animals with low-grade stomach irritation.

Another cause of acute gastritis is eating indigestible material like large bone fragments (mostly a problem for dogs not used to eating bones or when cooked bones are fed) or pieces of cloth, plastic, metal, rubber toys, golf balls and the like. If bones are the basis of the problem, simply give your pet fewer raw bones, supplementing with B vitamins to ensure adequate stomach acid.

The presence of large indigestible foreign objects often requires surgical removal, though sometimes they can be retrieved by passing a tube into the stomach. Cats often swallow sewing thread or knitting wool, which can get caught around their barbed tongues and pass down into the intestine while still hooked in the mouth. The unpleasant result can be a 'crawling' of the intestine up along the thread, which is often fatal. And if a needle is on the thread, it can penetrate the throat or mouth and cause the thread to get stuck, in addition to causing pain and possible infection.

Stop your pet swallowing such objects. Don't let pets play by themselves with any toy or object that could cause problems. If you suspect your animal has swallowed something dangerous, get professional help within a few hours or serious complications can ensue.

Do *not* use the treatment for vomiting or stomach upset before your visit to the vet, unless the vomiting is very excessive. If the swallowed material is small, not sharp or irregular, vomiting *may* get it out of the stomach. But if the object is sharp, pointed or very large, it would be too traumatic and dangerous for it to come up. Such objects must be removed surgically. In such a case,

use a treatment to control vomiting until you see the vet. If in doubt, do not encourage vomiting.

Treatment

The following treatment will help for simple acute gastritis *not* caused by foreign bodies. The symptoms are: pain in the abdomen (it hurts when you press the stomach, the animal doubles up with cramps and acts depressed); vomiting; and excessive drinking of water.

First, withhold all food for at least 24 hours and then reintroduce it slowly in small quantities. See the fasting instructions in chapter 15. Make fresh pure water available at all times or, if vomiting is part of the problem, offer one or more ice cubes to lick every couple of hours. (You don't want to aggravate vomiting and stomach irritation by encouraging too much drinking.) As a supplementary treatment make camomile tea. Pour a cup of boiling water over a tablespoon of the flowers; leave to soak for 15 minutes, strain, and dilute with an equal quantity of water. If the tea isn't accepted, just make the ice available.

The above treatment will suffice for mild upsets. For more serious upsets, one of the following is useful:

Herbal − peppermint (*Mentha piperita*): Pour a cup of boiling water over 2 teaspoons of leaves. Stand for 10 minutes, strain and add a teaspoon of honey. Give 1 to 2 tablespoons of this tea every 2 hours.

Herbal − ginseng (*Panax schinseng* or *P. quinquefolius*): Soak a capsule of the powdered root in ½ cup hot water for 15 minutes. Stir and administer 1 to 2 tablespoons every 2 hours.

Tissue Salt − *Natrum muriaticum* (Nat. mur.) 6X: Appropriate where indigestion is accompanied by excessive saliva. Give 1 or 2 tablets every hour until relief occurs.

Tissue Salt – *Magnesia phosphorica* (Mag. phos.) 6X: Indicated where there seem to be cramps (doubling up) every few minutes. Dissolve 2 tablets in $\frac{1}{2}$ cup hot water. Administer a teaspoon of this solution every 15 minutes until there is relief; then give a dose every 2 hours until the symptoms are gone.

CHRONIC GASTRITIS

This condition occurs in some animals as a long-term tendency to have digestive upsets, often after eating and sometimes once every few days. It can follow inadequate recovery from a previous severe attack of acute gastritis or may result from emotional stress, poor-quality or disagreeable food, drug toxicity or infections like feline infectious peritonitis or hepatitis. Sometimes there is no apparent cause.

Symptoms are poor digestion, tendency to vomit, pain, depression or hiding either immediately after eating or an hour or so later, loss of appetite and gas.

Treatment

The first and foremost treatment is to put the animal on a natural diet. I can't overemphasize the importance of diet because the illness may be the result of the very food your pet has been eating. Also, read the discussion under 'Allergies' to see if you must make further dietary restrictions. Particularly helpful in the nutritional line are B vitamins (in the brewer's yeast), unsaturated vegetable oil (olive oil is especially useful here) and lecithin (as lecithin granules and in egg yolks). A calcium supplement (bone meal) can also reduce intestinal muscle irritability.

A further treatment might include *one* of the following, as indicated:

Herbal – goldenseal (*Hydrastis canadensis*): Good for weak digestion, poor appetite and weight loss. Stir a teaspoon of the powdered root into a pint of boiling water. Let it stand until cool and pour off the clear yellow fluid. Use 2 to 4 teaspoons 3 times a day for several days. Later, only as symptoms may recur.

Herbal – garlic (*Allium sativum*): Especially useful for an animal that has a good strong appetite but gets upset with changes in the diet or is prone to gas and constipation. Make a cold extract by soaking 4 to 6 cut-up cloves in $\frac{1}{2}$ cup of cold water for 8 hours. Strain. Give 1 to 2 teaspoons 3 times a day until the problem is relieved.

Tissue Salt – *Calcarea phosphorica* (Calc. phos.) 6X: Indicated for the animal with pain after eating (may stop eating and hide) and excessive gas in the stomach (belching, abdominal swelling). Give 1 tablet 3 times a day for several days or weeks.

Tissue Salt – *Natrum phosphoricum* (Nat. phos.) 3X: Useful for pain that occurs 1 to 2 hours after eating rich or fatty foods. Also good for stomach problems associated with worms. Give 1 to 2 tablets twice a day for several weeks.

GASTRIC DILATION

This serious problem is seen mostly in the larger dog breeds. Its cause is unknown, though vets have found it to be linked with the feeding of commercial foods.

The symptoms of the condition are that after eating, the stomach (upper abdominal area) gets enlarged with liquid and gas, and sometimes feels like a tight drum. Generally, you will see excessive salivation, unsuccessful attempts to vomit and extreme restlessness and discomfort. This is an *emergency* situation, because the increased pressure on the walls of the stomach causes fluids to leak in from the blood with consequent dehydration, shock and possible death in a few hours. Another complication is that the stomach can rotate on itself and the twisting can completely block entry into or exit from the organ. Emergency surgery is often required at that point.

Prevention

Feeding a natural, home-prepared diet seems to be the best key to averting such problems. Feed two or three times a day instead of one large meal.

Treatment

When gastric dilation first occurs, it is a rather sudden and shocking situation. Get to your vet as soon as possible. The condition can be temporarily relieved at the surgery; however, it tends to recur. Each time the attack comes on sooner and with more severity. Eventually the animal is put to sleep because of the apparent hopelessness of the situation and the high cost of repeated medical measures.

This consideration prompts me to suggest alternative treatment, despite the severity of the condition. Once the owner has witnessed an attack, he or she can recognize the early symptoms and quickly intervene with one of the treatments suggested below. If relief does not follow shortly thereafter, emergency treatment is still an option.

Because of vomiting and the pressure closing off the opening to the stomach, I suggest only homeopathic preparations in this case. The tablets will act by dissolving in the mouth, even if they are not swallowed. You will need to plan ahead and order these in advance.

Homeopathic – *Nux moschata* 3X (nut-meg): Indicated for the dog with a greatly enlarged abdomen, belching or passing of gas, unsuccessful attempts to vomit, a dry mouth or thick saliva, legs that feel cool to the touch, disorientation, dizziness or sleepiness. Give 2 tablets every 15 minutes until there is relief, then every 1 or 2 hours until the condition has passed. Administer the tablets by crushing them to a powder within a folded piece of clean paper. Then use the paper to 'funnel' the powder on to the tongue or back of the throat. If you don't have the remedy on hand, in an emergency you can try putting a pinch of nutmeg from your spice collection directly on the tongue; it's not likely to be as effective as the homeopathic version, but it's worth trying.

Homeopathic – *Nux vomica* 3X (poison nut): Indicated for the animal with great restlessness, painful abdominal swelling, ineffectual vomiting and drooling. Give 2 tablets every 15 minutes as instructed for *Nux moschata*.

Homeopathic – *Carbo vegetabilis* 3X (charcoal): Dogs that may benefit from this remedy will have a less severe kind of attack, but already have had at least one serious episode from which they have not fully recovered. Thus, you'll see a pattern of recurring indigestion and gas, with periodic swelling of the stomach that causes breathing difficulty. This state of chronic ill health will produce progressive weakening, low energy and a cold body. *During an attack* give 2 tablets every hour till it is relieved; but you can start treatment for the general *pattern* even if there is no 'crisis' by giving 2 tablets 3 times a day for 2 or 3 weeks. (Once there is recovery give the tablets only as needed if the symptoms reappear later.)

Note: If you see favourable results with one of these treatments, bear in mind that using drugs like tranquillizers, antibiotics, stimulants or depressants immediately after a positive homeopathic response will very possibly cancel out the favourable response and lead to a return of the original condition. (See chapter 14 for a discussion of such interactions.) For this reason minimize or eliminate such treatment if the homeopathic remedies are doing the job.

STONES
See 'Bladder Problems'

TAPEWORMS
See 'Worms'

TEETH
See 'Dental Problems'

TICKS
See 'Skin Parasites'

TOXOPLASMOSIS

This disease deserves to be discussed in some detail, not so much because of its importance to cats (which usually recover from it without treatment, often without apparent symptoms), but because of its importance to unborn children. If a woman is infected for the first time during pregnancy, the foetus may be stillborn, born prematurely or born with serious damage to the brain, eyes or other parts of the body. Such problems are estimated to occur in 2 to 6 out of every 1,000 births in the United States. It is much less common in the U.K.

Before we consider this disease further, first let's put things into perspective. The toxoplasma protozoa infests almost all species of mammals and birds in the world. Infection ranges from 20 to 80 per cent of all domestic animals, depending on geographical area. In the United States, about 50 per cent of the human population is eventually affected. But despite the widespread occur-

rence of this little parasite, few infected individuals actually become *ill* from it. People who get clinically ill are mostly those whose immune systems have been suppressed by cancer chemotherapy, x-ray therapy or as a response to drugs used with organ grafts. Cats, too, are very rarely sick from toxoplasmosis. Those who get the disease show these symptoms: mucus- or blood-tinged diarrhoea; fever; hepatitis; and pneumonia (difficult breathing). They usually get over it on their own, developing a strong immunity that protects against further infection.

Commonly, both cat and person can acquire the parasite, and have *no symptoms whatsoever*. Here is where the danger lies: about one to three weeks after infection the cat will often start passing oocysts, egglike structures that can infect other individuals after a day or so of further development in the warm faeces or soil. The cat passes these oocysts until it develops immunity – in about two weeks. (If its immune system is depressed with cortisonelike drugs, however, the process can start up again.) These eggs can then be picked up by a pregnant woman who has not already had a chance to develop her own immunity. Thus, the disease spreads to the foetus, where it can cause the serious problems already mentioned.

Here are the ways this organism can infect pregnant women (and other people):

1. Through unintentionally ingesting a bit of cat faeces during the two weeks of oocyst shedding.

2. Through unintentionally ingesting soil contaminated within the previous year by an infected cat.

3. Through eating or preparing raw or undercooked meat that is infected. This is actually the most common route of entry for both people and cats. And even if your cat isn't fed raw meat, remember, freshly caught mice and birds aren't cooked!

If you think about it, there are several possibilities for spread. For instance, while changing a litter pan, digging in the soil or cleaning a sandbox you might wipe your mouth. Or, after doing one of these jobs, you might eat something before you've washed your hands. Does your cat walk from the litter tray to your kitchen counter, table or your pillow? Do you prepare salad on the same board used to trim raw meat?

If you are pregnant take special precautions. Don't feed your cat raw meat. If you eat meat yourself, be careful to cook it and to prepare it separately from foods to be eaten raw, like salads. Wash your hands well after any meat preparation, gardening, cat-stroking and the like. Unless you know your cat already is immune, persuade someone else to clean the litter tray, or use gloves and wash well afterward. Dispose of the contents in a sealed container (not on the ground). If you want to disinfect the tray, rinse it with boiling water or heat a metal one at 130°F for 30 minutes. Also control flies and cockroaches, because they can carry oocysts from the cat's faeces on to food.

If you want to keep your cat from ever getting toxoplasmosis in the first place (assuming he already hasn't had it), you would have to make some serious compromises. Raw meat, for example, is nutritionally superior to cooked, but to prevent toxoplasmosis, you'd always have to cook it. You would also have to keep your cat from hunting and keep him away from any soil possibly contaminated by other cats. Obviously, the only way you can manage these restrictions is by keeping him inside all the time, which is not such a healthy situation! The choice is yours, of course, but with reasonable precautions you should be all right, even if neither of you is yet immune.

ULCERS OF THE EYE
See 'Eye Problems'

UPPER RESPIRATORY INFECTIONS

The upper respiratory tract, which includes the nose, throat, larynx and trachea, is one of the favourite highways for germs interested in travelling inside the body. Many microorganisms and viruses dry out and masquerade as dust. Others come from secretions and scabs that dry out and break into small particles that, when stirred up, enter the air to be inhaled into the nose or throat.

In animals, upper respiratory infections often start and remain in the upper respiratory tract, causing such symptoms as a runny nose or eyes, a sore throat, coughing, inflammation of the mouth and sneezing. These infections resemble the human cold in many ways, but often deviate to produce their own unique symptoms, too.

We will consider three of the most common upper respiratory diseases found in companion animals: canine infectious tracheobronchitis, feline viral rhinotracheitis and feline calicivirus. (Distemper is covered as a separate entry.)

CANINE INFECTIOUS TRACHEOBRONCHITIS

Known as 'kennel cough' or 'canine respiratory disease complex', this condition is thought to be caused by a variety of viruses, perhaps complicated by bacterial growth as well. It's common where many stressed dogs, especially young ones, are in close contact. It crops up in boarding kennels, animal shelters, grooming establishments, veterinary hospitals, dog shows and pet shops.

The disease usually makes a clinical appearance about eight to ten days after exposure, with these typical symptoms: a dry, hacking, awful-sounding cough, perhaps with a clear, watery discharge from the eyes and nose or a partial loss of appetite. Generally speaking, it's not a serious condition, though in a tiny fraction of dogs there may be complications. I have rarely seen any.

The usual treatment consists of cough suppressants, antibiotics and perhaps a synthetic cortisone preparation. Though these measures may diminish the symptoms, it's generally recognized that the disease just has to 'run its course' of two or three weeks before recovery.

Treatment

You can assist the healing process by putting your pet on a fast, giving vitamins and using a herbal cough treatment.

Fasting on liquids only should begin when the symptoms appear and continue for 3 days. Follow the directions for fasting in chapter 15, taking care to reintroduce solid foods carefully and slowly.

Vitamins will help in several ways. Vitamin C is a good antiviral agent. Follow the directions for its use as described under 'Distemper, Chorea and Feline Panleucopenia'. Vitamin E will stimulate the immune response. Depending on the dog's size, give 50 to 100 I.U. of fresh d-alpha tocopherol from a capsule 3 times a day. Puncture the capsule and squeeze the oil right into the mouth. Taper off frequency at recovery. Vitamin A also stimulates immunity and helps to counteract stress and to strengthen the mucous membranes of the respiratory tract. Use $\frac{1}{4}$ to 1 teaspoon of fresh cod-liver oil 3 times a day (depending on the animal's size). Taper off at recovery.

Herbal treatment can consist either of a herbal or homeopathic cough syrup as sold at health food stores. Adjust the dose to your animal's weight. Or, try one of the herbs listed below.

Note: Herbal cough preparations typically contain several of the following: wild cherry bark, licorice, comfrey root, coltsfoot, mullein, slippery elm and horehound.

Herbal – peppermint (*Mentha piperita*): Best suited for the dog with a hoarse 'voice' and with coughing made worse by barking. Touching his throat is irritating and may bring on the cough. Make a strong infusion by soaking 3 tablespoons of dried leaves in 2 cups of boiling water for about 15 minutes (covered). Strain and add a teaspoon or two of honey. Give $\frac{1}{2}$ teaspoon to 1 tablespoon every 3 or 4 hours as needed to control the cough.

Herbal – mullein (*Verbascum thapsus*): Especially indicated where the cough is deep and hoarse and worse at night. Also where the throat seems sore to the touch or there is trouble swallowing. Soak a rounded teaspoon of the dried broken leaf in a cup of boiling water. After 20 minutes, strain and add a teaspoon of honey. Dose as above.

After recovery, your dog should be relatively immune for some time, perhaps a year or two. However, a similar virus could create the 'same' condition. Remember, stress seems to be the necessary factor for susceptibility to occur.

FELINE VIRAL RHINOTRACHEITIS (FVR)

This virus disease primarily affects the eyes and upper respiratory tracts of cats. Symptoms include sneezing attacks, coughing and drooling of thick saliva, as well as the presence of fever and a watery discharge from the eyes. Often the condition becomes more severe. The nose gets plugged up with a thick discharge, ulcers form on the eye surface (cornea), and the eyelids stick together with heavy discharges. The cat becomes thoroughly miserable, refusing to eat and unable to care for itself.

There is no standard treatment which shortens the disease. Usually antibiotics, fluid therapy, forced feeding, eye ointments and other measures are used to provide the best possible support for the ailing body. However, these cats are so out of sorts that they often resist handling and treatments. It can be a real challenge to provide adequate care.

Treatment

If you can catch the condition early, the following care may avert the more serious stage.

Give no solid food the first 2 to 3 days or until the temperature is back to normal. (The animal usually will not eat anyway.) Provide liquids as described under the section on fasting, in chapter 15. Give vitamin C ($\frac{1}{4}$ teaspoon sodium ascorbate powder, dissolved in pure water, every 4 hours), vitamin E (50 I.U. twice a day) and vitamin A ($\frac{1}{4}$ teaspoon cod-liver oil or 2,000 to 2,500 I.U. vitamin A from fish-liver oil sources, twice a day).

Every hour except during the night-time sleep give a tissue salt. Alternate *Ferrum phosphoricum* (Ferr. phos.) 6X (1 tablet every 2 hours) with *Natrum muriaticum* (Nat. mur.) 6X (1 tablet every 2 hours). Start with one; the next hour give the other, and so on. Crush the pill on a piece of clean folded paper and tap it into the mouth. As there is improvement, you can gradually decrease the frequency of treatment.

If the condition is very advanced when you start treatment, a different approach is needed.

Blend raw beef liver with enough water to make a soupy mix. Add 2 teaspoons of sodium ascorbate powder to every cup of this blend. Feed 1 teaspoon every hour to provide health-boosting nutrients, including B vitamins and about 150 milligrams of vitamin C with each dose.

If possible, clean the eyes and nose with warm salt water (allow $\frac{1}{2}$ teaspoon sea salt to $\frac{3}{4}$ pint spring or distilled water). Then put a drop of castor oil, cod-liver oil or olive oil in each eye; apply some to the nose, too (twice a day).

Give 1 tablet of tissue salt every hour (alternate, first using one, then the other): *Kali muriaticum* (Kali mur.) 6X and *Natrum muriaticum* (Nat. mur.) 6X. In addition, every morning and evening give 2 tablets *Calcarea phosphorica* (Calc. phos.) 6X (crushed is the easiest way). If you see improvement after a few days' treatment, but your patient continues to be depressed and will not eat, switch to a preparation made from goldenseal tincture (*Hydrastis canadensis*). Add 2 teaspoons of the powdered root to 1 or 2 ounces (2 to 4 tablespoons) vodka or brandy. Extract by letting the mixture sit 12 to 24 hours, shaking the bottle occasionally. Then add the following to a new, clean 1-ounce dropper bottle: 2 drops of the goldenseal tincture (let it settle first); 60 drops (1 teaspoon, full to brim) of vodka or (preferably) brandy; and 120 drops (2 teaspoons) of distilled or spring water. Cap the bottle and shake *vigorously* by hitting it hard against your hand 20 to 30 times so that it foams up. Give 2 drops of this preparation by mouth every 2 hours.

Once the cat is eating, encourage a variety of fresh and raw foods, especially meats, grated vegetables and brewer's yeast. Continue the vitamin C and eye treatment until recovery is complete.

FELINE CALICIVIRUS (FCV)

Sometimes this condition cannot be distinguished from the previous one, but generally the nose and the eyes are not so involved. Typical signs include pneumonia and ulcers of the tongue, the roof of the mouth and the end of the nose (above the lip). This condition is very difficult to treat because the mouth is so sore that the cat resists having anything put in it. You may need to wrap the cat up in a towel during treatment to keep from getting scratched (see chapter 15).

Treatment

Fast (as for the early stage of FVR) for the first couple of days. The cat will probably do so anyway.

Mix 1 tablespoon of brewer's yeast with 3 tablespoons of water. Add 1½ teaspoons vitamin C (as sodium ascorbate powder, which is less acidic than ascorbic acid). Mix well and administer 1 full teaspoon (or 5 ml with a plastic syringe) every 4 hours during the fast. This liquid is easy to administer and doesn't require opening the mouth very far. You can pull the cheek out to form a pocket for the fluid. Tilt the head slightly up and the liquid will run down the throat, initiating swallowing. If it doesn't run down, separate the teeth slightly.

In addition, 20 to 30 minutes before each feeding give 1 tablet of *Ferrum phosphoricum* (Ferr. phos.) 6X, crushed and dissolved in a teaspoon of pure water. The cat with an advanced case of mouth ulcers and pneumonia (difficult breathing, fluid sounds) may do better with *Silicea* 6X (for mouth ulcers) or *Kali phosphoricum* (Kali phos.) 6X (for weakness and prostration) instead of the Ferr. phos.

If pneumonia seems to have developed, it may be a good idea to use antibiotics, as sometimes bacteria will have 'moved in' on a weakened animal and further complicated the virus infection. They are not really indicated, however, when the condition

clearly just involves a virus and is, as yet, uncomplicated.

Once recovery begins, start tapering off with the other treatment, but continue the vitamin C for several days (250 milligrams 3 times a day). As soon as appetite returns and eating begins, use vitamin E (50 I.U. twice a day) and vitamin A (¼ teaspoon cod-liver oil twice a day) to rebuild the system.

URAEMIA
See 'Kidney failure'

VACCINATIONS

The prevention of disease by administering 'weakened' forms of the germ which causes it is a very popular and strongly supported method. Most often, after the vaccine organism is injected into the body, it will grow in the tissues (if it is a 'live' vaccine), producing a sort of 'mini-disease' that stimulates the immune response. This response is intended to protect the body against the real thing for a variable period of time – months or years. Sounds wonderful, doesn't it?

However, at the risk of being labelled a heretic, I must point out that there are some problems with vaccinations that should be understood by anyone interested in a holistic health approach. There are two things to consider: (1) vaccines are not always effective and (2) they may cause long-lasting health disturbances.

Vaccine ineffectiveness

There is an implicit assumption among many people that vaccines are 100 per cent effective. This belief can be so strong that a vet may tell you, 'Your dog can't have distemper (parvovirus, hepatitis, or whatever) because he was vaccinated against it. It must be something else.' But one thing I learned from my studies in immunology is that vaccines are far from 100 per cent effective. Obviously it is not just the injection of the vaccine that confers immunity; the response of the individual animal is the critical and necessary factor.

Several things can interfere with the ideal body response (production of antibodies and immunity). These include vaccinating when the animal is too young or is ill, weak or malnourished; using the wrong route or schedule of administration; and giving the vaccine to an animal with an immune system that has been depressed as a result of previous disease, inheritance or drug therapy.

For example, the unfortunate practice of giving vaccinations at the same time that anaesthetics are administered or surgery performed can introduce the vaccine organism at a time when the immune system will be depressed for several weeks. The concurrent use of corticosteroid drugs (to control skin itching, for instance) can also depress immunity and disease resistance.

Even if your animal seems to have a good response, there is no guarantee the disease will not occur. The immunity may be very short (for example, just a few months with the parvovirus vaccine) or a mutant germ may come along that will not be susceptible to the antibodies formed. Or if something weakens the immune system later on it may lack the ability to fully respond and the disease may be able to get a foothold. Such weakening factors include the kinds of things we've been discussing throughout this book, like stress, malnutrition, lack of vitamins, toxicity, drug effects and so on.

So we see that the effectiveness of vaccination is a complex phenomenon depending on many factors, not the least of which is the overall level of health as determined by the total lifestyle.

Possible harmful effects of vaccination

Besides sometimes being ineffective, vaccines can occasionally *cause* acute disease, or a chronic health problem over a long period. I often have noticed animals getting ill a few days after receiving vaccinations. Clinically speaking, the illness is indistinguishable from the disease the shot was supposed to protect against. It may be that the animal was in a weakened state and the vaccine virus therefore caused a more severe reaction than the 'mini-disease' intended. Whatever the reason, I have seen this problem most often after canine distemper virus, canine parvovirus, feline rhinotracheitis or feline calicivirus vaccines (which also sometimes cause a low-grade nose or eye irritation in cats).

Long-term effects are the more serious possibility. Over the years, doctors practising homeopathic medicine have accumulated information on the more subtle but stubborn problems of vaccination. To quote a contemporary writer on the subject, George Vithoulkas, 'The experience of astute homeopathic observers has shown conclusively that in a high percentage of cases, vaccination has a profoundly disturbing effect on the health of an individual, particularly in relation to chronic disease.'

This disorder 'engrafted' on to an individual by injection of a foreign disease is called 'vaccinosis' and in humans is associated with a wide range of conditions involving diverse parts of the body. In many cases homeopaths have found it necessary to 'antidote' the effects of vaccinations before full health can be restored.

Does this reaction occur in animals? I am convinced it does. If anything, animals may be vaccinated even more frequently than people. In fact, several cases for which I've been consulted were invariably made worse whenever a vaccination was given. I suspect that many skin problems at least partially reflect the body's response to frequent vaccination. Sometimes while an animal is improving after homeopathic treatment for a deeper condition, I will see a temporary rash of little pimples on the belly, just like that seen on puppies with distemper. I interpret this as an elimination of the foreign material introduced during vaccination.

After all, it is hardly natural for an animal to be repeatedly infected by the variety of diseases included in the typical vaccination schedules. In the natural state there may be frequent *exposure* through the usual routes, but not the massive invasion of the bloodstream that results from an injection.

What to do?

Since most people have little access to in-depth holistic alternatives, to be practical vaccination should be done for the more serious conditions. However, I suggest that (1) only a few vaccines be used (depending on what diseases are actually prevalent in your area), (2) that vaccines not be frequently repeated, and (3) that whenever possible (and there aren't many choices here) a 'killed' or inactivated vaccine be used in preference to a modified-live vaccine (which actually grows in the body). Here are some specific suggestions.

Dogs

Distemper and hepatitis vaccinations should be given at 9 and 12 weeks of age, followed by a 'booster' in a year. For the remainder of the dog's life, a distemper vaccination (by itself) given every three years is adequate protection. Leptospirosis, which is often included in these vaccines, is not very effective, as the immunity lasts only a few months.

Parvovirus might be considered under special conditions. For instance, if your dog will be exposed to large numbers of (possibly ill) animals, a vaccination is necessary. In that case, a series of two injections should be given about two weeks apart, before exposure. I do not recommend repeated and continuous immunization for all animals because the protective effect is good for only a few months and the long-term effect of this practice is uncertain at this time.

Cats

Distemper (feline panleucopenia) vaccine should be given at 9 and 12 weeks of age, with a repetition every five years. This is the only vaccination for cats I recommend at this time.

It is important to remember that the animal kept at a top level of health will have the most protection against disease. The exceptions to this seem to be the old, endemic virus diseases of dogs and cats like canine distemper and feline panleucopenia that are well established and virulent. Until alternatives are widely available to the public, it is prudent to vaccinate against them.

VOMITING

Vomiting is one of those symptoms of underlying illness that rarely occurs just by itself. Most often it is associated with an upset stomach, but it can also occur as part of poisoning, failed kidneys, drug reaction, pain or inflammation in some other area (like the peritoneum, pancreas or brain), or after surgery and other conditions. Therefore, it's always necessary to look beyond this one symptom to understand what the underlying situation is and to treat that.

However, there *are* times when nothing else seems to be wrong or where vomiting is by far the major problem. If not controlled, prolonged vomiting can lead to severe dehydration and the loss of certain salts, particularly sodium chloride and potassium chloride.

Treatment

The problem in treatment is that nothing given by mouth will remain in the stomach long enough to act, so the best way to administer treatment is by the use of crushed homeopathic tablets, which will act almost immediately through absorption in the mouth.

The first choice is *Ipecac* 3X (ipecacuanha). It is useful where there is persistent nausea and constant vomiting and where much saliva is generated because of the nausea. Give 1 tablet every hour for 4 treatments, then again only after each recurrence of vomiting. If *Ipecac* doesn't work, try the tissue salt *Ferrum phosphoricum* (Ferr. phos.) 6X on the same schedule as the *Ipecac*.

In addition, withhold all food and water during the vomiting period, allowing the animal occasionally to lick ice cubes. To replace fluids and salts (if there is dehydration), give a small enema every couple of hours as instructed in chapter 15. To each $\frac{3}{4}$ pint of enema water, add $\frac{1}{4}$ teaspoon of sea salt (or table salt as a second choice) and $\frac{1}{4}$ teaspoon potassium chloride (sold as a salt substitute in many markets). Given as an enema, the fluid will be retained and absorbed in a dehydrated animal.

WARTS

Dogs, especially, are prone to developing troublesome warts that sometimes itch and bleed. The problem is more common among older animals. Warts are not as easy to treat as you might think. However, here are some methods I've found helpful.

Tissue Salts – Use *one* of the following: *Kali muriaticum* (Kali mur.) 3X, *Natrum muriaticum* (Nat. mur.) 3X or *Natrum sulphuricum* (Nat. sulph.) 3X. Give 1 tablet 3

times a day for a couple of weeks. If you see no improvement, try another tissue salt for a couple of weeks, and so on.

Vitamin E: Some people have cleared up this problem in their dogs by regular application of vitamin E from a punctured capsule. It must be continued for several weeks to be effective. If you wish to use vitamin E locally along with a tissue salt, I suggest trying Nat. sulph. first.

Nutrition: The basic diet suggested in this book will be most helpful. Vitamin A (in the cod-liver oil) and the vitamin E supplements are especially indicated.

WEIGHT PROBLEMS

A survey done for Ralston Purina in 1975 revealed that 41 per cent of the respondents claimed their pets were overweight. Usually obesity is caused by over-feeding, feeding the wrong foods and lack of exercise. Overweight cannot be considered healthy. If excessive, it can strain the heart, make the circulation sluggish and seriously complicate other disorders.

The following diets will provide about two-thirds of the normal calorie requirements for your dog or cat (when used with the same weight guidelines and multiplier factors as in chapter 4). At the same time, they will supply higher percentages of protein, to compensate for a lesser intake of total nutrients. Because of the low calorie but high bulk content of the recipes, they will fill your animal's stomach while keeping its appetite reasonably satisfied. Thus, they can help your pet to lose weight gradually and safely, while getting enough of the basic nutrients it needs.

Feed the supplements as recommended earlier in the book. Vegetables especially

WEIGHT-LOSS DIET FOR CATS

$\frac{1}{2}$ *cup lean meat*

$\frac{1}{3}$ *cup cooked oatmeal*

2 tablespoons grated or chopped vegetables

2 tablespoons bran

daily supplements as recommended

Mix ingredients together and serve slightly warm.

Yield: about 1 cup

WEIGHT-LOSS DIET FOR DOGS

$\frac{1}{2}$ *cup lean meat*

$\frac{1}{4}$ *cup dry-curd cottage cheese*

1 cup cooked oatmeal

$\frac{1}{2}$ *cup grated or chopped vegetables*

$\frac{1}{2}$ *cup bran*

daily supplements as recommended

Mix ingredients together and serve slightly warm.

Yield: about $2\frac{3}{4}$ cups

useful on a weight loss regimen are leafy greens, broccoli, cauliflower, celery, lemon, onion and parsley.

Resist the temptation to feed extra snacks and treats that can add up to continued obesity for your pet. Sometimes people *create* overweight pets for psychological reasons – because they themselves have the same problem, because they enjoy watching the animal eat, and so on. See chapter 10 if this describes you!

If your animal has the opposite problem and is *underweight*, a different approach is needed. Use the basic diet in chapters 3 and 4 and treat with:

Herbal – alfalfa (*Medicago sativa*): Use 2 drops of the tincture 3 times a day for cats and small dogs. Continue treatment until the desired effect is seen – increased hunger and weight gain.

Another treatment suitable for older, run-down animals is:

Tissue Salt – *Calcarea phosphorica* (Calc. phos.) 6X: Especially good where there is apparently poor digestion or poor utilization of nutrients. Give 1 tablet twice a day for 3 or 4 weeks.

If the weight loss is sudden, there may be some infection or other cause which needs to be taken care of first. Have your vet investigate this possibility.

WORMS

Worms and internal parasites primarily are found in (1) the very young animal that has acquired them before or after birth from the mother (roundworms), (2) the young or mature animal that has numerous fleas or that eats other wild creatures (tapeworms are carried by fleas), or (3) the mature but run-down animal that is in a toxic state and is susceptible to parasites, both inside (roundworms, hookworms, whipworms, tapeworms) and out (fleas, lice, ticks).

How to identify worms

Tapeworms are indicated by the passage of flat segments which look like cream-coloured maggots, about $\frac{1}{4}$ to $\frac{1}{2}$ inch long. They do not crawl, but move by forming a sort of 'point' on one end. They can be seen on the freshly voided faeces or on the hair around the anus. After drying out, they look a lot like white rice kernels stuck under the tail.

Each tapeworm has a 'head', which stays attached to the lining of the small intestine, as well as dozens of egg-filled segments that will break off and pass out with the faeces when ripe. Many worming treatments result in the loss of most of the segments with apparent cure; however, the head can remain behind and regrow a new body which will begin passing segments again. Another problem is that animals get reinfested through swallowing fleas or eating wild creatures.

Roundworms are acquired by young animals from their mother, both before and after birth. You may safely assume that most young puppies and kittens have some. Most of the time the infestation is not apparent, therefore a microscopic examination of the faeces by your vet is necessary for a diagnosis. Be sure to ask if the infestation is light, medium or heavy, and what kind of worms were found.

Heavy roundworm infestation appears as an enlarged belly, poor weight gain and perhaps diarrhoea or vomiting. Sometimes whole worms are vomited or else passed out with the faeces. They resemble white spaghetti several inches long and will often move feebly when first voided. Usually, only young animals a few weeks old vomit worms.

Hookworms and whipworms are less common. They are more of a problem where crowded and insanitary conditions prevail. Severe hookworm infestation is serious because the worms suck the animal's blood and cause severe anaemia. In this kind of situation it may be best to seek professional help. In young animals with severe infestation, the loss of blood into the intestine causes the stool to look black and tarlike. It may also become fluid and foul smelling. The gums will become pale, reflecting the developing anaemia, and the animal will appear weak and thin.

Treatment

Recurrent parasite infestations indicate to me that the animal's resistance is not high. Unless the parasites are large in number or are causing a definite health problem, I prefer to approach treatment by indirect means, letting the body itself eliminate the problem. What the body needs most to do the job are *good* nutrition and *adequate* exercise. As the animal detoxifies and builds up strength on such a programme, many of the parasites will be sloughed off. If the need still remains after these basic measures, then direct treatment for the worms will be easier and more successful.

Nutrition should be restricted to the basic diet plan in chapters 3 and 4, using raw foods as much as possible (except for hard, indigestible grains or vegetables and pork or fish – which can carry parasites themselves). In addition, feed the following *every day:*

- Fresh, chopped or grated garlic. Mix ½ to 2 cloves into the food, depending on the animal's size.
- Bran. Add ½ to 2 teaspoons (depending on the animal's size) to the food. The roughage will help to carry out the worms.
- One of these vegetables: grated raw carrot, turnip or beets.

Also, make regular use of ground or flaked coconut. Fast the animal one day a week, giving it just large raw bones (cats, too). Not only will they stimulate the digestive tract, but the chewed bone material also will help to mechanically trap and carry out the worms.

Besides these dietary measures, also make use of the tissue salt *Natrum phosphoricum* (Nat. phos.) 6X, which stimulates the digestive system and returns acidity to normal, making the system less favourable for the parasites. Give 1 to 3 tablets twice a day for several weeks.

These measures alone have been successful in eliminating internal parasites in many animals I have treated. It is important to use the complete plan suggested here with a wholesome, home-prepared, non-commercial diet as the foundation. Note that in young animals a less-than-adequate protein level allows roundworms to increase to large numbers. Because a puppy or kitten needs more protein than an adult, be sure to use the high-protein recipes especially formulated for them in chapter 5.

If you find after four to six weeks of this programme that the parasites are still present, or if the condition was too severe to treat in this less strenuous way, more direct treatment against the worms is needed. There are several possible approaches (besides chemicals that may be harmful to the host as well as the parasite).

Homeopathic treatment: For *roundworms*, try one of these two remedies: *Chenopodium* 3X (Jerusalem oak) or *Cina* 3X (wormseed), given as 1 tablet twice a day for a week. Skip a week and then repeat this schedule. If you don't get satisfactory results with one, try the other in the same way.

For *tapeworms*, use *Filix mas* 3X (male fern), 1 tablet morning and night for several weeks.

Naturopathic and herbal treatment: The following is another effective method (adapted from the suggestions of herbalist Juliette de Bairacli Levy), though more involved and time-consuming than the homeopathic route. The same programme can be used for either tapeworms or roundworms. It consists basically of fasting and the use of repellent herbs, along with castor oil (to flush out the intestinal tract).

Start by feeding a special diet for 3 to 4 days, which will help weaken the worms by eliminating foods they prefer (fats, sugars, eggs, whole milk). Give two small meals a day, consisting of rolled oats (softened with water or skim milk), lightly boiled fish and a liberal sprinkling of nutritional yeast.

Next, fast the animal for 2 days primarily on water. If the animal is younger than six months, fast it for just a day on water with a bit of honey added for energy. On the first night of this fast give some castor oil to act as a purgative to help clear the bowels. Use ½ teaspoon for puppies less than three months and for all young cats; 1 teaspoon for puppies three to six months and adult cats; 1½ tablespoons for medium dogs; and 2 tablespoons for large dogs.

On the second day of the fast give herbal worming tablets (obtainable at many health food stores). Alternatively, make your own formula by combining equal parts of fresh grated garlic with powdered rue and wormwood (herbs) in Number 2 gelatin capsules (sold at chemists). Make this fresh each day or refrigerate it on account of the garlic. Dose according to product instructions or as follows (for the home-made mix): 3 to 5 capsules for small or young animals; 6 to 8 capsules for medium or large dogs.

About 30 minutes after giving the herbs, administer another dose of castor oil (same amount as before). Then wait another 30 minutes and feed a small amount (about a cup for a medium dog) or a warm, laxative, semi-liquid mixture of raw milk thickened with slippery elm powder, honey and rolled oats. If this is vomited, try again in 30 minutes. The slippery elm forms a smoothing jelly that helps remove the worms and eggs from the intestines.

For the next 3 days continue feeding this same mixture of milk, elm, honey and oats in 3 small meals a day. Each morning, at least ½ hour before feeding, give the herbs again, but cut the dose in half. Each evening it helps to give a mild cleansing laxative, such as ⅛ to ½ teaspoon (depending on body size) of powdered senna with a pinch of ginger. Give it in a capsule or mix into water or food.

Slowly return to a normal natural foods diet over the next few days. Stop giving the evening laxative once the animal is eating solid food and having bowel movements. For some time afterward include in the daily diet the foods recommended earlier (carrots, coconut, and so on).

During this period and for about 18 days after the fast, use fresh garlic regularly on the food or give it in gelatin capsules at about half the dose used in the worming capsules. Also, feed an occasional charcoal tablet (once every 2 or 3 days, but for no more than a month afterward) to absorb and remove any remaining impurities in the intestines.

With careful application of either of these programmes, in nearly all cases you should meet with success. If there is any evidence of continued infestation, or just to be certain all the worms are gone, have your vet check the stool about six to eight weeks after treatment, and periodically thereafter until you are sure the problem is resolved.

If by chance the parasites (especially tapeworms, which are more stubborn) are not satisfactorily controlled by this treatment, the animal can still be given chemical treatment. After the natural treatment, the worms will have been reduced in numbers and those that are left will be weaker. Also, the animal's resistance to either drug or parasite will be higher, so that the whole procedure is more likely to go well.

Remember also that persistent worm problems can be caused by reinfestation of the animal due to unsanitary contact with contaminated earth or groundwater or from swallowing fleas or eating wild creatures that can carry the tapeworm (but *not* from sniffing or interacting with other dogs and cats). Inadequate flea control is often a source of persistent tapeworm reinfestation.

A final word on parasites: read the section on animal-to-people diseases in chapter 11. Your parasitized animal can be a source of health problems for other animals or for children. Until the problem is cleared up, take special care to prevent contamination of the environment.

Special Guide to Handling Emergencies

Introduction (read in advance): The care you give an animal in the first few minutes of an emergency can make the difference between life and death. The first-aid remedies I suggest definitely work and will be tremendously helpful in that time between the beginning of the emergency and arrival at your vet's surgery. They are meant as temporary life-saving procedures to use while the vet is being called and transportation made ready. DO NOT use these methods as a way of delaying needed professional help. Instructions for more prolonged treatment apply only if you *cannot* reach medical care.

For this information to serve you, plan ahead and have supplies on hand in a convenient place. An emergency is not the time to begin assembling these tools and remedies or to start reading 'how to do it'. The information that follows is given in brief outline form, alphabetically, for quick perusal when needed. But you should study all the categories ahead of time so you can quickly find the right heading during a time of crisis.

Here is a list of supplies you should have on hand in order to make full use of my suggestions. See pages 269–70 for suppliers of the Rescue Remedy (a Bach flower essence formulation) and the homeopathic remedies. The tissue salts are sold at many health food stores and the other supplies are found in chemists.

Homeopathic remedies

- *Arnica* 6X – 1 bottle of 250 tablets
- Calendula tincture – 1-oz dropper bottle
- Calendula-hypericum ointment
- *Ledum* 6X – 1 bottle of 250 tablets
- *Urtica urens* tincture – 1-oz dropper bottle

Other remedies

- *Ferrum phosphoricum* (Ferr. phos.) 6X (tissue salt) – 1 bottle of 500 tablets
- Activated charcoal granules
- Rescue Remedy (Bach flower essence) (Prepare a solution: add 4 drops of stock to a 1-oz dropper bottle $\frac{1}{3}$ filled with brandy – as a preservative. Add enough distilled or spring water to fill the bottle and mix well. Make this diluted solution in advance and use it as recommended for Rescue Remedy treatment. Keeps indefinitely.)

Materials

- Elastic bandage – 3 inches wide
- Adhesive tape – 1-inch-wide roll
- 2 blankets – thick and strong
- Gauze pads – 1 package
- Plastic bowl – for preparing dilutions
- Water – for dilution (tap water okay)

WHAT TO DO IN EMERGENCIES

BREATHING STOPPED

Follow these steps:

1. *Apply Artificial Respiration Technique*. Open the mouth, pull out the tongue, check back into the throat to make sure no obstructions are present. Clear away mucus and blood if necessary. Replace the tongue, close the mouth and place your mouth over the nostrils. Exhale as you fill the animal's lungs, allowing it to exhale after. Do this 6 times a minute for dogs, 12 times a minute for cats. Inflate until you can see the chest rise.

2. *Administer Rescue Remedy*. Place 2 drops on the gums or tongue every 5 minutes until breathing is restored. Then every 30 minutes (if you can't reach help) for 4 treatments.

BREATHING AND HEART BOTH STOPPED

Listen at chest

Follow these steps:

1. *Apply Cardiopulmonary Resuscitation Technique*. Use the Artificial Respiration Technique (see 'Breathing Stopped') *and* the External Heart Massage Technique (see 'Heart Stopped') at the same time. This is easiest for two people.

2. *Administer Remedy*. Place 2 drops on the tongue or gums every 5 minutes until recovery of function, then every 30 minutes thereafter (if no help is available) for 4 doses.

3. *Apply acupressure*. If there is no voluntary restoration of function after 3 doses of Rescue Remedy, try this alternative. Use the edge of your thumbnail to put strong presure over the centre of the large pad of each rear foot. After a few seconds, release and apply pressure to the point on the nose shown in the diagram, using your nail or a pointed object like the cap of a ballpoint pen.

Alternate between acupressure and cardiopulmonary resuscitation. If two people are working, have each one apply one of the techniques continuously.

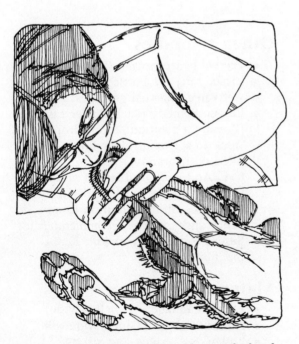

Artificial Respiration: Holding the mouth closed, breathe into the animal's nostrils. Allow it to exhale. Pace the breathing at 6 times a minute for dogs, 12 times a minute for cats.

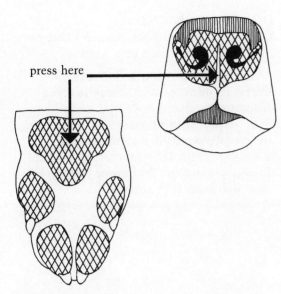

press here

Acupressure: Use the acupuncture points for resuscitation.

BURNS
'White' skin or scorched hair

Use one technique:

1. *Apply* Urtica urens *tincture*. Add 2 drops tincture to 1 ounce (2 full tablespoons) water. Saturate gauze with the solution and place over the burn. Do not remove, but keep gauze moistened. If necessary, hold in place with a bandage.

2. *Administer Rescue Remedy.* Add 4 drops from your preparation to 1 ounce (2 full tablespoons) water. Use as above with gauze. Also give internally, 2 drops on the tongue every 30 minutes.

CAR ACCIDENTS
Obvious injury; greasy or very dirty coat

Follow these steps:

1. *Move animal to safe place.* If the animal is found on the road, without bending its spine or changing its position, slide it on to a board or taut blanket and transport it as needed to a better location. You may need to tie a strip of cloth or wrap a pressure bandage around the mouth temporarily (as a muzzle) or put a blanket over the animal's head to keep it from biting someone.

2. *Administer Rescue Remedy.* Give 2 drops on the tongue every 15 minutes for 4 treatments (then 2 hours if necessary, until you can see the vet).

3. *Keep the animal warm and watch for shock* (see 'Shock').

CARDIOPULMONARY RESUSCITATION
See 'Breathing and heart both stopped'

CONVULSIONS
Stiffening or alternate rapid contraction/relaxation of muscles; thrashing about; frothing at the mouth

1. *Do not interfere with* or try to restrain the animal during convulsion.

2. *If breathing stops* after convulsion, use artificial respiration (see 'Breathing Stopped'). If the heart stops too, use cardiopulmonary resuscitation (see 'Breathing and Heart Both Stopped').

3. *Administer Rescue Remedy.* After the convulsion, give 2 drops every 15 minutes if the animal is frightened or disoriented.

4. *Consider poisoning* (see 'Poisoning').

CUTS
Lacerations, tears

Follow these steps:

1. *Flush out with clean water.* Remove

obvious debris like sticks, hair and gravel.

2. *Apply calendula lotion.* Add 2 drops calendula tincture to 1 ounce (2 full tablespoons) water; saturate gauze pads and bandage in place.

3. *Minor wounds* that do not need professional care should be washed with soap and water and dried carefully. Clip hair from the edges of the wound. Apply calendula-hypericum ointment twice a day until healed. Leave unbandaged.

FRACTURES

Leg 'bends' at sharp angle; animal won't use leg

1. *If the lower leg is obviously broken,* very carefully wrap a roll of clean newspaper or magazine around it and tape it to prevent unrolling. Do not try to set the leg yourself; just keep the lower end from swinging back and forth.

2. *If a wound is present* at the fracture site, cover it with clean gauze before applying a temporary splint.

3. *If the fracture is not apparent or is high up,* do not attempt to splint. Let the animal assume the posture most comfortable to it. A padded box may be best for transporting small animals to the vet. Walking on three legs may be best for a larger dog.

4. *Give* Arnica 6X, 1 to 2 tablets every hour for as many as 4 doses (if needed because of delayed help). If administration causes struggling and possible further injury, discontinue treatment.

GUNSHOT WOUNDS

Look for 2 holes opposite each other on the body; much pain and anxiety

1. *Give* Arnica 6X, 1 to 2 tablets every 15 minutes until there is relief from distress.

2. *Apply hand pressure with dry gauze* over the wound, if necessary, until bleeding stops. Or temporarily use the Pressure Bandage Technique (see 'Pressure Bandage Technique').

HEART STOPPED

No heartbeat felt or heard at chest

Follow these steps:

1. *Apply External Heart Massage Technique.* Place the animal with its right side down on a firm surface. Place one or both hands (depending on animal's size) over the lower chest directly behind the elbow. Press firmly and release at the rate of 70 times a minute (dogs and cats). *Caution:* Excessive pressure can fracture ribs.

2. *Administer Rescue Remedy.* Immediately put 2 drops in the side of the mouth, repeating every 5 minutes until there is a response. Then every 30 minutes (if no help is available) for 4 doses.

3. *If the heart does not start within a minute,* apply artificial respiration as well (see 'Breathing Stopped').

4. *Successful heart massage* (and respiration) can be estimated by the return of normal 'pink' colour to the gums.

Heart massage: using
both hands, press firmly
and release 70 times a
minute

HEAT STROKE
Animal found unconscious in hot car

Follow these steps:

1. *Remove immediately to a cool, shady area*. Use the car's shadow if necessary.

2. *Wet the animal with water*, continuously applied to cool the body as much as possible. Place ice packs around the body and head during transport to the vet.

3. *Administer Rescue Remedy*. Put 2 drops in the mouth every 10 minutes until you arrive.

HAEMORRHAGE
Bleeding from a wound or body opening

For skin wounds, use one of the following: *Arnica* 6X (1 tablet every 15 minutes until bleeding has stopped); *Ferrum phosphoricum* (Ferr. phos.) 6X (1 tablet every 15 minutes until bleeding has stopped); or, using direct pressure if necessary, locally apply either calendula lotion (2 drops tincture in 1 tablespoon water), crushed and powdered Ferr. phos. 6X or olive oil. If bleeding is still not controlled, use the pressure bandage (as described under its own heading) over a medicated gauze pad.

For internal bleeding, use either *Arnica* 6X or *Ferrum phosphoricum* (Ferr. phos.) 6X every hour for 4 treatments. Keep the animal calm. If hysteria is a problem, begin treatment by placing 2 drops of Rescue Remedy in the mouth every 5 minutes for 3 treatments. Then follow with the *Arnica* or Ferr. phos.

INSECT BITES
Bee and wasp stings; red painful swellings

For local use: For bee or wasp stings, apply a freshly sliced onion. For bee stings only, dab a drop of *Urtica urens* tincture directly on the sting.

Internally, for all insect bites give *Ledum* 6X, 1 tablet every 10 minutes until there is relief.

POISONING
Symptoms appear in three major forms: excess salivation, tears, frequent urination and defaecation; muscle twitching, trembling and convulsions; severe vomiting

Follow these steps:

1. *Give granular activated charcoal.* Mix 5 heaped teaspoons of granules in 1 cup water. Depending on the animal's size, give about $\frac{1}{4}$ to 1 cup by spoonfuls in the cheek pouch. If this causes excess struggle or worsens symptoms, discontinue. Your vet will be able to apply treatment under sedation or anaesthesia.

2. *Keep the animal warm and as quiet*

as possible. Stress has a very negative influence.

3. *Bring the suspected poisons and container* (if known) as well as any vomited material to the doctor for identification of the poison.

PRESSURE BANDAGE TECHNIQUE
To control haemorrhage, excessive bleeding; to keep gauze and medication in place

Follow these steps:

1. *Place dry or medicated gauze* over the wound and wrap an overlapping elastic bandage around it. Apply only slight tension to the bandage as excessive pressure (especially on a leg) can cut off blood flow like a tourniquet. If the wound is on the lower half of the leg, wrap all the way to and including the foot (to prevent swelling).

2. *Apply adhesive tape* to the bandage to keep it from unwinding.

3. *Remember, this is a temporary measure* until bleeding stops or you can reach the vet. Remove the bandage at once if swelling occurs below the bandage (as on a leg).

PUNCTURES
From teeth, claws, sharp objects

Follow these steps:

1. *Wash wound* with soap and water.

2. *Pull out* any embedded hair you see in the hole.

3. *Apply direct pressure* over the wound with gauze only if bleeding is excessive (see 'Pressure Bandage Tech-

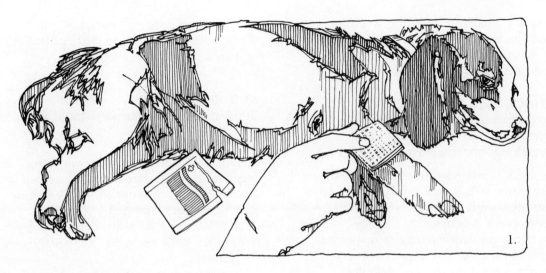

To control bleeding: Step 1: Place medicated gauze over the wound.

Step 2: Wind an elastic bandage around the wound to hold the gauze in place.

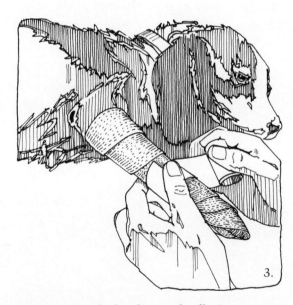

Step 3: Cover the bandage with adhesive tape to hold it securely.

nique'). Moderate bleeding will flush out the wound.

4. *Give* Ledum *6X*, 1 to 2 tablets every 2 hours for 4 doses.

SHOCK

Accompanies serious injuries. Symptoms are white gums, rapid breathing, unconsciousness

If much bruising or trauma is evident, use *Arnica* 6X, 1 to 2 tablets every 10 minutes, until response is seen. Then treat every 2 hours.

If internal haemorrhage is suspected, give *Arnica* 6X, 1 to 2 tablets every 30 minutes for 4 doses, then 2 tablets hourly thereafter.

If the animal is unconscious give Rescue Remedy, 2 drops in the mouth every 5 minutes until there is a re-sponse, then every 30 minutes.

Keep the animal warm with a blanket and in a horizontal position.

SUDDEN COLLAPSE
Sudden unconsciousness without warning

Follow these steps:

1. *Check to see if breathing or heart stopped.* If so, use treatment described under 'Breathing Stopped' or 'Breathing and Heart Both Stopped.'

2. *Use Rescue Remedy,* 2 drops every 5 minutes until response, and then every 30 minutes.

3. *Give a warm coffee enema* (for caffeine). Depending on the animal's size, use $\frac{1}{4}$ to 1 cup. Press gauze against the anus for 15 minutes to prevent fluid from coming out.

Where to Order Supplies

Suppliers of herbs

If you can't obtain herbs locally, you can order them by mail from the following companies:

Dene's Veterinary Herbal Products,
14 Goldstone Street,
Hove
Sussex (0273 25364)

Suppliers of seeds to grow your own herbs

Ashfield Herb Nursery
Hinstock
Market Drayton
Salop TF9 2NG

Gerard House
736 Christchurch Road
Boscombe
Bournemouth
Hants

Suffolk Herbs
Sawyers Farm
Little Conrard
Sudbury
Suffolk CO10 0NY

For more information about herbs, contact
The Herb Society
77 Great Peter Street,
London SW1P 2E2
(01-222 3634)

Suppliers of herbal remedies

A. Nelson & Co. Ltd
5 Endeavour Way
Wimbledon
London S19 9UH

Dene's Veterinary Herbal Products
14 Goldstone Street
Hove
Sussex

Suppliers of pet food

For non-meat, non-allergenic dry or frozen food, try your local health food store, or order by post from:

Dene's Veterinary Herbal Products
14 Goldstone Street
Hove
Sussex
(0273 25364)

Suppliers of flower essences

The original Bach flower essences are produced and sold by mail by:

Dr Edward Bach Centre
Mount Vernon
Sotwell
Wallingford
Oxfordshire
OX10 0PZ
(0491 39489)

The essences in the small stock bottles should be diluted by this standard method. Fill a clean 1-ounce dropper bottle $\frac{1}{3}$ full of brandy; add 2 drops of each stock essence selected for the animal (for the Rescue Remedy preparation, use 4 drops), and finish filling the bottle with distilled or spring water. Mix well and give 2 to 3 drops of this preparation (depending on the animal's size) 4 times a day for several weeks or months. The formula can be changed, if needed, as new indications appear for different treatment.

Suppliers of homeopathic remedies and tissue salts

Ainsworths Homeopathic Pharmacy
38 New Cavenish Street
London W1M 7LH

A. Nelson & Co. Ltd
5 Endeavour Way
Wimbledon
London S19 9UH

Weleda (U.K.) Ltd
Heanor Road
Ilkeston
Derbyshire E7 8R
(0602) 303151

Suppliers of grooming and hygiene products

For a flea comb with very fine teeth to capture fleas and other parasites, order by mail from:

Petcetera Etc Ltd
PO Box 112
Henley-in-Arden
Solihull
West Midlands B95 5HD
(0926 843030)

Recommended Reading

The following books are worthwhile resources for expanding your knowledge of issues and methods described throughout this word.

Handbook of the Bach Flower Remedies, by Philip M. Chancellor. London: C.W. Daniels, 1971.
Presents each of the 38 flower remedies developed by Dr Edward Bach with accompanying case histories. Fascinating reading and the most valuable guide to the use of this system.

The Complete Herbal Book for the Dog, by Juliette de Bairacli Levy. London: Faber, 1975.
A classic, now out of print. Valuable information and anecdotes on herbal therapy, natural feeding and health care. Oriented towards dogs, but much of it is adaptable to cats. Because the author suggests some herbs that are hard to obtain in this country, and emphasizes using large quantities of raw meat and fresh herbs, this book is less useful to urbanites. It is still available in public libraries.

The Treatment of Cats by Homeopathy, by K. Sheppard. London: Daniels, 1980.

The Treatment of Dogs by Homeopathy, by K. Sheppard. London: Daniels, 1980.
These two small volumes give brief indications for use of homeopathic medicines for lay treatment of common disorders of the dog and cat. Some of the information is valuable but the brevity of the descriptions is rather limiting.

The Homeopathic Treatment of Small Animals by Christopher Day. Wigmore Publications, London.

The Homeopathic Treatment of Dogs by George MacLeod. Homeopathic Development Foundation Ltd, 19A Cavendish Square, London.

Homeopathic First-Aid Treatment for Pets by Francis Hunter. Thorsons Publishers Ltd, Wellingborough.

Dried Foods, Biscuits and Quiches

Homemade dried food . . . for your pet and you

The following three recipes are for those who would like to feed a complete ready-made food comparable to the commercial sort from time to time, but who want to avoid the artificial additives, low-quality meat sources, inadequate fat levels, and other shortcomings of store-bought fare. People who are sometimes very busy or those who must occasionally leave their pet in a friend's care may find these kibbles an answer to their needs. They can also help to wean your pet off commercially dry foods and provide good teeth and gum exercise.

CAT AND DOG CRUNCHIES No. 1
(WITH MEAT)

1 pound minced chicken necks and gizzards (or other meat)
1 can chopped mackerel
2 cups full-fat soya flour
2 cups whole wheat flour
1 cup rye flour
1 cup maize meal

1 cup wheat germ
1 cup non-fat dried milk
¼ cup alfalfa powder
3 tablespoons bone meal (or 2 tablespoons dicalcium phosphate)
1 tablespoon sea salt or 2 tablespoons kelp powder
4 tablespoons oil or fat
1 tablespoon cod-liver oil
3 cloves garlic, minced
400 I.U. vitamin E
½ cup chopped onion (optional)
1 quart water
½ cup brewer's yeast

Mix all ingredients except the yeast to make firm dough. Spread flat on baking trays and roll to ¼- to ½-inch thickness. Bake at 350°F for 30 to 45 minutes. Cool, break into bite-size chunks and sprinkle with the yeast. (For cats you may want to cut the dough into small squares or ribbons before baking.)

Store in airtight containers. Keeps 2 to 3 days without refrigeration, longer with it. Supplement with a bit of fresh food (beansprouts, raw meat scraps, chopped vegetables) if fed on a regular basis.

CAT AND DOG CRUNCHIES No. 2
(VEGETARIAN)

> *2 quarts water*
>
> *2 cups whole grains (oatmeal, millet or cracked wheat, barley or corn, or any mixture of these)*
>
> *2 cups soya flour*
>
> *1 cup bran*
>
> *1 tablespoon sea salt*
>
> *¾ cup skimmed milk powder*
>
> *½ cup wheat germ*
>
> *½ cup brewer's yeast*
>
> *2 tablespoons alfalfa powder*
>
> *1 tablespoon kelp powder*
>
> *1 tablespoon bone meal or 2 teaspoons dicalcium phosphate*
>
> *½ cup oil*
>
> *1 teaspoon cod-liver oil*
>
> *400 I.U. vitamin E*

Slowly stir grains, soya flour and salt into 2 quarts of continuously boiling water. Cover and simmer 15 minutes or until done. Add more water if too dry. Cool slightly. Add remaining ingredients, stirring rapidly and thoroughly.

Spread thinly on a greased baking tray. Dry in the oven at 150° to 200°F until crisp. Break in pieces. (For cats you may cut the dough into small squares or ribbons before baking. Supplement with a little extra protein food, such as meat, tofu, eggs or cottage cheese if fed regularly to a cat.)

DOG CRUNCHIES
(VEGETARIAN, LOW-COST)

> *4 cups chicken food (or 7-grain cereal mix)*
>
> *2 cups soya flour*
>
> *½ cup buckwheat or whole wheat flour*
>
> *½ cup oil*
>
> *4 eggs*
>
> *1 tablespoon kelp powder*
>
> *1 tablespoon bone meal or ⅔ tablespoon dicalcium phosphate*
>
> *1 tablespoon brewer's yeast*
>
> *½ teaspoon cod-liver oil*
>
> *400 I.U. vitamin E*

Soak the chicken food and soya flour a few hours or overnight. Drain off part of the water, leaving enough to grind the mixture in a blender until smooth. Mix in remaining ingredients.

Spread thinly on greased baking trays. Bake at 350°F for 30 minutes or until toasted but not browned. If too soft, let dry in oven with heat off. Break into bite-size pieces. Supplement with fresh foods if fed regularly.

These recipes, along with the other recipes in this appendix, are adaptations, courtesy of Joan Harper, of recipes she introduced in the *Healthy Cat and Dog Cook Book* (copyright © 1975, 1976, 1978, 1979 by Joan Harper. Reprinted by permission of the publisher, E. P. Dutton), a good source of many creative ideas for preparing natural foods for pets.

Natural Treats

Biscuit treats can be a welcome change of pace for your pet as well as good aids for training and for cleaning and exercising the teeth and gums. Try the following recipes. Your animal will love them.

FAVOURITE BISCUITS

(Reprinted from *Prevention* magazine)

> 2 cups whole wheat flour
>
> ½ cup rye or buckwheat flour
>
> ½ cup brewer's yeast
>
> 1 cup bulgur
>
> ½ cup cornmeal
>
> ¼ cup parsley flakes
>
> ¼ cup dried milk
>
> 1 teaspoon dry yeast
>
> ¼ cup warm water
>
> 1 cup chicken broth
>
> 1 egg beaten with 1 tablespoon milk (glaze)

Combine flours, brewer's yeast, bulgur, cornmeal, parsley flakes and dried milk in a large bowl. In a small bowl, combine dry yeast and warm water. Stir until yeast is dissolved. Add chicken broth.

Stir liquid into dry ingredients, mixing well with hands. Dough will be very stiff. If necessary, add a little more water or stock. On a well-floured surface, roll out dough to ¼-inch thickness. Cut with knife or biscuit cutter into desired shapes.

Transfer biscuits to baking trays and brush lightly with egg glaze. Bake at 300°F for 45 minutes. Turn off heat and let biscuits dry out in oven overnight.

> *Yield: about 6 or 7 dozen biscuits*

WHEAT OR RYE BISCUITS

> 1 cup whole wheat or rye flour
>
> ¼ cup soya flour
>
> 3 tablespoons oil or lard
>
> ⅓ cup water
>
> ½ teaspoon bone meal

Mix flours. Mix oil or lard with water. Add liquid to flour and mix well. Roll out on baking tray and bake until golden brown at 350°F. Break into bite-size chunks (or pre-cut with biscuit cutter before baking).

DOG BISCUITS DELUXE

> 2 cups whole wheat flour
>
> ¼ cup cornmeal
>
> ½ cup soya flour
>
> 1 teaspoon bone meal
>
> 1 teaspoon sea salt
>
> ¼ cup sunflower seeds (or pumpkin seeds)
>
> 2 tablespoons, oil, melted butter or fat
>
> ¼ cup unsulphured molasses
>
> 2 eggs mixed with ¼ cup milk

Mix dry ingredients and seeds together. Add oil, molasses, and all but 1 tablespoon of egg/milk mixture. Add more milk if needed to make firm dough. Knead a few minutes, let dough rest ½ hour or more. Roll out to ½ inch. Cut into shapes and brush with the rest of the egg/milk mixture. Bake on baking trays at 350°F for 30 minutes or until lightly toasted. To make biscuits harder, leave them in the oven with the heat turned off for an hour or more.

Dishes to Share with Your Pet

Many casseroles and other dishes you prepare for yourself and your family make fine meals for your pet, too. But remember that an animal's protein needs (especially a cat's) are higher than yours. Therefore, mix extra protein foods into your animal's serving, as well as providing the daily supplements.

Lasagna, chilli, rice-bean casseroles, quiches, stews, omelets and many other standard main dishes are gourmet treats to a pet. Just be sure they are not too heavily spiced or fried and are used on an occasional rather than a daily basis.

Here are a couple of low-cost dishes you might like to serve both yourself and your animal.

QUICHE WITHOUT CRUST

For those who like to make the most of what's left over in the refrigerator, variations on this high-protein dish are sure to please both your animal and you. It's much like a quiche, but without a crust.

> *About 3 cups of what-have-you (cooked grains, crumbled tofu, cattage cheese, meat, chopped raw or cooked vegetables – especially courgettes, tomatoes, onions, spinach, broccoli; make a balanced combination)*
> *seasonings to taste (tamari, yeast, garlic)*
> *½ cup milk*
> *1 cup grated Cheddar or other cheese*
> *3 beaten eggs*
> *daily supplements as recommended*

Mix all ingredients except milk, cheese and eggs in a medium-size casserole dish. Scald milk in saucepan, then stir in cheese until melted. Add eggs to milk/cheese mixture and pour over rest of casserole. Bake at 350°F for 30 minutes or until firm. Supplements may be pre-mixed into casserole or mashed in when serving to your pet.

LENTIL LOAF

This tasty and inexpensive dish is reminiscent of meatloaf.

> *3 cups water or stock*
> *1 cup lentils*
> *2 cups rolled oats (or cornmeal)*
> *¼ cup soya flour*
> *¼ cup oil*
> *1 to 2 beaten eggs*
> *1 small onion, chopped*
> *1 clove garlic, minced*
> *daily supplements as recommended (except for oil)*
> *¼ cup tomato sauce or sugarless ketchup (optional)*

Slowly add lentils to boiling water or stock and simmer 20 minutes. Add oats and soya meal and let soak 10 minutes. Mix in the rest of the ingredients and turn into loaf tin. Top with ketchup or tomato sauce, if desired, and bake at 350°F for 30 minutes. Supplements may be pre-mixed into loaf or added when serving.

Acknowledgements

Producing a book is a lot like producing a film. It's a team effort. Yet the authors' or actors' names and faces appear so prominantly that we can easily overlook the tremendous contributions made by those working behind the scenes.

Not until we were fully immersed in this project did we start to realize just how many people were working on 'our' book besides us. One of the most prominent players in our field of vision was our very capable and supportive editor – Carol Keough. She carved away the excess, sanded the rough spots and polished the surface till the whole thing began to shine. If a book of this nature can be called artful, we owe it to Carol.

But our appreciation extends no less to the many dedicated people at Rodale Press who worked on this project, particularly to Mark Bricklin and John Feltman, whose encouragement got us started. Just as essential were Susan Rosenkrantz and the rest of the tireless team of fact-checkers whose job was to make sure every statement and reference was reliable and accurate. One of them – Holly Clemson – made no fewer than 70 phone calls to government agencies to confirm and clarify just what can and cannot go into pet food. Other researchers who dedicated their time and abilities include Martha Capwell, Sue Ann Gursky, Christy Kohler, Susan Nastasee and Joann Williams, along with department supervisors Carol Baldwin and Carol Matthews.

We could go on naming the contributors at Rodale – from the copy editors, nutritionists, typesetters, designers and illustrators to those who handled the mysteries of marketing, finance and promotion. We thank each and every one.

We are also indebted to many clients and colleagues whose shared commitment to natural healing has made all the difference. Special thanks go to the people who tested our recipes and reported their results. For their encouragement and cooperation I am grateful to my tireless clinic co-workers, Tootie Truesdell and Dottie Warner.

But some of the most important members of the 'crew' are some special people whose names you will find scattered throughout the book. They are those pioneers of humanity whose commitment to healing and communication have inspired, informed, challenged and taught us and many others. We particularly want to express our gratitude to the homeopath George Vithoulkas and the herbalist Juliette de Baıracli Levy for the major role each has played in expanding my understanding of natural means of healing. To J. Allen Boone, who is no longer alive and whom we met through his books, we give a heartfelt thanks for his courage and spirit in exploring the frontiers of communication and relationship with other species.

Lastly, to all the animals of the world – who feel, who suffer, who delight, who live – we offer our appreciation and the hope that this work will be of benefit. To them we dedicate this book.

RICHARD H. PITCAIRN, D.V.M., PH.D.
SUSAN HUBBLE PITCAIRN, M.S.

Index

Page numbers in **bold type** *indicate
Encyclopaedia section entries.*

Richard H. Pitcairn D.V.M., Ph.D., runs a very successful veterinary clinic in Eugene, Oregon, using nutritional therapy, homoeopathy and herbal remedies in preference to more orthodox veterinary treatments. His aim in writing this book is not to encourage owners to dispense with the guidance and clinical experience of a qualified vet, but to improve the quality of pet care and demonstrate that pet health is a direct reflection of nutrition and of the physical and emotional relationships between pets and owners.